30 DAYS to the FATHER'S HEART

TERRY MODICA

ISBN: 978-1-7375863-2-6

Cover design by Matthew Bourgeois
Text Design by Mary Tellier

Charis
PUBLISHING

Charis Publishing
charispublishing.com

Table of Contents

THE VICTORY OF ABBA'S FATHERHOOD

Subscribe to the Author's Blog
30DaysToTheFathersHeart.com/category/authors-blog

Watch the author's videos related to this book at
30DaysToTheFathersHeart.com/category/videos

INTRODUCTION

What Are You Seeking?

WHAT IS IT THAT you're seeking from God? Do you know that, if it's good and God doesn't have a better plan, you already have what you seek? It often takes time for it to be revealed and understood, but God has already granted it.

Most of us don't have the level of faith that makes waiting for God's help a joyful, peaceful time. That's because we don't fully trust God.

When you've cried over unanswered prayers, who did you blame? For most of my life, I blamed myself. God could not possibly be at fault. He was perfect. He was all-good. He loved me unconditionally. So I worked hard at my spiritual growth. I wanted to have faith that was at least the size of a tiny mustard seed. Apparently, according to Jesus, only a little bit of faith is enough to move mountains. "Nothing would be impossible for you," he said (see Matthew 17:20). And apparently my faith was smaller than that.

During my young adult years, after a major conversion experience in which I recommitted myself to Christ, people told me about miracles they received. However, when I prayed for miracles, nothing happened. "It must be me," I thought. "Something's wrong with my faith." I was so sure of this that when others came together to pray for anything amazing, I left the room afraid that my lack of faith would somehow prevent them from receiving what they asked for from God.

Determined to find my way into the mustard seed-sized faith that can move mountains, I immersed myself in scripture studies, prayer groups, parish events, and anything else that seemed faith-building. Many good fruits came from this daily effort, including a few answered prayers, but not enough. Faith had to be better than this!

Deep down, when we try and try but fail to have the kind of faith that gets results from our prayer requests, we don't really blame ourselves. We blame God. He is, after all, way more powerful than we are. He can make miracles happen despite our smaller-than-mustard-seed faith.

This raises terrible questions, such as: Has God abandoned me? Is he ignoring me? Does he care about others more than he cares about me? We ask because we *feel* abandoned, ignored, and uncared for, and we don't want to believe that God would do that to us.

This leads to many tears. One day as I cried because I felt ignored by God, an image of a cardboard box came to mind. It wasn't a very big box—about the size of a microwave oven. I wondered what might be in it.

"You have put Me in a box," I heard in my own inner voice, but I knew it was not my voice. "You have been limiting Me. You see Me as less than *I Am*. Open the box and let Me out."

Gladly! I visualized the lid of the box opening up and I imagined God escaping from it and expanding larger and larger until he filled the universe.

This began a life-long quest to unpack who God really is and what he is really like. God as a loving, doting, perfect Father who desires more than we do for our prayers to be answered. God as the infinite, unlimited, all-powerful Father who wants to use his mightiness for our benefit. God as the Father who solves our problems and lifts us up above them.

In the parishes where I've worked in adult faith formation and through Good News Ministries (the Catholic faith-building ministry that my husband, Ralph, and I founded in 1995), I've made it my goal to help people meet the real Father. Everywhere, I see the need for spiritual healing that comes from perceiving God as less than he is.

We limit the size of our faith by projecting onto God the imperfections that we've witnessed in the humans around us. However, because no one—not even the best of parents—can be God for us, we yearn to be fathered by him, and at the same time we have a hard time seeing him as more than what we have witnessed in others.

Furthermore, fatherhood has been severely undermined in society. And this has diluted people's understanding of the True God. The world today desperately needs to be converted to Christ, but our power as Christians to change the world for Christ is weakened by our own distrust in God the Father.

This book, *30 Days to the Father's Heart*, is written to help you experience the wonderfulness of the True Father so that your faith can be set free to reach its full potential. It's an inspirational guide to healing that will enable you to experience God the Father as he truly is, using scriptures, true life stories, and theological reflection. In it, we'll identify and overcome the most common misconceptions that interfere with faith in God.

This book is filled with true stories from my own personal journey and the experiences of others. Although each situation is unique, the feelings, blessings, and problems they generate are universal. It's my hope that the stories will assure you that you are not alone in your pain. This realization is often the beginning of healing. Storytelling helps make the truth sink deeper into our hearts where real change occurs.

To be effective, we need to be honest. Some people have expressed discomfort over the frankness of my personal stories. "Are you being hurtful to your parents?" they wondered. Rest assured that my parents read this book during its development, and my dad (who has since passed away) helped me to remember some of the details more accurately. They were/are both happy that this book will help others get to know the deep love of God the Father more fully.

The chapters are short to give you time to reflect on each new discovery you make. Use this book as a private, in-home 30-day retreat. It can also be used in parish discussion groups that are set up to offer friendly support and complete confidentiality. Each chapter will generate new insights that will forever change how you view God as your True Father.

My friendship with the Father deepened as I wrote this book. I pray that yours will, too—to astounding new heights of joy and depths of intimacy and an ever-widening trust in the Father's love for you.

In God's smile,
Terry Modica

For this reason I kneel before the Father, from whom every family in heaven and on Earth derives its name. I pray that out of his glorious riches he may strengthen you with power through his Spirit in your inner being, so that Christ may dwell in your hearts through faith. And I pray that you, being rooted and established in love, may have power, together with all the Lord's holy people, to grasp how wide and long and high and deep is the love of Christ, and to know this love that surpasses knowledge–that you may be filled to the measure of all the fullness of God. (Ephesians 3:14-19 NIV)

DAY 1

Tears for Abba

DO YOU REMEMBER crying because your daddy wasn't there for you when you needed him? Or your mama? You've been carrying around a father-wound and a mother-wound that God wants to heal. Let me introduce you to Abba-Daddy Who Wipes Away Your Tears.

> *I pray that you, being rooted and established in love, may have power, together with all the Lord's holy people, to grasp how wide and long and high and deep is the love of Christ, and to know this love that surpasses knowledge–that you may be filled to the measure of all the fullness of God. (Ephesians 3:17b-19 NIV)*

My earliest memory is a scene in the kitchen. From my seat in the baby's high chair, I see Mommy washing dishes. Daddy comes into the room demanding that she serve him a bowl of "wife-dipped" ice cream (he always called it "wife-dipped" ice cream because he wanted her to serve him). I'm not old enough to understand why the tone of his voice disturbs me nor why Mommy gets upset. What I do remember—and rather vividly—is a ball of ice cream flying across the room, thrust from her spoon toward my father.

Although loud fighting was not common in my childhood home,

their quarrel that day became permanently etched in my psyche. Sixty-plus years later, I still tense up when I witness people argue loudly with each other. I want to intervene. I want to bring peace. And at the same time, I feel completely incapable of making a difference because deep inside I'm still that two-year-old surprised by the scoop of ice cream flying across the room.

The next life-changing event that I remember occurred four years later. At six years old, a child's brain develops an ability to understand her environment and reason out what's good, what's bad, and what should be but is not. At six years old, I came to a devastating conclusion: My daddy was not the warm, friendly, understanding, compassionate listener that I needed him to be. Whatever triggered this realization is lost in the past, but I remember grieving deeply and making the decision, which held for the rest of my life, that I would never again call him "Daddy." The name didn't fit. "Dad" was more acceptable. It felt less intimate. It acknowledged his fatherhood while representing the sad lack of father-daughter closeness.

My dad was basically a good father. His flaws tell only part of the story. He loved his wife and children dearly, and I knew it. He was not abusive. He made it a priority to attend my school events. He figured out ways for the family to have fun together, including awesome vacations, despite being poor. He taught us how to have a balanced life. And most importantly, with my mother he introduced me to Christ and taught me to pray.

The problem was: I had discovered that my father was not *The* Father.

Seeking the Father

Every person is created by God to know him, to love him, to serve him in this world, and to be happy with him forever in Heaven. Saint Paul wrote, *"Praise be to the God and Father of our Lord Jesus Christ, who has blessed us in the heavenly realms with every spiritual blessing in Christ.* ***For he chose us in him before the creation of the world*** *to be holy and blameless in his sight"* (Ephesians 1:3-4 NIV; emphasis mine).

You and I were created to be like our Divine Father; we were made in his image (Genesis 1:26). Therefore, since the moment of our entrance into this unholy world, we instinctively have been seeking the Perfect Father who made us. However, until we learn how to have a close, intimate relationship with God as our Father, we will keep looking for him in his closest representatives: fathers, mothers, aunts and uncles, foster parents, grandparents, teachers, best friends, clergy, etc.

In my forty-plus years of ministry, I've encountered many who are seeking the Perfect Father in the people around them without consciously realizing that this is why they continually feel disappointed and hurt. Many of us end up in divorces and other broken relationships because of this. It's also why ministers and priests disappoint us: We look to them for the best examples of God's Fatherhood, but they are all imperfect. Sadly, their failure to be the God that we want them to be causes indignation and outrage, a reduction in donations to the Church, separation from the parish, and—all too often—separation from the very God we're seeking.

No one can love us the way God loves us. Everyone whom we rely on for the love and care and support we need are imperfect representatives of God the Father.

Throughout my childhood, I expected my daddy to be God. Of course, I didn't realize this because I thought I had already found God. Jesus has been my Savior and a close companion for as long as I can remember. When I was a child, having a close relationship with Jesus seemed to be enough. In reality, it was not.

It would take another twenty years before I came to know God as my Father. Meanwhile, my dad, like all human fathers, continued to fail to be the Father for whom I deeply longed. Although he did a lot of things right, every imperfection stood out as a big reminder that he failed to be what I wished him to be. My mother wasn't perfect either, and her shortcomings contributed to my false images of God. So did the third grade teacher who embarrassed me in front of the class. And, after I became an adult, the policeman who gave me a speeding ticket instead of letting me go with just a warning. (And so forth with every human authority figure.)

Created to be loved

Father God gave us life and created us to be loved. Ever since he created the Earth, he's been looking forward to having a close, loving relationship with you. You are God's handiwork (see Ephesians 2:10).

Deep in the soul of every child is an awareness that his or her life comes from God *"the Creator of the heavens, who stretches them out, who spreads out the Earth with all that springs from it, who gives breath to its people, and life to those who walk on it"* (Isaiah 42:5 NIV).

Every child instinctively knows that God exists and that he is the source of love and that he is perfect. Want proof of this? Consider how strong is the impulse to expect perfection from humans. We have all been seeking him (although unconsciously) in the people around us since our babyhood—especially in those who were our first representatives of his Fatherhood.

God created us for love. Psychologists have long recognized that the need to be loved is the strongest of psychological needs. When we feel unloved, we are profoundly sad, emotionally hungry, and shaken to the core. It can lead to despair, and it's a very short walk between despair and suicide.

God designed into the very fabric of our being a natural yearning to receive *his* love, to be embraced securely by *his* caring compassion, so that we cling to him all the way into eternity. We were born with a divine knowledge of what love is supposed to feel like, what it's supposed to look like, and how it's supposed to be shared.

Have you ever watched a small child follow his or her parent? One day during weekday Mass, God taught me about his Fatherhood as I watched a young mother and her two pre-school sons. The older boy was getting too rambunctious, so she stood up to take him outside. She signaled the younger one to stay in his seat. As she walked toward the door, he watched her steadily. Nothing else mattered. His instinct was to jump up and run after her, but he fought it. Up he stood and then obediently sat down. Then up again when his mom opened the door to leave. He started to move toward her but then returned to his seat. It became especially hard for him when she disappeared from view, and finally he gave in to his inner yearning and ran after her.

In the animal world, this is called "imprinting." The first creature that a freshly hatched duckling sees becomes its mother, which it dutifully follows everywhere even if the mother waddles across a busy street in front of oncoming traffic. Fortunately, human parents are a lot smarter than ducks.

When you and I were little, we had the same instinct to follow our parents. It's a built-in survival mechanism. It's the primal example of trust. Jesus used this as an example of how we adults should trust Father God. He said in effect: *"Unless you become like little children, you will never be able to follow your Father to Heaven"* (adapted from Matthew 18:3).

However, since our human parents were not perfect—because they were not God—following them sometimes led us smack into the oncoming traffic of worldly ideas, misunderstandings, and arguments that caused ice cream to fly. And sometimes it crashed us into their anger, their unhealed wounds, and, for some readers, their deliberate abuses.

We all need healing

Take a few minutes to think of some of the ways that the imperfections of your parents (or guardians) and other authority figures have caused you to suffer. Do you remember crying because your daddy wasn't there for you when you needed him? Or your mama? Did a father-figure punish you when you didn't deserve it (or maybe you did deserve it but at the time you felt innocent)? Did a parent fail to come see you at a school event? Were both your parents away at work when you needed a hug after a bad day at school? Was your father separated from you by divorce or death or long travels for his job? Was an important person in your life too drunk to notice your needs? Or too busy?

Pause to bring these hurts to mind. Father God wants to heal them!

This exercise of remembering is not meant to ignore what was good about these people. We're setting the stage for a closer relationship with God the Ultimate Parent. We're not fault-finding; we're seeking God. We need to recall the imperfections of humans because this is how we overcome our false images of the Divine Father. This is how we open ourselves to the healing love of the only parent who is perfect. Even the best of parents unintentionally hurt their children because of human limitations and because of how they, too, were treated by their own imperfect parents.

(1) Next, think about the examples of insufficient love that you learned by witnessing the imperfections of others. Do you have a spouse who was unfaithful to you? Or a boss who never deals with problems in the company? Or parents who changed after you became an adult, as we see in Debbie's story? She says:

"All my childhood memories are wonderful of my parents. Sure, we were disciplined, and at times I felt things were unfair, especially when I was a teenager, but for the most part I know that all the discipline was for my own good. Unfortunately, in their last years, my parents seemed to be fighting verbally with one another. What is so hard for me is wondering, because I grew up thinking they were the best parents and in love with each other, how could they be so unkind to one another in their last years? My heart is broken not seeing them love each other openly on a daily basis."

(2) Listen to how that translates into her relationship with God:

"I want to see God Our Father as the one I call on throughout the day (a hard habit for me to form). My question is: How do we become more childlike, trusting God in our daily life?"

(3) Who has taught you to be distrustful? Cynical? Guarded? Charmaine says:

"It is so difficult for me to totally trust God, to surrender all to him. I keep trying to fix me but to no avail. You see, when as a child, my siblings called me bad names and I cannot remember ever being defended by either parent."

(4) Who has taught you to be jealous? Do you believe that God favors others more than you? That he answers the prayers of others while saying "no" to you? Listen to Tonia's story:

"I continually remember the time during my senior year of high school that I wanted to become a dental assistant. At the time, our city did not offer classes and I would have to go to a city that was quite a distance. My parents refused my request. However, my oldest sister, who was the perfect daughter at the top of her high school and college graduating classes, was never refused when she asked to go away just as far. I felt like the child who is always walking in her shadow but never good enough!"

(5) Who has rejected you and made you fear abandonment? Kay lived in a loving home, and yet:

"There was always an emotional distancing from my Dad. He and my Mom shared an amazing love for each other that I, as their only child, never really felt a part of. I felt protected, I felt loved, but I also felt like the 'third wheel.' As a result, while I believed in

God the Father, he was a distant supervisor of my life and not at all someone I would go to for comfort and solace. Mom and Dad had frequent arguments that scared me because I feared abandonment. These arguments were always followed by long periods of silence. My life, up until my Dad died, was colored by issues of abandonment, rejection, fear of his anger, lack of warmth, criticism, and other concerns, all of which shaped my thinking and beliefs about God the Father.

"When my Dad died, I was given the opportunity to care for my Mother who was in the late stages of Alzheimer's. I developed a whole new perspective of my Dad and a great deal of respect for the man that he was. That perspective allowed me to develop a different relationship with God the Father and a great love for the comfort and guidance he offers for me and all his children."

(6) Who made you feel "not good enough"? Note: There is another side of God that we must also consider. Although we refer to him in manly terms, God is not limited to manly traits. He is both a Father and a Mother to us. He has the nurturing qualities of motherhood as much as he has the protective qualities of fatherhood. What is your ideal image of the perfect mother? God is the source of that. He has given us the perfect example of motherhood in the flesh in the Mother of Jesus. And yet, as Maureen's story tells us, we feel like we're missing out on the motherly love of God:

"I know my mother loved me, but I don't remember her being loving toward me. I only remember her being judgmental and distant, unlike my father. I have no trouble relating to Abba-Father. He is my everything, just as in my childhood my father was kind and self-effacing. But even at the ripe old age of 72, I struggle with mother issues."

(7) And what about other authority figures? Priests and ministers are charged with a very special responsibility of representing God. They are supposed to be our spiritual fathers. Mary says:

"I personally have had an awakening in my relationship with priests as representations of God. Growing up I was told they were 'God on Earth for us' and so I have had more than a few disappointments finding out they were really 'only human.'"

The key to knowing the Father's Heart

Recalling the sources of our poor images of Father God is key to getting to know him as he really is. However, part of the healing process is to also remember how our parents (and others in positions of authority) revealed the truth about God. For example, my dad represented God's Fatherhood very well in his protection of the family. I grew up feeling the love that inspired his protectiveness. A favorite memory comes from the time when Ralph and I were dating. We were high school sweethearts. Ralph's father was very suspicious of me due to his own protectiveness.

When Ralph drove me home from our dates, we usually talked for hours parked in the driveway. When my family vacated the living room by going to bed, Ralph and I brought our discussion (and smooching) indoors.

Around 10:00 one night, while Ralph and I cuddled on the couch, deep in conversation, the phone rang. My parents had just gone to bed. Dad answered the phone. Ralph's father was calling to find out if Ralph was with me. And then he insisted, quite irately, that Ralph should be sent home immediately.

What happened next made me feel very good about my dad. He defended Ralph! He protected our right to be together. He made a difference by standing up for us.

Any scary experience during childhood can become a misconception about God. And the reverse is true: The ways that we felt protected when we were young can become trust in God.

My dad counseled a man who was mentally unstable. He tried to help him spiritually while a psychiatrist dealt with his problems psychologically and medically. Unfortunately, this man became violent and attacked his psychiatrist, beating him into a veritable human vegetable with a hammer to his skull. While he was still on the loose, the police informed my dad that he might come after him next. So my dad sent me and my sister and brother to the house across the street.

We watched from a window as police cars patrolled the area. From the vantage point of safety, the situation seemed like an adventure, like I was living out a cop show on television.

Years later, when faced with a challenge that involves taking risks, I have enough trust in God to feel exhilarated by the adventure. Certainly, there is some degree of worrying about what's going to happen, but if I've sensed the Father's calling or go-ahead in the troublesome situation, I trust that he is protecting me. I trust that he has a plan that's so good, even if things go wrong they will turn out to be used for good (as Romans 8:28 promises).

Because I grew up feeling protected by my parents, when I've needed God's protection, I have felt it. Think now about your own father, mother, and other significant parental influences. In what ways did they portray or represent God's wonderfulness? Laura shares this:

"I grew up with a dad that expected perfection. If he said jump, you asked how high on the way up. If you brought home an "A" from school, why not an "A+"? But he also was the one who told you that you sang the best in your class, and I believed it! As I have grown I have realized he just wanted the best for me."

It's good to think about what our parents did right more often than you think about their shortcomings. Father God revealed himself to you through these important people, and he continues to do so whenever you remember the good times. A good spiritual exercise when you're feeling low is to ask yourself: "What misconception about Father God is contributing to how I feel?" Then pull up a memory of your dad or mom or someone else (it could be anyone else, including friends) doing something for you or saying something to you that made you feel good. God speaks through such memories. He, too, wants you to feel good.

Father God wants to heal your heart

Jeanie, whom I met through my ministry, told me, "Even though my dad was a good provider, never hit me, and I knew he loved me, I was afraid of him due to how I saw him act in stressful times when things didn't go his way."

No matter how old we are today, for every unhealed wound of the past, there's a little child in us who still cries out to be nurtured and comforted by The-One-Who-Is-The-Perfect-Daddy—the one whom Jesus called "Abba" as he cried out for help during his great emotional agony in the Garden of Gethsemane just before he went to the Cross. We want Abba to hold us in a protective embrace and make every hurt go away.

The problem is, he's invisible. He's not physically touchable. It takes a lot of time and effort to learn how to feel his embrace. In the past, we turned to our human dad and mom (and others) and found them to be insufficient. Humans cannot give us everything we need nor fulfill every longing.

This has handicapped our understanding of the total sufficiency of God. On the one hand, we know that God is quite sufficient for our every need and every good desire. On the other hand, to some degree, each of us sees him as less than he is.

The truth is: God is more sufficient than we can imagine. As Ephesians 3:20 points out, he is able to do *immeasurably* more for us than we could ever ask for or even imagine. And he wants to reveal more of himself to you now.

This book is written to introduce you to Daddy Who Wipes Away Your Tears. In whatever ways your parents and other authority figures have failed to represent Father God's true nature, he wants to enter into your heart more deeply and heal you. He wants to enable you to receive from him more of the goodness and love that you long for. He has been waiting for this day. He is inviting you to reach out to him and accept more from him—more than you know is possible.

Today's Exercise: List the Hurts You Want God to Heal

To get started, list the ways you've been hurt or failed by parents and other authority figures (teachers, clergy, etc.). Do this in writing. There are writing exercises for each day of the journey as you travel deeper into the Father's heart. As you proceed, your Loving Father's healing embrace will be unveiled.

DAY 2

Healing Your Image of God's Fatherhood

JESUS MADE KNOWN to us what the Father made known to him. He calls us "friends" because we are the Father's friends. The way Jesus loves us reveals to us what Abba-Father is like. We long to be embraced by and protected by his Fatherhood, but there's a disconnect we need to overcome. So Jesus wants to give us healing from the wrong images we have of God's Fatherhood.

> *No one knows who the Son is except the Father, and no one knows who the Father is except the Son and those to whom the Son chooses to reveal him. (Luke 10:22 NIV)*

Which Person of the Holy Trinity feels closest to you? Who has the deepest relationship with you? Whom do you turn to first?

For most of us, it's not the Father.

Jesus is our Friend, our Brother, our Savior. He's the center of our worship during Mass. He's the one we receive in the Eucharist. We can easily visualize him by reading the Gospels. We're reminded of what he did for us every time we gaze upon crucifixes in church and at home. Jesus has been the subject of artwork far more often than any other Person of the Trinity—he was so human!

Perhaps it's the Holy Spirit who's the most difficult to feel close to. The Holy Spirit is, after all, *called* a "spirit," and this sounds so ethereal, so other-worldly, so intangible. And yet, if we've been through a Life in the Spirit Seminar or if we've had other experiences of good faith formation about the Third Person of the Trinity, he is the one we rely on for understanding and wisdom, for the right words to speak as Jesus promised (see Luke 12:12), and for help in our efforts to grow in holiness. The Holy Spirit is known as The Helper—how nice!

God the Father is the scary one. We think of him as the one who punishes us when we sin. We believe that he expects perfection from us. And he's too far away up there in Heaven to help us with our little daily problems. Right?

I had a wonderful relationship with Jesus since my earliest childhood, as far back as I can recall. I grew up believing that Jesus was my Best Friend. When I felt lonely, I turned to Jesus. When I felt misunderstood by my father, Jesus sat with me in my room while I cried on my bed. When I forgot a homework deadline and felt panicked and sick to my stomach about it, I knew that Jesus loved me anyway. He encouraged me to do better, building my confidence (not my guilt).

God the Father, on the other hand, could increase my guilt (a mistaken idea that we'll cover more fully in future chapters). I thought of him as The Big Disciplinarian. He loved me, of course, in the same way that all parents who discipline their children are loving them when they scold and dole out punishments. I reasoned that, because I got enough discipline from my dad, why should I spend any time with God the Father? My parents didn't offer me friendship, so it never occurred to me that I could have a friendship with God as my Father. Jesus was the one for that.

I learned early on that Jesus said in John 15:15, *"From now on, I call you my friends. You did not choose Me; I chose you!"* This meant a lot to me because (for example) in gym class I was usually the last kid to be chosen for sports teams. I was sure that the team captains would have preferred to not choose me at all. But Jesus, the God who came to save the world, chose me. ME! Jesus wanted me for a friend. Wow!

However, this was a very limited understanding of John 15:15. I missed the point that Jesus was making about the Father. Read the whole verse: *I no longer call you servants, because a servant does not know his master's business. Instead, I have called you friends, for everything that I learned* ***from my Father*** *I have made known to you"* (NIV, emphasis mine).

The reason why Jesus calls us "friends" is because he *learned this from his Father*. In fact, everything he taught he learned from the Father. Jesus made known to us what the Father had made known to him—because we are the Father's friends.

Let me put this another way. Jesus had a friendship with his Father—not just a sonship. And what Jesus had, Jesus gave. If we are a friend of Jesus, it should be easy to experience friendship with the Father. But this was unimaginable to me.

Like many who are reading this, I never experienced a close friendship with my dad. The idea of confiding in him, and feeling heard and understood like I experienced with my true friends—this was a concept that was so foreign to me, I didn't even imagine it.

So, neither could I imagine that God the Father could be a friend.

The spiritual director I had when I became an adult recognized the importance of this problem. She led me through a visualization in which Jesus introduced me to the True Father. In my prayer-imagination, I "saw" Jesus greet me at the door to the throne room of God. He opened the door and invited me in. I walked on a red carpet crossing over a vast, shiny floor. Then I arrived at the base of an enormous throne.

Sitting on the throne was a very big Father. I expected a stern expression. But he was smiling at me! Then, with the gentlest of voices, he invited me to sit on his lap. How could I? He was too large. He offered to lift me up, and when I gave him my hand, suddenly he seemed very reachable. The next moment, I was cuddled by him like a beloved child. I could feel the fabric of his kingly garments. I could feel the warmth of his chest against my cheek. I could feel the love in his heart. No question about it: I was loved. I was his beloved little girl.

That experience was the beginning of a Father-daughter friendship that has deepened ever since. It was the first step in the healing of my image of God's Fatherhood. There have been many other milestones along the way. I'll share them with you as we proceed through this book.

Right now the Father wants you to know that you are his beloved child and he is favoring you with an opportunity for true friendship. He says to you, *"You are precious in my eyes, and honored, and I love you. Do not be afraid, for I am with you"* (adapted from Isaiah 43:4-5).

The Father is giving you total love and kindness and mercy. *"And so we know and rely on the love God has for us. God is love. Whoever lives in love lives in God, and God in them"* (1 John 4:16 NIV). Love isn't love apart from God. Love is God actively giving himself to us. Even the love we have for others is God loving them through us.

It's impossible for God to be untrue to himself. Therefore, he loves us even when we don't deserve it. *"He makes his sun to rise on the bad and the good, and sends rain on the righteous and the unrighteous"* (Matthew 5:45). As Bishop Robert Barron points out: "The sun doesn't ask who deserves its warmth or its light before it shines. It just shines, and both good and bad people receive it. Neither does the rain inquire as to the moral rectitude of those upon whom it showers its life-giving goodness. It just pours—and both just and unjust people receive it."

The Father gave us Jesus so we won't have to face punishment for our sins. *"For God did not send his Son into the world to condemn the world, but to save the world through him"* (John 3:17 NIV).

The Father cares about us so much that he gave us a way to escape from the punishment we deserve. *"This is how God showed his love among us: He sent his one and only Son into the world that we might live through him. This is love: not that we loved God, but that he loved us and sent his Son as an atoning sacrifice for our sins"* (1 John 4:9-10 NIV).

"The Father of Jesus Christ is love, right through. That's all God is; that's all he knows how to do. He is not like us: unstable, changing, moving from one attitude to another. No, God simply is love." (Bishop Robert Barron).

He is completely patient with us regardless of how imperfect we are. Scripture tells us to think often of his kindness, tolerance, and patience, because the kindness of God leads us to repentance (see Romans 2:4). God knows that we overcome sin much more easily through his kindness than through punishments.

He's intimately and infinitely concerned about our daily trials. *"Blessed be the Lord, who daily bears us up; God is our salvation"* (Psalm 68:19 ESV). And *"the Lord knows how to rescue the godly from trials"* (2 Peter 2:9 NIV).

So why doesn't it feel like he's this wonderful? It's because our image of his Fatherhood has been tainted. We see him through eyes that first saw the imperfections of human parents. We need to differentiate human traits from divine traits. We need to stop projecting onto God that which is not godly. We need to make ourselves available to the truth so we can let God heal our image of him.

God can only be known by our hearts, the center of our soul, where love resides. He cannot be known by the mind because he is much more than we could ever imagine: much better, much more caring, much more available to fill in the gaps left by insufficient human love. To grasp the "more" of him requires that we abandon all of our incorrect ideas, images, and concepts of God. To enter into his healing embrace, we must overcome misconceptions. We must stop projecting human images onto the Abba-Father.

God is not your enemy

"I blame God for being stuck where I am spiritually," Felisha told me. "He gives me as much as I deserve, which in my mind isn't much." Insight into why she thinks this way is found in understanding her childhood: "I struggled to make my parents proud of me, and God is even harder to please than they were! I have loads of experiences from my past that I am sure contributed to this idea that I won't receive much from God. I pray daily, but always as a beggar at God's feet, expecting little help from him—obviously the damage from my childhood is real."

Felisha received her first images of what God the Father is like from parents who were hard to please. They loved her, but—like all parents and every other human being—insufficiently.

She felt loved but *conditionally*. She heard the message, whether it was intended or not, that she should always "do as we say or else . . . " The "or else" was a discipline that made her feel crushed and stripped of her self-esteem.

"The damage began in my childhood," she continued, "but certain other experiences also helped reinforce the idea that I couldn't be special to anyone. The same is true of God. I must obey or else. Since I am far from perfect and fail him hundreds of times a day, how could he possibly love me very much when I don't love myself very much either?"

This happens all over the world. Gift Nyirenda in Malawi (central Africa) said, "My father was the least person I liked in our family. I thought he was always watching out for new mistakes from me so that he could give out proper punishment. That blinded my image of who God the Father really is, and even after my father's death it is still hard to reconcile my life with the reality [of who God is]."

Every person has injuries and scars from being loved incompletely during childhood—even if our fathers completely earned the "Best Dad" trophies that we gave them for Father's Day and even if our mothers were saints who stayed on the pedestals we hoisted them onto during early childhood.

At the very least, they punished us (we were imperfect, too!) and this didn't feel good. It's nearly impossible for a child to understand that punishment is not a withdrawal of love. We were disciplined for our own good, but at the time it happened, we focused on how good it would feel to continue doing whatever the punishment was trying to stop. The person punishing us was, at that moment, our enemy (because he or she was "against" us). Thus we unwittingly developed an unholy fear of God as Father: The implication is that he's our enemy, not a benefactor, when we sin.

No wonder people stay away from the Sacrament of Confession! And yet, there is no shame in this sacrament. There is healing—reconciliation—with God. There is power. There is a very special gift from God: the supernatural grace to grow stronger in resisting the sins we confess.

> *You have been my help . . . my father and my mother have forsaken me, / But the LORD will take me up. / Teach me Your way, O LORD, / And lead me . . . (Psalm 27:9-11 NASB).*

God becomes our enemy only if we become his enemy first—deliberately opposing him, doing whatever we want to do, following our own idea of what is right and wrong—knowing full well that God has a different idea. And since enemies are to be feared, thinking of God as the enemy explains why so many people who prefer the ways of the world are so hard to evangelize. They don't want to have a relationship with God. They fear him and so they get angry at anyone who represents God and his ways.

It's true that God does get angry. We see it in the Old Testament. We see it in the New Testament when Jesus drove the greedy merchants out of the temple. God gets angry when others hurt us without remorse. God gets angry when he watches his children suffering from the terrible repercussions of sin.

However, if we want to be holy, we need to recognize that God is for us, not against us, even when we sin (see Romans 8:31). He appreciates the remorse we feel and our determination to do better. This is the true Father. And so we need to heal our image of God as a father who gets angry at us or pulls away from us whenever we fail to be his perfect child. If the father figures in our lives were unhappy with us because we failed to live up to their expectations, our tainted image of God tells us that he, too, is unhappy with us.

Likewise, if our dads died during our childhood or left the family or traveled often for their jobs, we unconsciously assume that Father God, too, won't be close when we need his help. Lyra grew up without a father. He had died when she was two years old. How do you suppose this affected her relationship with God? As you read her story, look for the imperfect traits of the humans in her life that became a false image of God's Fatherhood:

"My mother became our 2-in-1 parent, providing for all our needs. Because my mother was not home most of the time, she would warn us to be good always or else God would get angry. That was how I have perceived God: a punitive one. I thought we're supposed to earn God's favor. For me then, God was a distant Father who would grant my prayers when I'm good and punish me when I failed."

Imperfect trait #1: Her father was absent. The image of God that this implied: The Father is distant. God is not the doting Father she needs and longs for.

Imperfect trait #2: Her mother could not be home whenever Lyra needed her. The implication: God the Loving Parent is not closely involved in our lives, not available to reassure us when times get tough, and not aware of all our needs.

Imperfect trait #3: Her mother described God as a Father who watches for his children to fail at being good and gets angry as soon as they do. Implication: God only answers our prayers when we earn his approval by being perfectly good, and if our prayers are not answered, then that's proof that we're bad. Since Lyra was imperfect, she could never be good enough for God. She could not rely on his help, which is a false image that was reinforced by imperfect trait #2 above.

Have you ever thought something like this? "God is a good Father, all powerful and all understanding, but what if I am in this mess because it's me who is at fault? I'm not good enough in his eyes. I miss all his blessings because I am lazy, pleasure-seeking, greedy, envious, selfish, etc. And worst of all, now it's too late and no prayer can change the situation."

Lyra says, "I blamed my father for dying early. I blamed God for letting all the unfortunate things happen to us, and I blamed myself for being inadequate. It took me forty-four years to discover God's unlimited and unconditional love. I had limited him by locking him in a bottle: I treated him like a magic genie who grants my wishes if I've been good."

She continues, "Now that I have finally found a relationship with him, the desire to know him more gets greater every day. Now when I cry to him, it's not because I want to blame but because I need rest and healing. Although sometimes I still fail to trust him fully, when I cry my heart out to him, he makes his presence felt in various ways that I could never have imagined. He truly is a loving Father."

Healing begins

The first step in the healing process is to see yourself the way God sees you: with perfect love. Keep in mind that the Devil does not want you to know the truth. We have an enemy who uses our wounds and traumas and brokenness to do all he can to obscure the Lord's goodness and the Divine Love that's flowing—already flowing!—into your life in a deeper way. Our enemy wants us to doubt God's goodness and love. But God gave us the Divine Word (the Bible) to make the truth clear. For example:

> *Love is patient, love is kind. It does not envy, it does not boast, it is not proud. It does not dishonor others, it is not self-seeking, it is not easily angered, it keeps no record of wrongs. Love does not delight in evil but rejoices with the truth. It always protects, always trusts, always hopes, always perseveres. (1 Corinthians 13:4-7)*

In other words, God is saying to you right now:

> *I love you so much that I'm happy to be patient with you! No matter what you've done wrong, I long to give you My kindness. I am not like those who rejected you because they envied you. I do not boastfully lord it over you like others have done, but as your Lord I do boast to the angels and saints about how wonderful you are. Yes, I know how messed up you still are, but when I look at you, I look through the sacrifice that My Son made for you. Your sins were nailed to that Cross, and because you love My Son, that makes all the difference. On My Son is what is ugly about you. I see what is beautiful in you.*
>
> *I am humble of heart in all of my dealings with you. I will*

never dishonor you before others–regardless of what you have done. When you fail to see Me as I really am, I am dishonored by it but I am not self-seeking; I am you-seeking. When you sin, instead of becoming quickly angered, I consider how much you want to be holy and I smile about the future because you will conquer this sin with the help of My Holy Spirit. When you ask Me to forgive you, your sin is wiped from the Book of Life; I no longer keep a record of what you did wrong. And before you repented, remember that trouble you got into that felt like a punishment? I did not delight in that. And when you realized the truth, I rejoiced.

No matter what you've done wrong, as long as you humbly turn to Me now and surrender your will to My Divine Will, I am at your side to protect you. I trust you far more than you trust yourself. And no matter what you're still doing wrong without yet repenting, I always have hope in you. My love for you will pursue you all the way, if necessary, to the moment when we meet at the gates of Heaven and we can finally and fully embrace in that perfect love for which you have been deeply longing.

The second step in the healing process is to realize that we are all loved incompletely, insufficiently, imperfectly by the humans who are called by God to love us as much as he loves us. And we love them incompletely, insufficiently, imperfectly, too. To find the joy and peace and healing that comes from God's perfect love, we need to identify the imperfections of humans and turn them into a powerful reminder that Father God is better and bigger than all that. They are, in fact, evidence that he is reaching out to us. He is using them to invite us to realize that only he can give us the fullness of love and goodness and help for which we long. Abba-Father wants us to depend only on God (and here I speak of the fullness of God, the entire Trinity).

We long for the fullness of God's love because we instinctively know that we're supposed to have it. *"I have loved you with an everlasting love"* (Jeremiah 31:3 NIV). He designed us to know and receive his love. He created us because he has been loving us everlastingly, timelessly, desiring to have a precious Father-child relationship with us ever since and *before* we were conceived in our mother's womb. *"For you created my inmost being; you knit me together in my mother's womb"* (Psalm 139:13 NIV).

Our Divine Father brought us into existence so that he could love us with his whole heart, his whole soul, his whole mind, and his whole strength. Jesus told us to *"love God with all your heart, with all your soul, with all your mind, and with all your strength"* (see Mark 12:30) because this is the nature of God! This is the kind of love he has for us. For *you!*

Father God wants to heal your wounded heart. As he says in Jeremiah 31:3-4 (adapted for this moment): *"I have loved you with an everlasting love; I have drawn you close to Me with unfailing kindness. I will build you up again, my precious child."*

He is with you right now to correct the bad messages that have cut you down. Let him point out your goodness and your giftedness. He sees your goodness even when you cannot. Yes, he sees your sins, too. Yes, he sees your every flaw. But because you have allowed Jesus to be your Savior, when the Father looks at you, he sees you through the filter of the Son's sacrifice on the Cross. He sees your sins nailed to the Cross. He sees you as the cleansed saint that the Sacraments have re-created you to be.

Psalm 139:14 (NIV) is a prayer you might want to say every day if you need healing from a bad self-image: *"I praise you because I am fearfully and wonderfully made; your works are wonderful . . . "*

Why is it hard to imagine that Father God sees us as so wonderful? Because childhood punishments and the imperfect views of us that came from parents and other father-figures have tainted not only our image of God but also our image of ourselves. True, we sin and make plenty of mistakes and fail in other ways. But we are much more than that, and God knows this better than we do.

So if the first step toward healing our image of God's Fatherhood is to embrace the imperfections of others as a reminder to expect perfection only from God, then the second step is to embrace our own imperfections as learning experiences, realizing that God is delighted to help us become who he designed us to be: wonderful masterpieces made in his image.

The third step is to distrust our memories. They are not giving us an accurate picture of God.

Memories are unreliable. They are tainted by our emotions and desires and fears. For example, children usually remember only part of what the parents did or said. And what they do remember is tainted by their partial understanding of their parents' motives. So, it's not surprising that my son remembers trying to get my attention and being pushed away.

The reality is: I worked from home as a freelance writer so that I could be readily available to the children. Ralph and I sacrificed expensive vacations and other big purchases for this. But my son was too young to understand this. In his thinking, if he could see me, he could get attention from me. However, we had rules about interruptions. Whenever I got writing assignments, I had deadlines to keep and I tried to teach my children to respect this.

Thus, when a child needed my attention, if the interruption would disrespect my work, I would say, "No, not right now," and I would give him or her my undivided attention as soon as possible. My son only remembered me saying, "No." His emotional needs were not met fast enough to satisfy his youthful impatience, and so his emotions highlighted the part of the conversation that he disliked the most. As time passed, this emotional highlighting became what psychologists call "implicit" memory.

We all have implicit memories that differ from reality. The problem is, our implicit memories not only affect our relationship with our parents (or whomever triggered the emotional reaction), they also interfere with our relationship with Father God. Accurate or not, what we remember is what we project onto God.

Therefore, **the fourth step** toward healing is to consciously differentiate our human parents from God the Perfect Parent. Ask yourself: What is my image of God the Father? Who is he to me?

On Day 23 of this journey into the Father's heart, we will go a lot deeper into healing. But it starts here. And each day between now and then will lay the groundwork for the healing that you've been praying for.

Today's Exercise: The Box of Differentiation

Here's an exercise that will introduce you to God the Father as he really is. Take a sheet of paper (this is your "box") and draw a line down the middle. In the left column, list every imperfect trait that you've experienced from your human father. You can also do this with regards to your mother, a boss, or any other person in authority over you.

The traits could be long-term personality traits or short-term, temporary traits that were triggered by unusual circumstances. Add it to the list if it got stuck in your memory, because anything that has not been forgotten is very likely affecting your relationship with the Father.

For example, words you might choose are: absent, not a good listener, abusive, short-tempered, too demanding, liar, or undependable.

If you have trouble getting started because you had wonderful parents and were never hurt or disappointed by any authority figure, follow Bill's example:

"I sat in front of my divided 'list' page in order to write down my late father's imperfect traits—not that he was overweight, etc., but significant ones. I looked at that page, and looked, and thought: He was a good Dad, a great Dad. He was strict with us four boys and he smoked, but I couldn't think of anything to write. He developed some new traits as he neared his final 85th year, but I didn't hold him as responsible as I do frailty and senility. But then I thought: I ought to put myself in that left column and re-think the exercise. I did and found several items to list."

So feel free to think outside the box when writing inside the box of your writing exercise. What are the quick answers that come to mind when you read these questions?

1. Recall a time when you suffered because of someone's behavior. Name that behavior.
2. Think of a time when you felt disappointed, let down, or discouraged. What negative trait(s) caused that problem?
3. What traits in yourself or in others have worked against hope?
4. Did/do you live with anyone who made promises that were insincere?
5. Who made/makes you feel inferior? What trait(s) caused that feeling?
6. Who has been deceitfully charming or manipulative in order to get his own way?
7. Did any authority figure in your life demand respect without earning it?
8. Have your plans or dreams been squashed by a bully or control freak?
9. Were you frequently criticized and belittled?
10. Did you have to "walk on eggshells" when talking to a parent because you were unable to be open and share yourself freely?
11. Was a parent so lost in alcohol or other addictions that you didn't

get the attention you needed?

12. Did a parent have unpredictable mood swings, one minute happy and sweet and the next minute throwing a temper tantrum, thus making the gentle side unreliable?
13. Did anyone show cruelty, inflicting physical harm on you or someone else in your family or pets?
14. Which of the following traits were missing from your relationship with your dad? If he was absent from your life, apply these questions to the closest father substitute.
    - Was he your hero? A man of courage, perseverance, and integrity?
    - Did you feel secure and safe?
    - Did he live humbly?
    - Did he teach you how to pray and have faith in God?
    - Did he teach you the truth about the wrong messages of the world?
    - Did he provide you with a moral compass and teach you how to exhibit high moral values with courage?
    - Was he the voice of reason when you had problems, offering solutions or a new perspective?

After pondering these questions and any others that come to mind, use the left column of your paper to write a list (each five words or less) of everything that describes your father's human imperfections. You may expand this to include any important parental figure. And don't get stalled by your emotions. As difficult and sad as this exercise might feel now, forge ahead. By the end of this chapter, your healing will begin. Do this exercise now—before reading the remainder of this chapter.

* * *

When finished, in the right column next to each imperfect trait, list the opposite trait. For example, next to "absent" write "always with me." Next to "abusive" you might choose to put "safe." In the example that Bill gave about his dad's old age senility, he wrote, "God is ageless and changeless in all his traits."

Do this now and then continue reading. Trust me, it will be more effective if you don't read ahead.

***

After filling in the right column, read out loud the list you put there, beginning with "God is . . . " For example, "God is always with me. God is safe."

What you've just accomplished is the very important therapy of differentiating humans from God and Earthly parents from your Divine Father. You've stopped projecting onto God what humans have modeled.

Use this list as a meditation and repeatedly mull over each trait that you named in the column on the right. One at a time, ask yourself: How fully do I believe that God the Father is like this? Mark which ones you need to understand more fully. Then ask Jesus to introduce you to this Perfect Daddy. Visualize it with your imagination during prayer. Invent your own divine throne room or any other scene where it feels good, safe, and friendly to meet the Father. And remember this place! Revisit it whenever you want to feel close to your Divine Daddy.

The final step toward healing is to let God fill in the gaps left by human imperfections. This began for me during a major crisis of faith. I was certain that God had abandoned me and my family.

God, why have You abandoned me?

Ralph and I wanted to move to a better neighborhood so our two young children could grow up in a safe environment. We prayed confidently for our house to sell quickly. Eight months later, our house was still on the market. I wondered: *Why is God ignoring us?* I couldn't shake the sense that he had abandoned us.

Surely God could see what this long wait was doing to our family.

One Sunday on the way to church, I pointed out a house that had sold in just two weeks. I said, "Our house is at least as good. Why do all the other houses sell except ours? We asked for God's help from the very beginning. But did that make any difference?"

Ralph shook his head. "The guys at work never ask for his help and everything seems to work out great for them."

I replied, "I feel like if we had never asked for God's help, we would have sold our house a long time ago." Our faith was eroding fast.

When we arrived at the church parking lot, I stared at the doors. What would I do if I couldn't find God in there? The feeling of being abandoned had been growing over the past several weeks.

We entered the building and were greeted by Sister Cathy, who had been praying for us. She asked, "Have you sold your house yet?"

"No," I answered and hurried on before the tears could flow. Taking a seat, I prayed, *Oh God, let me know You haven't abandoned us. Show me that You're going to answer our prayers.*

Then the Mass began. The congregation sang, "I am your God. No longer be afraid. I know your every need; My love will never end."

My voice cracked and my eyes blurred with tears. My soul cried out, *But I am afraid, Lord! I'm afraid what I want isn't important to You. In all this waiting I feel only torment. Your love never ends for everyone else. God, why have You abandoned me?*

I barely managed to stay in church. To keep from weeping, I thought about a needlepoint project I was designing at home.

Finally, Mass ended. On the way home I told Ralph, "I don't know if I'll be able to go back next week. This feeling that God is ignoring us is destroying my faith, maybe beyond repair. If God doesn't do something soon, I can't see how I'll ever be able to trust him again."

Ralph silently gripped the wheel.

I continued. "Intellectually, I believe God is holding up the sale of our house for some good reason that only he knows. But spiritually, I feel abandoned. If only I could hear God assuring us that it's all for the best."

That afternoon two couples came by to look at the house, but again, no one wanted to buy it. The next day we got a call from the woman who owned the house that we hoped to buy after selling the old one.

"Any interest on your house yet?" she asked.

"No."

"A family came through here yesterday. They really like the place. They'll probably draw up a contract this week. You know I'd rather sell it to you, but I'll have to take the first good offer I get."

"Well," I tried to laugh. "If your house really is the one God thinks is best for us, they won't buy it." I said it more out of habit than belief. Inside, I was panicking. We were going to lose the house we wanted because God was ignoring our prayers.

After I hung up, my heart thumped forlornly while my hand still cradled the receiver. I needed someone to talk to. I needed help overcoming this crisis of faith. But whom could I call? Who had enough faith and was willing to listen to me?

I remembered my brief encounter with Sister Cathy. She had seemed genuinely interested and she had counseling skills. I called her and set up an appointment for Tuesday afternoon.

Another wait. Tuesday afternoon came slowly and I spent the time wondering what my faith would be like when all this waiting was finally over.

As we sat together at the kitchen table in her convent, I told Sister Cathy why I felt so discouraged.

"Depression is anger turned inward," she said. "Who do you really feel angry toward?"

I shrugged. "God, I guess. But I know I shouldn't. It's just that, well, it seems like he answers everyone's prayers but mine."

"Sometimes we project toward God images or feelings we have toward friends. For example, a son who's never known his father's love often finds it hard to understand God's love."

That made sense, but I couldn't see how it applied to me. It wasn't my family or friends who were interfering with the selling of our house. It was God.

Driving home, I thought about what she'd said. I wondered, *Have I ever felt abandoned by friends?* Yes. There were times when I'd been hurt because my friends had let me down.

"But God's not like that!" I exclaimed. "He's a Friend with a capital F, the only true Friend!" The real source of my problem became clear. Because friends had abandoned me, I expected God to do the same. But God is not like human friends!

As if a switch had been thrown, I saw God in a whole new light. Joy flooded in and replaced months of depression. It was still another month before we sold our house, but for the first time, I was able to wait without worry. In the end, we got our proof that God had never abandoned us. We sold our house for a better price. God saved for us the house we wanted. And mortgage rates had dropped.

More than that, the timing was also perfect for the family who bought our old house and for the one who sold us our new home. In the end, my faith was stronger than ever.

DAY 3

The Name of Abba, Like No Other Name

THERE ARE MANY names for God in scripture. Let's look at the one that Jesus used: Abba. Then let's find your own special name for God to help heal your relationship with him.

> *For those who are led by the Spirit of God are the children of God. The Spirit you received does not make you slaves, so that you live in fear again; rather, the Spirit you received brought about your adoption to sonship. And by him we cry, "Abba, Father." The Spirit himself testifies with our spirit that we are God's children. (Romans 8:14-16 NIV)*

My dad has a favorite memory about my childhood, which he likes to retell often. It was the day I became old enough to notice the man who was preaching up front in church. I stood up on the pew, pointed and exclaimed, "That's my daddy!"

My dad was the pastor of a Protestant congregation. He beamed with pride at his little girl's pronouncement, even though I had interrupted his sermon.

Unknowingly, I had preached my own sermon that day with those three simple words. As Abba-Father's children, we have good reason to exclaim every single day, "That's my Daddy!" If you're not already doing this, let's begin. It will make a difference.

Imagine that you're sitting in church and the pastor finishes reading the Gospel passage and looks up at the congregation, ready to explain what you just heard. Suddenly the image of an elderly gentleman transposes itself over the pastor. The pastor is hidden completely. What you see is God the Father. You know it's him. No doubt about it! Your innermost spirit recognizes him.

God himself has come to explain the Gospel passage!

His voice is calm, soothing, and gentle yet full of certainty. You can see in his face that he is yearning—deeply yearning—for everyone (even the small children) to understand what he is saying. You have never before heard the Bible explained with such clarity. How beautiful he makes the truth sound! Even the part that used to be difficult for you to believe as true, now you know for sure that it is true and you feel very blessed to finally see it from God's perspective. You can't help but smile and nod your head as the truth sinks in.

Your smile has caught his eye. He looks directly at you and returns your grin with the biggest, happiest smile you have ever seen. You can feel his gaze penetrating deeply into your soul. You know he can see all your faults, but he is still grinning with delight! He sees everything that is good in you and (you know this with all of your heart) he is very pleased with you.

As he turns back to the rest of the congregation to continue the homily, he winks at you.

Now you feel like standing up and shouting, "That's my ___!" Daddy. Father. Papa. Abba. What name do you use? Your choice can affect your confidence in him.

We have emotional attachments to certain names. Who was your favorite person during childhood—someone who cared about you, someone you enjoyed, someone who was safe and uplifting?

When you meet a new acquaintance with the same name today, do you automatically have good feelings about this person?

Who bullied you?

A stranger today with the same name might have to wait for you to process your inner distrust as you carefully watch for proof of goodness. Though this process might happen so quickly you don't realize you're doing it, it's a normal psychological phenomenon.

At around the age of six, I stopped calling my father "Daddy" because it seemed to express a warmth between us that existed only in my wishful thinking. Nor did I want to call him "Father" because that sounded too formal, too cold and stand-offish, and my relationship with him was better than that.

What does the name "Father" feel like to you? What does praying to "Our *Father* who art in Heaven" do for your desire to feel closer to God? Does this name exude trust? The kind of trust that dwells in your heart and affects your behaviors?

Trust does not reside in your intellectual-thinking head where you know the truth about God. How much of your life—your daily decisions, moods, and words—gives evidence that you trust God? Trusting him so much that you would follow him across a dangerous highway while traffic is speeding toward you?

A prayer life based on intimacy with the Father

Many people don't know that God is speaking to them every day in a fatherly way. Do you recognize when he's hugging you and comforting you and is being everything else that we look for in a daddy?

Charmaine calls him "Papa God." She says, "Some years ago I remember coming home very distressed from my job, crying out to him, and he scooped me into his bosom to comfort me. If only I could have stayed there! Recently, I asked him for a hug. I received it in the arms of a complete stranger. The next day, the Holy Spirit confirmed that this had been the hug that I had asked for."

That's my Daddy! And yours, too.

When I need a hug from God, I sometimes return to the throne room where I had first climbed onto his lap. Visualizations like this are very helpful, especially after prayerfully asking the Holy Spirit to anoint your imagination. I also visit my Divine Daddy in the visualization of a sunny, green field surrounded by colorful wildflowers. In this meditation, the Father is sitting on a quilted blanket on the ground. He's inviting me to join him, and I do. He already knows what's bothering me, so I snuggle into his embrace and let him hold me.

This is more than just a mental exercise. It's very real. I'm sure of it, because I always feel better afterward.

When you imagine being alone with Father God, where do you go? What does the scene look like? The more details you add to what you visualize, the more effective the meditation becomes.

When you finish the encounter, do you feel more loved? Do you feel heard? Do you feel like you benefited from the experience? If so, trust those feelings. If you had been unable to force yourself to feel better before meeting up with the Father, you can be sure that the reason you feel better afterward is because you really, truly did spend time with your divine Daddy.

But what if you cannot imagine being alone with Father God? What if your attempts to meditate on and feel his presence keep failing? Remember that Jesus said (John 14:7 NIV), *"If you really know me, you will know my Father as well. From now on, you do know him and have seen him."* So focus on Jesus and let him reveal the Father to you. Listen to Liddy's story and see the Father in Jesus:

"I recall when I was very young, probably in my teens, that I felt so unloved (in my family of 6, I was the 5th child). I was crying uncontrollably on my bed and I wished God would take me Home. I didn't belong here on Earth. Then something made me turn and look behind me. There was the figure of Jesus with outstretched arms! And this wonderful peace filled me. He did not touch me or hold me, and when I looked again there was nothing. But this peaceful love enfolded me."

God as Liddy's Father reached out to her through her relationship with Jesus.

One of the clues that God is speaking to you in a fatherly way is what happens when you feel heard. As you pour out your grief to God—your tears or your troubles—how do you know that he is truly listening?

To answer this, consider: Was your human father a good listener? And your mother and the priest in the confessional and others you've turned to when you needed to be heard? Could you approach each of them with confidence in their desire to believe you and understand you and listen to your heart as well as to your words?

If you can say yes to that last question, you probably have no difficulty feeling heard by God. You're very blessed! Many who are reading this have not had the same experience. Yet.

God, of course, hears every word we say and every thought we don't speak. He understands us better than we understand ourselves. And he sees it all through the lens of "the big picture"—the entire situation, including the needs of everyone who's affected by it. He knows what's transitory and he knows how to lead us into the eternal if only we would respond to his voice.

A very important part of being heard well is receiving well the responses that come to us. We learn to do this—poorly or appropriately—from our human relationships. If the father-figures in your life have genuinely listened to you and understood you, it's likely that you find it fairly easy to entrust your heart to God and believe that he cares. And you behave accordingly.

The best possible scenario is when the person we're speaking to is strongly connected to the Holy Spirit, actively listening to both the Spirit and to us at the same time. When that happens, we can trust that God will speak to us through that person.

But ask yourself this: Do you have any automatic *distrust?* A built-in protection mechanism that keeps you guarded in case the other person does not really have your best interests at heart? If you do, it's affecting your ability to receive all that the Father wants to give to you and say to you through this other person.

Consider what it means to be truly heard. A lot of people seem to be listening to us, but if they become judgmental about what they hear, they have not listened well. When we feel misjudged after being open and honest, it's because the person we're talking to is listening more to his or her own ideas, faults, and presumptions than to us.

How has this affected your relationship with God?

Felisha, who says she never feels "the comfort of his closeness," described her father as a good listener but very judgmental and her mother as extremely controlling and more judgmental toward her than to anyone else. When asked what her stumbling block is in her relationship with God, she answered with frustration, saying: "I can't understand how a loving Father, seeing a child of his trying to reach him, would not bend down and pick her up."

There's a direct connection between how her parents "listened" to her and why she thinks that God ignores her when she reaches out to him. She did not learn what being listened to is really like. She says, "I know that God listens when I speak to him, but he is like one of those people we see on TV who waves away journalists, saying 'NO COMMENT!'"

Judgmentalism creates a very wrong impression about God. God is, of course, the ultimate Judge. Psalm 75:7 (NIV) says, *"It is God who judges: He brings one down, he exalts another."* Saint Peter preached that everyone has to "give account to him who is ready to judge the living and the dead" (1 Peter 4:5 NIV). However, if we think of ourselves as deserving of punishment even after we repent, we've forgotten why Jesus died on the Cross.

This train of thought is actually from the Devil. Satan is the Accuser, not God. Satan wants us to feel so bad about ourselves that we believe God can't or won't be gentle with us. Satan does not want us to realize that God is, in truth, a loving Father who bends down into our sinful messes to pick us up and cradle us gently next to his heart.

Yes, Abba-Father is The Judge. But that does *not* mean he is judgmental.

Judgmentalism teaches that God doesn't care about us nearly as much as he cares about laws and rules and regulations. Judgmentalism teaches that God does not hear our hearts, that he does not consider our motives, and that he does not notice how much we actually desire to be holy even though we are sinning.

In reality, a good judge listens very well. A good judge takes everything into consideration. Psalm 119:137 says, *"You are just, O Lord, and your judgment is right."* God is never judgmental but he does make fair judgments—more accurate judgments than any human can make. His heart goes out to everyone who genuinely wants to be lifted from sin. When he sees his child reaching up to him to be pulled out of her messes, of course he bends down to pick her up!

For our relationship with Abba-Father to be healed, we need to unlearn what judgmentalism taught us and learn how to recognize God the Father as the Good Judge. Then we will be able to proclaim with delight: "That's my Daddy!"

Find your special prayer-name for God

We know that God is supposed to be completely trustable, but when your prayers are not answered, how do you feel about God (not *think*, but *feel* about him)? Do you feel abandoned? Ignored? Rejected? To whatever extent we feel this way about God, that's how much we don't trust him. And how do you suppose that makes *him* feel?

Servant of God Luisa Piccarreta (1865-1947), also known as the "Little Daughter of the Divine Will," was an incredible mystic. Jesus told her:

> I feel sad when they think that I am severe, and that I make more use of Justice than of Mercy. They act with Me as if I were to strike them at each circumstance. Oh! how

> dishonored I feel by these ones. . . . by just taking a look at my life, they can but notice that I did only one act of Justice—when, in order to defend the house of my Father, I took the ropes and snapped them to the right and to the left, to drive out the profaners. Everything else, then, was all Mercy: Mercy my conception, my birth, my words, my works, my steps, the Blood I shed, my pains—everything in Me was merciful love. Yet, they fear Me, while they should fear themselves more than Me. (June 9, 1922)

Remember, Jesus revealed God the Father through the way he treated people. Like Father, like Son. Re-read what Jesus told Luisa Piccarreta, but this time recognize the feelings of Abba-Father.

Now think of a prayer request you've recently offered up to God. Imagine making the same request to the person who was your best childhood friend. Let's further imagine that this person has been given supernatural powers. Knowing how good and caring your friend was to you, what do you suppose he or she would do with your request? And probably pretty fast, too, right?

Okay, so try nicknaming God with that person's name. My best, longest childhood friend was Mary Cleary. It just doesn't seem suitable to pray to God and call him Mary. It does help, however, to project onto God the qualities about Mary Cleary that I enjoyed so much.

It was my friend Mary who introduced me to the fun of bowling. "You'll like it," she told me.

"Let's go!" I trusted her. I believed her. No question about it, I would enjoy bowling. So I asked my dad for permission and he told me, "No."

Oops, my dad had disappointed me again. I felt personally rejected when he rejected my request. Making matters worse, he offered no explanation.

As a teenager, I had become bold when Dad's responses made no sense to me. So I demanded to know, "Why not?"

Of course, he didn't like this and responded with anger. I began to cry. Finally, the truth came out: He said he was trying to protect me. He didn't like bowling because he wasn't good at it, and he was sure that I wouldn't like it either.

Joe had a similar experience:

> I'll never forget when my father and mother forbade me from joining the Boy Scouts. My heart was set on it, but what my father didn't understand, he didn't permit. I blamed him for being an ignorant immigrant who never got to eighth grade. It wasn't until much later that I realized the big picture: His love was protection from what he didn't know and understand.

God as our Good Father wants to protect us, too, but unlike our human parents, God understands everything. When he says no to us, he's taking into consideration the big picture—the *whole* picture. How it would affect our future. How it would affect others. Whether or not it will lead to sin.

We need to remind ourselves of this whenever we allow old wounds, consciously or unconsciously, to project onto God the limited knowledge of humans.

Happily, my dad changed his mind when he heard himself explain his reason for saying no to my desire to go bowling. And guess what! I enjoyed bowling very much despite all the gutter balls I rolled. If I had trusted my dad's feelings about bowling, though, I would have felt discouraged by my low score. But because I trusted my friend's enthusiasm for the game, I enjoyed it immensely. That's what a best friend can do.

It's taken me a lifetime to see Abba-Father as a best friend. Some grown-up daughters have a best-friend relationship with their dads. I can't imagine what that's like. If you have the same difficulty, it's time to be healed from relating to Father God as if he were a disciplinarian who has limited understanding and limited compassion. It's time to develop a relationship with him that's a close friendship. A good friend doesn't reject you over bad bowling. And this is the kind of friendship that the Divine Father wants to have with you.

It's very healing to project onto God the loving traits of the best friends we've known. Did your friends understand you when you shared your deepest thoughts with them? Abba-Father understands you better than all others. Did your friends ever criticize you when you were open and vulnerable with them? Your Divine Father does *not* do *this*, but if there is something to criticize, he wraps you in his loving arms and invites you to improve without making you feel bad about yourself.

Did your childhood friends enjoy hanging out with you? What

about the friends you have today? Why do they feel good in your presence? Abba-Father likes being with you for the same reasons.

Which friends have been strong supports for you? Like: "I've got your back. No matter what others think of you, I'm on your side." Abba-Father is definitely saying that to you right now.

How do I know this is true? Because I rely on it! For example, whenever someone falsely accuses me or refuses to believe me, my first reaction is to defend myself. I want to argue in an attempt to change the other person's mind. (A normal human reaction, right?) But I've learned that this rarely works. More importantly, I need to stop caring about what others think of me and focus only on what God thinks of me. Instead of trying to protect my reputation (which is what motivated me to argue), I should let Father God protect me.

When I turn to him and ask him to defend me, everything changes. God's love fills me and this brings with it a peace that is inexplicable. Sometimes the other person hears or receives the truth from God that I had wanted to argue them into believing. But when they don't, it doesn't matter because God is comforting me. I visit him on the blanket in the field and tell him what the other person accused me of. I do this with insecurity, because I wonder if there is any truth to the accusation. "Maybe I feel defensive because I don't want to hear the truth," I tell him. "What do You think about me?"

And then, if there's a wrong I need to admit and fix, Abba-Father reassures me that I am much more than this one sin or this one mistake. He reminds me of what is good about me, what the other person had failed to see in me. His perfect love fills the entire conversation.

I'm able to do this healing meditation because I've had good friends who defended me.

Making the connection between our friends' loving traits and God's is an excellent spiritual exercise. However, we can't take this so far as to use their names when praying to God. That would sound silly and be too distracting. And yet, names are important. Think about how you feel when you contact an important person (a boss, the leader of your favorite ministry, the owner of a business you've sent a complaint to, and such), and you get a reply that includes your name—not in some formal way (like "Dear so-and-so"), but embedded in the message itself. It indicates that you matter. You feel connected.

God says to you, *"Do not fear, for I have redeemed you; I have summoned you by name; you are mine"* (Isaiah 43:1 NIV). When you summon

God by name, what do you call him? Does it make you feel connected? And connected closely enough?

Remember what I shared with you, in Day 1, about why I could no longer call my father "Daddy." The name didn't fit because it felt too intimate, so I chose "Dad." I considered calling him "Father," but that was too formal. This carries into my relationship with the Divine Father. I can't call God "Dad" because that totally projects my human dad onto him. The name "Father" seems too formal. And the name "Daddy" is tainted by memories of feeling disappointed in and disconnected from my dad. So, what name would help me in my relationship with God the Father?

What works for me might not work well for you. For some people, the name "Father" conveys loving respect while for others it makes God seem distant. A good step deeper into the Father's heart is choosing a name for him that summons all the wonderful and perfect fatherhood that you long for.

What did Jesus call him during those private all-nighters of deep prayer? It seems likely that he called him "Abba."

"Abba" was the Aramaic word for "father" in the traditional liturgies and prayers of the Jews whenever they referred to God *in a family context*. It did not literally mean "Daddy"; it had no connotation as a term of endearment or a child-like relationship with God. It was simply what sons and daughters called their dads throughout their lives.

The Gospel writer Mark tells us that Jesus used this name for the Father while agonizing in the Garden of Gethsemane. In great emotional angst, Jesus called out: "Abba! Father! All things are possible for You; remove this cup from Me." And then he added, *"Yet not what I will, but what You will"* (Mark 14:36 NASB). Since "abba" means "father," it's as if Jesus cried out, *"Father! Father!"* Interestingly, it's only Mark who shows Jesus using the name Abba; what was Mark's reason for pointing this out? What did he intend to teach?

One of the reasons why Jesus was killed is because he closely aligned himself to God the Father. He repeatedly emphasized that he came from the Father and did and said only what the Father wanted him to do and say. His opponents thought, "Blasphemy! Jesus is merely human like everybody else. It's impossible that he could be both human and divine at the same time."

In using "Abba! Father!" as the cry of Jesus, Mark wrote both the

Aramaic word for "father" and the Greek word. His use of the Aramaic name "Abba" referenced the Jewish liturgies that Jesus had grown up with. By coupling this with the everyday Greek word for father, Mark was reaching out to both Jews and Gentiles, making it clear that God was the same God for both. And Mark was saying that God was not only the father of Jesus, he was *The* Father—the Father of us all.

This very pointedly asserts that God's Fatherhood was very important to Jesus, both theologically and in the family sense—including in the hour of his greatest emotional need. Look at the depth of trust this implies: "Abba! Father! All things are possible for You; remove this cup from Me; yet not what I will, but what You will."

When you pray the Lord's Prayer, "Our Father, who art in Heaven . . . ," do you feel that same level of deep trust? I don't—not automatically. But when I pray, "Abba, my True Father, my Divine Daddy in Heaven . . . ," what a difference this makes!

Maybe you'd prefer to call him Papa or Pops or Paw. Choose a name that is powerfully intimate for you, a name that does not remind you of your own human father unless he doted on you so much that he really was a good representation of the compassionate trustworthiness of God.

There are two more times in the New Testament when God is called "Abba." Paul used it in Galatians 4:6 and Romans 8:15 to emphasize the special son/daughter relationship we have with the Divine Father who loves us so much that he adopted us into his family. It's an adoption that gives us full privileges and inheritance. (We'll get into this more deeply in a later chapter.)

In other words, God is trustworthy in a very fatherly way and in the best sense of the word "fatherly." The *Catechism of the Catholic Church* helps us understand this (in paragraph 239):

"By calling God "Father," the language of faith indicates . . . that he is goodness and loving care for all his children . . . The language of faith thus draws on the human experience of parents, who are in a way the first representatives of God for man. But this experience also tells us that human parents are fallible and can disfigure the face of fatherhood and motherhood . . . He transcends human fatherhood and motherhood, although he is their origin and standard: no one is father as God is Father."

Meditating with Our Father

We can learn much about who God the Abba-Father really is by meditating on the words Jesus gave us when he taught us how to pray:

Our Father,

Abba, Papa, my perfect Daddy, the same Father who sent angels to minister to Jesus in the Garden of Gethsemane . . .

Who art in Heaven,

because You are divine, You are Creator of all, You fathered me, gave life to me and want to spend eternity with me, because Heaven wouldn't be the same without me, and You long to enjoy it with me . . .

Hallowed be Thy name,

for Your very name is holy and You want me to call you "Abba-Father," sanctifying the title of Father, teaching me and showing the world what true fatherhood is meant to be . . .

Thy Kingdom come,

because You have adopted me and honored me with the privilege of being Your prince/princess, generously giving to me the inheritance of all the valuables of Your Kingdom, and You desire that I live in this inheritance right now . . .

Thy will be done,

because everything You will is good and everything You desire for me is blessed . . .

On Earth as it is in Heaven,

because You care about every nuance of my Earthly life, every moment, every problem I face, every person I meet, every opportunity to use the gifts and talents You have given me . . .

Give us this day our daily bread,

because You care about every hunger I have and You want to feed me with the nourishment that satisfies, purifies, heals, and blesses me. You want to give me Your Son, Jesus, Who is the Bread of Life, Who is teaching me to trust You more by making me rely only on You, one day at a time, moment by moment . . .

Forgive us our sins as we forgive those who sin against us,
because it pains You to see me enslaved to my sins and chained to the sins of others, since You want only what is good for me . . .

Lead us not into temptation but deliver us from evil,
for this is what I truly want, and You as my Abba-Father want to protect me and strengthen me in the midst of the evils of this world. You want to rescue me through Jesus from demonic strongholds and influences . . .

Amen!

Saint Francis of Assisi meditated on the nature of Abba by writing his own prayer inspired by the Our Father prayer:

O OUR most holy FATHER
Our Creator, Redeemer, Consoler, and Savior,

WHO ARE IN HEAVEN:
In the angels and in the saints,
Enlightening them to love, because You, Lord, are light
Inflaming them to love, because You, Lord are love
Dwelling in them and filling them with happiness
because You, Lord, are the Supreme Good,
the Eternal Good
from Whom comes all good
without Whom there is no good.

HALLOWED BE YOUR NAME:
May our knowledge of You become ever clearer
That we may know the breadth of Your blessings
the length of Your promises
the height of Your majesty
the depth of Your judgments.

YOUR KINGDOM COME:
So that You may rule in us through Your grace
and enable us to come to Your kingdom
where there is an unclouded vision of You
a perfect love of You
a blessed companionship with You
an eternal enjoyment of You.

YOUR WILL BE DONE ON EARTH AS IT IS IN HEAVEN:
That we may love You with our whole heart by always thinking of You
with our whole soul by always desiring You
with our whole mind by directing all our intentions to You and by seeking Your glory in everything
and with our whole strength by spending all our energies and affections
of soul and body
in the service of Your love
and of nothing else
and may we love our neighbors as ourselves
by drawing them all with our whole strength to Your love
by rejoicing in the good fortunes of others as well as our own
and by sympathizing with the misfortunes of others
and by giving offense to no one.

GIVE US THIS DAY:
in memory and understanding and reverence
of the love which our Lord Jesus Christ had for us
and of those things that He said and did and suffered for us.

OUR DAILY BREAD:
Your own Beloved Son, our Lord Jesus Christ,

AND FORGIVE US OUR TRESPASSES:
Through Your ineffable mercy
through the power of the Passion of Your Beloved Son
together with the merits and intercession of the Blessed Virgin Mary
and all Your chosen ones

AS WE FORGIVE THOSE WHO TRESPASS AGAINST US:
And whatever we do not forgive perfectly,
do you, Lord, enable us to forgive to the full
so that we may truly love our enemies
and fervently intercede for them before You
returning no one evil for evil
and striving to help everyone in You.

AND LEAD US NOT INTO TEMPTATION:
Hidden or obvious,
Sudden or persistent.

BUT DELIVER US FROM EVIL:
Past, present, and to come.

Amen.

Today's Exercise:
That's my Daddy!

Now write your own version of the Our Father prayer, and finish off each sentence with the exclamation, "That's my Daddy!" For example:

Our Father, You are in Heaven where You see everything that is going on in my life, and because You care so much about me, You are working a plan for my benefit, not disaster.
That's my Daddy!

Hallowed be Thy name. I worship You because You are holy.
That's my Daddy!

And so forth.

By writing it down, it becomes much more meaningful. Meditate on it daily. Bring it to mind when you're reciting the Our Father prayer in church where we go through it too fast for a deep meditation. Once your own version becomes so well known to you that it floods your worship when the recitation of the Our Father begins, you'll automatically become cognizant of Abba's nearness. And your heart will exclaim, "That's my Daddy!"

DAY 4

Words That Make a Difference

WHAT WORDS DO YOU use that imply something about God that really came from the ungodly traits of the humans in your life? This is what we'll look at now because it can make all the difference between a safe, healthy friendship with Abba-Father and a relationship that's handicapped by misconceptions.

> *"Because of the devastation of the afflicted, because of the groaning of the needy, / Now I will arise," says the LORD; "I will set him in the safety for which he longs." / The words of the LORD are pure words; / As silver tried in a furnace on the Earth, refined seven times. (Psalm 12:5-6 NASB)*

The Christmas of my first bicycle was both delightful and frustrating. Delightful because I finally received what I'd been begging for. Frustrating because my younger sister got a bike too.

Whenever I had pleaded, "*Please* can I have a bicycle," my parents told me that I wasn't old enough. So you can imagine how I felt when my sister got her bike the same day I did, even though she was two years younger than me.

"Unfair!" I cried.

I can empathize with the first laborers in Jesus' parable about the vineyard workers (see Matthew 20:1-16). The landowner hired them early in the morning and agreed to pay them a denarius (the usual wage for a day's work). He hired more workers at noon, still more at mid-afternoon, and a few more just one hour before quitting time. Then the landowner, a.k.a. God, paid everyone the same amount. In relating this to my bicycle, I had "worked" longer than my sister at growing old enough for a bike.

"Unfair!" cried the men who had worked the longest. "Some of those other guys worked only one hour and paid them the same amount you gave to us. That's not fair!"

But the employer replied, "I am not being unfair to you, friend." (Friend? Is this how God treats his friends? As Saint Teresa of Jesus said, "If this is how You treat Your friends, no wonder You have so few of them.")

Jesus continued the parable, still sounding very unfair, with the landowner saying: "I gave you what you agreed to. So what if I want to give those who were hired last the same as I gave you? I can do whatever I want with my money."

Very unfair! Hmm, that even sounds like my human father scolding me for being unhappy about waiting an extra two years for my bike. It also sounds like God is being tricky. Even miserly. As if he's saving money by cheating his full-time workers out of what they deserve.

And then comes the stinger: "Or are you envious because I am generous?"

Yup, that's me! I commit the sin of envy every time God makes easy for someone what I have worked hard for or prayed many years for. The little girl who waited too long for a bike has become the lady who cries "Unfair!" at the blessings of others.

You see, while I'm waiting on the Lord to give me what the Bible assures me he has promised, I'm vulnerable to the idea that God doesn't care about me as much as he cares about others. I can usually resist this false message, but not when I see someone else get what I want.

But what does the word "fair" really mean? To my parents, it meant treating everyone equally. My dad often reiterated that it was very important to him that he treats each of his three children equally. This meant, on that particular Christmas morning, that both me and my sister got our first bikes at the same time. I knew that this was not the true definition of "equal." To be treated equally, my sister and I would have been given our first bikes based on age, not "at the same time."

Thus, my image of God became: He is a Father who is unfair while claiming to be fair.

So let's ask: Does "fair" mean the same thing to Father God as it did to my human father? And to you and me?

What point was Jesus making with this parable? To find the answer, we have to look past the way the parable makes us feel when we put ourselves into the work shoes of the first laborers. Jesus is revealing the Father's compassion toward the underdog. The disadvantaged ones.

Consider the type of person who often gets turned down when applying for a job: the weak, the sick, the disabled, the "too" old and the "too" young, and other targets of discrimination, such as criminals or anyone with a bad reputation. Jesus is asking you: "In what ways do you feel discriminated against? The Father is going to give you more than what anyone else would give you! Who has overlooked you? The Father is going to give you special treatment! Who has rejected you because you don't match their expectations or because they don't understand your capabilities? The Father has a special mission for you."

Turn off the auto-responses that control your feelings

If our focus remains on the first laborers of the parable, we miss the opportunity to learn that God wants to give us more than what's "fair." That's the trouble. We get stuck in feelings that are based on wrong images of God's Fatherhood.

Malformed unconscious beliefs control us with auto-responses that are inappropriate for the situations that trigger them. We need to take control away from the misconceptions that have been limiting our understanding of Abba-Father.

The image of God as a Father who is unfair is, in fact, very unfair to him. This is *not* who he really is. He is a caring Father who is genuinely interested in you. He is generously doting on your unique needs. He is concerned about you while also remaining concerned about everyone else in your life. He gives you what you are ready to receive as soon as you are ready for it. He is never late, not even when we think he is. His timing is always perfectly suited for our lives and for the journeys of our faith growth.

However, it's possible to know this as a fact and yet not as a belief. Here's an example of how this happens:

God has taught me the truth of his perfect timing for many years. It's uncanny how often he reveals his hand in the timing of nearly everything I do. Despite this, sometimes I react to circumstances instead of act on what I know is true. My auto-response tells me that the Father is a God who answers prayers with, "Okay, you can have what you want, but first you'll have to wait until someone else catches up." It tells me: "Anyone else who might be impacted by your prayer request has to reach the point of asking for it, too, wanting it as much as you do. Until then, you have to wait." In other words, I think that I'm handicapped by the spiritual handicaps of others.

"Unfair!" I cry.

We have a lot of misconceptions about how our Divine Father treats us. These mistaken ideas often come from words that have been tainted by misuse, such as "fair." Another tainted word is "love."

Nancy didn't know the real meaning of love. Despite several years of therapy for the abuses she had suffered during childhood, she needed spiritual healing to discover God's love for her. She needed to learn that God's love was different than what she had grown up with.

Her father had been mentally unstable. When Nancy was five years old, he was committed to a psychiatric hospital. After that, one of her older brothers began to molest her and another brother physically and emotionally abused her. The image of God she unconsciously learned from her dad was that he is a Father who is not there to defend you when you need him most; he is not protective. From her brothers, she learned that love means being a victim. When she heard the words in church that describe Jesus as Victim, she identified with him but in a painful, non-healing way.

Furthermore, her mom often said while spanking the kids (just like many other parents do because it's true), "It's because I love you that I have to do this to you!" So of course, to Nancy, all love was suspicious. Even God's.

She says, "To this day, I have trust issues." When her second husband molested her daughter, "That was the final straw. I felt, right then and there, that I couldn't trust *any* male. I wanted to die, and I made my final attempt on the highway." Thanks to the therapy she received, her suicidal impulses were overcome, but she needed to learn how to trust God. She could not do that without first learning that there are men who are trustworthy.

After she came to me for spiritual healing, I introduced her to my husband, Ralph, and we included her in some of our family activities. We wanted to show her what God's love is really like. I led her through some inner healing exercises, and these began to make a difference. However, she distrusted my love for her. She wondered, "When is the abuse going to start?" To protect herself, she tried to push me away with anger and false accusations.

Of course, the abuse she expected from me never happened. But that didn't stop her from reacting to me as if I were about to hurt her. Our friendship was a minefield, and it didn't take much for an explosion to get triggered. Despite learning that I was safe, her emotional auto-responses overruled her intellect. And the same auto-responses also affected her understanding of how God loves her.

Meanwhile, the Holy Spirit inspired me to stand my ground patiently, quietly, calmly, and Jesus gave me the strength to do it. When time and again I did not treat her in the harmful way that she expected, she began to understand the difference between the manipulative, so-called "love" of her childhood traumas and the safe, unconditional love of Abba-Father.

Words of love do not mean the same to the abused as they do to the non-abused. More than anyone else, those reading this book who've been abused (especially during childhood) have more to overcome, more to reprogram, more to learn and relearn about who Abba-Father really is and what his love is truly like.

Nancy and I talked a lot about the true meaning of love and how God designed relationships to be. We differentiated Abba's unconditional love from every other relationship she'd ever had. Over the course of several years, she learned the truth about love, forgot it when circumstances triggered auto-responses, relearned the truth, and gradually became stronger in it.

It took a lot of reprogramming to deactivate the bombs in her minefield, and today there are still situations that trigger unhelpful auto-responses. She's had to repeatedly practice what she learned. She's had to persist in reexamining her auto-responses, relearning the truth, and reinforcing appropriate responses. It's a learning curve that needs to continue for the rest of her Earthly life. She explains:

> Trust is an imprint that we learn as young children. We trust Mom and then Dad. When those building blocks are missing, trust has to be a conscious effort, done every day. It never becomes natural after those imprinting years are long over. Unless God comes in and does a miracle, trusting others has to be put on just like someone who, after losing his legs in a car accident, has to put on prosthetic legs in order to walk. It's a lifetime struggle. I will never trust the way a child in a safe home learns to trust. I have accepted this fact and I do my best to just trust God because he is the most important figure in my life. As for trusting others, I lean on my crutch of trusting him first. But it will always be a struggle for me, just like a person who has to live a life with no legs.

If she hadn't persisted through spiritual healing with determination and the help of a professional therapist, she never would have made the progress that she did. And then, to continue progressing, Nancy relied on constant prayer, the Bible, spiritual books and talks, and Holy Mass: the essential sources of growth for all of us.

Anyone who has been abused needs the threefold approach that helped Nancy: (1) psychological counseling from a qualified therapist, (2) persistence and determination and conscious effort, and (3) spiritual healing. Without these, it's common to get stuck in the auto-responses that control our feelings.

Rout out your misconceptions about Abba-Father

All of us—everyone—can deepen our relationship with Father God and increase our trust in him by paying attention to our auto-responses whenever it seems like God is not loving us the way he should. Even the words that we rotely and obediently recite in church can trigger wrong ideas. For example, when the intercessory prayers of Mass and other group events are read, how does the congregation respond? A very common formula is: "Lord, hear our prayer." What happens with that on the subconscious level of faith?

The implication could easily be: "Lord, You don't hear us unless we ask You to hear our prayer." Think about it. If this is what you believe, change the formula. Mentally or out loud change it to: "Lord, thank You for hearing our prayers." Do you notice the change in your spirit?

What other words do you use frequently that imply something about God that is simply not true? These nuances can make all the difference between a safe, healthy friendship with Abba-Father and a relationship that's handicapped by misconceptions.

The Holy Spirit has provided us with tools that free us from malformed auto-responses. It's like having a treasure map and a magnifying glass to search for what has been hidden. Only when they are exposed can we conquer them. Let's uncover the subtle, hidden misconceptions that have been influencing you.

God is good. We know that. We profess it out loud. But whether we actually believe it or not is proven in the tests of everyday life. Our reactions to stressful situations—our behaviors during difficulties—reveal a lot about our unconscious beliefs.

For example, do you *really* believe that God is good all the time? That it's impossible for him to sin against you (or against the loved ones for whom you've been praying)? If you do, then why do you get stressed out by the situations that you've entrusted to him?

Or how about this: Do you *really* believe that God is omniscient (all-knowing)? If you do, then why tell him how to fix your problems or how to change your spouse or how to convert your adult child who has left the Church?

Admittedly, we understand Abba-Father imperfectly. So we compensate by adding to the end of our prayers, "But You know what's best. Thy will be done." Later, our joyless response to the hardships of life betray our inner handicaps. We still have unconscious messages undermining our faith. "Thy will be done" means, deep down, something like: "Thy will be done because I have no say in the matter anyway. Thy will is not fair, but You are God and I cannot control You, so I'm unhappy. Now I'll pray a Novena of the Rosary to get the Blessed Mother to change Your mind."

We accept his will and we don't accept it—both at the same time!

In scripture, God is described as the Rock whose works are perfect. All of his ways are just. He is faithful and he does no wrong. He is upright and just (see Deuteronomy 32:40). In human logic, where one plus two equals three, "God's ways are just" is added to the injustices we suffer even after we pray and therefore equals a definition of "fair" that is not fair to us at all.

Yet we know that God is faithful and does no wrong. We know he is a Father who is always "fair" and "just." So how do we make sense of the times he seems unfair? We blame ourselves. Our auto-response belief is that we don't get what we want because of God's justice. We don't deserve to be treated better.

This is why our auto-responses can tell us that we must wait for others to become ready for divine help when we give our prayer requests to the Father. They further tell us that we must wait patiently or else we're sinning and the Father gets upset with us.

But who can be patient under those circumstances? It's not our fault that we're ready while others are not. We now have someone else to blame. Hooray.

Every malformed, below-surface thought process hampers our relationship with Abba-Father. Unless we pay attention to what's happening underneath and rout out what is wrong, we remain stuck there. The good news is: Once exposed to the light of the scriptures and the revelations that are readily supplied by the Holy Spirit, they lose their hold on us. Our faith grows.

To enjoy a close, fun, helpful intimacy with the Father, we need to understand him as he really is. We need to reprogram our thought processes and consciously choose to live in the truth of God's goodness. We need to do this repeatedly until we form a healthy, holy auto-response.

Reprogramming involves understanding the scriptures better and reading them in the context of the bigger picture or lesson that's connected to them. This is what we've been doing with the parable of the vineyard workers. As I said before, Jesus was revealing the Father's compassion toward the underdog. In this light, "fair" and "just" describe a God of compassion, mercy, and love. I like that! It's not about the bike at all. Nor wages. It's about unconditional, merciful love.

Let's look at how knowing this can affect our prayer requests. When we pray, we can experience the peace that overcomes stress by reminding ourselves that God is fair and just and that therefore he doesn't withhold anything good from us, not even if we've had a long, dark past of doing evil. What matters, in his eyes, is how much—right now—*we* want what *he* wants.

So, what does he want? He wants to say yes to the desires of our heart. He wants to say yes to our prayer requests, as long as what we want is not sinful. But he wants to give us even more than we've asked for. His "yes" might come with a "but not now" or "not this way."

And he wants us to learn something valuable, something that will increase our holiness, something that will also help others. When we want this too, we appreciate how fair Abba-Father truly is. We relax. We discover joy even before our prayers are answered.

The divine logic is: "God's ways are just." Add to this his forgiveness for the injustices that we've repented from, and now one plus two equals "he only wants what's best for me," which equals far more than we can ever imagine. Therefore, "I can trust him with 'Thy will be done' and truly be at peace with that."

The formula is simple: To free ourselves to enjoy a close, trusting relationship with Abba-Father, we must first identify and then clear up our misconceptions about him.

Today's Exercise:
Reprogram your thought processes

To find the errors that control your auto-responses, listen to how you complain. Every complaint carries within it a clue about how you see Abba as less than he really is, such as less caring, less powerful, less attentive, or whatever the "less" is that has been diminishing your relationship with him. These clues are important!

Today's exercise will help you detect the misconceptions that have been affecting you. Write a letter to the Father. Name your toughest prayer request—that situation that has been going on for far too long—and complain to him about how he is or is not handling it. Complain, complain, complain! (This is not sinful; he can handle it and he knows that your innermost desire is to be healed.) Write down why you're upset with him, but if you don't feel upset with him, dig deeper by finishing this sentence: "I trust You, Father, but I wish You would ___."

Write it fast, unfiltered. Be honest. Be brutally honest. Don't hold anything back.

Describe your feelings—they contain wonderful clues. How do you feel about waiting so long for your prayer to be answered? Even if you think you know why God wants you to wait so long, how do you feel about that?

Maybe you're waiting for God to zap someone into loving you the way they should. You know that God won't force them against their free will. So how does *that* make you feel? God is surely powerful enough and creative enough to get around their free will somehow.

But nothing has changed. Or maybe it got worse. Complain to God about his (apparent) lack of intervention.

Write this letter to God now before finishing this chapter. Write it, don't just think it. The second half of this exercise will shed light on what you wrote.

* * *

Watch your words

My first spiritual director, Irene Huber, frequently taught that "what you say is what you get." She wanted everyone to pay attention to the words we use, because our choice of words can impact us emotionally and spiritually. In her healing ministry, she had discovered that when people came to her saying, "I'm sick," they were less likely to receive a miracle than if they said, "I've been diagnosed with or have the symptoms of a sickness."

We can either own the illness or take ownership of God's concern and compassion for us in our illness. By choosing our words carefully as we describe what we're seeking from him, our focus shifts from the limitations of the illness to the potential of the healing.

To say, "I have ___," is to admit ownership of it. Which is truer for you? "I have faith" or "I have fear"? Do you have a fear that if your prayers are not answered, disaster will strike? Do you have a fear of God disappointing you? Or any other fear that's based on a misconception about God?

I'm sure you want to say, "I have faith," but when you react to situations that challenge your trust in God, reacting so spontaneously that you don't have time to choose your words carefully, what comes out of your mouth? For example: "I'm feeling very worried about this situation. I'm afraid it's going to get worse." This does not mean you have no faith. It simply means that you're routing out a misconception that's been controlling you.

Look again at the letter to God that you wrote in today's exercise.

1. What did you take ownership of with the words you wrote? (For example: "I have fear that this terrible situation will last forever.")
2. Which sentences can be rewritten to start with "I am ___" or "I have ___"? (For example, change "You know what is best, Father, but I sometimes feel angry about the injustice of it. I can't imag-

ine why You haven't done anything about it yet" to "I am angry because You seem unconcerned about the injustice. I have doubts that You truly care.")

3. What clues about your understanding of Father God do these sentences reveal? (For example, if you wrote "I am angry because You seem unconcerned about the injustice, I have doubts that You truly care," ask yourself: "Which humans in my life treated me unjustly long ago?" And then remind yourself: "Ahhh, but Father God is much better than them! Of course he cares! He hates the injustice far more than I do."
4. Which sentences proclaim correct understandings and which ones are raising flags about misconceptions? (Highlight in yellow what is true about Abba-Father, and cross out the misconceptions. Circle the parts that need further clarification.)

Our choice of words when praying to the Father can reveal a lot. In your prayer exercise:

1. Were you demanding or trusting? (Perhaps both?)
2. Did you tell God how to solve a problem? How humble were you in sharing your ideas with him? How much of the problem-solving did you leave up to him?
3. What do your demands (or strong preferences) and problem-solving ideas indicate about your conceptions of God?
4. Which words obscure what Abba-Father is really like?

By unEarthing the indicators of a lesser faith, your faith will grow. Identify the wrong messages that some of your words imply. Then seek out the truth from scriptures, a spiritual director, or a friend who has mature faith. Post the truth on sticky notes by your desk and on the bathroom mirror. Turn them into memorized mantras that you repeat often and out loud. This will reprogram your auto-responses.

Rewrite your prayer request with carefully chosen words of faith, even quoting scripture. Let this become your mantra in the particular situation that's covered by this prayer. And guess what will happen! Your new way of praying will improve your prayer words and build your faith during other situations as well.

DAY 5

The Safest Father in the World

THE PATH TO HEAVEN is the journey of becoming a little child who sleeps without fear in the Father's arms. How safe do you feel with God the Father? Are you able to climb up onto his lap and into his arms to feel his protective concern for you? He wants you to feel his powerful arms wrapping around you and creating a zone of extreme peace with you at the center.

> *The proof of our existence is that God–somebody who is higher, somebody who is greater–is holding us, protecting us. (Saint Teresa of Calcutta)*

No one is loved fully in any human relationship. This is a normal flaw of the human condition. And it's the source of much of our anguish. It's why Jesus told us to forgive seventy times seven times (Matthew 18:22); in other words: more than we think is enough. And sometimes we have to do this repeatedly—even daily—with the same person!

Therefore, because we project onto God what we've learned from humans, it's difficult (though not impossible) to fully believe that God loves us completely in every possible way despite our own flaws. It's *especially* difficult if we hold within us any misconceptions about how *safe* God is.

If we fear him at all (speaking not in the biblical sense of the word "fear," which by definition is a very humbling awe of God)—if we fear God for any reason, at any moment, this is a red flag alerting us to our need to discover more about how safe God really is. If we're afraid of being disappointed by his handling of our prayer requests or if we're afraid we're not good enough to receive his doting, fatherly love, we need to open ourselves to what it means to be "safe in God."

For Nancy, whose dad had abandoned the family through mental illness, leaving her unprotected from the abuse of her brothers, feeling safe with God seemed impossible. However, her traumatic childhood was not the only reason why she felt unsafe with the Father. It's the same with us: There are multiple reasons that were layered on top of each other throughout our lives. Healing requires identifying them and turning each of them over to Jesus, one at a time.

Nancy says, "One of the big reasons why I struggled to believe that Father God loved me was because I had asked him to heal my six-year-old niece Shelley, my Mom, and even my ex-husband Buck. I yearned for them to be healed and live. But all three times, God said, 'No,' at best, but worse, I thought he didn't even care enough to hear my cries. They all died! I was devastated."

But then one day as she turned this over to Jesus, he impressed upon her: "Nancy, the goal of life isn't about living a long life on this side of Heaven. The goal is to get on the inside of Heaven's gate. Your loved ones were each asked, and they all gave me their yes to coming Home. They all knew you wanted them to live, and they did live and are alive here and now. Remember, the Kingdom of Heaven is here and now. They are still with you."

Nancy explains how this healed her: "Since I believe in life after death, the sting of their death was healed by this realization. Of course, it didn't happen in a day. But over time it did help the healing process."

Let's look at how safe you feel with Father God. Are you able to imagine yourself sitting on his lap? When you pray, are you able to imagine being warmly embraced by him? If not, then the goal of this chapter is to make it possible. Otherwise, the goal of this chapter is to identify any remnants of fear, because perfect love casts out all fear, and God wants you to know that he loves you that much.

There is no fear in love. But perfect love drives out fear, because fear has to do with punishment. The one who fears is not made perfect in love. (1 John 4:18 NIV)

This scripture explains that God, because his love is perfect, drives out fear. He drives it out! He does not use the fear of punishment to convince us to change from sin to saintliness. Let that sink in. This is not what we instinctively believe because every good parent punishes their children when they misbehave.

It's true that we do deserve to be punished for our sins, but Jesus took our punishment for us when he allowed himself to be crucified for our salvation. If we accept his sacrifice as a gift, then we need to realize what Jesus hopes we'll do with the gift. He wants us to live in the freedom that his sufferings obtained for us: freedom to be fully loved, freedom from the fear of punishment, and freedom to enjoy Abba as the wonderful Father that he truly is.

If instead we don't feel safe with God, it's because we have not yet been made perfect in love. Notice that I did not say, " . . . because we have not yet *become* perfect in love." We cannot achieve this for ourselves. God is the one who perfects us. How? By filling us to overflowing with his perfect love. (Scripturally speaking, the word "perfect" means "complete, full, whole.")

So, if fear controls us in any unhealthy, unholy way, it's a big red warning flag alerting us to the fact that we have not yet allowed God to fill us with his perfect love. He is completely, fully, wholeheartedly in love with us, and we must choose to open ourselves fully to it. That's why you're reading this book. (God is very pleased!) Every time we go to the Sacrament of Confession, we open ourselves more fully to God's perfect love. And it happens in countless other ways too.

By the way, loving others is a lot easier when we first know that we are deeply and totally loved by God.

Abba-Father desires that we go straight to him for the love we seek. No human parent, spouse, or friend will ever love us completely, not until they have entered into the fullness of God's love in Heaven. So, our Perfect Father wants to fill in the gaps. In the Old Testament, he said, *"I have loved you with an everlasting love; I have drawn you with unfailing kindness. I will build you up again . . . "* (Jeremiah 31:3b-4a NIV).

But wait. I detect a contradiction. Jesus said that whatever we ask for in *his* name, the Father will give it to us (see John 16:23). That means we must go through Jesus to reach the Father, right? Is this because the Father is too fearsome for the direct approach?

For some of us, it might mean exactly that. We feel safer when Jesus is our Mediator. The root of this feeling probably comes from learning that a good mediator can protect us from someone's anger or punishment or disapproval or injustice. My dad was a good mediator when he fielded that late-night phone call from Ralph's impatient father. I'm sure you can think of several mediators during your life who made you feel protected.

Gifford remembers his mother as a mediator. He says, "I used to look at my father as someone to fear, a person I could not request something from unless I reached him through my mother." This indirect approach caused delays that led young Gifford to feel disappointed and depressed. Later, he learned that, during the delays, his parents had discussed his needs. And so he learned that good comes from waiting patiently, because their discussions were based on their love for him.

In other words, by asking his mother to mediate for him, he learned that his father loved him very much. This is what happens when Jesus serves as our Mediator. It brings us closer to the Father. We discover how very much Abba-Father cares about us.

A very healing meditation is to visualize Jesus mediating for you. Start by recalling an incident from your childhood in which you felt unloved. Close your eyes and return to the scene. How old are you? Where are you? How do you feel? What happened that made you feel this way?

Then invite Jesus to come into the scene. What does he say to you? For example, a common punishment is to send children to their rooms. When my parents scolded me for a wrong-doing and banished me to my room, I felt rejected, ignored, and abandoned. I understood where I had erred, but at that moment the only thing on my mind was a deep yearning for at least one of my parents to come to my room and hug me, reassure me that they still loved me, and discuss calmly how I needed to change. And, most of all, I wanted them to affirm what I did right. In other words, I needed Abba-Father's perfect love.

Years later when I brought this into a healing meditation with Jesus, he listened closely to my needs. (By the way, before beginning any healing meditation, pray and ask the Holy Spirit to anoint your imagination. That's key. I'll guide you through this in today's exercise at the end of this chapter. And if what you visualize or hear makes you feel uncomfortable, or if you just can't "see" Jesus because you're not a visual person or for any other reason, quit trying and meet with a spiritual director, or a mature Christian who has an inner healing ministry, or a Christ-centered therapist.)

After I told Jesus what I had needed from my parents when they sent me to my room, I visualized him leaving my bedroom (after asking my permission—God is such a respectful gentleman!) to fetch my parents. He brought them in, one by one, and asked me to tell them what I needed. In this imaginary encounter, my parents listened and then asked for my forgiveness. I gave it to them, we hugged, and I asked God to forgive them too. Afterward, the little girl in me no longer felt like crying about being sent to my room. Jesus had truly healed me through the meditation. And most importantly, I no longer feared that Father God might "send me to my room," a.k.a., punish me by rejecting me and abandoning me.

Today, I don't need to bring Jesus into the meditation. When someone disturbs me or a situation frightens me, I close my eyes and visualize Abba-Father sitting on that blanket in the field of flowers that I described earlier. I run to him, plop myself next to him, and snuggle into his side while he wraps his protective arms around me, smiling at me all the while. I tell him what's bothering me, and I don't leave until he has comforted me with wisdom, reassurance, or simply his wonderful embrace.

Sadly, traumatic experiences make the healing process much harder. If your relationship with the Father has been damaged by trauma, until you work through the healing process, you will probably always feel unsafe with him and you will need Jesus to continue being your Mediator. If you get stuck there, ironically Jesus is separating you from the Father. You have unintentionally placed him *between* you and the Father. The good news is: Since Jesus and the Father are one God, there really is no such separation.

To feel closer to the Father's heart of parental love for you, it's very healing to see Jesus as not only a Mediator but as your *pathway* to the Father.

Jesus wants to help you go straight to the Father's parental heart so you will know how very dear you are to him. Jesus knows that this will fill in the gaps of your human parents' imperfect, insufficient love. He wants you to be able to climb up onto Abba's lap and feel the safety and security of his concern for you. He wants you to feel his powerful arms wrapping around you and creating a zone of extreme peace with you at the center.

Make straight the path to Abba's Heart

John the Baptizer preached, *"Make straight the way of the Lord"* (see John 1:23). To anyone living in Israel at the time, this was a message of safety. Today, we tend to see it only as a call to take no detours on our journey of faith.

In John's time, as it was for Isaiah whom he quoted (*"make straight in the desert a highway for our God"* from Isaiah 40:3), the roads or highways were paths that had been forged by previous generations. They were *not* straight because travelers had to wend their way around hills and dunes. However, danger lurked behind every mound because they might be hiding a thief or an enemy ready to pounce. So, travelers made wide sweeps through potentially dangerous areas, always keeping in view the far side of the hills, allowing themselves room for evasive action.

They took the safest route. Not the shortest route. Heading straight through the area could have been disastrous. So, when Isaiah and John declared that people should make a straight way to the Lord, they were declaring that the Lord was safe.

As mentioned previously, those who were abused during childhood have more to overcome and relearn about who Abba-Father really is and what his love is truly like. The visualization that worked so well for me, when Jesus introduced me to the Father and the Father pulled me up onto his lap, usually does not work for those who experienced trauma, especially when it was physical abuse.

The woman whose brothers began to abuse her when her father was taken from the home (Nancy) had been so traumatized that she could not even go to the Sacrament of Confession. It required being alone with a man, and this triggered severe panic attacks. After many inner healing sessions coupled with weekly counseling by a professional therapist, and by getting to know my husband Ralph as a friend in social outings, she gradually felt safer and safer around men. She returned to Confession and even began to enjoy this sacrament.

Abuse is but one way that a person might be violated. Any behavior from others that disrespects our personal dignity is a violation of who we are as children of God. We're violated when a thief steals from us. And when anyone wrongly condemns us by false accusations, we are violated just as much as the truth itself is violated.

Many years ago, in the front yard of my New Jersey home was a row of evergreen trees that I cultivated. They had reached the height of about seven feet when a car careened around the corner and drove directly into them, knocking two of them down. The driver backed off of them and quickly drove away. The trees survived and are now quite tall and beautiful, but I felt surprisingly very violated.

The car was red, and for days I watched for a red car to pass by my house so that I could track down the driver. I don't know what I would have done had I found him, but it became an obsession. I took walks nearly every day in the hope of finding this car parked in a neighbor's driveway. Although the physical exercise was good for me, the mental exercise was not.

I asked Jesus to help me find this car. He answered the prayer by asking me to forgive the driver. He sternly but gently told me to let go of my need to find him. That was not easy for me. I had to force myself to obey him, but when I did, I received a healing. I no longer felt violated.

Why did tree damage disturb me so much? The damage was not permanent. I only needed to prop the trees up with supports to give them time to recover. What made me feel violated was the unwillingness of the driver to stop and apologize. I wanted him to show me that he cared.

When it seems like God doesn't care about you, what feels violated?

In a subconscious way, the tree incident connected to times when my personal dignity felt violated because someone didn't care about me. It reopened an old wound from the time my dad forgot to pick me up at the shopping mall. I was a young teenager alone, waiting, feeling abandoned and a little scared. My mother didn't drive; I had to depend on my father who was very preoccupied with his work. We had no cell phones in those days, and I did not want to go off in search of a pay phone in case my father showed up while I was away from the predetermined pickup location.

He finally remembered me after he came home from work at the end of the afternoon and realized that I was not there. Undoubtedly he felt bad about forgetting me, but by then I was feeling too frightened, hurt, and mad to realize it. My importance as his daughter had been violated. It felt like he didn't care. Of course, he really did care but being forgotten is a form of personal violation.

When we feel violated, we feel very unsafe. Although my dad never again forgot about me after promising to pick me up, I continued to feel unsafe. Eventually, I matured enough to forgive him so that

I could heal. I can now wait for a ride without the fear of abandonment if the driver is late. I've even had other tree incidents (damage of one sort or another done to my property) without wanting to track down the perpetrator to make them apologize. But in my relationship with Father God, I needed to do more than forgive my father before I could feel totally safe.

Keep in mind that forgiving is not only for the benefit of others. It's a gift that you give to yourself. It's the gift of freedom: You will no longer be chained to the source of the hurt. The more difficult giving forgiveness is, the bigger the gift will be because your newfound freedom will be that much more meaningful. But don't try it by yourself. The Holy Spirit will empower you to forgive if you ask for help.

Also keep in mind that forgiving does not mean forgetting. Remember enough to stay safe without dwelling on what happened. By forgiving you will become free to remember without anger, fear, and stress. Then you will be able to find a new pathway to a new place of peace and joy. You will be able to persist in reaching this new place despite what happened to you.

Learning to feel safe with Abba-Father

Have you noticed that it's easier to feel closer to God outdoors in the beauty of nature? It happens this way because creation is an expression of the beauty of God himself. God is more beautiful than we can imagine. Any image of him that makes him seem ugly in any way (such as a grumpy, frowning old man) is a lie from Satan who wants to take over as your father.

To conquer Satan's tricks, find an image of fatherhood that makes you feel safe, and project that onto Father God.

When Nancy was struggling to feel safe with Father God, I asked her if she knew any kind-hearted old men. She thought about this for a while. Unable to identify anyone from her life who fit this description and made her feel safe, she considered her favorite TV shows. She remembered "The Waltons" and Grandpa Walton (played by actor Will Geer). "To this day," she says, "Father God looks like Will Geer to me."

Feeling unsafe with Abba comes in many forms, often without an obvious connection to safety. For example, when we feel frustrated about a lack of opportunities to make our dreams come true, deep down we might be feeling unsafe with God. In my own experiences, it seemed like God gave me talents, training, desires, goals, and dreams and then refused to give me opportunities to use them! At best, he let me use them only partially and only in small ways. I felt like a caged bird prevented from flying with the wings that God had given me.

Here's how feeling unsafe leads to feeling caged: When we've been violated, someone else has taken control—to our detriment. We are imprisoned by the demands they make on us when they force us to do something against our will. They have stolen our freedom to be who we really are and do what we prefer to do.

Forgiving the perpetrators puts us back in control. Regardless of whether or not they are actually remorseful, forgiving them frees us from the control they've had over our thoughts and emotions. And it frees us to heal the damage they've done to our relationship with Abba-Father.

However, to enter into the healing process, we must first identify the wrong perceptions about God that were generated by the lack of safety.

What makes you feel unsafe with God? Has he seemed uncaring? Has he asked you to do something that led to trouble and misery? Did you put into his hands a job interview or house sale or a travel opportunity and then suffer dashed hopes? Did you entrust a loved one to him but he/she died or abandoned the relationship anyway?

Let's look at the proof that God *is* safe and is *always* safe.

1. **Abba-Father never violates our freedom; he never tries to control us.** Proof of this is the free will that he's given us. He never interferes with our freedom to choose sin instead of holiness, even though he wants more than anything for us to be holy like him. Whatever we do, he lets us do it because he has no desire to control us.

2. **Abba-Father has no desire to invade us nor force himself upon us.** Consider the lost souls who remain far from God. He could easily break them in order to humble them, but he waits for them to realize how broken they have made themselves.
3. **Abba-Father never violates our personhood.** Consider how Jesus treated the woman caught in adultery (see John 8:1-11). He protected her from being stoned, which was what the law

prescribed for her sin. And then he gently, tenderly asked her, "Where are your accusers now?" After pointing out that none of them had condemned her, he said, "Neither do I. You are free to go; stop sinning." He acknowledged that she had sinned without disrespecting her dignity.

4. **Abba-Father makes no demands against our will.** Consider the last time the Lord asked you to do something and you opted not to do it. He might have asked through the priest who requested larger donations, or through a call for more catechists that awakened a desire in your heart until you reasoned that you had no time for it, or through an aging parent who needs more help from you. God did not punish you when you said "no." Problems were caused by your "no," but it was not God who caused them. And when you changed your mind and did what he asked, it was not because he forced it. It was because you went through some sort of process that shed new light or convicted you with a genuine desire to say yes. Right?

God does put pressure on us to do things his way. He did issue those ten commandments. Jesus did give a whole sermon about rules (see Matthew 5, 6 and 7). But every rule and every commandment are for our own good. We benefit from behaving the way God tells us to live. Never does he coerce us, though. We are safe with him. Completely safe.

The caged feeling that I suffered was not caused by God. I needed to deprogram my misconceptions about God. So I focused on the truth: Abba-Father never inspires in me desires, goals and dreams in order to torture me by frustrating me with closed doors. Other forces are at work: the free will decisions and prejudices of people who failed to believe in my dreams.

Some of the blockages were indeed God's "fault"—a happy fault, a blessing, because the timing was not right yet. I had to learn to see Abba-Father not as a father violating my right to use my talents and training but as a father who cares so much that he protected me from situations that I was not ready to handle. He also protected me from being exposed to what *others* were not ready to handle, for if I had freely proceeded, they would have caused problems that I could not have foreseen.

My cage door finally swung wide open one day during daily

Mass. Actually, it felt more like the cage bars dissolved away. This book is one of the results. And although there are still people in my life who are not yet cooperating with God's plans for me, I am safely resting in Abba's lap while we wait together for their progress. It's an active waiting that has kept me joyfully on an adventure of using my talents and training in other ways.

Today's Exercise: Create a visualization

When you do today's spiritual exercise, start with the idea that, to the Father, you are the only person in the world. Put aside the reality that there are billions of other people seeking his attention. God does not have the limitations that parents have when too many people and tasks and responsibilities prevent them from giving undivided attention to their children.

Nancy says, "I used to pray to God thinking that *if* my prayers made it to the office in Heaven, my message was laying in an in-basket on an angel's desk. Or, if God did get it, that it was in a stack under more important prayers like praying for a war to end or praying for a loved one who was dying. I just didn't think my prayers were his top priority. But when someone told me that, to God, I am the only person he's focused on, then my prayers became more fervent because now I knew he indeed heard them and has put them on the *top* of his list of priorities."

Early in this book I shared the story of how I met the True Father by visualizing Jesus taking me to the Father in his throne room. I also shared with you the imaginary field where I often go to sit with the Father on a blanket in a peaceful field. These are sacred spaces where I am alone with Abba-Father and he is giving me his undivided attention. Do you have a sacred space in your imagination yet? Let's go there now. We'll design one if you don't have it yet.

(1) Pray the following or something like it.

In the name of Jesus Christ, I offer my imagination to You, Holy Spirit. Anoint my imagination to receive inspired ideas. Help me to visualize a place where I can safely sit with God the Father and feel his love and realize how very precious I am to him.

Jesus said: "No one knows the Son except the Father, and no one knows the Father except the Son and those to whom the Son chooses to reveal him. Come to me, all you who are weary and burdened, and I will give you rest. Take my yoke upon you and learn from me, for I am gentle and humble in heart, and you will find rest for your souls." (Matthew 11:27-29 NIV)

Lord Jesus, reveal the Father to me.

(2) After reading this paragraph, close your eyes and think about a beautiful place where you feel peaceful. You can use my imagery of the throne room or come up with your own scene. Notice that Jesus is standing next to you. He is smiling at you. He is happy that he can now introduce the Father to you in a new and more truth-filled way. What is he saying to you?

(3) Imagine that Jesus is pointing out the Father to you. What do you see? If you have trouble seeing the Father or if the visualization becomes disturbing, say the name of Jesus over and over again until you feel peaceful. If the peacefulness never comes, stop and set up an appointment with a spiritual director or a Christian therapist who can lead you through this.

(4) Go to the Father. Take your time. Take as much time as you need to approach him and hug him or climb up onto his lap or sit next to him. What do you see? Details are important because they help make the experience more real. (And it *is* real because you asked the Holy Spirit to anoint your imagination.) How bright is the scene? What else do you see? What is the Father wearing? Does he have a beard? Are his eyes sparkling? Is he smiling? Keep adding details to the scene.

(5) Talk to Abba-Father about the fears you still have. Do this within the visualization. Afterward, write down everything you remember saying.

(6) Here's what Abba-Father says in response to you (adapted from Hosea 11:3,8,9).

It was I who taught you, **[insert your name]**, to walk,
taking you by the arms;
though you did not realize
it was I who healed you.
How can I give you up, **[insert your name]**?
How can I hand you over to those who mistreat you?

My heart is overwhelmed;
  My compassion is stirred up.
I will not give vent to My anger,
  nor will I destroy **[insert your name]**;
For I am God and not a man,
  the Holy One who is with you.

Be Satisfied with Me *(attributed to St. Anthony of Padua)*

Everyone longs to give themselves completely to someone,
To have a deep soul relationship with another,
To be loved thoroughly and exclusively.
But God, to a Christian, says,

"No, not until you are satisfied, fulfilled and content
With being loved by Me alone,
With giving yourself totally and unreservedly to Me,
With having an intensely personal and unique relationship
With Me alone.
Discovering that only in Me is your satisfaction to be found,
Will you be capable of the perfect human relationship
That I have planned for you.
You will never be united with another until you are united
With Me alone,
Exclusive of anyone or anything else,
Exclusive of any other desires or longings.

I want you to stop planning,
Stop wishing,
And allow Me to give you the most thrilling plan existing,
One that you cannot imagine.
Please allow Me to bring it to you.
You just keep watching Me, expecting the greatest things.
Keep experiencing the satisfaction that I Am.
Keep listening and learning the things I tell you.
You just wait.
That's all.
Don't be anxious.
Don't worry.
Don't look at the things you think you want;

You just keep looking off and away up to Me,
Or you'll miss what I want to show you.
And then when you are ready,
I'll surprise you with a love far more wonderful than any
You could dream of.
You see, until you are ready and until
The one I have for you is ready
(I am working even at this moment to have you both ready at the same time),
Until you are both satisfied exclusively with Me
And the life I prepared for you,
You won't be able to experience the love that
Exemplified your relationship with Me.
And this is the perfect love.

And dear one, I want you to have this most wonderful love,
I want you to see in the flesh a picture of your
Relationship with Me,
And to enjoy materially and concretely
The everlasting union of beauty, perfection and love
That I offer you with Myself.
Know that I love utterly.
I Am God.
Believe it and be satisfied."

DAY 6

The Father Heals Us of Fear

IN TODAY'S WORLD, more and more people fear God due to the lifestyles they have chosen and the decisions they have made. Their inner child thinks they will be punished, and shame tells them that they need to hide from God. At the same time, Abba is reaching out with the love of a father who knows that erring children need extra attention, while Jesus the Savior is actively and continually seeking the lost sheep who are hiding from the Father.

What are you ashamed of? Does thinking about it make you want to run to the Father or away from the Father?

> *Then the man and his wife heard the sound of the Lord God as he was walking in the garden in the cool of the day, and they hid from the Lord God among the trees of the garden. (Genesis 3:8 NIV)*

Fear is our enemy. Not God. Abba's love is the cure for all of our traumas and every fear, every worry, every anxiety. The safe and perfect love that we do not receive from humans is readily available from him. Do we really believe this? It seems that most people do not.

It's not something that is taught often enough in religious education classrooms, homilies, and adult faith formation events. I've met many good, faith-filled people who are ridden with anxiety. The reason, in many cases, is that we tend to expect—even demand—that our peace and joy come from other people doing what they are called to do (i.e., love as they should with the love of Christ).

A wife expects her husband to love her faithfully, listen to her because he cares, and humbly apologize when he's wronged her. The husband expects his wife to be supportive of him in his trials, love him no matter what mood he's in, and humbly apologize when she's wronged him. The truth is: This is the love that God calls for in the Vocation of Marriage, so of course it's expected. The fact is: Everyone fails. Humans will always disappoint us.

Only God's love is perfect. And it requires spiritual and emotional discipline to turn to him and let his more-than-enough love become our more-than-enough peace and joy.

Abba's touch is very healing, but people run and hide from it. And yet, despite their best efforts to make a good life for themselves, hiding from God actually increases their fear, worry, and anxiety. If they don't recognize this as a wake-up call but continue trying to hide from the God who sees all and knows all, their thought processes become irrational. Their inner soul, which knew God from the day of their conception, is in conflict with their minds and their wills.

As Saint Augustine so famously said to God, "You arouse us so that praising You may bring us joy, because You have made us and drawn us to Yourself, and our heart is restless until it rests in You."

Felisha, who in chapter two said that her parents were hard to please "and God is even harder to please than they were," was ruled by fear, anxiety, and negativity from a very young age. "I was a sad and very pessimistic person," she says, "even though I didn't really have a reason to feel so bad all the time, especially not in later years." Then, as an adult, she heard a talk on the subject and continued to seek and listen to several more. It changed her life. "I thank God that I no longer wake up every morning with dark clouds obstructing the light in my life," she says.

One of the tools she learned to use is scripture: She finds a verse that speaks to her fears and repeats it aloud to herself until the fear loses its hold on her. Later in this chapter we'll cover other ways we can let Abba-Father heal us from fear.

The downward spiral of fear

By God's grace and love, we learn to overcome all of our fears. However, to receive his grace and live in the joy of his love, we need to stop fearing God. This is hard to do if we've been crippled by shame.

It happens even in the best of families. A child is raised in a church-going family with Christ-centered values. As she enters into adulthood, she chooses to accept the ways of the world that are contrary to the ways of God. So, she begins to hide—she hides from the truth and she hides from God and she sometimes even hides from her family. What she's really trying to do is hide from is the contradiction of choosing a lifestyle that was not part of her upbringing.

For many, this leads to becoming inactive in the faith. Deep down, they know that something is wrong in their relationship with God, but shame tells them to be afraid of him. They feel safer not going to church. They feel more and more uneasy around churchgoers. They might even become argumentative in order to justify their faithless decisions. If you know someone who's like this, remember that the louder they argue, the more fearful they are of the truth that they're hiding from.

Fighting for their right to be wrong is a form of hiding that we see a lot of today. Consider what might happen to those who adamantly fight for abortion, gay marriage, gender change, and other controversial moral issues. What if they choose to open their minds to the possibility of being wrong? What if they were to investigate what the Church teaches about these issues? What if they even went so far as to humbly examine why the teachings are really for their benefit, how they are based on love, and how they make the world a better place when implemented?

Unless they also know that Abba loves them unconditionally, many feel terrible shame about the wrong beliefs they have been clinging to. Unless someone helps them realize that seeking forgiveness would free them to enter fully into his love, most fight shame by becoming more adamantly opposed to whichever truths make them feel uncomfortable. And unless they reach out for God's mercy and learn how to receive it, most are afraid (often pushing this fear down into their subconscious) of crumbling under the weight of their own self-disapproval. They are fighting off poor self-esteem or depression, and what they don't realize is that they are really fighting against the Father who highly esteems them.

In other words, their fear of God sends them into hiding from the very Father who can provide everything they need. But facing the truth—with fear standing in the way—can be a very difficult struggle. Meanwhile, the world is telling us to not struggle with it but to give in to the desires of our flesh-nature. In fearing shame, they don't know the secret to becoming shameless.

In Matthew 15:21-28, a Canaanite woman with a demonized daughter goes to Jesus for help. The disciples try to shoo her away. Even Jesus apparently dismisses her. But she is "shameless" about persisting with her request, and Jesus approves. Saint John Chrysostom extolled her as a model to emulate: "[She is] shameless with a goodly shamelessness." Unlike this single-minded mother, he pointed out, "When we fail to obtain, we desist; whereas it ought to make us more urgent."

The Canaanite mother exemplifies the proper attitude toward God: a combination of humility and boldness, of deference and defiance. This is a combination that leans on God's goodness and depends on close intimacy with him.

It's not easy to reach this point when we're hiding from God, fearful of the truth. For example, the parents of aborted children who are willing to face the truth about what they have done need to find their way to God's mercy, but it's such a terrible truth that it's easy to fall back into self-protectively arguing that abortion is a good choice.

Similarly, the young man or teenage girl who feels attracted to someone of the same gender needs to know God's mercy—and his help as well—to figure out what is the healthiest, holiest way to deal with the attraction.

No one likes to realize that they have done wrong or have held the wrong beliefs. Those who humbly and courageously face it recover from shame and become happier than they ever were before. Those who hide from the truth perpetuate their shame and, in an effort to feel better about themselves, blame others.

Michael grew up in a loving, faith-filled home. But a terrible tragedy that occurred while he was in grade school began to undermine his faith and the close relationship he had with his parents.

His religious education teacher, the mother of a classmate, was a special lady. She taught the children in her home, mothering them and making sure that everyone enjoyed learning what she taught. But then, midway through the year, she was decapitated in a terrible car accident.

Death—especially when unexpected—can be a major fear-generator. For Michael, it was unnoticeable at first, but his teacher's death translated into the fear of losing his own parents.

Fast forward to Michael's high school years. In health class, he learned that people who are overweight and lead stressful lives and eat a lot of red meat are prone to heart attacks. His dad was overweight, worked in a stressful job, and loved to eat burgers and steaks. Michael asked him to change—but to no avail. Unable to control that which he feared, he diverted the energy of fear into anorexia. He couldn't stop his dad from overeating, so Michael began to under-eat.

His parents soon noticed his unhealthy behavior and took him to a therapist. Michael returned to his normal diet. However, his underlying fear of losing his father had not been uncovered.

After going off to college, Michael began to explore the occult despite hearing throughout his childhood that it's a demonic counterfeit to what God offers. The idea of gaining supernatural powers attracted him.

The promise of gaining power through occult practices is especially appealing to those who feel powerless. Occult powers are the devil's counterfeit of life in the Holy Spirit. When demons are given the opportunity, they pull people away from God's love.

Fear is a very common fruit of demonic invasion. Michael began to fear his parents. Even when they showed him unconditional love and gentle compassion, as soon as they were out of his sight, fear took over again.

Deep down, Michael still held within him the faith-based teachings of his childhood. He recognized that his decisions were contrary to the ways of God. But rather than face the shame that he feared, he withdrew in avoidance. And rather than discover the fear of death that motivated his fascination with the occult, he cut himself off from his parents. If any tragedy were to hit them, he wouldn't have to know about it.

But this, too, was shameful. He had to find a way to justify hiding from his parents, so he focused on bad memories from his childhood, exaggerated them, and repressed the good memories. He condemned his parents for treatment that never happened and incidents that he remembered incorrectly. (Exorcists report that one of the common signs of demonic influence is the warping of memories.)

It's a tragic story that has variations being lived out by many adult children of faith-filled, Christ-centered, church-going parents.

More than ever, people today need to learn what it means to be loved by Abba-Father. He desires to bring his unbelieving sons and daughters to Jesus, the Son he sent to Earth to die for them. How will he do it? What's his plan?

When Jesus walked the Earth, his love and mercy and compassionate concern taught—for everyone who wanted to learn the truth—that Abba-Father is real, that the Father is all-powerful, and that the Father cares. But what about today?

The good news is: Jesus is *still* here on Earth—*in us*. We are now the ones walking with the Father. We are now the ones representing the Father. We are now the ones who are called to reveal, through our behavior, what God the Father is really like. He is calling upon us to bring unbelievers to his Son. As his beloved children, we have testimonies of soul-changing miracles that need to be shared openly and often.

Today's Exercise, Part 1: Your testimony

Take some time now to reflect on some of the amazing ways that Abba-Father has revealed himself to you. In what ways are you different than you used to be because you trust God? This is your testimony. Write it down so that it becomes easier to remember and to share. When people see how joyful and peaceful you are because you know that Abba is taking good care of you, and if you share the stories that prove it, they get the opportunity to learn what it means to be loved by the heavenly Father.

Don't continue reading until after taking note of how the Father has revealed himself to you. You'll miss out on a very necessary step if you skip this exercise.

* * *

Abba offers freedom from fear

Michael wanted to have his parents' love for many years to come, but he got caught in a trap that denied him the freedom to receive that love. It also turned him away from the perfect love of Abba-Father. That's what fear does. It steals our freedom by lying to us.

Whether a fear is small or huge, it disempowers us at the very time we're seeking to gain control. For example, the fear of not being able to find employment after being laid off from a job can pull us away from God's help by convincing us that we're failures. Fear lies to us, and so we lose the freedom to be who we truly are and to do what we're gifted and called by God to do.

Abba-Father, in contrast, freely gives us freedom: freedom from sin through Christ, and then freedom to be his adopted children—with all that this includes.

Saint John tells us in his first epistle: *"There is no fear in love. But perfect love drives out fear, because fear has to do with punishment. The one who fears is not made perfect in love" (1 John 4:18 NIV).* What are you afraid of?

When we understand what it means to be loved by Abba-Father, fear dissipates. How much anxiety we have is an indicator of how well we understand (or remember) Abba's love. To overcome anxiety, first identify the misconceptions you're believing about God, then ask the Holy Spirit to fill you with the truth about each misconception.

Remember that when we look at Jesus, we see the Father (as explained in John 14). The Father and the Son are fully united, one in being, one in purpose, one in answering our prayers. Jesus came to Earth to reveal the Father's true nature to everyone who is open to receiving his perfect love. He said, *"No one knows the Son except the Father, and no one knows the Father except the Son and those to whom the Son chooses to reveal him"* (Matthew 11:27 NIV).

Then Jesus said, *"Take my yoke upon you and learn from me"* (Matthew 11:28). Since Jesus is yoked to the Father, doing only what he sees the Father doing, he is inviting us to be yoked to the Father *with him*. This seems burdensome if we prefer to go our own way and stay in charge of our own lives, but Jesus says, *"Surprise! This is actually the easy way to live. This is a light burden."* Why? Because when we're not pulling away from Jesus and we are cooperating with Jesus, going with him wherever he wants to go, he carries the weight of the burden.

Fear does not want us to know that the Father cares so much about us that he wants what is truly best for us. Examine the role that fear has been playing in your life. Ask yourself, "What's keeping me from fully trusting in God's goodness toward me? How does fear play into this?"

Then look at Jesus. He readily gave miracles to all who asked for help. Why? Because Abba-Father desired to provide the miracles. Jesus told us that if we have a close relationship with the Father, we will receive whatever we need.

Jesus said, *"Do not worry, saying, 'What shall we eat?' or 'What shall we drink?' or 'What shall we wear?' Your heavenly Father knows that you need them. Seek his kingdom first. Rely on him above all else. Turn to him before trying anything else. Cling to nothing but your Father, and you will be given everything you need."* (See Matthew 6:31-32.)

Fear says this is not true. Fear says that God will disappoint us.

Which voice do you believe? When you're not thinking but you're simply reacting to a problem, what do your actions and attitudes reveal about your understanding of Abba's love?

The traps of fear are rampant, but the love of the Father is always abundant.

Fear's trap #1: If you react by taking matters into your own hands, you're believing lies about God.

> **Defeat the fear:** One good way to overcome this is to find scriptures that show God handling a bigger problem. Since he did that for those people in the Bible, he will certainly help you; after all, he gave his Son Jesus to you knowing full well that Jesus would have to suffer and die for you.

Fear's trap #2: If you entrust the problem to God and then take it back by worrying about it, fear is telling you that God can't or won't do enough good with it.

> **Defeat the fear:** The best way to deal with this is to see yourself as God's partner in dealing with the problem. What can you do to help solve the problem? Pray about it. Convert the energy of worry into an action plan. Then sit with it for a while before acting upon it, waiting to find out if the Holy Spirit anoints the plan with divine energy. You'll know when that happens, because divine energy brings with it joy and hope and opportunities to implement the plan.

Fear's trap #3: If you repeatedly complain or lose your temper, you haven't let Abba heal your wounds. Your complaints are a cry for help. Your temper is a cry of pain.

> **Defeat the fear:** Let God heal you through a counselor or

a good friend who is solid in the Faith or through a spiritual director.

Fear's trap #4: If you're waiting for someone else to comfort you or to solve the problem by making a change, you haven't discovered that the Father's love can more than make up for what someone else is not doing.

> **Defeat the fear:** Increase the time you spend in meaningful prayer and meditation, which will take your focus off of others and put it where it belongs.

Fear's trap #5: If you get depressed and it lasts more than a day or two, what do you wish you could control but cannot?

> **Defeat the fear:** Ask God to reveal to you the bigger picture that he sees. "All things work together for the good of those who love the Lord" (see Romans 8:28)—so what benefits might come from the troubles you're enduring? Write down all possible answers and revisit this list whenever you need a boost in hope.

Fear's trap #6: If you know that God always walks with you during hard times but you're avoiding a person or a situation that will stir up trouble, fear is telling you that it will be irredeemably disastrous, or you will suffer unbearably.

> **Defeat the fear:** Give God your "yes" about accepting whatever cross he knows is coming. Ask Jesus to help you carry it. Unite yourself to Jesus on his Cross by seeing the connection between what happens to you and what happened to him. By doing this, all of your sufferings will become redemptive. Praise God for the opportunity to serve him while so closely united to Jesus.

Charmaine shares how she defeats fear. She says, "When I am excessively anxious and fearful, Papa God always urges me to praise him. It's hard to keep focused in those moments, but he would not ask this of me if he knew that I could not do it. So, when I praise him consciously and from my heart, it brings the most immense peace. What I am learning is that instead of trying to desperately rid myself of the anxiety, Papa God is actually using this to draw me closer to him, to a more intimate relationship with him, while teaching me about me."

What signs of anxiety do you see in your reactions to problems? What is fear telling you? What is Abba-Father lovingly saying to you that casts out the fear?

Today's Exercise, Part 2: Replace your fears with the Father's love

Remember that fear always lies. Think of the word "fear" (F-E-A-R) as False Evidence Appearing Real. Fear uses just enough of the truth to capture our attention and our trust, and once we trust fear, it leads us away from the truth. For example, fear tells us: "Yes, God does work miracles, but remember the miracle that you asked for and didn't get. This is proof that God is not interested in you." In this hypothesis, what feels like proof is really the *fear* that God is not interested in you.

When we don't fight the fear, it controls us and harms our relationship with the Father. The damage is automatic unless we deliberately stop the process. Since the lie that fear tells is hidden behind a truth, (as we see in the example described in the previous paragraph), we very easily—and automatically—allow the lie to control our faith and dictate our lives. And thus fear disempowers us.

This is easily cured! We need only to identify the lie that fear is telling us, renounce it in the name of Jesus, and ask the Holy Spirit (the Spirit of Truth) to reveal the truth to us. And then be still and listen.

I'll lead you through that process now. Get out that writing pad again.

1. Describe a fear that has been controlling your life.
2. Then pray, asking the Father to speak to you through his Holy Spirit.
3. Circle or underline the words in the description of your fear that might possibly be a lie.
4. Pray again and listen for reasons why you, as the beloved son or daughter of the Perfect Father, do not need to be afraid.
5. Write these reasons as a love letter from the Father to you.

When you hear the truth, you will recognize it, because Jesus gave you the Holy Spirit. Is it something that helps you grow stronger in faith? Does it give you peace—but more than peace, does it bring your blood pressure down? Does it put you in touch with Abba's love? Then trust it! And act on it!

You can add to #4 above by thumbing through the Bible and turning scriptures into a very reassuring prayer.

Try this one. Adapt it for your needs (for example, "though an army besiege me" might be changed to "though financial troubles besiege me").

The Lord is my light and my salvation -
whom shall I fear?
The Lord is the stronghold of my life -
of whom shall I be afraid?
When the wicked advance against me
to devour me,
it is my enemies and my foes
who will stumble and fall.
Though an army besiege me
my heart will not fear;
though war break out against me,
even then I will be confident.

One thing I ask from the Lord,
this only do I seek:
that I may dwell in the house of the Lord
all the days of my life,
to gaze on the beauty of the Lord
and to seek him in his temple.

Psalm 27:1-4 (NIV)

In other words, to overcome fears, stay in Abba's arms at all times!

DAY 7

When Doubts Tell Us God Doesn't Care

WHAT DOUBTS ABOUT God the Father do you have? These are undermining your faith, and today we're going to find a way to overcome them.

Jesus said to them, "A prophet is not without honor except in his own town and in his own home." And he did not do many miracles there because of their lack of faith. (Matthew 13:57-58 NIV)

What if you lived in Nazareth when Jesus came into town after he had become famous for his healing and preaching ministry?

Matthew 13:54-58 shows the disbelief of people who thought they knew Jesus but their preconceptions interfered with their faith. "He's just the carpenter's son," someone said in disgust. "Who does he think he is?"

Joseph had passed away long ago, and still they describe Jesus as "the carpenter's son." Was Jesus so unnoticeable as a carpenter in his own name that he hadn't even earned a good reputation as a business owner?

Nazareth was a small town. Everyone knew each other. Why were his neighbors so surprised at his wisdom when he gave a teaching in the synagogue? Had he been just a quiet, unappealing young man before the Holy Spirit filled him at his baptism? It's hard to imagine Jesus as someone who was "just" so ordinary that no one expected greatness from him.

And he did not do many miracles there because of their lack of faith (verse 58).

Imagine that it's a few months prior to this scene, and you are traveling outside of Nazareth to visit a relative in Capernaum. During your visit, you hear that Jesus has been preaching on a nearby hillside. Your relatives and their friends tell you about healings they had experienced, and you see the evidence. You know they are not lying or exaggerating. So you go to the hillside to see this Jesus for yourself, and when he teaches, you notice that he speaks with authority. You can sense love and truth behind his words.

Then you return home to Nazareth. You tell your neighbors what you had witnessed in Capernaum. But they don't believe you. In fact, they scoff at you for falling prey to superstitious nonsense.

"Don't you remember playing with Jesus when he was a little boy?" they ask. "He's no different than you and me. And remember how ordinary he was, learning the carpentry business from his father Joseph's side?"

How would their disbelief affect your beliefs? Do the doubts of others ever undermine your faith?

The influence of spiritual prejudices

So far in this book, we've been digging up the misconceptions we have about Abba-Father that originated in human failures. Now let's look at preconceptions. Preconceptions originate in prejudices that we've been influenced to believe. How affected are you by spiritual prejudices?

Let's continue with our Nazareth story to find out.

Imagine that Jesus arrives in Nazareth and you rush out to see him because you're sure that he's going to work miracles like you had witnessed in Capernaum (a preconception). But nothing supernatural happens (reality has contradicted your preconception). You hear a rumor that he laid his hands on a few sick people and healed them (see Mark 6:5), but you hadn't witnessed this yourself. How do you feel about Jesus now? Did the clash between preconception and reality confuse you? Do you feel angry? Disappointed?

How do you feel now about the conversations you had when you returned home from Capernaum and told people about Jesus? Do you feel embarrassed? Belittled? Inferior? Wrong? Are you doubting yourself?

Jesus is walking down the street, passing by shops, probably on his way to the town well. It's a busy place. Will you go to Jesus and ask him for an answer to your prayers? Or will you shy away, afraid that the townspeople will scoff at you again? Do you even believe that he will give you what you ask for? Or has your confidence in him changed?

Look, there goes a crippled man who's brave enough to approach Jesus. Hope exhilarates you, because now you and your neighbors will see proof that Jesus really does do miracles! But no, what's this? The man is arguing with Jesus, and Jesus turns away from him. Jesus looks sad. Surely it's because he's unhappy about the man's condition. So why is he walking away from him? Apparently, Jesus doesn't really care about him. This would explain why people are rejecting him.

Today, all of us have sought help from Jesus without getting it. If Jesus could walk away from a crippled man, why would he answer *your* prayers? Isn't that one of the reasons why you struggle with doubts?

The world says that Jesus is not divine. Many of those who do believe in his divinity proceed to live as if God doesn't really care. It seems like he sees our pain and walks away. The alternative is more disturbing: He sees our pain and stays, but apparently he's okay with our suffering, so he does nothing.

And if Jesus doesn't care, then neither does the Father who sent him.

We know that this is *not* right, but we struggle with it. We too readily conclude (in our hearts and in our actions if not also in our thoughts) that when our prayers are not answered, it's because God doesn't care. Or he doesn't care *enough*. Every disappointment, every long waiting, every novena and marathon of prayers reinforces that God's caring only goes so far as to say, "It's better for you if you don't get what you're asking for." He's the stern father who makes us mow the lawn in the hot sun when our friends are inviting us to go swimming in their refreshing, crystal clear pool.

Charmaine knows that it's important to balance our lives. She learned to alleviate her sufferings with laughter and singing along with songs on the radio and even dancing to the rhythm of the music. But eventually, everything became too serious. She wondered: "How do I have fun without feeling guilty, without thinking that something bad will happen after?"

Her questions are rooted in doubts about the true nature of Abba-Father. She explains: "It is so difficult for me to totally trust him, to surrender all to him. You see, I was called names as a child by my siblings and cannot remember ever being defended by either parent." Their lack of concern was reinforced by the many wrong messages of her father's alcoholism and abusiveness.

This translated into doubts about God: "I did not trust him completely. I could not believe in his goodness. Something bad must happen. I believed that he said one thing but would do another, especially when bad things would happen."

Developing a personal relationship with God has not come easy for her. She says, "By his grace I am developing one. There are lots of things I have to let go of: my pride, my will, self-righteousness, impatience, and feeling that I am running out of time and I must change *now*. I never blamed God for the things that went wrong in my life. I believed that the faults were all mine and thus I had to fix me."

We all need to work on overcoming our sinful tendencies, day by day, until the end of our Earthly lives, as part of growing closer to Abba-Father. However, did you catch the contradiction in her statements of belief? This contradiction is a clue to where she needs to focus her healing.

"By God's grace, I'm developing a personal relationship with him," she said. And yet she added: "I have to fix me."

What is God's grace? It's the gift of his active intervention in our troubles. A gift! We cannot earn grace. We receive it. When we meditate on God's concern for us, we open ourselves to his grace. Our self-improvement needs to be done in partnership with Abba-Father. Our desire to be holy needs to be tied to his desire to bless us. And because of that desire, he gave us the Holy Spirit. It is the Holy Spirit who changes us (after we've given him permission to do so). He needs only our cooperation and determination to improve.

Charmaine wanted to know: "How do I have fun without feeling guilty, without thinking that something bad will happen after?" Let's look at these two common misconceptions separately.

The suspicion that something bad will always follow happy times is best handled by overcoming fear, as prescribed in the previous chapter. The fear that good times turn into bad times is common in families that have suffered abuse. If you have this fear, go back to Exercise #2 of Day 6 and do it again for this fear.

The guilty feeling that comes from having fun is cured by understanding the fun-loving nature of our Father.

Overcoming doubts

Did your human dad (or father substitute) play games with you? This question has two connotations: (1) emotional games such as "I'll reward you with my love and attention after you finish your homework, and better yet, after you get an A+ on the exam," and (2) fun games such as sports, cards, board games, video games, and swimming in a refreshing, crystal clear pool.

Trust is built when people play fun games together. The camaraderie of it forges a bond like nothing else can.

For our trust in Abba-Father to deepen, we need to discover that he knows how to have fun. He's the Daddy who says the lawn can wait and then he drives us to the swimming pool and splashes in the water with us.

Have you noticed the activities of this fun-loving God in your life?

It's an accurate image of God the Father. Who do you think invented fun? God, of course! He designed his children to have a playful spirit.

One of my favorite activities for relaxation and restoration is boating. When the dolphins play—and they definitely have a spirit of fun—alongside our boat, it's a gift from Abba's playfulness. When the seagulls follow us, gliding on the air above the wake behind the boat, they're hungry and they're watching for lunch to splash up from the churned water. And it's fun to watch. Abba called those birds over to our boat.

When we owned our own boat, Ralph often joked that, when we're on the water, I'm a storm magnet. We've been caught in the rain and thunder and lightning too many times, but God has always kept us safe.

It's an exciting adventure when you know that you're doing it with a fun-loving Abba.

One of my favorite memories is only a favorite because of how funny it was. We were boating on the far side of Tampa Bay near our home in Florida. The peaceful weather suddenly turned into a severe storm. The squall line between us and home port was too dangerous to pass through, so we headed for the nearest dock to ride out the winds and torrential rains in safety.

However, the dock belonged to a wealthy man who came running up to us, getting drenched by the rain. He was worried, I guess, that we were going to damage his dock. After we showed him how well we had secured the lines, he invited us to come into his house. *Wow, how hospitable!* we thought. As it turned out, he only wanted to keep a close eye on us. He ushered us into a room directly off his patio. He gave us a couple of towels, turned the television on to a continual weather report, and sat there quietly watching it as we waited for the storm to pass. I thought it was hilarious that he should think that Ralph and I might be thieves.

Since he was not interested in conversation, he never learned what kind of people we really are. He remained clueless about us, but God knew us and God still laughs with me whenever I think about this story.

Today's Exercise, Part 1: Laugh

Charmaine discovered that Father God "has the heartiest, most robust laugh ever." When he rejoices, he *really* rejoices!

What funny stories do you have from your own life? Write down a few words that identify each incident (for example, "the rich man's dock incident"). Where is God in these stories? Identify his presence in them and then imagine the two of you laughing together.

* * *

Abba wants to relieve your suffering

God designed us to enjoy life. A corollary truth is: He designed us to understand that relief from suffering is important. This is who he is. He is a healer, not a destroyer. He is no sadist. He enjoys life and he enjoys sharing his joy with us. While it's true that Jesus spoke about carrying crosses, and it's true that our agonies unite us to Jesus, and it's true that hardships can lead to important lessons and purifications, Father God does not enjoy watching us suffer. He rejoices when our pain is healed.

For many years I suffered the rejection of someone who is very important to me. I lifted him up to the Lord every day during my morning prayers. In church, I offered up the Mass for him and prayed for our reconciliation. Countless friends prayed the Rosary for him and remembered us in their daily prayers. We all knew that God was bigger than the problems that divided us. And yet, two decades passed and the rejection remained as deep and divisive as ever.

Sometimes I wondered if all those prayers made any difference: What would happen if I stopped interceding for him? But the pain in my heart wouldn't let me quit. Daily this precious soul needed to be lifted up to the Lord, so I faithfully continued to pray and hope and wait and endure the pain of rejection.

One year on his birthday, I asked God to give me a sign that the prayers made a difference. Immediately, Abba, my Divine Doting Daddy, began to minister to me. He didn't reassure me that the end of the suffering would soon come, though I had very much hoped he would. But he did relieve my suffering by filling me with an awareness of how dear I am to him. He reassured me of his love for me (even though I was not doubting this). And he let me know that he appreciates my sacrifice.

You see, at the root of the rejection was my passion for serving the Lord. The Devil hates me and wishes to retaliate against my ministry. Because he could not stop me from making a difference for the Kingdom of God, he found an opportunity to hurt me through the rejection of a loved one. For a season I even heard the whispered lie, "If you shut down Good News Ministries, I will release my hold on this person." Of course, this only drove me to serve the Lord with more passion.

The passion to remain in Christ does not remove the sting of being rejected. But Abba-Father compensates for that. Whatever the cause of your suffering, remember this: The Father is doting on you. He is right now reassuring you of his unrelenting love. He is appreciating the sacrifices you have made.

However, it can be difficult to feel God's appreciation. This is not because he's ignoring us. It's because we don't believe it. Where does this doubt come from?

Sometimes it comes from our misunderstandings about humility and pride. It's prideful to think about how wonderful we are, right? But Abba-Father is telling you *right now* what is wonderful about you.

Can you hear him? Or is "humility" interfering?

True humility recognizes that God knows us so well that he even knows what is wonderful about us. True humility recognizes that our wonderfulness comes from God himself. We were made in his image. Jesus gave us the Holy Spirit to empower us to grow in holiness and overcome the sins that hide our wonderfulness. True humility accepts these truths as we rely on his help.

What else causes you to doubt? Disbelief in the goodness of God? How about someone else's disbelief in your goodness? Let neither self-focus nor self-abasement keep you from receiving and enjoying the appreciation that God is beaming at you. Abba-Daddy wants to reassure us that he cares very much about how we feel.

Today's Exercise, Part 2: Be reassured that God cares about your concerns

Abba-Father designed us to enjoy doing works that serve as an outlet for the gifts and talents he's given us. Are you fulfilled in your work? He also designed into us the desire to earn enough to take good care of our families. If we have financial problems, it's not because God doesn't care. Perhaps he's teaching us to get our priorities right. Have we purchased more than we should because the world has made it seem good to keep buying new, bigger, and better? Or perhaps it's the injustices of others that have caused our problems. Have we forgiven them? And have we asked Abba-Father to show us the hidden blessings that he has provided?

What are the unanswered prayers you have? What are you concerned about? Take time now to list the biggest concerns you have. Then think about: "Why am I so concerned about these?"

* * *

Next, focus on this answer: "Because I care." Where do you think this concern came from? God, of course! When we care about others and we want to see a problem get resolved, we are sharing in God's true nature.

Since this is how God designed you, of course he wants to make a difference in everything that you're concerned about. Your loving concern is union with his compassion. This union is itself a form of prayer. In fact, it's a mutual communication of what God wants to do.

Can we care *too much* and maybe even get in the way of God's work? In truth, there is no such thing as caring "too much." Ask this: Is it possible for God to care too much? I've never heard anyone complain that he cares too much. If we care so much that it hurts, we are joining Jesus in his Passion when he cared so much that he suffered excruciating pain and died for us.

Yes, caring "too much" can get in the way of God's work, but only if we take matters into our own hands in order to stop the suffering of our passion. Or if we reject the relief that God offers because we want things to turn out differently.

He wants to answer all of our prayers and relieve all of our concerns, but usually not as fast as we want him to. He waits on the free will cooperation of everyone who's involved. He wants the best for everyone. So, he's already working a plan (a plan for good, not disaster—see Jeremiah 29:11) and in the meantime he's already doing more than we can ask for or imagine (see Ephesians 3:20). A good prayer life with quiet meditation time makes it clear what this "more" is while we wait.

What have you learned while waiting? What blessings have come from the wait? What have you become stronger in? And what about those who have been delaying God's plan? What have they become stronger in?

Today's Exercise, Part 3: Finding proof that God cares

Next, take the list of your concerns, which you wrote about in part 2 of today's exercise. This time rewrite them into sentences thanking God for being concerned. Use the following sentence-starter, replacing the name "Abba-Father" with whichever name for him that you like:

Thank you, Abba-Father, for being concerned about ___.

* * *

The importance of good friends who have strong faith

Most of us live in Nazareth. Our whole society is Nazareth. To fully believe that Jesus is showing us that Abba-Father cares, we need to find other faith-filled believers and spend a lot of time with them.

To have unquestionable trust in Abba's helpfulness, we need to gather with them in prayer groups and volunteer work and social get-togethers.

Let's return to Capernaum. This time, imagine that you're with Jairus, the synagogue leader. His daughter has just died, but Jesus tells him, "Don't be afraid; just believe! She will be healed."

When you and Jairus arrive with Jesus at his house, Jesus chases out the neighbors and relatives who are wailing and mourning. Notice how he reacts to their scoffing. "Stop wailing," Jesus tells them. "She is not dead but asleep." Of course, they don't believe him. They mock him. Everyone knows the girl is cold dead.

Jesus does not let anyone enter into the house with him except Peter, John and James, and Jairus and his wife, and *you.* After Jesus closes the door and the disbelievers are shut out, you look hopefully at this amazingly confident man. You cannot hear the wailing anymore. You can only hear the breathing of each person in the room. Nothing is distracting you from noticing the love on the face of Jesus. And the peace. And his tender smile as he reaches for the dead girl's hand and says, "My child, get up!"

She stirs. Her spirit returns to her body, and she pops up off the bed. She glances quickly at the strangers and announces to her parents, "*What's there to eat around here? I'm starving.*" (See Luke 8:40-56.)

To stop doubting that Abba-Father cares about your concerns, we need to leave Nazareth, pass through Capernaum, and move to Bethany. Here is where the closest friends of Jesus will become our friends. Bethany is where Jesus raised one of his friends from the dead.

Bethany can be any of the "hot spots" around the globe where miracles are common. Hot spots are locations where the Holy Spirit's fire is vibrantly active because whole communities of believers meet regularly to feed their faith and help each other overcome doubts. Join them online if that's the only way you can do it. In person is better.

The larger the group of faith-filled believers that surround us, the easier it is to feel the presence of Abba-Father ministering to us, speaking to us, and embracing us. Hopefully your church community is full of believers who are alive in the faith. Worshiping with them should be an experience that makes connecting to God a supernatural reality. This is the way God designed church to be—read the Book of Acts.

Unfortunately, in-person, Spirit-filled prayer groups are not always possible.

What do we do then? How do we reach the level of faith where we know, always and under all circumstances, that Abba-Father cares?

We can travel to Bethany spiritually. It's important that we seek out friends who want the same level of faith or have already achieved it. We create a Bethany with them. The worldly people we associate with will drag us down and take our eyes off of God. They are incapable of strengthening our faith. The same is true for Christians who are weak and disinterested in faith growth. However, finding our Bethany friends and building good relationships with them will require giving up personal agendas and normal activities if they interfere with spending time with our Bethany friends. This is not easy, but it's a lot easier than trying to reach higher levels of faith by ourselves.

In the experiences of Bethany friendships, our confidence grows. Doubts give way to increased trust. Insecurities about Abba's love disappear under the compassionate guidance of friends who have already overcome similar doubts.

Meanwhile, there *is* something very helpful that you can do alone. Pray:

Holy Spirit, teach me the truth.
Lord Jesus, deliver me from the doubts and false teachings of the world.
Abba-Father, I cannot escape from them on my own. Carry me.

DAY 8

Dealing with Disappointment

RARELY ARE OUR PRAYERS answered instantly. And there are good reasons for this. Divine reasons. If we could see it from God's perspective, we'd be grateful for the journey of waiting. But our first instinct is to see it from our own limited perspective. And this leads to disappointment.

> *Yet those who wait for the LORD / Will gain new strength; / They will mount up with wings like eagles, / They will run and not get tired, / They will walk and not become weary. (Isaiah 40:31 NASB)*

When I was 17, one of my favorite rock stars performed in a small, nearby city. This was an opportunity I did not want to miss. Afraid that my parents would forbid it, a friend and I bought tickets and arranged transportation. I reasoned that if I had already spent my money for it, surely my parents wouldn't stop me from going.

They did.

I cried. I cajoled. I explained that the tickets were not refundable, that my friend was allowed to go but only if she had a companion, and that I was mature enough now to handle a rock concert without getting into drugs or anything else bad that they thought might happen at the concert.

None of this mattered. The answer was still "NO."

Although they were rightfully protecting me, I didn't see it that way at the time. I felt old enough and mature enough and safe enough to go to a rock concert without an adult. It took me a long time to forgive them for that.

We do the same thing with God. Even when we get older and more mature, our hearts can get so fixated on a goal that sometimes we try to trick God into saying yes. Oh, we probably don't think of it as tricking him. We know that this would be wrong. But if we assume that the only way to get what we want is to plan it ourselves, spend time and money on it, and *then* pray about it, we're definitely trying to trick him (however unconscious this might be).

Have you ever prayed something like this *after* starting a new venture? "Oh Lord, look at the good this is doing already. You know this project is a blessing to others. But I need Your extra help now. I can't see any reason why You wouldn't want me to continue doing this, especially if You help me get it done." Did you forget to seek the Holy Spirit's guidance *before* you got started?

First we make up our minds about what we think is best, and then we ask the Lord to help us do what we've already decided is right. I've seen this trick used to justify getting divorced. I know people who've had abortions this way.

It's manipulative, and God won't be manipulated. And self-made agendas are always inferior to God's plans, no matter how sensible they seem.

Sometimes we try to manipulate the *truth*. For example: "I know I'm supposed to get married instead of living with my sweetheart, but we really do love each other, and if it's loving, it can't be sinful." But truth is unchangeable, no matter how we try to change it. Sin is destructive, no matter how we try to justify it. Including when we sin in the name of love.

Underneath the self-justification and the manipulation are the desire to be in control instead of surrendering to God, the hope of avoiding disappointment, and the prideful fear of being wrong. Ironically, in trying to get what we want outside of God's will, inevitably we get into situations that we cannot control, we end up disappointed, and we suffer from wasted time and money or some other valued commodity. And in the process, our understanding of the Father's protective love gets lost or damaged.

Even after we've matured beyond trying to manipulate God, disappointments from the past might still be affecting our relationship with Abba-Father today. To find out, ask yourself: "Am I expecting to be disappointed in my prayer requests? Or do I trust Abba-Father so much that I'm actually pleased when he says 'no' or 'not yet' to my ideas?"

The Spiritual Success Principle

God answers prayers in one of three ways: "Yes," "Not right now," or "I have something better in mind." When we trust God, we gladly accept any answer he gives to us. But how do we know what his answer is? First, we need to have a personal relationship with the Holy Spirit because the Father gave us the Holy Spirit to be our Helper and Teacher. When our souls are submitted to the Holy Spirit, we become able to recognize the voice of God. In addition to this, we also need friends or a spiritual director who can help us know when guidance from the Father is not just something we conjured up. (We all have the human desire to fill in the blanks of God's messages when we don't hear him well. This is us being in control. This is us trying to manipulate the situation.)

Jeanie describes how she hears God's answer to her prayer requests: "I wait either for my request to be granted at a later date or for him to answer it in a totally different way. It amazes me what happens. The answer is something I never expected. Sometimes he changed the circumstances so that the problem was eliminated, and sometimes he took me out of the situation without me having to do anything."

Waiting on God for guidance can seem tricky. It's so easy to mess it up. How should we do it? How do we wait without fear and anxiety but with faith and hope?

I'm the kind of person who doesn't like to sit still while waiting on God to direct me. I go knocking on doors, so to speak, to find out which opportunity God will open. This works successfully, but it usually involves wasted time while I stand in front of doors that never open. The Holy Spirit has been teaching me a better way: Think about it all you want, pray to receive clarity, and move forward when circumstances fall into place. Meanwhile, stay busy with what you already have in your life and enjoy it.

That is the Spiritual Success Principle.

Knocking on doors (looking for opportunities to fulfill your dream or reach your objective) does work as long as you don't knock so hard that you break the door down. Or get bruised knuckles.

When circumstances begin to fall into place, we often wonder, "Is this just a coincidence? Am I reading too much into it? I need more confirmation from God before I can act on this." The desire for confirmation is a holy one but it can also turn us into procrastinators. Again, talking it over with a good friend who is mature in faith or a spiritual director is often necessary. But in the end, the decision is yours. It's another lesson in trusting God. Whenever you think that God might be telling you to do something, go ahead and move forward with it while asking God to redirect you if you're misunderstanding his will.

My prayer for this is: "Father God, it seems like it's a good idea to ___. It seems like it meets with Your approval. Therefore, I'm going to act on it, but please, if ever I go in the wrong direction, grab me by the ankles so I cannot move forward without tripping. Then turn me toward the direction You want me to go."

This is another way to apply the Spiritual Success Principle. It always works, but at the moment of tripping, we might conclude that God is failing us. Fiona felt sure that God wanted her to have a job that opened up because "everything seemed to be falling into place perfectly."

"But," she bemoaned, "humiliation and failure were lined up for me instead. It wasn't as though I wanted the job in the first place. My judgment wasn't clouded by my own agenda or enthusiasm. The way things were happening, everything seemed to indicate that it was God's will that I should go for it. I honestly don't care that I did not get the job. I was disappointed because I thought that the Lord was showing me that he was leading me to a new phase in my walk with him—one where he would lead and I would know that he was nudging me in one direction or another and I would be given the grace to follow."

One of the clues that we are following God's plan is the passion we feel about it. Psalm 37:4 tells us to *"Take delight in the LORD, and he will give you the desires of your heart"* (NIV). This doesn't mean that he *fulfills* the desires of our heart as if he were a magic genie making our wishes come true. It means that he *places within us* the desires that he plans to fulfill. What do you feel passionate about? Where do you think that passion came from? Something in your circumstances triggered it but it originated in the passionate heart of the Father.

If everything falls into place but you don't feel a passionate desire to do it, like what happened to Fiona, don't move forward in it until you examine *why* you don't have a desire for it. Submit yourself to the Father. Surrender to him your lack of desire. Then ask the Holy Spirit to set you on fire with a passion for it, if it is the Father's will. If you've truly surrendered all of your reasons for not wanting to do it, it won't be long before a supernatural passion for it wells up within you.

Jason discovered the Spiritual Success Principle when he applied for college. He had worked very hard during high school in order to pursue aerospace engineering. His scores were high, he took Advanced Placement courses, and he participated in clubs and sports. And with God on his side, even though there were a lot of students applying to the same university, he felt sure that he'd get in.

He waited eagerly for his letter of acceptance to arrive. When it finally did, he opened it confidently, ready to get on with celebrating his admission acceptance. But it was a rejection.

Three fellow students were accepted. Jason knew for a fact that their grades and SAT scores were not as good as his. Did the admissions department make a mistake? Did God? Jason was so disappointed and shocked that he called to ask if an error had been made. He was told that there were many good candidates, and they tried to vary which ones they accepted. He was then told to keep up his grades at whatever college he chose and then reapply for the second semester. A number of students would drop out in the first semester and, due to his excellent record, he should have no problem getting in at that time. The admissions director even told Jason to contact him personally.

So, off he went to another college and kept up his hard work. As the semester progressed, he decided not to reapply to his first choice, because this other college had a much higher-rated aerospace program and he had great professors who were mentoring him well. He was very happy there and realized that this is where Father God had placed him. It was such a good fit!

God is so good and so caring that he does the same type of intervention for those who are not advanced enough in faith yet to think about asking him for help. Charmaine did not have the kind of relationship she has now with the Father when she traveled into the

United States to help a friend. She decided, without prayer, to apply for a six-month visa.

"We both expected Immigration to allow me a six-month stay, as was the usual. I was given three." She felt disappointed but, "As it turned out, because of personality differences, I was more than happy to return home after the three months."

While she was packing to fly to the U.S., the Holy Spirit told her not to take along her gold jewelry. But she dismissed the message as just her own imagination. In less than a month they were stolen. Even this became a blessing in Abba-Father's loving hands. "I know now," she says, "that I was being stripped of worldly attachments." Detachment from worldly goods enables us to become more attached to God. This too is an example of the Spiritual Success Principle.

Today's Exercise, Part 1: Disappointment

Think of a time when you felt disappointed by God. Write the story of what happened.

* * *

Every child experiences the disappointment of wanting something, wishing for it with all their heart, and not getting it. We learn disappointment at a very young age. The baby who is hungry and not immediately fed experiences disappointment. The toddler who cries to be held and is ignored by well-meaning but busy and distracted parents experiences disappointment and, deep down, never forgets.

When my children were growing up, Ralph and I believed that it's important and holy to sacrifice the income of one of the parents (me) to raise the children and be there for them when they are not in school. When our finances got frighteningly tight and the children were old enough to mind themselves for a couple of hours after school, I took a job as a staff writer for my diocese's weekly newspaper. But when David and Tammy's grades began to slip and we noticed other clues revealing that my absence was making a difference, I quit the job. Knowing that God wanted me to give more attention to my children, I asked God to honor my obedience by helping us pay the bills—and he did, somehow, of course.

I took up freelance writing, giving me lots of time to spend with the kids. The rule was: If Mom is working at her typewriter (or later, her computer) and you need her attention, respect her needs, and wait. She will get back to you shortly.

But David didn't understand it that way. He didn't want to wait, so he felt rejected and neglected. Even though he soon got the attention he sought, what he remembered later was the rejection.

In our relationship with God, we feel the same child-to-parent disappointment. Every prayer that goes unanswered the way we want it to and as fast as we want it to reinforces the experience of rejection, neglect, and disappointment. Even though we know that God has a better plan, the feelings of rejection and disappointment can sneak up on us and undermine our closeness to Abba.

In the heat of the moment, frustration takes over. We're tired of dealing with problems that we had hoped God would miraculously fix by now. This feeling makes it easy to forget the promises of God. We forget the miracles that happened in the past. We forget the blessing-filled attention that he gave us. If we could shut out the disappointment to recall previous times of his divine intervention, our faith and our patience would get a boost.

Parents disappoint their children usually because they understand something that the children do not. Perhaps a child keeps begging to go on an expensive vacation to Disney World and you know that the family cannot afford it. How do you feel? You want to give it to your child; you want to see all of your children happily enjoying the sights and sounds and rides of Disney entertainment. But you know that it would mean sacrificing their enrollment in Catholic school or some other benefit that's more valuable than enjoying a few days of entertainment.

In our relationship with Abba-Father, it's healing to remember that God knows more and understands more than we do about whatever it is we are wishing for, dreaming of, and hoping for. He always wants what is best for us. And, like we do when we have to disappoint our own children, he feels the disappointment with us. Like every good parent, our Heavenly Daddy wants to see us enjoying the sights and sounds of a well-lived Earthly life.

The difference between hoping and wishing

When you experience the kind of disappointments that come with suffering, do you get angry at God? This anger means that you believe in him and trust him, and you're surprised that he has apparently let you down. It means that you feel close enough to him to hope for a good outcome.

Hope is not wishful thinking. It's the awareness of God's goodness and expecting to be able to enjoy that goodness. Hope means celebrating what is certainly going to happen before it happens. This certainty comes from realizing the bigger picture, i.e., the biggest picture of all: The Father sent the Son to us so that we can get to Heaven and spend eternity with him, and he gave us the Holy Spirit to help us while we're still on Earth. In other words, the Father cares so much about us that he gives us everything we need to experience his goodness forever.

Daddy-God is telling you, "Look! I am bigger than any and all of the problems you're suffering!"

He cares about you more than anyone else ever could. He cares about everything that's bothering you, even you more than you do yourself. He is infinitely more powerful and more insightful and cleverer than you are. And he has a much better idea of how to resolve your problems.

There's always great reason to hope!

Psalm 23:1-6 (NIV) reinforces this:

The Lord is my shepherd, I lack nothing.
He makes me lie down in green pastures,
he leads me beside quiet waters,
he refreshes my soul . . .
Even though I walk
through the darkest valley,
I will fear no evil,
for you are with me;
your rod and your staff,
they comfort me . . .
Surely your goodness and love will follow me
all the days of my life,
and I will dwell in the house of the Lord
forever.

We often think of Jesus as the Good Shepherd, but remember that King David wrote this beautiful psalm long before Jesus was born. He wrote it about God the Father. Like David, we can trust the Father because he is greater than any evils we endure. He brings light into darkness, protects us in battle, and provides rest in our exhaustion.

To "dwell in the house of the Lord forever" means that, because of his love for us and our love for him, we remain in him every moment; he sanctifies every moment, engulfing every situation with his mighty presence.

Hope is the fruit of trusting in God's love. To say, "I hope he will help me" is to say, "Of course he will help me, but I can't see the proof of it yet."

Hope involves waiting. Hope is telling you that God has already answered your prayers. He began to act the moment you turned to him for help. He even planned what to do about it before you knew you had a problem!

Hope is what enables us to have peace while we wait to see the results. Hope enables us to have patience while we wait on God's perfect timing, remembering that he cares about us *and* everyone else who's involved.

Wishful thinking, on the other hand, is hoping without faith. Hope requires faith. Our hope for answered prayers is based on who God is and what his ultimate plans are and our desire to be in those plans. We cannot see the future, but we trust the One who does see the future. As Saint Paul said in Romans 8:24, "Hope that is seen is no hope at all. Who hopes for what they already have?"

To increase your hope, spend time reflecting on all the reasons why you can trust God. Go back to the second column in the Box of Differentiation that you wrote on Day 2. You will discover that you have more than enough hope to endure your current problems while God works his grand plan. Meditating on this will give you the healing and peace that will strengthen you for the journey of waiting.

Hope produces joy. If your feeling of disappointment has not yet been converted into joy, ask for the supernatural help of the Holy Spirit.

> *May the God of hope fill you with all joy and peace as you trust in him, so that you may overflow with hope by the power of the Holy Spirit. (Romans 15:13 NIV)*

What have you longed for in prayer? Even if that prayer is never answered in your lifetime, what's your reason for continuing to hope? In the answer to that lies a healthy, happy relationship with Abba-Father. It's where you're sitting on his lap and feeling loved and protected.

Abba never stops doing good for us

Our Divine Father is always helping us. He is always doing good to us and for us. But unless we can see it during times of trial and stress, it's easy to doubt it.

When bad things happen, do you sometimes wonder: "Where is God?" Don't trust your feelings. Trust God. Your feelings will tell you, "God has abandoned you." Feelings change; God and his love for you never change. Love is not love unless love is given. Because God *is* love, it's utterly impossible for him to withdraw his loving presence from you.

> *For I am convinced that neither death nor life, neither angels nor demons, neither the present nor the future, nor any powers, neither height nor depth, nor anything else in all creation, will be able to separate us from the love of God that is in Christ Jesus our Lord. (Romans 8:38-39 NIV)*

God is actively using your trials to refine and define you. Trust him. Let him turn bad into good.

> *And we know that in all things God works for the good of those who love him, who have been called according to his purpose. (Romans 8:28 NIV)*

God also intends that what you gain from your trials will influence and change the lives of others. It's never only about us. The good that God does for us is not much good unless he multiplies it through us. Often he turns our experiences into a ministry that influences others. It might be a parish ministry, it might be an online ministry, it might be something huge, or it might be a personal ministry of using your gifts and talents with your next-door neighbor. But the help that God gives through answered prayer is never intended to benefit just one person.

Don't try to hurry the process of turning bad into good; you'll only get frustrated because you can't speed up the process, no matter how you try. Remember what happened to Joseph in the Old Testament (starting with Genesis 37). After his brothers dropped him into the depths of a pit to get rid of him, there was nothing he could do about it. He couldn't climb out, jump out, levitate out, or talk his way out. All he could do was pray and wait upon the Lord.

What happened next might not have seemed like the answer to

his prayers: He was sold into slavery. But in the long run (20-plus years), God's plan was awesome. Joseph endured a lot, including unjust imprisonment, until finally he was made the Pharaoh's overseer, in charge of the whole land of Egypt. It would be another nine years until his brothers came to him seeking food because of a famine. (Joseph had wisely ordered the storing of extra food supplies during the years of good crops.) Thus, he became a sort of messiah for the Hebrew people.

Joseph learned a lot during those three decades. He grew spiritually mature. God endowed him with mystical gifts (the interpretation of dreams). Likewise, as we wait for our prayers to be answered, we need to be alert to new revelations. God always offers us amazing new discoveries. Suffering usually is rewarded with mystical gifts. These wonderful blessings are the first installments of the good that the Father pulls from bad experiences.

One day when I was begging God to take action in a problem that seemed unending, he increased my faith (and patience) by inspiring me to look at the empty air in the room around me. The air was not really empty. Molecules of oxygen filled the space around me, as well as dust and human skin cells and dog dander and pollen from outdoors.

More than that, the air was filled with God himself. Suddenly I realized that everything around us is always "pregnant" with God's activity. Like the air, we are surrounded by Abba's goodness. Like me in my prayer chair, we are living *in* his helpfulness. Like a pregnancy, growth occurs while we wait. God's plans are unseen for a while, but they are nonetheless under development.

I think one of the most disappointing verses in scripture is John 14:13. Jesus said, "I will do whatever you ask when you pray in My name, so that the Father may be glorified in the Son." *Whatever?* How many times have you seen this *not* answered? I feel the sting of unanswered prayers every day.

"Come on, Jesus. You promised! Let's glorify the Father!"

Nothing changes. More disappointment.

We need new eyes.

My friend Elyse, a long-time member of my prayer support team, often tells me, "God always answers your prayers, Terry." Really? Whenever she says that, I wonder what she sees that I don't.

Remember what I said earlier in this chapter about the importance of having friends? Elyse is an example of that for me. When I asked her to cover in prayer a very long and difficult problem, she not only prayed for that, she also prayed for words that could lift my spirit.

She said, "Waiting on the Lord is hard to do, but his timing is always amazing to me. He certainly knows the desires of your heart. So, it's ok to release the dream into his hands, which I know you have done, and see what happens. You, dear sister, have been on an incredible and exciting journey. Of course, there have been obstacles, disappointments, dreams dashed. But look at all the wonderful things God is accomplishing through your obedience and determination. His Holy Spirit is alive and well in you!"

I never saw it that way before. God had probably tried to tell me this directly, but I didn't hear him until Elyse spoke it. I couldn't see what God was doing in my long stretch of waiting until I saw it through her eyes.

Disappointment happens when our eyes remain fixated on our goals, our dreams, or our desires. Joy happens when we put our focus back on the Lord and learn to look at each situation through his eyes. This life (this pre-Heaven pilgrimage) will always have obstacles, disappointments, and dashed dreams—even when we stay completely within God's plans, pursuing goals that he inspired. The important thing is not what is disappointing but what God is accomplishing despite the disappointments.

Blessed are those whose strength is in you,
whose hearts are set on pilgrimage.
As they pass through the Valley of Baka,
they make it a place of springs;
the autumn rains also cover it with pools.
They go from strength to strength,
till each appears before God in Zion.
(Psalm 84:5-7 NIV)

These verses describe a spiritual law that affects everyone in the Kingdom of God: We pass through the Valley of Baka on the way to greatness. The Hebrew word *bakah* means "to weep, to bemoan."

Abba-Father will produce greatness from every situation that we turn over to him. We can choose to live in this greatness (which exists even before we see it), for this is where we experience his tremendous love for us. Or we can live in continual disappointment, which is a nasty-smelling waft from the pits of hell, deteriorating our friendship with the Father. It's Satan who wants us to be disappointed, not God.

St. Augustine summed it up well: "Our Father: at this name love is aroused in us . . . and the confidence of obtaining what we are about to ask . . . What would he not give to his children who ask, since he has already granted them the gift of being his children?"

Overcoming obstacles

There are a myriad of reasons why good goals and holy desires meet with delays and obstacles. Some have to do with the wrong decisions we have made. Some have to do with the sins of others. Some happen because we live in an imperfect world; we're not in Heaven yet. Some occur because the Earth is a battlefield with demons fighting against the good that God has planned. And some are part of God's overarching plan.

I hate delays and obstacles. When Ralph and I built our house in 2012, we suffered from so many permit and construction delays that completing the project seemed impossible. We had to seriously discern which of the above-mentioned reasons for the delays we were dealing with. Had we made a wrong decision in starting the project? The stress was enormous. The problems were potentially disastrous financially.

Our Good Father had foreknown what would happen. In his great love for us, he gave clear signs at the very beginning that the decision was good and that all would end up well. One such sign was the unlikely event of both the land surveyor and the scientist from the Environmental Protection Agency showing up at the same time. The property's owner gave us only two weeks to investigate whether or not to purchase the land. Our builder informed us that the EPA would take a month to get out there. But when the scientist showed up at the same time as the land surveyor, which made his job easier, Ralph and I knew that God's hand was in it. Remembering this is what gave us the courage to persevere with hope during every delay and obstacle.

Here is one very valuable lesson that I learned from the experience; I pass it on to you to multiply the blessing: An obstacle is just a temporary problem seeking God's solution.

The good of waiting

Nearly every answered prayer requires waiting. Disappointment comes from expecting the wait to be as short as we wish it could be.

We're always waiting for something, right? Life is full of one wait after another and multiple waits simultaneously. Waiting feels like a bad thing, because we wait with impatience. Impatience comes from the worry that our worst fears might be realized or that disappointment will be the end result or that when good does happen, it won't be good enough.

Another problem with waiting, for many people, is the tendency to blame ourselves for the delay or (worse) for never getting the help that's needed. The reasoning goes like this: God is good, so if my prayers are still not answered, it's because I'm the one who is not good. I shouldn't feel disappointed in God because the delay is my fault. I have disappointed God by being not good enough. The bad situations are the result of making a bad decision or they are a punishment for my past laziness or sins.

Stop that train of thought! This is Satan accusing you. He wants you to feel discouraged and, at the same time, keep your focus on yourself instead of God. The truth is: Even if you committed the worse sin in the world, if you repented of it, God is not blinded by it. If you pray with a spirit of love and with good (holy) motivations, you are praying like a saint.

As Charmaine's story illustrates, we don't have to be perfect to receive God's help. (It's impossible anyway, so why let the devil trick you into feeling bad about your imperfections?) God's responsiveness to your prayer requests is not controlled by your decisions and your behaviors. God's helpfulness is not dictated by how good you are.

Love is not love if it's not actively loving you, and because God is love, it's utterly impossible for him to withhold from you the answer to your prayers. Unanswered prayers are not dead prayers. Unanswered prayers are not evidence that God doesn't care (although the devil wants you to think he's uncaring). Unanswered prayers are merely answered prayers still waiting for time to catch up to reality. The reality is: God began working on a plan for many blessings to result from your prayer request before you even began to pray about it, and he will surely see it through to completion. In the meantime, you're only waiting for time to catch up to this reality.

The belief that waiting is bad is a misconception. Waiting is actually a good thing! Even Heaven waits. This seems odd because, in eternity, time as we know it is meaningless. In eternity, all is "now." And yet, those who have gone there before us are waiting for the time when we will join them. Saints pray for us and wait with us for the fruits of their prayers.

Since everything in Heaven is good, waiting must be good.

> *The Lord is not slow in keeping his promise, as some understand slowness. Instead he is patient with you, not wanting anyone to perish, but everyone to come to repentance. (2 Peter 3:9 NIV)*

The author of this verse was referring to the promised Second Coming of Christ, but we can learn from it an important principle about waiting: In every promise that God has made, waiting is always beneficial. More people will benefit. More lessons will be learned. More blessings will be given to us during the wait.

Abba-Father gives us the Holy Spirit to teach us how to overcome the obstacles and to guide us to the goal. Wallowing in disappointment and all the negative feelings that come with it only paralyzes us. Relying on the Holy Spirit makes even the biggest of (divinely inspired) dreams come true in Abba's perfect timing.

When Ralph and I built our house, we knew it wasn't God who put up the obstacles. Since we had seen the Father's loving hand in the start of the project, we pushed forward and, with inspired guidance from the Holy Spirit, found our way around and over every obstacle. In October of 2012, we moved into our new home. Two weeks later, my parents moved into it, too, so that we could become their caregivers.

As it turned out, some of the obstacles were blessings in disguise, because they forced us to change some of the original design plans. The changes created a better environment for sharing the house with my parents. Abba-Father had taken our house plans and adapted them without waiting for us to ask him to do it. He knew that we didn't have the foresight to ask.

Today's Exercise, Part 2: Blessings

Revisit what you wrote in Part 1 of today's exercise. Look again at your description of a time when you felt disappointed by God. Next, name some of the blessings that came from that trial.

Abba-Father is so caring!

DAY 9

Abba's Hidden Love in Our Confusion

When we try hard to discern God's will and then proceed with what we perceive as his guidance only to meet with failure, we understandably get lost in confusion. We wonder: "What happened? Why didn't this work out? I was following God. I was trusting God. And he led me into disaster! But this is not God's nature; perhaps I'm projecting onto him what a human has done to misguide me. Or is it my fault? Did I misinterpret his guidance?" More confusion.

> *"For I know the plans I have for you," declares the Lord, "plans to prosper you and not to harm you, plans to give you hope and a future. (Jeremiah 29:11 NIV)*

In the previous chapter, I shared the story of how Ralph and I built our house despite many obstacles. But there was one more coming straight at us—one that was both unexpected and devastating. It hit us just days before the closing date for the new house, just a couple of days before moving in. Ralph got laid off from work.

"Huh? How could that happen?" we wondered. "Where was God's protection? I don't understand. The timing couldn't be worse."

The bank's loan officer asked for proof of Ralph's employment right *after* he lost the job. God could have made him ask beforehand, so why didn't he? Instead, the loan officer found out about the loss of income. The bank would not grant us a mortgage. We were going to be stuck with a big construction loan and no house for it.

It looked like Father God was standing in the doorway of our new house, arms crossed, like a big, bully bouncer at a night club, telling us, "No, you can't get in." And it felt like God was towering over Ralph saying, "No, you can't have this job anymore." And there was no changing his mind. No way for Ralph to get his job back, no way to find a new job in time to save the house.

Sometimes we misinterpret the sternness of the Father as meanness. Like he's a bully and he's scowling at us no matter how well we behave. This happens because, when we were children, our human parents seemed very mean to us when in firm sternness they rightfully disciplined us. In truth, Abba-Father's sternness comes from his authority, and, like any king, what he says from his position of authority is what matters. It is not open for debate.

However, it's also true that Abba-Father, unlike many human parents, actually delights in us when we question him. This is appropriate in a healthy father-child relationship as long as the child is not questioning his authority but genuinely wants to learn and the parent has time and patience for it.

Abba-Father is always watching out for us, always planning what is good for us. It is much more beneficial for us that he applies his kingly authority for our sake, in the implementation of his plans, than it is to have to manage things on our own. If this is what we really want, then we'll discover the secret to living in the joy and peace of being under God's authority. It's as simple as one, two, three:

1. We give Father God the benefit of the doubt.
2. We choose to trust him.
3. And then we relax knowing that he's got everything under control even when things look chaotic.

As Ralph and I faced the huge losses of good employment and the house we had just finished building, we turned to God in prayer, still reeling from shock. The prayer was short and straight from the heart: "Help! What do we do now?"

Our Good Father did not delay his response. He told me, "Ralph's lay-off is an answer to your many prayers begging me to free him from the huge stress of working for that company."

My reply: "So this is my fault then?"

I thought about my daily prayers spanning several years, asking for Ralph to be delivered from the job that made him miserable. "But now, Lord? You chose *now* to set him free from this suffering? I had expected You to help him find a replacement job. It would be much better, You know, to move him from one job to the next without a gap in time and income."

Of course, God did know that—and more, much more about the situation. For reasons we would only later find out, it was better for Ralph to retire early. But it was too soon to know this. The confusion continued.

God also knew that there was no need to panic. The loan officer called back and asked about *my* income. It was, when combined with Ralph's retirement 401k fund, enough to grant us the mortgage. We'd have to cut back on other expenses, but we could afford to keep the house.

Our new prayer became: "Dear Lord, help Ralph find a new job before his severance package runs out." God answered this prayer even though he knew that it would be better for Ralph to retire now. The new job started exactly when the severance package ended. God's perfect timing (though we had wanted it sooner).

And then, two years later, he was laid off from this company too. And thus began his early retirement, which enabled him to help me with the responsibilities of caring for my elderly parents. Soon after, a checkup with the doctor revealed a problem with his heart. The stresses of working in the fast-paced corporate world could have killed him.

The origins of our confusion

Felisha felt very confused when God's guidance led her to a job she didn't get.

"I had what I thought was an excellent opportunity," she says, "for a full-time job with many perks. The greatest perk would have been that my husband and I could live together all the time instead of only on weekends. I did not want the job, but it was a good opportunity, so I discussed it with my husband, and I took it before the Lord."

She waited on the Lord and prayed and sought his will. "During my prayer times, I received many confirmations from the Word of

God assuring me that the battle was the Lord's, etc. My trust and faith in God were at the highest point. I did my best to prepare for the exam that was required to get the job. I took it very seriously, trusting that God would make the impossible possible."

When it came time for the test, "I failed miserably. Even though I was the *only* candidate who sat for the exam, I did not get the job. Since then, I don't know how to discern God's will for me. My prayer life has really suffered, and I feel horribly let down by God. When I think about trusting him, I tell myself, 'Don't be too sure that he's going to keep his word.' A horrible experience! It was such an ordeal and so humiliating."

Often, confusion originates with the idea that we have understood his guidance correctly, when in fact we did not. Listen to the example of Jeannette and Gerald's story:

Jeannette shares, "After living in one city for 27 years, my husband and I decided he would take a promotion within the company he worked for, although it would require him to move to another city. The good points were that we were going to be empty nesters in two years, and we looked forward to new adventures in a different area, plus my husband would have a new challenge for several years before he retired, plus one of the places he would travel to was our hometown where both of our aging parents still lived. All of these things sounded good to us."

In trying to discern God's will, she says, "We talked to our youngest son who was a sophomore in high school. Since he had lived here his entire life, had long-time classmates and friends, and was on the basketball team at school, if he vehemently objected, we would not make the move. As it turned out, he thought it would be exciting to meet new friends and get onto one of the five basketball teams of this new and larger parochial high school. So, my husband accepted the job and we made plans to move. We put our home on the market and house-hunted in the new city. When spring arrived, my son was treated to a going away party by his basketball team."

Then came the confusion. "Our home was not selling, and I could not find one in the new city that met our criteria. There had been one possibility: We found a builder who had a lot that we liked. But as time passed, the lot was sold to someone else. Then, in addition to the housing situation not working out in a timely manner, we needed to pay a large non-refundable deposit to the parochial high school that my son would attend for his junior year."

Not knowing what else to do, Gerald asked his company if he could accept the new position right away but delay moving for two years until their son would graduate from high school. They agreed.

Jeannette says, "In light of these disharmonious things, we asked God for clarity as to how we should proceed. We finally told God that if our home sold before the school deposit was due, we'd put the deposit down in the new city, taking the sale of our house as a "go-ahead" sign from him. If it did not sell, we would stay back for two years and let our son graduate from his current high school. As it turned out, our home did not sell. We told our son about the situation. His reaction was a bit of a surprise to us. He was glad that we would not be moving. He said he got to thinking about how he'd miss his friends and everything else in his current situation. However, he did not tell us because he did not want to ruin his dad's opportunity. Now he was glad of our change of plans and looked forward to staying put."

Eventually the realtor that Jeannette and Gerald had used in the new city called to report that the builder's lot they had liked so much had become available. The person who was going to build on it had a job change and could no longer do it.

"Are you interested?" the realtor asked. The only problem she saw with it was that it would take about a year to build the house after everything was approved. Jeannette and Gerard were pleased; this was not a problem at all. They saw it as God's timing and thanked him. As it turned out, there were "snags" along the way that delayed the building process, and the house was not completed until their son went off to college. God's perfect timing had guided the plan and he protected Jeannette and Gerard from making a mistake even while they were unaware of his help.

Often our confusion comes from projecting our own assumptions or hopes into whatever God is trying to say and do. This happens to me. My thoughts are rich with ideas, and if I don't hear Abba-Father fast enough or clearly enough, my brain fills in the blanks.

To counter this, I have found this Increase/Decrease prayer to be very helpful: *"Abba-Father, renew me in your Holy Spirit. Holy Spirit, increase in me the desire and energy to do ___ if it is the Father's Divine Will. If it is not Your will, or not at this time, then whenever I think about proceeding with it, drain me of energy and decrease in me the desire to do it."* After that,

I have to pay attention to my energy level.

Here's a true example of how this works: Before starting this book, the Increase/Decrease prayer increased my energy, the flow of ideas, and my desire to write it so much that eventually the book overtook my busy schedule. I just had to take time off for it.

On other occasions, when I begin to implement a plan and I feel lethargic about it, my first inclination is to force myself to do it anyway just to get it done—in the name of self-discipline. But this, I've learned, is usually the wrong response. I need to trust the lack of energy as an answer to the Increase/Decrease prayer.

A lack of energy could have other causes, too. As a fail-safe measure, I ask Abba-Father to give me a divine push in the right direction if I'm misunderstanding his guidance.

We also need to consider that our Enemy might be interfering. When I began editing the final draft of this book, I lost all energy and inspiration for chapter two. So, I prayed the Increase/Decrease prayer, but that did not work. Finally, I tried some spiritual warfare prayers. I sent "any demons who are interfering" to the foot of the Cross of Jesus to be covered by his blood. That worked! The energy and inspiration began to flow again.

(Note: Do not attempt to handle demons without proper training, except for using the basic tools that Jesus has given us through the Church, such as holy water, the Rosary, and repeating the name Jesus out loud.)

Why does God allow us to get confused?

God blesses our confusions. It's part of the humbling process of realizing that our understanding of God's guidance is tainted by the limitations of our perceptions. Confusion is a sign that we're getting mixed messages and we cannot sort out which is the Father's voice. Not until we repent of choosing for ourselves what we think God "should" do. And perhaps we also need to repent of other sins because our sins give the devil permission to confuse us.

Our confusion is worsened by:

- The half-truth messages of fear. (For example, "What if I don't get a new job? We'll end up losing our house!") The cure: Ask the Holy Spirit to help you identify the lie that the fear is telling you so that you can realize the opposite, the truth that the Father is revealing.

- Resentment toward people who contributed to the problem. ("I got laid off because the manager above me was prejudiced against me. It's his fault.") The cure: Forgive them.
- Anger because we did not get what we wanted. Mix this with pride and it's a very hard confusion to overcome. The cure: Forgive God and accept responsibility for misinterpreting his guidance or, when appropriate, choose to persevere until his full plan is viewable in hindsight.

This is why we should not try to discern God's will on our own. God values one-on-one interaction with us, but he also wants to clarify and confirm his plans through others. A spiritual director, counselor, or a community of Christ-centered, Spirit-filled friends can help us get pointed in the right direction when we need the extra help—especially when our personal prayer time does not bring clarity and we need to make a decision without further delay, or when we make every effort to discern God's will correctly and we still remain confused.

Even while we are in a state of confusion, we can relax in the security of knowing that Abba-Father is with us and cares very much about us. It helps to remember that God will make good come from everything—including confusion. The question is not: "Why is God confusing me?" Rather, the true question is: "What does God want me to learn from this?" Confusion turns into peaceful joy when we discover the answer to this one.

Think of confusion as a grey fog covering the path that you're traveling. You're on the right path, but you can't see how everything is already in place ahead of you, right where they need to be. The fog hides the trees and flowers that make the journey beautiful. It hides the cottage that the Father has provided for shelter. It hides the destination that he wants you to reach. They are all just beyond your view.

Nor can you see the fork in the road. You've asked for Abba's protection from wrong decisions. Therefore, he's directing your feet in the right direction, and although the left side of the fork is where you think you should be headed, he's got you going up the right side of the fork. Something about this doesn't seem right, and the fog makes this feeling turn scary. But really it is very good!

Then you crash into a hard wall. You didn't see yourself headed toward it. It's God's protection preventing you from going the wrong way! However, this might not become visible to you until later, when you can look back.

In the journey of following Abba-Father through the fog of confusion, we are being tested and tried. The test is for our benefit. We learn from it just how much our trust in the Father has grown (or not).

I often joke, "God, you duped me, and I allowed myself to be duped."

God "duped" me into wanting a priest-friend to become the first chaplain of Good News Ministries. We later discovered that alcoholism was handicapping him emotionally and in his ministry. Both of his parents had been alcoholics, and he had become an alcoholic himself. Abba-Father knew that we would never have invited him to move to Florida if, during our 20 years of prior friendship, we had discovered his alcoholism and understood the effects of codependency. Abba-Father also knew how much more effective in helping others I would become after learning how to deal with our friend's problems.

I could also say that Abba-Father "duped" us into moving from New Jersey to Florida in order to start this ministry in 1995. We had no idea about this plan. We thought we were moving just to get away from snow and high taxes. It was a good "duping," but it changed our lives in more ways than we had been able to predict.

In 1994, Ralph and I had served on the core team of a different Good News Ministries. The New Jersey group planned a week-long evangelization school for our parish, to be held in November. To our surprise, we never got to be part of that great event. Instead, God inspired our family to move to Florida. This was very confusing.

The Holy Spirit energized us with a desire to move. At first, we tried to find a new house in the same town. We envisioned staying in our beloved parish and continuing with the New Jersey School of Evangelization. Remember what I said earlier about God being a good Father who protects us from going in wrong directions? There were many forks in the fog-filled path that he put us on. It was all very confusing, but gradually the inexplicable desire to sell our house pushed us farther and farther south until we landed in Florida.

On January 30, 1995, we found ourselves in a restaurant near our new home, standing in front of Charlie Osburn, the man who had trained the New Jersey team. He had come here to give a seminar. (Was this timing and location just a coincidence?) Recognizing us, he pointed out to us a core team that the Lord had already put together for a Good News Ministries of Tampa Bay. The new ministry was still only a dream and a prayer for these people. They had been praying the Rosary for two years asking God to provide leaders.

Charlie asked, "Will you be those leaders?" We said yes and questioned our sanity because we had seen the work that goes into this.

Our Wise Father knew that we would have said "no" if Charlie had invited us to start Good News Ministries of Tampa Bay while we still lived in New Jersey.

God often confirms his guidance through circumstances. Be on the alert! When situations happen outside of your control, God is planning something good that seems (at first) very confusing. Ride it out. Keep praying. Trust your Wise Father. Even if the Devil is behind the confusing, God is allowing it so that he can humiliate the Devil by raising you up in an awesome, better-than-expected plan.

As Gift Nyirenda says, "We prefer to control our destiny, forgetting God's role and hand in all of this. God never has a plan of fear, pain, and suffering for us. Jesus Christ took it all on the Cross then opened a way for us to reconcile ourselves to God through an advocate, the Holy Spirit. When the Holy Spirit speaks to us, all we need to do is cooperate."

Today's Exercise: Journey from confusion to blessings

We gain new spiritual strength only through a process that at times is too confusing to understand. This growth happens not by God making everything easy but by us responding to God's invitation to walk through the difficulties with him. We need to remember this when we want to run away from the confusion or away from God for apparently causing the confusion. Our Good Father wants us to walk with him through the grey fog all the way to the blessings that he knows are waiting for us. He's inviting us to a more intimate Father-child relationship.

Saint Theodora Guerin knew this. She said, "The way is not yet clear. Grope along slowly. Do not press matters; be patient, be trustful. With Jesus, what shall we have to fear?" As you meditate on this, remember that Jesus takes us to the Father. Jesus reveals the Father to us. So, we can rightfully say, "With the Father, what shall I have to fear?"

To us, the fog looks like a curse; a hardship to get rid of. But to our Good Father, it's an adventure of journeying hand-in-hand. He sees what's ahead. He wants to make sure that we don't miss it! Think of him like a treasure hunter who has memorized the treasure map. Just keep clinging to his hand. Keep going. With Abba-Father at your side, you'll reach the treasures that he's very eager to give you.

The Bible shows countless evidence that God rejoices in this Father-child partnership. The prophet Elisha required Naaman to wash himself seven times in the Jordan River to be healed of leprosy. (See 2 Kings 5.) The idea confused Naaman so much that he almost didn't do it. He had expected Elisha to call upon his God, wave his hand, and provide an instant cure. When he didn't get what he expected, he got hot-headed and angry. Fortunately, his servants convinced him to give it a try. (They were the community God spoke through to get Naaman pointed in the right direction when he needed the extra help.) After he accepted his own part in the plan and cooperated with the instructions, he received his healing.

It's not as if Elisha wasn't able to provide an instant healing. In 2 Kings 6, he said one short prayer and all the soldiers of the enemy were blinded (verse 18). Later, he said another short prayer and they were all instantly healed (verse 20).

Why then did God, through Elisha, want Naaman to journey through confusion before reaching his cure?

In John 9:1-7, Jesus healed a blind man by spitting on the ground and making a mud paste with his saliva. I'll bet this man was confused by this at least just a little, huh? Jesus applied the mud to the man's eyes and then instructed him to wash it off in the Pool of Siloam. Only after complying with Jesus' strange way of dealing with it did he receive his healing.

At other times, Jesus healed people with only a word or a gesture. Why did Jesus give this particular man something to do first? Because the Father had a special plan for him. The Bible does not give us the follow-up story; we can only guess at what God had in mind for him. Perhaps this very intimate encounter with Jesus set him on the path of becoming an evangelizer who could heal people's hearts when they were doubting that God truly cares.

Abba-Father has gifted us with freedom, intelligence, and creativity to participate in what he is doing. He enjoys involving us in the process. At first, we might suffer the uncertainty of traveling blindly on a fog-filled road. But it's not because God delights in confusing us.

It's because there's something to learn from it and he's giving us the opportunity to discover it.

We learn more from mistakes than from easy successes.

In big problems, look for small blessings. Eventually you'll be able to see huge blessings, but until then, look for the small clues about the Father's helpful involvement. This will sustain you by bringing you relief and encouragement. Small blessings are seeds that Abba-Father has planted. Cultivate them.

Instead of focusing on what didn't go right, take a deep breath, and forgive God or yourself or whomever has triggered anger, frustration, or doubt. And then ask the Holy Spirit to help you notice and identify any good that has come from the journey of walking through the trial. Be sure to look carefully enough to see the smallest of blessings. Small things often float past us like dust in the air around us, capturing our attention only when the light hits the particles from just the right angle.

What blessings can you identify from the confusing problem that has been on your mind while reading this chapter? Write them down.

* * *

Every one of these blessings is a seed that Abba-Father has planted for you. They will sprout and grow from the attention you give to them. Protect these seeds by looking at what you wrote today, and add more to the list as the days go by. Enrich the soil of your spiritual life by feeding your soul (for example, by daily Mass, monthly Confession, meditating on scriptures, studying Church teachings, listening to and singing along with praise and worship music, etc.)

Thus, these small blessings will grow and gain strength. They will change the landscape of your life. In fact, the trial that was so frustrating will eventually evolve. The fog of confusion will lift. Although the journey might be long, you'll finally see a scenario or a solution that's better than what you had ever envisioned.

When Dawn retired from a career of 34 years in education, she was not ready to quit being a teacher. "I was still too young to retire," she says about the confusion she felt. "But after a year of retirement, God put me in a place that was a blessing—working in a Catholic school. I love my second career! Don't get me wrong, I loved my first career and cared for my students, but things had started to become a job, not fun or rewarding. I never expected to be where I am today. God knew all along that I would be blessed, happy, and able to grow spiritually here. I will be forever grateful that he heard my disappointment about retiring and granted me the job I currently have."

The cure for confusion

Abba-Father does not enjoy putting us through the torments of confusion. He gave us a way out—for example, in Acts 1:7-8 (NIV). When Jesus was ready to ascend to Heaven, his disciples questioned him, trying to clear up their confusion about God's plans. They asked him, "Lord, are you going to restore the kingdom to Israel now?"

He replied: "It is not for you to know the times or dates the Father has set by his own authority. But you will receive power when the Holy Spirit comes on you."

Abba-Father's authority is key here. We need to trust it. He doesn't always clear up our confusion, but he does always make clear his presence and his involvement. But we can only see it if we seek it.

More important than knowing what to expect is to know that *God* knows. One of my favorite mottos is: "I don't know what the future holds, but I know Who holds the future."

God gives us whatever we need for doing our best and enjoying this Earthly life in the most beneficial way. When we are confused, when we have unanswered questions, the Holy Spirit is our aid and our ally. The Holy Spirit is the divine authority of God activating his helpfulness in our journey of becoming more and more like Christ.

Jesus said that the Holy Spirit will teach us everything we need to know (see John 14:26). This does not mean that we become all-knowing; it means that we can trust the all-knowingness of God and safely believe that he will teach us what we need to know when we need to know it. His knowledge will assist us. And if it seems like he's not helping us, it means that we can ask the Holy Spirit to help us understand how we are projecting onto the Father some human traits that seem to limit his help.

What if we find ourselves in a failure or in a troubling situation after trying to discern and follow God's will? If we tried our best, we need to forgive ourselves and trust God: The journey is not over yet. And if the failure comes from our sinful decisions, we need to go to the Sacrament of Confession to receive God's forgiveness too.

Examining where we went wrong can increase our confusion—at first. In truth, this is the path to peaceful joy. Instead of feeling bad about getting it wrong, we need to remind ourselves that, for as long as we live on Earth, we're imperfect interpreters of God's will—and this is okay! God does not hold it against us. So, why should we? What really matters is that we try our best. And each day, our best becomes a little better than it was the day before. The Father is delighted with every little step we take in our wobbly walk closer to the innermost depths of his heart.

With God on our side, confusion is simply a temporary fog. We can peacefully wait for the Holy Spirit to teach us what we need to know at the time we need to know it. It rarely comes sooner because our Good Father is teaching us to trust him more.

If we don't take this introspective route, confusion can become a tactic of the enemy. Paul told the Galatians:

> *"I am astonished that you are so quickly deserting the one who called you to live in the grace of Christ and are turning to a different gospel–which is really no gospel at all. Evidently some people are throwing you into confusion and are trying to pervert the gospel of Christ." (Galatians 1:6-7 NIV)*

Merry was born in Indonesia but, due to racism, she never liked being Indonesian. She says, "When I stayed in Australia for seven years, I loved every minute of it. I felt more at home there than I did back in Indonesia." Then she fell in love with an Indonesian man. She describes how this caused confusion, which later led to many blessings: "The man I was about to marry needed to reside in Indonesia in order to continue his father's business. Also, because he is the only son, his parents hoped he would take care of them in their old age."

She continues: "Against all of my family's advice, I decided to move back to Indonesia, the country I disliked. I gave up the bright future for my career and decided to help my new husband with his factory." She chose love above her own wants.

"Well, things have not turned out as well as I expected," she says. "During very difficult times, I have wondered if I made a mistake going back to Indonesia. Especially when I saw that all of my sisters in Australia are able to afford houses and cars while I am trying to save this struggling business."

However, when she turned away from the sources of her confusion to find out what Abba-Father was doing, she realized that God has been blessing her with more important things, which money cannot buy. "I was blessed with two children, and through loving them and forgiving them, I learned so much from them. At the beginning, I thought children were a burden: more financial responsibility and more moral responsibility teaching them good human values. But now I often realize that the children are teaching me lots of wisdom. I've learned from them how to live in the now. I've learned from them how to forgive by seeing how they forgive me even after I was verbally mean to them. In loving them, I feel as if I am giving myself the love that I didn't have much of during childhood. I have become a much better person because of them."

Merry has described multiple big blessings. But that's not all! She reports, "Being in Indonesia also means that I get to be closer to my parents. I didn't have good relationships with them, but watching them try to love my difficult brother, I can forgive them for what they have done or have not done to me, because I can see that they have love. They just don't know how to express their love because they didn't receive much love from their parents either."

And there's more. Merry says, "Spiritually I feel that, by being put into very difficult and humbling situations, I learned to see things from the 'poor beggar' point of view instead of judging people for not being as good as I assumed they should be."

Then she notes, "I believe that I wouldn't have learned so much if I had stayed in Australia and lived my own carefree life."

Every day there is something to be confused about. Remember that confusion isn't evidence that God doesn't care. Or that God cares but we're too blind to see it. It's just an opportunity. Our Good Father always wants confusion to become a source of new blessings.

When anxiety, fear, and anger about the uncertainties of God's guidance hide the blessings, it's time to stop what we're doing and sit still with the Lord. I've found that the best place for this is in church during Mass or during Adoration of the Blessed Sacrament. Here is where we are most closely connected to God. The Holy Spirit has greater access to our thought processes. It's a place where we put our focus on Jesus, which removes our focus from the grey fog of confusion and the dark elements in it that frighten us.

Clarity arises from this change of focus. Even in the continued unknowing of a challenging situation, we more clearly understand that Abba-Father is watching out for us. He is taking good care of us. He is forging for us a future that will resemble what we had feared but which will soon produce special blessings that we cannot yet imagine. Rather than dread the future we fear, we can look for the blessings. Every little blessing is evidence that a very big blessing is waiting for us. Rejoice in this truth. Give God your thanks for it now; don't wait until the fog clears. This exchange of love will lift your spirits. And then this, too, will become one of the blessings you get to enjoy.

DAY 10

The Discipline of Abba-Father

IN THIS DAY OF our journey deeper and deeper into the Father's Heart, let's look at how much we're influenced by the fear of punishment. Does the discipline of a good father always mean punishment? Could it be that we wrongly interpret the pain of discipline as a bad thing?

Do we want to hide from God when he disciplines us? Or do we run to him with thanksgiving because he has taught us something valuable?

> *Endure hardship as discipline; God is treating you as his children. For what children are not disciplined by their father? If you are not disciplined–and everyone undergoes discipline–then you are not legitimate, not true sons and daughters at all. Moreover, we have all had human fathers who disciplined us and we respected them for it. How much more should we submit to the Father of spirits and live! They disciplined us for a little while as they thought best; but God disciplines us for our good, in order that we may share in his holiness. No discipline seems pleasant at the time, but painful. Later on, however, it produces a harvest of righteousness and peace for those who have been trained by it. (Hebrews 12:7-11 NIV)*

Very early in life I realized that if I learned from other people's mistakes, I could avoid getting into trouble with my parents. When my brother or sister got punished, I observed what they had done wrong and determined not to do the same thing. This didn't protect me from making my own mistakes and erring in other ways, but it did set me on a lifelong course of making it a top priority to learn the easy way how to do what's right.

During my childhood, this earned me the reputation of being a "goodie-goodie" amongst my friends. Sometimes even "holier than thou" because I also prayed a lot and thought everyone should do likewise. It puzzled me why people used these nicknames as if they were insulting me. I didn't know it yet, but they were mocking the divine calling, which we all have, to become saints.

Somewhere along the way of maturing into an adult, avoiding the punishment of my dad grew into the desire to do only what God the Father wants me to do—"nothing more and nothing less" (as I say in my morning prayers)—even when it doesn't make sense or when it goes against my personal inclinations. My plan is to keep getting better and better at this (with the Holy Spirit's help).

"Do whatever he tells you" (from John 2:5) was the theme of a conference that Ralph and I attended in 1993. It beckoned us in giant letters painted across a wide banner above the stage. As we would later find out, this was the first clue that God was going to send us to Florida to become founders of Good News Ministries of Tampa Bay. But we had to go through a formation process—one that Abba himself designed.

The key skills of holy living are listening to, waiting for, and discovering God's Divine Will. This process requires a lot of time, the humility of self-doubt, plenty of mistakes and a desire to learn from our mistakes. Therefore, we should be forgiving and patient with ourselves when we err. Abba-Father is—but not forever; we all arrive at the day of reckoning when we discover that our unrepented sins have become "what you reap is what you sow":

> *Do not be deceived: God cannot be mocked. A man reaps what he sows. Whoever sows to please their flesh, from the flesh will reap destruction; whoever sows to please the Spirit, from the Spirit will reap eternal life (Galatians 6:7-8 NIV).*

Why is obedience so difficult at times? Why do we rebel? The answer lies in the question of what motivates our obedience: Is it the fear of punishment? Or is it a genuine love for God? If it's the fear of punishment, of course we want to rebel from that kind of Father! If it's love, we want to please our Father just like any child who wants to do good deeds for a parent out of sheer appreciation.

If it's love, our obedience is grounded in the confidence that God knows what's best for us. But do our decisions always show this confidence?

Every teaching of Jesus, every law that Jesus came to fulfill, every command that Jesus gave: These were not restrictions of our fun or free will. They were protections against evil.

> *But the righteous live forever, / and their reward is with the Lord; / the Most High takes care of them. / Therefore they will receive a glorious crown / and a beautiful diadem from the hand of the Lord, / because with his right hand he will cover them, / and with his arm he will shield them. (Wisdom 5:15-16 NRSV)*

The Father always has our best interests at heart. He only wants to bless us and to bless others through us. The teachings of Christ are an embrace by Abba-Father's love, and it is felt by those who want to be holy, that is, unless we've been made numb by the fear of punishment doled out from a Father upon whom we've projected human traits.

Have you thought that perhaps a disease you suffer from or the lack of healing despite many prayers is God's punishment for sin? Or that his disapproval was revealed through a car accident, or the fire that burned down the house, or the loss of a job, or any other hardship?

Terrible things happen merely because we are living on Earth instead of in Heaven, not because God is punishing us. But sometimes what we suffer is a reaping of what we've sown, like the knee pain caused by being overweight, or like the absence of friends caused by lying to them. In effect, we are punishing ourselves—and God permits this because he knows that good can come from it and he won't override our free will decisions even though he knows the consequences that we will face. This might sound unloving but wait till you see the good that comes from it!

The role of repentance in discipline

When we think of God as The Punisher, our natural inclination is to live in self-protection mode. We convince ourselves and others that what we're doing that *feels* wrong is really *not* wrong. To avoid punishment (or so we think), we choose to believe that sin is not sin—which is the heresy of moral relativism. When we sin, we justify ourselves, blame others for our mistakes, and hide from our need to repent.

The word "repent" usually carries with it the idea that we are bad, and so we prefer to believe that we are okay no matter what we've done. But "repent" actually means "to change direction" after realizing that where we've been going (or what we've been doing) is wrong.

In other words (and it's healing to know this), it's the direction we're headed in that's bad, not us.

God made each of us good! Yes, even you and even the worst person in the world. Holiness is our core nature, our true nature. On the sixth day of creation, God said, "Let us make humans next—*in our image, in our likeness.*" God's traits are at the core of our nature! He looked over everything he had created—including *you*—and declared it "very good." (See Genesis 1:26-31.)

Sin—*even when we don't believe it's a sin*—interrupts our goodness. It interrupts our relationship with our Good Father, so he sent Jesus the Savior to redirect us away from the path to Hell and toward the path to Heaven. Jesus took our sins upon his sinless self and nailed them to the Cross with his Body. He conquered sin for us by letting our sins destroy him, dying for us. Then he overcame this destruction through his resurrection. When we embrace this truth, we are set free to be who we really are (made in the image of our Father).

> *Therefore, there is now no condemnation for those who are in Christ Jesus, because through Christ Jesus the law of the Spirit who gives life has set you free from the law of sin and death. (Romans 8:1-2 NIV)*

> *We are saints who still need a lot of purification, but we are not bad people. We are cherished children of a caring Father. "Those whom I love I rebuke and discipline," he says. "So be earnest and repent." (Revelation 3:19 NIV)*

Most of us tend to think that the word "discipline" is a synonym for "punishment." But the discipline of Abba-Father is best described as "formation"—like a potter shaping a beautiful clay vase that will someday hold sweet-smelling flowers.

> *Indeed, we have sinned, "Yet you, LORD, are our Father. / We are the clay, you are the potter; / we are all the work of your hand." (Isaiah 64:8 NIV)*

> *But the pot he was shaping from the clay was marred in his hands; so the potter formed it into another pot, shaping it as seemed best to him (Jeremiah 18:4 NIV).*

Our Loving Father reshapes our lives in order to bring our best selves out from within.

There are three phases in the disciplinary process. First, marred by our own sins, we suffer the consequences of wrong decisions. For example, a man who is attached to the things of this world—his house, his car, his books, his plans—suffers greatly when he loses them. In this phase, it's all about what *we* want. We want the suffering to end, and our prayers are meant to convince God to fix things.

What God does, however, is hold in his hands our brokenness and all of our potential for what we could become. While he waits for us to surrender to his potter's wheel, he lets us continue to damage ourselves until we decide we are willing to enter the second phase.

Now it becomes all about what *God* wants. We seek the face of God. And he smiles as he accepts from us the gift of misshapen clay that came from our poor decisions, our woundedness, and our rebellions. Our prayers are meant to serve God.

This is when the man in our example decides that he really doesn't need all of his worldly stuff. More than anything else, he wants to have an intimate relationship with God as a personal friend and a caring Father. Now the Father is free to reshape the man's life into something more useful, something that looks different than before.

There is one more stage. The third stage is when the new life—the reshaped pot—benefits others. It becomes all about the sufferings of others and what we can do to help. Our prayers are meant to detach us from everything self-centered. We seek to be the hands and face of God. (We will cover this in more depth in a later chapter.)

The real meaning of discipline

My dad was the family disciplinarian. He often told us that Mom was the one who understood the psychology of children and he only understood that he was elected to mete out the punishment. "Wait till your father gets home" is the way many mothers get their kids to behave if she can't do it with reasoning and rewards (unless the father no longer lives in the home; we'll cover this later, too). And so, when my dad came through the front door ready to relax after a long day of work and he was greeted by the need to discipline children, you can guess why I formed an image of the Father as short-tempered, unhappy, and tired of his children's stupid disobedience.

We all learned as children that upsetting the Father usually results in punishment.

Indeed, God's discipline sometimes is very punishing—but not because God is quick-tempered and tired of our sinfulness. Scripture tells us, *"Return to the LORD your God, for he is gracious and merciful, slow to anger, and abounding in steadfast love; and he relents over disaster"* (Joel 2:13 ESV).

Discipline feels punishing due to our own attitude, not God's. How reluctant are we to change? Do we hate our broken lives yet continue in our old ways despite how miserable we feel? Or are we willing to learn what Abba-Father is teaching us through it?

The word "discipline" actually means "train" or "prepare by instruction" as in teaching one how to do a task or get something done. It comes from the Latin word *disciplina*, which means instruction or knowledge. It shares the same root as *discipulus* from which we get the word "disciple."

During the Middle English years (c. 1100-1500), the word "discipline" became associated with mortification by scourging yourself as penance for sins. It's a perversion of what discipline is meant to be. And it still lingers: Instead of feeling good that we have learned something through discipline, we feel guilty. We are not gracious and merciful to ourselves. Even after going to Confession and hearing Jesus say, through the priest, "Your sins are forgiven," we beat ourselves up for what we did wrong.

Abba as Potter does not smash the sinner to reshape him. That would be unloving. To appreciate the discipline of Abba-Father, we must first focus on his merciful love instead of seeing him as a chastiser who never forgets how we erred. This change in our thinking isn't easy because we've been trained to chastise ourselves. And it's not easy because we realize that God is all-knowing and therefore it's impossible for him to forget our sins. Right? Therefore, we should not forget about them either. Do you have a problem forgiving yourself? If so, this is probably why.

One day I asked God if he really could forget our sins after we've repented and reconciled with him in the Sacrament of Confession. He replied, "Do you remember being born?"

"No, of course not," I said.

"But you know you were born."

"Yes, of course."

"In the same way, I know all the ways you have sinned, but I do not remember any of it since you repented and asked for My forgiveness. I have not dealt with you according to your sins or repaid you according to your iniquities. For as high as the Heavens are above the Earth, so great is My loving devotion to you. As far as the east is from the west, that's how far I have removed your transgressions from you. As a father has compassion on his children, so I have compassion on you. For I know how I formed you. I remember that you are weak, like dust." (See Psalm 103:10-14.)

Before moving forward from here, let me interject a question that I'm often asked: "*How* do you have conversations like that with him? How do you get him to answer your questions like a human being would?" I used to ask others the same question.

Hearing Abba-Father conversationally comes from many years of clearing out my misconceptions about him while learning to trust him more and more. It comes from being "baptized in" or anointed by the Holy Spirit through the Catholic Charismatic Renewal, for this makes all the difference between trying to succeed on my own and receiving supernatural help.

It also comes from my imagination. I ask the Holy Spirit to anoint my imagination every time I do a visual meditation or ask God a question. Then I trust that my submissive willingness to learn the truth is all that the Father needs to reach my heart with his words. His voice has my permission to reach the ears of my soul.

And it comes from scriptures too. Notice that his answer to my question above came from Psalm 103. I don't have the Bible memorized; I merely have read it enough and listened to it proclaimed in Sunday and daily Mass for many years. The idea or principle of a scripture comes to mind, not the chapter and verse. Later, I research it and find the scriptures that help answer my question.

The whole conversation takes place, usually, over the course of days and sometimes months. At first, I hear the short answer in my heart or soul or imagination (whichever you want to call it). This begins a process of continued reflection about it. More is revealed through a book I'm reading, or a comment made by my husband or a friend, or a hawk flying by, or anything that God in his infinite creativity chooses.

As long as what we hear during prayer does not contradict the Bible or the teachings of the Catholic Church, we can trust that it is God's voice and not the Devil's.

But could it be our own inner voice? Might it be our own will—our own desires or expectations? The answer lies in this: Does it require us to be submissive to the Father's will? Is it free of self-defensiveness and self-justification? Are we willing to bend our will and have our minds changed? Does it cause an "aha!" moment of a wonderful revelation, which feels good even though we discover we had been wrong about something? If the answers to these questions are "yes," then we can trust that we're listening to God's voice and not our own.

When the conversation feels like I'm the clay and the Divine Potter is reshaping me into becoming more like him, I know I can trust what I'm hearing.

Anyone who has entered the first phase of disciplinary growth, as described earlier in this chapter, has jumped onto the potter's wheel. Proverbs 3:32 (NASB) says, *"For the devious are an abomination to the LORD; / But he is intimate with the upright."* The devious are those who don't seek God at all. They plot and plan everything without him; they decide for themselves what is sinful and what is not.

The upright are those who seek God and want to embrace Divine Will—even though they obey him imperfectly. Saintliness is not about avoiding all sins. It's about accepting the Father's discipline like the clay pot accepts the potter's hands. We want him to lovingly (and yes, gently) reshape our own will so that it looks more and more like his.

It's a lifelong purification. It's an intimacy with the Potter who can make wonderful and beautiful treasures out of broken pieces.

Hidden blessings

Every rebuke from Abba-Father is a blessing. We know that he does everything for our good, but do we fully believe it? Not usually.

During hardships, we demand that he quickly bring a stop to everything that's painful. We seek his helping hand and, if we can't see it, we feel abandoned or punished.

In truth, he never abandons us. Even when we are unfaithful to God, he remains faithful to us because he cannot forsake himself. It's impossible for him to stop loving us. He is always good and can never do evil (see 2 Timothy 2:13).

> Saint John of the Cross explained it this way: *"God sustains every soul and dwells in it substantially, even though it be that of the greatest sinner in the world, and this union is natural. The supernatural union exists when God's will and the soul's will are in conformity. Therefore, the soul rests transformed in God through love."*

A very common question raised by hardships is, "Why me? Why do I have to suffer this?" There's an old cliché that contributes to the pain of this: "There but for the grace of God go I." We think it when we see someone else suffer. I wish I could erase this saying from the planet! For me and for many others it implies that God did not give his grace to that person who is suffering. With this possibility in the back of our minds, we could easily conclude that when it's our turn to say, "Why me?" it's because God has withdrawn his grace from us.

Not so!

Let's change the cliché to: "By the grace of God, he/she can get through this. I wonder if I can help." And change the "Why me?" to: "By the grace of God, I can get through this. I look forward to finding out how he will help me."

Not everything bad that happens is a punishment. But all—*everything*—is used by our loving Abba-Father to teach us something. For example, the sins we commit become lessons that strengthen us to resist sin. *"Those whom I love I rebuke and discipline. So be earnest and repent"* (Revelation 3:19 NIV). We learn from the troubles we caused when we gave into temptations.

The second type of lesson comes after making wrong decisions. We seek God's guidance but interpret it incorrectly. This is not a sin; it's a mistake. But mistakes can be as destructive as sins. We hate to admit our mistakes as much as we hate to admit that we've sinned. "*Humble yourselves, therefore, under God's mighty hand, that he may lift you up in due time. Cast all your anxiety on him because he cares for you"* (1 Peter 5:6-7 NIV).

And the third kind of lesson comes from being hurt by the sins and mistakes of others. God protects us, but not always in the way we want. He makes us stronger and teaches us to love our enemies. *"I will make you a wall to this people, a fortified wall of bronze; they will fight against you but will not overcome you, for I am with you to rescue and save you"* (Jeremiah 15:20 NIV).

In each case, we benefit because we learn something valuable.

Today's Exercise: Find the Mercy in God's Discipline

One day I requested the prayers of a man (I'll call him "Luke") whose ministry was to help Christians discover new levels of freedom in their faith journeys. I hoped he would become a prayer partner for my work in Good News Ministries. However, Luke did not understand the purpose of our prayer sessions. He treated me as if I personally needed the same kind of help that everyone else came to get. He used a prayer formula he had learned and blamed me for the lack of results.

When our one-hour session timed out, I left feeling cut off, unserved, and unheard. Frustrated and hurt, the little girl in me who had felt unheard by her daddy wanted to cry. Before starting my car to drive home, I turned to Abba. "Bless what just happened, Father! Make good come from it. What do you want me to learn from it?"

Was Luke right about anything that I had rejected during our meeting? "No," he answered. But there were three lessons to learn.

One: I had committed the sin of arrogance. I had not humbled myself before the Lord to ask whether or not I should even go to Luke in the first place. Lesson learned: Remember to pray about every decision, even ones that seem obvious; God knows far more than I do about it.

Two: I had made a wrong assumption about Luke. Lesson learned: See the first lesson above.

Three: Luke was doing a ministry that requires supernatural faith. By that I mean relying on the gifts of the Holy Spirit that come from what many call the "Baptism of the Spirit." During our session, his comments seemed to lack the inspiration of the Holy Spirit. He followed a formula. At first, I dismissed this as just my imagination, hoping to be wrong. After all, Luke supposedly knew what to do. And

I was determined to find the help that I had requested.

Lesson learned: Look for the personal relationship with the Holy Spirit others have before getting involved with them in ministry. The more inspired by the Spirit they are, the freer I can be with them and the more I'll be able to accomplish with them.

Abba-Father disciplined me well. I did not feel condemned by him. I felt stronger. It would take me a while before I could fully forgive Luke because the little girl in me cried about his disappointing and surprising lack of hearing me and understanding my needs.

When bad things happen to you, remember that you are being trained and reshaped, like an athlete in training. Ask yourself: How is the experience making me stronger?

Next, ask where the mercy is. Abba-Father's discipline always—definitely *always*–includes mercy. If we think we're being punished unmercifully, we're believing a lie that Satan is using to make us feel miserable and to falsify the image of God's Fatherhood. It's the devil, not God, who punishes his victims unmercifully.

When we look for and identify where God's mercy is making good come from bad, we find the smiling face of our dear Abba-Father.

What is troubling you most right now? Describe it in a sentence or two on paper. Then make a list of what you have learned from this trouble so far. How is it making you stronger? How is God reshaping you?

DAY 11

How to Recognize the Father's Voice

FEELING CLOSE TO Abba-Father even while we are being disciplined—*especially* while we are being disciplined—comes from knowing how precious we are to the Father. Discipline is meant to be an exchange of love. In a trusting relationship, we are glad to receive instructions that will purify us. And the Father, who wants only what is best for us, is glad that we are glad—just as any good parent is happy when the child accepts the lesson being taught. But to reach this level of trust, we need to know how to differentiate the Father's voice from other voices.

> *As soon as Jesus was baptized, he went up out of the water. At that moment heaven was opened, and he saw the Spirit of God descending like a dove and alighting on him. And a voice from heaven said, "This is my Son, whom I love; with him I am well pleased." (Matthew 3:16-17 NIV).*

Do you know why Jesus was baptized? He wasn't in need of repentance like everyone else who came to hear John the Baptizer.

Thirty years prior, Jesus had humbled himself to become one of us, uniting himself to sinners so that he could take onto himself the punishment of our sins. Now here, at the initiation of his public ministry, he surrendered himself to the baptismal water so that when we are baptized, he is there in the water with us, raising us up to a new life, the holy life, everlasting life.

Everything that Jesus did is meant to reveal, by his example, not only what God the Father is really like, but also who *we* are. As the Son of God, he shows the children of God what the Father created us to be like and how we can live as children of God.

So, when Jesus was baptized and the Holy Spirit descended upon him and the Father said, "You are my beloved Son; with you I am well pleased," he showed us by example what happens at every person's baptism.

The Holy Spirit descended upon *you* and the Father said about *you*: "You are my beloved child; with you I am well pleased!"

Do you find this hard to believe? Yes, it's true that he knows what we do wrong. Yes, he knows how we have sinned and which sins we have not yet repented from. But he also knows how much you want to be one of his true children. He knows that you want to be holy. He knows that you're working at it, improving from day to day or perhaps from week to week. The Father is very pleased with you because you are not rejecting him but are seeking to grow closer to him. The Father is very pleased with you because you are interested in healing your image of him. The Father is very pleased that you want to spend eternity with him.

What do you think the Father's voice sounds like when he tells you that he is pleased with you? Can you bring to mind a parent or teacher or coach who praised you because something you did or said was very pleasing? Project that person's voice and smile onto God the Father.

But what about your sins? What does the Father's voice sound like when you sin? Is it scolding? Belittling? Frightening?

There's a huge difference between the scolding voice of a human parent and Abba-Father's corrective voice. The Devil likes to counterfeit the Father's role. The Devil abuses our memories of getting scolded by humans who were displeased with us. He knows how to push your buttons and make you feel belittled and frightened of God's displeasure.

The good news is: There's an easy way to spot the difference between the Father's reprimands and any other voice. When the Father calls our attention to what we've done wrong, we actually feel delighted. We feel the goodness behind the call to repent.

I can remember my dad yelling at me for not helping Mom do the household chores. He succeeded in making me change my ways, but I resented him for not pitching in to help alongside me. Abba-Father, on the other hand, is able to call my attention to a sin I'm committing and at the same time give me strength to overcome the sin. He's on my side! He does the chores with me. He supports me and renews me whenever I'm weak or tired.

There is so much love in the gift of his assistance that my heart melts. Any resistance I have against repenting dissolves away in his embrace.

God in his wonderfully compassionate goodness empowers us to make necessary changes. This is especially evident in the Sacrament of Confession because, as a sacrament, it provides a supernatural grace that is not available during one-on-one, alone-with-God confessions.

Here's an example: One day, when I went to Confession, I happened to be mad at my husband. I confessed other sins, but I did not want to stop being angry at Ralph. I figured that my anger could be used as leverage to make Ralph do what I wanted him to do.

After I named my other sins, the priest asked, "Is there anything else?" (This is another advantage of going to Confession. During one-on-one time with God, it's a lot easier to pretend that there is nothing else to repent from.)

Reluctantly, I nodded my head.

After explaining the whole situation to the priest—including why Ralph was in the wrong—he asked, "Do you want to stop being angry at him?"

I tried to shake my head "no." But I knew God was waiting for my "yes." I felt no condemnation. I felt no fear of punishment. What I felt was God waiting patiently. And a loving nudge to take the next step.

Almost imperceptibly, I nodded. "Okay, yes," I said to the priest. "I don't want to stop being angry at Ralph, but okay, I sort of do. Just a little."

"That is all that God needs!" the priest replied. And he continued with the prayers of the sacrament. Through the priest, Jesus gave me absolution. Through my tiny bit of willingness to change, Abba-Father gave me peace. Peace! Suddenly I no longer felt angry at all. Through no effort of my own except a slight nod of the head, my heart changed.

The Accuser's voice

When we hear any accusatory voice, we should never listen to it. Not at all. Never ever. It's the sound of condemnation. If it makes you feel belittled, unworthy of love, undeserving of good things, or unable to receive forgiveness, that's not Father God speaking.

Always prayerfully discern the voice that whispers in your mind and the message that comes to you through the people in your life. If it agrees with what God says about you, believe it.

Or here's an easier way to discern whose voice is trying to get your attention: If it's loving, if it's affirming, if it builds you up, if it acknowledges that you are good and helps bring out the best in you even though you are far from perfect—believe it.

In Philippians 4:4-7, we read that if we rejoice in the Lord always (trusting him, grateful that he is with us through good times and bad), *"the peace of God, which transcends all understanding, will guard your hearts and your minds in Christ Jesus"* (NIV).

The Accuser's voice wounds your heart and confuses your mind. And it lacks the peace of God. Remember that Jesus said, *"The thief comes only to steal and kill and destroy; I have come that they may have life, and have it to the full"* (John 10:10 NIV).

Continuing with verse 8 of Philippians 4, we see another clue about what God says about you: "Whatever is true, whatever is noble, whatever is right, whatever is pure, whatever is lovely, whatever is admirable—if anything is excellent or praiseworthy—think about such things." This scripture is advising us to think about such things because they are all reflections of the true nature of God. Therefore, because *we* were made in the image and likeness of God, they describe *our own* true nature. It may take the rest of our Earthly lives to become fully who God created us to be (which is the journey of sainthood), but know this:

Whenever the Father speaks to you, he speaks to whatever is true in you, whatever is noble, what is right, pure, lovely, admirable, excellent, and praiseworthy in you.

On the other hand, if the voice disagrees with Abba's nature and what he has said about you, reject it. It's Satan accusing you. And he's a liar. Jesus called him the father of lies (see John 8:44). Satan wants to undermine your relationship with God the Father so that he can become your spiritual father.

For example, Abba-Father would never say to you, "You're a sinner; therefore, I do not love you." Or, "You're a failure." Or, "You're not good enough." Nor would he ever communicate words of shame to you. I've said this before and I'll say it again because it's so vital to your relationship with the Father: The Father created you as "good" (see Genesis 1:26-31). You were made in the image of God, and he always sees the good in you. When he invites repentance, it is with encouragement, never shame.

There is no condemnation for us if we are in Christ Jesus, because Jesus has set us free from the law of sin and the punishment of death. He gave us his own Holy Spirit (see Romans 8:1-2), and therefore when the Father looks at us, he sees the Holy Spirit and he sees our desire to grow in holiness. Even if that desire is nearly imperceptible, he sees it. He smiles at you and embraces you and affirms what is good in you.

Only those who have no such desire should worry about condemnation. There are many who claim to believe in Jesus but, lacking a desire to be holy, they do not remain in him. They do not follow him. Even demons believe in Jesus—which is why they work so hard to pull us away from him.

This is the only unforgivable sin: To reject the desire to be holy. Jesus said, ***"Truly I tell you, people can be forgiven all their sins and every slander they utter, but whoever blasphemes against the Holy Spirit will never be forgiven; they are guilty of an eternal sin"*** (Mark 3:28-29 NIV). Heaven is only for the holy. No one who deliberately rejects holiness will want to spend eternity with God and the saints.

Isn't it ironic that we live in a world where holiness is mocked ("She acts like she's holier than thou.") and sin is glorified ("If it feels right to you, do it.") even in our own churches?

Every person who rejects Jesus and the path of holiness was created with an inherent desire to seek God and to do good, but they've been taught to go against their true nature. Jesus took to the Cross the sins of evildoers, and the Holy Spirit wants to enliven in them what is holy. That's the plan.

However, they have heard the Accuser's voice condemn them. People often live up to (or down to) what is expected of them. "You will never amount to much with bad school marks like these" might start as a parent's imperfect attempt to inspire greatness, but the Accuser shouts, "You will never amount to much!" every time the child makes a mistake, and so a lie becomes a life-long misconception about us *and* about Father God's goodness.

Jesus has given us the power to silence the Accuser. We can succeed just like he did when he was tempted. He told Satan the truth as God had revealed it. Saint James tells us to resist the Devil and he will flee (see James 4:7). Resistance is not passive. Nor does resistance mean pushing the accusations out of your mind, which can be oh so hard to do. And resistance is not a form of self-defense.

Saint Teresa of Avila said:

> When the Devil reminds you of your past, remind him of his future! The Devil will try to upset you by accusing you of being unworthy of the blessings that you have received. Simply remain cheerful and do your best to ignore the Devil's nagging. If need be, even laugh at the absurdity of the situation. Satan, the epitome of sin itself, accuses you of unworthiness!

To resist the Devil and make him stop his accusations, we do what he doesn't want us to do. We confidently rejoice in who we are to Abba-Father. We crush his lies by quoting scriptures out loud or by doing the opposite of what the Devil wants us to do.

Today's Exercise, Part 1: Silence the lies

Write down some of the accusations or condemnatory statements that have been said to you or about you. Also list some of the bad things that you think about yourself. While you're doing this, if any of it disturbs you, stop and say, "Aha! That is the voice of the Accuser!" You are allowed to reject every one of them as a lie. In fact, renouncing these lies is exactly what Abba-Father wants you to do so that you can hear his compassionate, fatherly voice more clearly. So do this exercise now, before continuing with this day.

***

The Father's voice

Probably a few of the things you listed above contain a half-truth about you. We all make mistakes. We all have faults. We all love others imperfectly. But while the Accuser condemns us for what is wrong about us, Abba-Father praises us for what is right about us. And that's not all! If we desire it, the Father addresses what is wrong in what we have done and empowers us to grow in holiness. He blesses us with lessons to learn from our mistakes. He increases our compassion for others so that we become less likely to sin against them.

Our Divine Daddy looks at our willingness to change—no matter how tiny our willingness is—and rejoices.

> *The LORD your God is in your midst, a mighty one who will save; he will rejoice over you with gladness; he will quiet you by his love; he will exult over you with loud singing (Zephaniah 3:17 ESV).*

Loud singing! Can you hear your Heavenly Father singing over you with loudness?

A silent father is a difficult father to know.

Jesus said, *"My sheep hear my voice, and I know them, and they follow Me"* (John 10:27 ESV). Now remember, everything he said and did came from the Father. Jesus was the Word of the Father made flesh (see John 1:1-5). Therefore, whenever you think that Jesus is speaking to you—either through a scripture, a song, a homily, direct revelation, or a friend—it is the Father you hear. He speaks through Jesus who is the Word of God.

Let's also realize the Holy Spirit's role in this. Jesus said, *"But the Advocate, the Holy Spirit, whom the Father will send in my name, will teach you all things and will remind you of everything I have said to you"* (John 14:26 NIV). In other words, the Holy Spirit brings us the messages of the Father. Ever since the first Pentecost after Jesus' resurrection, the Spirit of God has been that Person of the Holy Trinity who empowers Christians to hear and understand the voice of the Father.

In the Sacrament of our Baptisms, we received all three Persons of the Holy Trinity. The voice of the Father is therefore already in us. Jesus frees us from the Accuser so we can hear the Father. The Holy Spirit enables us to understand the Father.

You might be wondering: Which Person of the Holy Trinity should we be praying to and listening for? Aren't they all equal? Don't we pray to the Father through the Son with the help of the Holy Spirit? Does God care how we address our prayers?

It doesn't really matter which One of the Trinity you pray to, since they are all the same God. Each Person of God relates to us in a different way for a different purpose. For example, Jesus is our Savior, not the Father nor the Holy Spirit, and yet both Father and Holy Spirit are key to the salvation plan as much as Jesus is. Another example: The Father fathered us in our mother's womb. We are his children. But Jesus and the Holy Spirit are totally involved in this.

For what we want to accomplish in this book, we're focusing on the First Person of the Trinity. However, we also need a personal relationship with Jesus and with the Holy Spirit. They help us heal and they lead us deeper and deeper into the Father's heart.

Don't get hung up on which is which. When God speaks to you or ministers to you or blesses you, all three Persons are involved.

How to recognize the Father's voice

Sheep really do know whose voice to follow, and they come running—not sauntering, not procrastinating—but running to the shepherd when they hear him. We need that kind of relationship with Jesus because, when we run to him, we are running to the Father. When Jesus calls, it is the Father calling.

To more fully understand this, take a few minutes to go to YouTube and search for "my sheep hear my voice." This will locate several videos of sheep responding to their shepherd. Watch a couple of them. My favorite one is called *Do sheep only obey their Master's voice?* by Way2Much Productions. Find it on YouTube by typing it this way, with the quotation marks as is:

"my sheep hear my voice" Way2Much

It gives me goosebumps every time I watch this video, and a tear or two of joy.

The more time we spend with Jesus the Good Shepherd, the easier it becomes to recognize when God is speaking to us and to discern what he's actually saying. We accomplish this by reading the Bible, going to church, attending parish missions and other adult faith formation opportunities, reading spiritual books (like this one), and listening to videos and podcasts that do not contradict the Bible and Church teachings (like my *Footsteps to Heaven* podcasts at footstepstoheaven.com).

Meanwhile, here are three questions that can help you sort the Father's voice from your own imagination and from any other voice. First, though: Do a background check. Make sure that the message passes the test of: Does it contradict scripture or Church teachings? If you don't know the answer to that, ask clergy or a spiritual director or a friend who is knowledgeable about such things.

And then . . .

1. **Is it affirming?** Even when Abba-Father chastises us because we have sinned, he is always full of awareness of what is good in us, and he speaks to us with a desire to bring out that goodness and to strengthen us in it.
2. **Do you feel uplifted?** Abba's messages always include or begin with some version of, "I am here to help you. I care about you. You are My beloved." When Jesus told someone, "Go and sin no more," it was with the Father's belief that this person could and would embrace a life of holiness. It was a command based on hope—the kind of hope that knows the future. Therefore, it was more than a command. It was a message that completed a healing.
3. **Do you feel loved?** Every time Abba-Father speaks to us, he is loving us, completely and unconditionally. Jesus did not come to save us from the Father's wrath; that's an old misconception about God. Jesus came to reveal the Father's love. Focusing on what is wrong with us does not accomplish the Father's plan. Berating us for our sins does not make us holy. Rather, the more fully we understand, accept, and return the Father's generous love, the holier we become. Sin becomes easier to resist.

These questions are ideal when we're asking the Lord for guidance. They identify the false guidance of wolves who want to devour the sheep and the poor guidance of half-hearted shepherds who might inadvertently lead the sheep astray.

When I was around ten or eleven years old, I asked my parents, "Do miracles happen today like they did in the Bible?" My family belonged to a mainstream Protestant denomination. My dad was a minister and therefore should have known the answer, right? Well, that's what I expected. However, neither of my parents had ever witnessed the supernatural the way the first Christians did in the Book of Acts.

"No," they answered me. "That was just for getting the Church started." In other words, today we no longer need to raise people from the dead or heal the lame or multiply food. That showiness of God converted a lot of people in the beginning, but now we have a well-established Church.

My inner lamb did not recognize that voice. I knew they were wrong. I thought, "Of course we still need miracles today. Of course there are still a lot of people to convert."

I looked around the sheepfold for another voice. This was before the days of Christian television channels and long before the Internet made it easy to search for testimonies and photos of miracles. So, by the time I was 14, since I couldn't find anyone in church who believed in miracles, I began looking outside the church. I discovered that there are many who claim to experience the supernatural: psychics, astrologers, tarot card readers, and the like. At the library, I found nothing about Saints (lots of miracles there but I wasn't Catholic yet and I didn't even think to research Saints), nor anything about modern-day activities of the Holy Spirit (again, I didn't know how to look for it).

What I did find were plenty of books on the occult.

I read them avidly. Thus began my journey away from the Good Shepherd. What I learned was exciting and I shared it with my sister and friends. We formed a "psychic club" to experiment with what I was reading. By the time I was 20 and moved away from home as a newlywed, I had lost all interest in the One who had been my Best Friend since my earliest childhood. I still believed in Jesus, but I no longer spent any time with him.

A friend named Janet gave me a book that explained how the ghosts I contacted in séances were really demons. Since I no longer recognized the voice of the Good Shepherd, I didn't believe it.

In my senior year of high school, I started dating Ralph. I wanted to get him involved in my occult activities, but as soon as he tried it, he saw a demon and ran out of the house because it was trying to suck him into something like a "black hole." That should have warned me, but I shrugged it off.

My friend Ed also tried to warn me. I didn't believe him either. He became a priest in 1975, the same year Ralph and I got married. A couple of years later, Father Ed spent a week of his vacation with us. He didn't try to set me straight about the occult, though. My mind was closed.

That weekend, I drove him to a Catholic Church because he wanted to celebrate Mass. Father Ed asked me, "Are you planning to attend Mass?"

"Sure," I said. "I want to see you do your priest thing."

I'll share the rest of this story in the next chapter. What's important to know today is that when my friend explained to me what and who the Eucharist is, a miracle happened. I recognized the voice of God speaking through my friend. I heard the voice of the Good Shepherd, and I ran to him like the sheep in the YouTube video. I wanted to be fed by him all the time, and several months later, I officially became Catholic so that I could participate freely and fully in the miracle of the Eucharist.

We don't have to put hard work into recognizing the voice of God. Abba-Father desires to be heard. He makes it easy. All we have to do is give him our yes, however slight the nod of our head. That's the first step.

The hardest part of this is letting go of old ideas and replacing misconceptions with the truth. That's exactly what you're doing now! The Father is very pleased with you. Very pleased.

Listen with the ears of your soul for the familiar sound of truth; it's the Father's voice speaking through the Holy Spirit who is the Spirit of Truth, and your soul recognizes him. Practice listening every day while your trust in the Father grows through shedding your misconceptions about him. During every private prayer time, ask the Holy Spirit to anoint your imagination, and then trust what comes to mind as long as it passes the tests that I named earlier in this chapter.

Today's Exercise, Part 2: What is Abba-Father telling you?

Revisit what you wrote in part 1 of today's exercise. Now write what Abba-Father says about each one of those accusations. Imagine the Father looking like an adorable old gentleman, and he's sitting next to you. He's reassuring you: "Trust your instincts," he's saying. "Why do those accusations make you feel condemned or belittled? They make you feel bad; that's not My voice you're hearing. What would be a loving counterpoint to each of those accusations? That's My voice!"

For example, if you wrote, "My third-grade teacher accused me of cheating on a test and would not let me explain why I was innocent," the counterpoint could be, "I studied hard for that test; I am a hard worker and I love getting good grades through my own honest efforts."

And the Father says to you, "I am delighted that you studied hard for that test! You are indeed a hard worker. It's wonderful how much you enjoyed getting good grades through your own honest efforts. That's the kind of daughter (or son) that I created you to be."

If there is any truth to what your accusers said about you, how would a loving parent defend you and at the same time guide you to change? That's the Father's voice.

For example: "You cheated on the exam at work because you wanted to get that promotion. But notice that it has made you feel bad about yourself. You really do prefer to do well through your own honest efforts. I am very pleased about that! Now go to the Sacrament of Confession and remember to forgive yourself."

Ask the Holy Spirit to help you fully accept the truth of your goodness. Then notice that you have received a miracle of healing!

DAY 12

Communion with the Father during Eucharistic Adoration

JESUS' MISSION IS to take us to the Father. He did this by dying for us, taking our sins upon himself as he suffered the torture of the Cross. But he also did this by living for us. Through his incarnated life as a man on Earth, he guided us to our Heavenly Father. And because we have so many misconceptions about the Father's treatment of us, Jesus demonstrated what the Father is like by being an example of his true nature. And he didn't stop there. Today he connects us to the Father every time we open ourselves to the gift of Holy Communion.

> *Jesus gave them this answer: "Very truly I tell you, the Son can do nothing by himself; he can do only what he sees his Father doing, because whatever the Father does the Son also does. For the Father loves the Son and shows him all he does. Yes, and he will show him even greater works than these, so that you will be amazed. (John 15:19-20 NIV)*

Jesus has been revealing the Father to you all of your life, and he will continue to do so. I think he might even do this for all of eternity, for we will never fully know God, since he is more—always more, infinitely more—than any human could ever understand. I think it's likely that the Saints in Heaven are still learning. That might be one of the great joys of Heaven!

So, let's discover what Jesus wants to reveal to us today. Let's investigate how the Holy Eucharist, which is Jesus himself, reveals the Father to us.

Who do you pray to most often: Father, Son, or Holy Spirit?

For most of us, it's the Son because Jesus himself told us to ask in *his* name: *"And I will do whatever you ask in my name, so that the Father may be glorified in the Son. You may ask me for anything in my name, and I will do it"* (John 14:13-14 NIV).

Do you realize that every time you entrust your needs, prayer requests, and intercessory intentions to Jesus, it is ultimately the Father whom you're addressing? Jesus makes this clear: *"I am not saying that I will ask the Father on your behalf. No, the Father himself loves you because you have loved me and have believed that I came from God"* (John 16:26-27 NIV).

Jesus is our Mediator while we are still on Earth. Hebrews 5:2 reminds us that the high priests of the Old Covenant were appointed to represent the people in matters related to God. Jesus is the fulfillment of that priesthood, becoming the one mediator between God and humankind (see 1 Timothy 2:5) so that those who follow him can be adopted by the Father and receive his eternal inheritance (see Hebrews 9:15).

Prayer is meant to be a spiritual communion with God in his fullness. But on our own we can never achieve this. So, the Father sent the Son to become our Mediator. Jesus hears our prayers, accepts them, and carries them to the Father. He adds his own love and redemptive power to what our hearts desire (if they are holy desires). And because we desire to be heard by God *and also* to hear God's responses, Jesus speaks the Father's words to us through the Holy Spirit.

Jesus explained in John 14:16-17 that the Father would give us a Helper (an Advocate) who will be with us forever. Jesus called this aide the Spirit of Truth. It's the Holy Spirit emanating from the love of the Father and the Son. The Holy Spirit is, in effect, the love-energy (i.e., the power) of God responding to our prayers. The Spirit of God delivers to us Abba-Father's answers to our prayers.

And when we don't know what to pray because of the intensity of the problem or because we don't have enough information upon which to base our prayers—what then?

> *. . . [T]he Spirit helps us in our weakness. We do not know what we ought to pray for, but the Spirit himself intercedes for us through wordless groans. And he who searches our hearts knows the mind of the Spirit, because the Spirit intercedes for God's people in accordance with the will of God. (Romans 8:26-27 NIV)*

So, you see, the Holy Spirit goes the extra mile for us. Not only does he deliver Father God's words to us and helps us to interpret those words, but he delivers to the Father the wordless yearnings that dwell deep in our hearts. This works most effectively when we have an active, personal relationship with the Spirit. The indwelling, fully active presence of the Spirit within us resonates with all that is holy and beautiful in our wordless longings. Have you ever heard the hum that comes from two objects resonating at just the right frequency?

To understand this better, consider how the strings of a piano resonate to produce beautiful music. Scientifically speaking, every object has a natural frequency at which it is able to vibrate. When the piano player hits a key, the key hits a string. If the piano has been properly tuned, hitting the string causes a vibration that matches this particular string's natural frequency. The string begins to vibrate with ever increasing amplitude (it resonates), creating a sound that we can hear.

Similarly, when the Holy Spirit prays within us (if we have been properly tuned), "the Spirit himself intercedes for us through wordless groans." The Holy Spirit resonates with what is holy in us (what is "in accordance with the will of God"). This produces a beautiful sound that the Father hears and responds to.

Therefore, a good way to start a prayer request can be: "Abba-Father, in the name of Jesus Christ and in the power of the Holy Spirit, I humbly ask for . . . "

A most intimate way to pray

One of the most intimate ways to pray is what we in the Catholic Church call "Eucharistic Adoration" or "Adoration of the Blessed Sacrament." During this form of prayer, we're in the presence of Christ as truly as if we had been following him around Galilee two millennia ago. He is fully present in the bread that, through the miracle of "transubstantiation," now has only the form of bread because the substance is Jesus himself.

My first encounter with Jesus in the Eucharist happened when I attended my first Catholic Mass in 1977. An old friend who had become a priest visited Ralph and me for a week's vacation. During his stay, Father Ed wanted me to take him to a Catholic Church so he could celebrate the Holy Mass. I thought it would be fun to watch him do his priestly thing. He, however, knowing that I was a Protestant, had to explain why I should stay in the pew and not get in line to receive Communion.

"But if you came to my church," I said, "we wouldn't deny our communion to you."

"Mass is not a communion service," he said. "The bread and wine of your services are just symbols. Your communion service is a remembering of the Last Supper of Jesus. The Catholic Mass is that and so much more!" Then he explained the miracle of transubstantiation.

> *Jesus said, ". . . For my flesh is real food and my blood is real drink. Whoever eats my flesh and drinks my blood remains in me, and I in them. Just as the living Father sent me and I live because of the Father, so the one who feeds on me will live because of me." (John 6:55-57 NIV)*

During Mass, I listened attentively to the consecration prayers that Father Ed spoke. Wow! Something much more intense than my Protestant services was happening here. When Father Ed held up in adoration the bread-now-flesh of Christ and said, "Behold the Lamb of God!" my heart reached out to Jesus with an insatiable yearning to become united to him. This was prayer without words; an exchange of love beyond description. I felt suddenly *alive* in faith!

Until that moment, I had lost all interest in Christ due to my involvement in the occult for the past seven years. Thanks to the Good Lord, my whole life began to change when I encountered Jesus in the Eucharist.

Participating in the Holy Mass should always result in some kind of change within us. Who can truly encounter Jesus and not be transformed by it?

Every time we see the Eucharist lifted up above the altar during the consecration prayers, if we're paying attention and fully participating, we are worshiping Jesus in an exchange of intimate, Divine

Love. This is a powerful moment of Eucharistic Adoration. What do you do with it?

There's an old, mostly forgotten tradition that needs to be brought back by everyone at Mass. When the newly transubstantiated Host is held up by the priest and he proclaims, "Behold the Lamb of God," we should quietly but enthusiastically adore Jesus with the words of Saint Thomas: "My Lord and My God!" (John 20:28). Or remind yourself: "This is *my* precious Lord and God!" And then adore Jesus: "Thank You for Your sacrifice, which I cannot even comprehend."

Then the liturgy progresses and soon Jesus in the Eucharist is lifted up before us and to us alone. We're given a one-on-one encounter with God. "The Body of Christ," announces the minister of the Eucharist.

We agree, saying, "Yes, I do believe!" (in the word "amen") and we consume the Body of Jesus into our own body and his Blood mingles with our own blood. Now our entire self is involved in this prayer of divine union.

If we're careful to stay in that spirit of prayer instead of thinking about what we'll do after Mass, and if we don't fall prey to some other distraction, we enter into what I call "the Golden Moment." We consume Jesus, and God's grace fully consumes us. Our Earthly life is more Heaven-connected than at any other time.

What do you want to say to Abba-Father during the Golden Moment? Can you hear him ministering to you? Can you feel his immersive embrace?

Make the divine encounter last longer

Saint Gabriel Brochero (1593-1649) said, "The Consecrated Host is a miracle of love; it is a prodigy of love; it is a wonder of love; it is a complement of love; and it is the most finished proof of His infinite love towards me, towards you, towards mankind."

This Golden Moment is an encounter with God that we can experience every day if we have access to daily Mass. But the time of adoration during Mass is usually all too brief. Is it enough?

No, not if we want more from the Father than what we get from going to Holy Mass. There is always more of God to experience. There is always more that the Father wants to give to us, more that the Holy Spirit wants to say to us, and more need for Jesus to serve as our Mediator. There's more love, more comfort, more help available.

So, the Church gives us Adoration of the Blessed Sacrament as an opportunity to make the divine encounter last longer. What a powerful moment it is when the Body of Christ is given to us for our adoration! We watch as Jesus, in the form of bread (the "host"), is reverently placed on the altar, usually in a vessel that's shaped like a cross. This vessel is called a *monstrance*, from the Latin word meaning "to show."

This gift makes God available to all who avail themselves of it. He provides it for no other purpose than love, worship, and communication.

When is your next opportunity? Prepare for it now by reading the following meditation.

The chapel is quiet. The smell of incense awakens your senses. On the altar, Jesus the Eucharist is waiting for you. You find a place to kneel in reverence.

This is a very special time. As you gaze at the Host, knowing that this is Jesus in the flesh, look *into* the Host. Look *through* the Host and let your heart and mind travel *beyond* the Host. The Father is there! He's waiting for you with a big smile on his face. His arms are reaching out to you to immerse you in his safe, protective embrace.

Jesus is once again leading you to the Father. This is his purpose! He has no other mission.

As you gaze into and beyond the Host, you are entering into another dimension of space and time. Picture yourself getting up and walking to the monstrance, still focused on Jesus in the Host. On the other side of Jesus, beyond the monstrance, is Heaven! Imagine that the Host is a portal (if you've seen any sci-fi movies about portals to other dimensions, use that image). Next imagine yourself jumping through it.

You've landed in the Father's Divine Lap. His strong, protective arms hold you securely and warmly. He is greeting you with the biggest, friendliest, most approving smile you have ever seen!

> *For this is what the Lord says: "As a mother caresses her baby, so I will comfort you: I will carry you at my breast and rock you in my lap" (adapted by St. Therese of Lisieux from Isaiah 66:12-13).*

If you try to become aware of this communion with the Father but it eludes you, ask Jesus in the Host to breathe on you the gifts of his Holy Spirit. Picture it: Imagine Jesus standing in front of the altar. He's looking at you with eyes full of tender compassion. He is smiling at you! He is delighted that you are spending this time with him.

Realize that you are also seeing the *Father's* tender compassion. In Jesus, you are seeing the *Father's* smile. The *Father* is very delighted with you.

Jesus speaks to you with a gentle but firm voice: "Receive My Holy Spirit." He raises his right hand toward you and gives you a blessing. This is the Father blessing you!

Do you desire to receive this gift? More than ever before? Abba-Father is giving you the desire of your heart. As Jesus assures, *"What father would give his child a stone when asked for bread? Your Father in heaven cares much more than any human parent and will give the Holy Spirit to all those who ask for it"* (see Luke 11:11-13).

The Holy Spirit will make it easier for you to experience communion with the Father. The Holy Spirit will carry his voice to the ears of your heart.

On the other side of the Host is the Father's joy. The Father's healing. The Father's love for you, which is full and complete. Spend time lingering with him. Enjoy being doted on by the Divine Daddy who created you.

The Eucharist at Mass enhanced

After we've spent time adoring Jesus in the Blessed Sacrament and encountering Abba-Father there, celebrating Mass can become a much more powerful experience of the Father's nearness.

Notice that all of the prayers led by the presider during Mass are directed to the Father. Participate in the Mass with this in mind. Remain aware of how you and the priest are speaking to the Father.

Many of the prayers of the Eucharistic Liturgy are *about* Jesus, not *to* Jesus. The prayers are directed to the Father. Have you noticed that? In fact, the entire celebration of Mass is an intimate dialog with the Father:

1. The first hymn, which unites the children of God in song, begins the conversation. Do you sing? It doesn't matter to Abba-Father what your voice sounds like. Remember, he gave you that voice and meant for it to sing praises that glorify him in an exchange of love. If you're off-key, so what? The Father is delighted that you've opened your mouth.

2. In the Penitential Rite, we seek the Father's forgiveness for our sins—and he readily gives it. Have you prepared for this by bringing to mind your sins? The opportunity for this is usually so short during Mass that it's important we think about it before arriving at church.
3. Abba-Father speaks to us through the Holy Spirit as we listen to the scriptures and the homily. But what if the homily is boring or off-topic? Abba-Father wants to give you the best possible experience of his active involvement in your worship, so expect the Holy Spirit to deliver a message that comes directly from the heart of the Father—even if it is spoken only within your heart.
4. During the intercessory prayers, we give to our Father the needs of others. None of the prayers about us (the people) are directed to Jesus. They all go directly to the Father through Jesus.
5. The miracle of the Eucharist occurs because of the Father. It is the Father who gives Jesus to us by transforming bread and wine into the Body and Blood of our Savior. It happens when the priest asks the Holy Spirit to come down upon the bread and wine (during the prayers of consecration):

    Therefore, O Lord, we humbly implore You by the same Spirit: Graciously make holy these gifts we have brought to You for consecration, that they may become the Body and Blood of Your Son our Lord Jesus Christ, at whose command we celebrate these mysteries. (from Eucharistic Prayers III)

By the time we say the "amen" that acknowledges our belief in the truth of this, we have been transformed. By the grace of God, we have been purified. Now, in receiving and consuming Jesus in the Eucharist, we are temporarily detached from this world. We are fully united to God, however briefly it might last.

This is not a moment to be squandered. Enjoy it! Be conscious of the presence of your Divine Daddy. He is very delighted that you are here and that you have chosen to worship him and enter into the mysteries of Christ's purifying, Eucharistic gift.

While you are still in the state of grace, having repented of your sins and being made worthy by Jesus Christ (having prayed sincerely, "Lord, I am not worthy . . . but say the word and my soul shall be healed"), and having received Jesus in the Holy Communion of the Blessed Sacrament, make full use of this special moment. You are pure! Give Abba-Father your love with all your heart, with all your soul, and with all your mind (as Jesus tells us to do in Luke 10:27). What a glorious moment this is! He is loving you with all of *his* heart, with all of *his* soul, and with all of *his* mind.

Over the years, I've discovered that during Mass is when I'm able to hear God most clearly. I've learned to take seriously the ideas and inspirations that come after the prayers of consecration have begun, for they have usually proven true over the test of time.

When I'm feeling depressed or troubled, I'm most eager to get to Mass because I know that it will give me the comforting embrace of Abba-Father. When someone rejects me or disbelieves me or falsely accuses me of wrong thinking, it is in the Eucharistic Liturgy where I most easily find my Divine Daddy's encouragement and affirmation.

If you are unable to receive Jesus in the Holy Eucharist, run—don't walk—to the nearest priest to remedy whatever has been holding you back. For example, any unrepented sin makes receiving Jesus in the Eucharist a blasphemy against his holiness. So, go to the Sacrament of Confession as soon as possible.

Another obstacle is getting remarried without first obtaining an annulment of the previous marriage. It means you might be living in the terrible sin of adultery, so apply for the annulment despite all reasons to avoid it. An annulment will prove (to yourself as well as to everyone else in the Church, which is very healing) that your previous marriage was never valid. God had not put you two together. God did not recognize that marriage, so you are free to be married to someone else. (And by the way, children brought into this world through a non-valid marriage are nonetheless considered valid by God. They are true children.)

Just don't ever let anything stop you from receiving all that the Father wants to give to you. Don't let the Devil encourage sin. Don't be held back by anyone's un-divine thinking. Again I say: If you are unable to receive Jesus in the Holy Eucharist, run—don't walk—to the nearest priest to remedy whatever has been holding you back.

Today's Exercise: Pray the "Our Father" for deeper communion

Let's end this chapter with one more meditation. Previously in this book, we visited the "Our Father" prayer in a new and deeper way. Since this prayer is an important part of Mass, let's do it again with yet another adaptation. Be sure to add your own words to it. At Mass we recite this prayer too quickly. If you do this exercise often, the prayer will become a more meaningful part of your encounter with Abba-Father.

OUR FATHER—Daddy, Father of us all, You love all of your children, even those who don't know You.

WHO IS IN HEAVEN—You are Lord over all. Eventually, we will all come face-to-face with Your infinite love and realize how poorly we have loved others like You have loved us. Help me to discover Your love here on Earth.

HOLY IS YOUR NAME—Help me to revere You and to recognize Your great mercy. Likewise, I ask You to help those who, because of their involvement in evil, are most in need of Your mercy. Help us all to turn away from everything that is not of You.

YOUR KINGDOM COME—Whatever is fighting against Your kingdom, our Savior Jesus has already defeated it through the Cross and his Resurrection. May his Precious Blood cover every evil-doer for whom I am praying: Break Satan's strongholds and heal their minds and souls.

YOUR WILL BE DONE ON Earth AS IT IS IN HEAVEN—Help me to know Your will, clearly and accurately, and fill me with a zeal for doing what You ask of me. Give me special graces to hear and grasp Your will more profoundly.

GIVE US TODAY OUR DAILY BREAD—You know what I need for recognizing Your Divine Will and what I need to enter into it and remain in it. Help me to receive everything You want to give me. Feed me Your Love.

FORGIVE US OUR SINS—Forgive me for succumbing to temptation and for allowing myself to be confused about what is right and what is wrong. Forgive me for contributing to evil in the world by my unloving actions and by my lack of loving actions.

AS WE FORGIVE THOSE WHO SIN AGAINST US—Lord, I do forgive. I ask You, merciful Father, to forgive those who have inflicted evil upon me. Break the chains of hatred and violence that hold so many people in Satan's grip.

DO NOT SUBJECT US TO THE FINAL TEST—Do not let anyone for whom I'm praying die before they have recognized and accepted Your love. Help us all to become like Jesus, who is the human embodiment of Perfect Love.

DELIVER US FROM EVIL—Deliver me and the whole world from all tactics of the Devil. Rescue evildoers from living as Satan's instruments; set them free to enjoy Jesus Christ here on Earth and then eternally in Heaven.

AMEN!

DAY 13

Children of God by Adoption

UP UNTIL NOW IN this 30-day journey into the Father's heart, we've been focusing on who he really is as our Divine Daddy. Now we're going to shift to who *we* are to ***him***. What does it mean to be God's children by adoption?

Discovering this can help you make the transition to seeing Father God as a Divine Daddy who chose to adopt you because you are so very, very important to him (instead of seeing him through the lens of your experiences with humans). You are more precious to Father God than you know. He is more actively reaching out to you than you realize.

I wish I could sit down with you face to face and lead you through an inner healing. However, it's impossible to do it through a book that's written for all kinds of different people with all kinds of different father-wounds. This book, when read in its entirety, is designed to be a process of inner healing that slowly unfolds within you like a blossoming flower. If you've not been doing the prescribed spiritual exercises, you're cheating yourself of this opportunity; go back and start over to receive all that the Father longs to give to you.

In this day of the journey into the Father's heart, we're going to build your confidence in how good he is to you by helping you see yourself through his eyes.

> *"For those who are led by the Spirit of God are the children of God. The Spirit you received does not make you slaves, so that you live in fear again; rather, the Spirit you received brought about your adoption to sonship. And by him we cry, "Abba, Father." The Spirit himself testifies with our spirit that we are God's children. Now if we are children, then we are heirs–heirs of God and co-heirs with Christ, if indeed we share in his sufferings in order that we may also share in his glory." (Romans 8:14-17 NIV)*

St. Teresa of Avila wrote, in 1563:

> Up until now, I thought I needed others, and I had more trust in help from the world. Now, I understand clearly that all this help is like little sticks of dry rosemary and that in being attached to it there is no security; for when some weight of contradiction or criticism comes along, these little sticks break. So, I have experienced that the true remedy against a fall is to be attached to the Cross and trust in him who placed himself upon it. I discover that he is the true friend, and through this friendship I find in myself a dominion by which it seems to me I could resist, providing God doesn't fail me, anyone who might be against me.
>
> Though now I understand this truth so clearly, *I used to be very fond of being liked. No longer does being liked matter to me; rather, it seems in part to weary me* [emphasis mine], except in the case of those with whom I discuss my soul or whom I am thinking of helping. For I desire that the former like me so they might bear with me and that the latter do so that they might be more inclined to believe what I tell them about the vanity of everything.

I highlight the italicized part of St. Teresa's quote above because, I confess, I'm too easily sent into an emotional tailspin whenever someone misunderstands me or makes wrong assumptions about me. Their rejection of who I truly am feels like I've been smacked by a monster octopus that has captured me in its tentacles and is squeezing the life out of me. The monster won't release me until I agree with what it says about me. But even that doesn't free me. If I comply with its demands, I'm crushed by its powerful grip into a smaller version of who I really am.

The truth is: It's only God's opinion of us that really matters. This truth rescues me every time.

However, knowing this truth does not protect me from getting sucked into an emotional tailspin. That's because the spinning began as far back as I can remember. I grew up feeling misunderstood by my father.

My beliefs and my opinions didn't matter to him. He only wanted compliance from me. His own insecurities were demanding that he have the first and last word on everything. (Undoubtedly this did not happen all the time, but it's what influenced my memories of him and therefore my image of Father God.) Anything else from me was "sassing back," he said, regardless of my tone of voice (and in fact, I did become sassy in an immature attempt to be heard).

Today there are a number of other people who keep me locked in the grip of their wrong assumptions. It's a normal part of living on this side of Heaven's gate.

The good news is: Although the door between them and me might be locked tight, Father God has given me other doors, and they are wide open. The Light of Christ is beaming brightly through these "Daddy Doors." Some lead to Godly friendships and some are very special because they lead to God alone.

He is doing the same for you.

Everyone has been misunderstood by their parents as well as their friends, their boss, coworkers, spouse, children, and all other significant relationships. A sign that we still need healing from it is the tendency to include in our prayer requests a lot of explanation, reasoning, logic, and more talk than listening. A good way to overcome this is to pause and add:

"But You, oh Lord, know me better than I know myself. You understand the situation better than I ever will. You know what is good in me and see it more clearly than I do. Help me to see myself the way You do through Your eyes of unconditional love."

Pray with Psalm 139:1-6 (NIV):

You have searched me, Lord,
and you know me.
You know when I sit and when I rise;

you perceive my thoughts from afar.
You discern my going out and my lying down;
you are familiar with all my ways.
Before a word is on my tongue
you, Lord, know it completely.
You hem me in behind and before,
and you lay your hand upon me.
Such knowledge is too wonderful for me,
too lofty for me to attain.

The monster octopus squeezed me to crush me. In contrast, Father God hems us in with his loving care like a hug that empowers us to heal and to gain new freedom to be who we really are as his beloved children, created good, made in his image.

During my childhood, God gave me others who listened well enough to understand me most of the time—my grandparents modeled Abba-Father's listening ear, as did my friends. They were the Daddy Doors that God gave me.

My dad didn't try to figure me out. When our points of view differed, he rarely asked me questions about why I thought what I thought. He was the father, he knew better than I did, end of discussion.

Then I met Ralph (we were high school seniors). Not only did my new boyfriend understand me, he also enjoyed hearing everything I told him! It didn't take long for me to fall in love with him.

One evening at the end of a date, we missed the curfew. We were parked in the driveway, talking about a million different things. Technically, I was home before the curfew. But my father was livid. He didn't want to hear any excuses. I couldn't reassure him that Ralph and I had done nothing wrong except lose track of time. He forbade me to continue dating Ralph for a while—I no longer remember how long this punishment was to last; it might have been a week, but it seemed like forever.

The next day, Ralph knocked on the door to speak to my father privately. This surprised and amazed me. They talked behind the closed door of my dad's office for several long minutes. When they emerged, Ralph was smiling, and my father announced that we could resume dating. Later, I asked Ralph what he had said to my father; he wouldn't tell me.

Ralph had worked a miracle. He was my knight in shining

armor. He had come to my rescue and somehow accomplished with my dad what I could not.

This is what love does, what our Divine Daddy does. He comes to the defense of his adopted children. He lifts up the downtrodden and stands up for the misunderstood. He heals the brokenhearted. He sets us free from the fears and frustrations that imprison us. He serves as an open door when other doors have been slammed closed.

As you can guess, Ralph's shiny armor eventually rusted. He, too, has misunderstood me. No human can be all that we need, nor even come close to it, all of the time. Every spouse needs more than what their sweetheart can provide. Every marriage suffers from misunderstandings. Life's hardships pile up like too much baggage. Sufferings wear us down. We lose the strength that had made the relationship strong in the beginning. What then?

Most marriages that fail, I've noticed, fall apart because at least one of the spouses has failed to discover that only God can be all that we need—*for all* that we need. Without God as our most significant and greatest source of love, we demand too much from our spouses, and eventually they break or run or hide.

Divine courage

Abba, whose Fatherly love surpasses all understanding, has put into place a plan that rescues us from the many deficiencies of human relationships. Think again about his plan: He comes to our defense. He lifts us up when we feel downtrodden. He gives us compassionate understanding. He heals our broken hearts. He sets us free from the fears and frustrations that imprison us.

This love is the spirit of adoption. It is our Divine Daddy being a protective father despite our shortcomings.

To more deeply experience Abba-Father's love, we need to realize what it means to be adopted by him. St. Teresa experienced it this way (continuing with the next paragraph of her quote above):

> In the very severe trials and persecutions and opposition I experienced these past months, God has given me great courage; and the greater these trials were the greater was the courage, without my growing tired of suffering. Toward persons who spoke evil of me, not only did I feel I bore no harsh feelings, but it seemed to me I gained new love for

them. I don't know how this came about; it was a blessing given by the hand of the Lord.

Courage is a gift from Abba-Father. The world's definition of courage is very insufficient. It's much, much more than bravery. Courage from Abba-Father is the confidence that comes from knowing that we are loved and accepted and cherished by the One whose opinion is the only viewpoint that really matters.

When we feel wrongly judged or criticized by a parental voice in an old memory or by a coworker or boss today, we don't need to be afraid of what others think. We can safely listen to criticism with a willingness to learn from it, as long as we simultaneously listen for Abba's voice reaching us through the comforting presence of the Holy Spirit. The Father always softens the blow. The truth that's been packaged in criticism is unwrapped and given to us as a blessing when Abba-Father hands it to us.

Knowing that we're protected by Abba, we are free to safely recognize that sometimes our critics teach us something valuable, even when they are wrongly projecting their own faults onto us. By remaining aware that we are loved, accepted, and valued by God, we can discern the difference between human judgmentalism and the Father's invitation to improve ourselves. Then we become free to love the people who oppose us without demanding that they believe us. This is divine courage!

Divine courage looks like this: We don't defend ourselves; we let the Father do that. We don't argue with our opponents; we quietly ask the Holy Spirit to enlighten them. We don't linger in hurt feelings, nor do we feel crushed by the monster octopus; we let the peace of Christ influence our mood.

What it means to be adopted by Abba-Father

To know the Father as our "Holy Knight in shining armor"—to know him as a Father who defends us and uplifts us in the face of opposition—we need to better understand how the spirit of adoption works.

But first let's look at why we need the spirit of adoption. Since God created us, doesn't that mean that we're his children from the start? Yes—*and* not fully.

Jesus is the only real Son of the Father, because he is the only one who is truly like the Father in every way. But the Father yearns for all of us to become like him. What parent has not hoped that their offspring will follow in his footsteps? What Christian parent has not hoped that their children will grow up in the faith and remain united to them in faith and family ties? This desire comes from God himself. It's part of his character. He longs for us to unite to him in every way, just like Jesus did.

This is why the Father sent Jesus to Earth. This is why Jesus became human like us. When we choose to follow Jesus, he leads us to the Father. When we accept the fact that we need a Savior and we allow Jesus to take our sins to his Cross, we are resurrected with him into the life of a true son or daughter of Abba-Father.

> *"See what great love the Father has lavished on us, that we should be called children of God! And that is what we are!" (1 John 3:1 NIV)*

> *"His divine power has given us everything we need for a godly life through our knowledge of him who called us by his own glory and goodness. Through these he has given us his very great and precious promises, so that through them you may participate in the divine nature, having escaped the corruption in the world caused by evil desires." (2 Peter 1:3-4 NIV)*

Our Dear Divine Daddy has adopted us because of his tremendous love for us and because he values us and cherishes us. However, we are not perfect children. We are not like Jesus in every way—yet. That will only happen in the next life after we've been purged of everything that is not like Jesus.

> *"Beloved, we are God's children now, and what we will be has not yet appeared; but we know that when he appears we shall be like him, because we shall see him as he is." (1 John 3:2 ESV)*

How amazingly wonderful and generous that Abba-Father adopts us regardless of our imperfections! He is full of compassion and mercy.

> *"You are my beloved child, in whom I am well pleased" (from Matthew 3:17).*

When Jesus became one of us, he united himself to us in every way except sin. Everything he did, he did it on behalf of the Father—for us. This includes what happens in our baptisms.

On Day 11 of this 30-day journey into the Father's Heart, we took a close look at the baptism of Jesus. Now let's look more deeply into our own baptisms.

Why are Christians baptized? The first thing that probably comes to your mind is the textbook answer. The *Catechism of the Catholic Church* states in paragraph #1213:

> Holy Baptism is the basis of the whole Christian life, the gateway to life in the Spirit (*vitae spiritualis ianua*), and the door which gives access to the other sacraments. Through Baptism we are freed from sin and reborn as sons of God; we become members of Christ, are incorporated into the Church and made sharers in her mission: "Baptism is the sacrament of regeneration through water in the word."

And #1215 states:

> This sacrament is also called "the washing of regeneration and renewal by the Holy Spirit," for it signifies and actually brings about the birth of water and the Spirit without which no one "can enter the Kingdom of God."

A brief history lesson

Do you know the connection between Baptism and the Sacrament of Confirmation? The latter is often mistakenly described as the sacrament that gives us the Holy Spirit. But in fact, we receive the fullness of Father, Son, and Holy Spirit in the Sacrament of Baptism. And as described above, Baptism gives birth to our adoption into God's family through "renewal by the Holy Spirit."

Confirmation is also mistakenly described as the sacrament that gives us the anointing of the Holy Spirit to empower us to serve God. And yet, children who have not received Confirmation but who have been raised in a Christ-centered home often exhibit the empowerment of the Holy Spirit. Haven't you said (or heard someone say), "My baby is seeing angels!" Or, "My little boy shows amazing wisdom when he talks about matters of the faith."

And the Charismatic Renewal includes the "Baptism of the Spirit" regardless of whether or not the person has received the Sacrament of Confirmation. This is not a substitute for Confirmation. Rather, it's an awakening of our life in the Spirit, which began with our baptisms.

Confirmation is the sacrament that's the most difficult to explain, and here's why. In many dioceses of the Latin Rite of the Catholic Church, Confirmation takes place several years after First Holy Communion. This often makes it feel like a sort of "graduation" from religious education classes. We hamper the Church's mission with this attitude.

From the days of the early Church through the Middle Ages, Confirmation was closely linked with baptism.

> *When the apostles in Jerusalem heard that Samaria had accepted the word of God, they sent Peter and John to Samaria. When they arrived, they prayed for the new believers there that they might receive the Holy Spirit, because the Holy Spirit had not yet come on any of them; they had simply been baptized in the name of the Lord Jesus. Then Peter and John placed their hands on them, and they received the Holy Spirit. (Acts 8:14-17 NIV)*

Bishops have always been the ones who administer Confirmation because the bishop *confirms* that the baptismal rite was valid. Baptisms can be administered by anyone, including a parent or other lay person (in emergency cases, otherwise by clergy), but not Confirmation. This sacrament can only be conferred by a bishop or else by a priest who has been given special permission by the bishop to represent him.

Throughout most of Church history, families celebrated the Sacrament of Baptism as the first part of initiation into the Faith. Then they waited for the bishop to come to town and confirm the baptism. After that, they believed, the newly adopted member of God's family was ready for First Holy Communion.

In Acts 8 (above), we see this happen. The "apostles in Jerusalem" were bishops. Peter was the head bishop (the Church later named this role "pope," an affectionate Greek word for "father"). He and another apostle, John, traveled to a community of new Christians. The Samaritan Christians had been baptized but only in the name of Jesus, not Father and Holy Spirit. So, Peter and John laid hands on them to confirm and complete their baptism. Adoption into God's family was verified by manifestations or charisms (supernatural gifts) of the Holy Spirit.

Since the earliest days, Confirmation was administered to babies before their first birthday, after Baptism and before First Holy Communion. It is still done this way in the Eastern Churches, the

Orthodox Church and other Catholic Rites that are in union with the Pope. And this same order is still used in the Latin Rite for anyone over the age of seven who has not yet been baptized.

As populations grew and the Christian kingdom spread, bishops were no longer as readily available, so confirmations took place at older ages. After the Fourth Lateran Council (1213-1215 A.D.), Communion, which continued to be given only after Confirmation, was to be administered only when the child reached the age of reason. After the 13th century, the age of Confirmation and Communion began to be delayed further, from seven, to twelve, and then to fifteen.

Then in 1910 (which is only recent history) Pope St. Pius X increased devotion to the Holy Eucharist by pushing Confirmation and First Communion back to early childhood, i.e., as soon as the child was old enough to understand what these sacraments mean.

However, it often happened that Confirmation was not available when the child was ready for First Communion. So, after two millennia of providing Baptism, then Confirmation, and then First Communion, in 1932 official permission was given to change the order "where necessary."

Originally intended to be an exception, it became more and more the accepted practice. We've lost the 2000-year-old understanding of Confirmation's connection to Baptism. Catechists have had the difficult task of explaining why Confirmation is a sacrament for teenagers. Thus, it is often mistakenly perceived as the time when the Holy Spirit is given to Christians. And for many it's not much more than a graduation ceremony as teenagers look forward to getting out of school and being set free from forced catechesis.

When Paul placed his hands on them, the Holy Spirit came on them, and they spoke in tongues and prophesied. (Acts 19:6 NIV)

Have you ever witnessed the baptismal grace of Confirmation like this? The Holy Spirit is given to us by the Father and the Son to enable us to become holy (resist sin) and be effective in the Church's mission of changing the world by bringing the Light of Christ into the darkness. Wouldn't it be great if children knew early on that they can have this benefit? And imagine if they were taught in all years of religious education how to use it in everyday life. Just think of how much they could learn from the Holy Spirit (the Spirit of Truth) while their minds are still open and they have not yet become rebellious teenagers.

Here's a little-known fact: Due to the true nature of the Sacrament of Confirmation, young children may request that the bishop confer this sacrament upon them as soon they are old enough to understand what it means, have been suitably instructed, and are able to renew their baptismal promises (Canon 891 of the *Code of Canon Law for the Latin Rite,* dioceses of the United States).

The benefits of Baptism

We are baptized so that the Father can re-create us. We are plunged into this sacrament as children of Adam and Eve from whom we inherited their Original Sin. The best way to be baptized has always been full immersion in water because it's easier to understand what's happening spiritually than when a little water is poured over the head. This plunging represents death (drowning). The Father then raises us up in resurrection power to a new life as his adopted children. Now we are united fully to all of God and we receive *his holy* inheritance.

When Jesus was baptized in the Jordan River, he united himself to us. Since we (not Jesus) are the ones who need to repent, he stood in proxy for us as John the Baptizer dunked him. This was the first act—the first miracle—of his public ministry.

We receive the benefits of this gift when we choose to accept what he did for us. The Sacrament of Baptism, by itself, does not guarantee that we will end up in Heaven. We are free to reject the Father's adoption of us.

Whenever parents have a baby baptized, the parents and godparents, in union with Christ and on behalf of the child, provide the benefits of baptism to the child. In so doing, they are committing themselves to the extremely important and necessary responsibility of teaching the child how to accept the benefits of his or her baptism. This is why the Church says "no" to the baptisms of children who will not be raised in the Faith. It's pointless to baptize a child who will not be taught what it means to be baptized.

Many grandparents today worry about the eternal souls of grandchildren who have not been baptized. We might as well also worry about the souls of the parents and the children who are not learning and living the faith. To think that the Sacrament of Baptism will ensure their salvation is to treat this sacrament like it's magic. Instead, let's pray for their salvation every day, remembering that God hears our prayers for mercy.

Our knowledge is limited: We cannot be sure that an unbaptized child who dies will not reach Heaven any more than we can be sure that a baptized child will reach Heaven. Let's leave their fate up to our brilliant and creative Father who wants them to reach Heaven even more than we want it.

Today's Exercise: Name why God is a good Father to you

Let's think about what happened after Jesus was baptized. The Holy Spirit descended on him so that he could proceed with his ministry in all the power of his Father. The same thing happens to us—and for the same purpose. In our baptisms, we received the Holy Spirit, first of all to help us become more like Jesus so we can have God's power in our battles against temptations, and secondly to continue the mission of Christ with the power of the Father.

And then what happened? Abba-Father's voice boomed from Heaven, saying, "This is my beloved Son, in whom I am well pleased." This, too, is repeated for us. Abba-Father said the same thing about *you* when he adopted you. And if you have accepted the gift of your baptism and all that it entails, the Father is very pleased with you *right now*.

As our Adoptive Father, he's not looking at our imperfections. He's looking at who we really are, deep in our hearts, in our souls. He's not ignorant of our imperfections, which keep leading us back into sin. That's not his focus. Jesus, his Perfect Son, took our sins upon himself so that the Father could see us at our best. When the Father looks at our sins, he sees them through the filter of Christ's sacrifice on the Cross.

We all need a Daddy who focuses on what's best in us. We become our best when what is good in us is acknowledged and appreciated.

No human father can look beyond the skin. No human parent can see the heart of gold that's underneath our imperfections. Only Abba-Father can do that. And so, he gladly adopts us and takes over the role of fatherhood. He desires to give us the very best. He wants us to experience the very best that a father can bring to the relationship.

With this in mind, finish the following sentence, writing down as many examples as you can remember. (Hint: Ask the Holy Spirit to help you think of more examples.)

I know God is a good Father to me because:

DAY 14

The Father Sees You as a Gift

FATHER GOD CREATED you to be a treasure, a gift to be cherished. To be a gift means that we're blessing someone. We're making the lives of others better. Abba-Father designed each of us, at the very moment of our conception, to be gifts for the world—sacred gifts through which he could work. He answers the prayers of others through us. He heals through the giftedness of people in the medical field. He builds homes through the giftedness of laborers. Rarely does he do anything apart from the gifts that he designed into people. God values our partnership in accomplishing his will.

> *Every good and perfect gift is from above, coming down from the Father of the heavenly lights, who does not change like shifting shadows. (James 1:17 NIV)*

Our Divine Daddy enjoys sharing his gifts. And you are one of his most precious gifts!

Acknowledging that we are gifts to the world is not prideful if we also acknowledge the Giver of the gifts. Being a gift is a very humble position because a gift is always something that is handed over to others. God is the Giver. Others are served by the gift that we are.

Note: By the time you reach the end of this chapter, you will be able to see yourself as a treasure, a gift that the Father cherishes. However, if you find yourself stuck in thinking that God focuses only on what is wrong with you, and that you're trash instead of a treasure, re-read this chapter—more slowly. Turn the entire chapter into a spiritual exercise by reading over and over again the parts about being God's gift to others—until you begin to believe that it's true about you. And if that doesn't get you unstuck, please see a therapist; your wounds run deep and cannot be healed by this book alone. But be assured that the Father does want to heal you!

Let's start by remembering what we learned about ourselves from our childhood, especially: Did your experiences teach you that you are a gift? Psalm 127:3 tells us that children are a gift from the Lord. That's what I learned as a child. My husband Ralph, however, had been taught something very different. His dad often said to him and his six siblings, "Children are liabilities until you turn eighteen and move out."

Ralph explains: "When we did something good, he'd say, 'You're a good kid.' But when we messed up, he'd yell at us and tell us that we were liabilities."

How do you think this affected Ralph's perception of God the Father?

His dad loved to play with the children. He loved them and cherished them. However, he often became quite gruff, easily losing his temper. To avoid getting yelled at, Ralph fixed whatever got broken before his dad discovered it. He learned to hide in the background. He felt happiest when he was quietly ignored.

In his relationship with God, this translated to: "I think I'm supposed to be perfect, and when my flaws show, I think I must hide from God and cover up my mistakes quickly."

Ralph's childhood experiences forged the idea that he was basically good but nothing special. And yet, he's very intelligent and scientifically-minded, which enabled him to become a highly skilled computer engineer with mechanical and electrical expertise. Before leaving the corporate world, he reached the national level where he served as a highly respected support tech for the field techs. Often, a client awaiting repairs wanted no one but Ralph to tackle the problem.

He was (and still is!) good at using the talents and intelligence that Abba-Father designed into him. Nevertheless, instead of recognizing that he was one of God's gifts to the world, he thought of himself as just a cog in a machine. The companies he worked for reinforced it by thinking of their employees as "tools" (as many companies do). And what's a tool? It's a *thing* that can be replaced.

So, Ralph believed: "If I disappear, someone else will replace me. I'm nothing special."

When clients thanked him for sharing his special knowledge, instead of seeing their appreciation as God expressing his own gratefulness through them, he focused on how much he didn't know. He insisted that he was inadequate and unimportant—which seemed like humility but in actuality was woundedness. When complimented, he wondered, "Are they trying to butter me up? What's their hidden motive?" Gradually he's learned to feel more comfortable about the good things that people say about him, but he's had to fight the old inner voice that says, "You're good, but you're really a liability."

You are a gift to Jesus

Do you know that the Father gave you to Jesus as a gift to him? If you've made Jesus your Lord and Savior, and if you desire to follow him and grow in holiness with the help of the Holy Spirit, then it's true. The Father has adopted you into his family and has given you to Jesus as a gift of love. This is why Jesus prayed (italics are mine for emphasis): *"Father, I desire that they also, whom you have given me, may be with me where I am, to see my glory that you have given me because you loved me before the foundation of the world"* (John 17:24 NIV).

Consider how the first apostles were a gift to Jesus: What giftedness did the Father design into them for the sake of blessing his Divine Son?

This question might not be readily answered because we tend to focus on how Jesus is a gift from the Father to us (to all humankind). And we tend to wrap giftedness up in terms of services that we render, the good deeds that we do, the talents that we utilize, and the love that we bring. However, sharing our giftedness is only half of the picture.

We *are* a gift.

The Father gave to Jesus the gift of close friends. Peter, James, and John were the only apostles whom Jesus took up Mount Tabor to witness his miraculous transfiguration and his divine meeting with Moses and Elijah. And they were the only ones he took with him into the Garden of Gethsemane for emotional support as he agonized over his impending crucifixion. Obviously, he treasured their friendship on a very personal level. And we know that Martha, Mary, and Lazarus were other close friends.

The Father also gave to Jesus the gift of *your* friendship. Stop and think about that for a while. How much you love Jesus, how much you follow him, how much you adore him in the Holy Eucharist—that's how much you are a gift to Jesus. And the Father is very pleased! The giver of the gift wants to see his gift make a difference. See it enjoyed. See it be a blessing. You know how he feels. You feel the same way when you give a present to a loved one.

There are many ways that we are a gift to Jesus. Let's take as an example the apostles again. The Father gifted the first apostles with lives that put them in the right place at the right time to assist with the arrival of the long-awaited Messiah and the continuation of his mission afterward. You, too, were created by the Father for this time and place. It was no accident. Regardless of the circumstances of your conception, the Father gifted you with a life that is meant to be a blessing to Jesus in the world today.

How about their curiosity and willingness to learn? These, too, were ways that they were a gift to Jesus. In the same way, *you* are a gift to Jesus. And their talents: What talents did they have that made them a gift to Jesus while he lived on Earth? We like to joke that Peter was untalented as a fisherman, as evidenced by Jesus intervening a couple of times because Peter had failed to catch anything. However, let's not forget that before Peter met Jesus, he had supported his family with his fishing business for years. It's likely that he helped provide many of the meals that Jesus and his entourage enjoyed.

Today's Exercise, Part 1: Describe your giftedness

In what ways are you a gift from the Father to Jesus? Write it down. Describe your giftedness. (Don't skip this exercise. What comes next will be affected by what you write.)

* * *

When you finish writing about your giftedness, look at it again, but this time, extend it out to the world: How you bless Jesus is how you bless the world. Jesus is giving you to others as a gift that helps make the world a better place. He had asked the Father for this.

"As you sent me into the world," he prayed, *"I have sent them into the world"* (John 17:18 NIV).

However, when we fail to see ourselves in this light, we can end up feeling resentful, especially if our giftedness gets used more than we'd like or if it's shared with people we don't like serving. It's too easy to feel like we're being taken advantage of. What we can give could be easily abused.

The difference between the Father seeing us as a gift for the world and being abused by the world is our attitude. Are we willing to be God's gift to others? A gift that is freely given brings great joy to the giver and to God. But if we view ourselves as a cog in a machine, we feel pushed, driven by other forces. And no one likes to get pushed around.

To the Father, you are precious, uniquely valuable, and irreplaceable. That's the definition of a wonderful gift! A masterpiece! No one else can bless others the way you can—no one who ever lived and no one who ever will live. Abba-Father designed you to be like nobody but him. You are gifted with God's own giftedness (his goodness, his character traits, a portion of his talents) in a unique combination that matches no one else, ever.

We are happiest when we get to be who we really are, putting our giftedness to good use. Our life on Earth is meant to be spent unpacking our gifts as we become more and more like our Father. Since God is infinite, every person in the world could be like the Father and still be uniquely different than all other persons!

Cogs in machinery can be replaced. Gifts can be substituted, but never replaced.

Ralph is a wonderful gift—a huge blessing—to countless people. And I'm privileged to experience this in our relationship and in watching how he blesses others. God has blessed me through him for many years regardless of the imperfections of our marriage and the flaws that he brings to it—as do I. If I had never met him, I probably would have married someone else and enjoyed his giftedness, but he would not have been Ralph. He is irreplaceable. This sounds very obvious, but it's a lesson in realizing how important all of us are in the giftedness that the Father designed into us.

After my parents moved into our home so that we could take care of them, Ralph became a gift to them (as well as to me) in the tasks of caregiving. As every caregiver knows, it's easy to feel pushed and driven by outside forces, but Ralph is not a cog that could be replaced. No one else in the family can work through the maze of Medicaid paperwork like he does. No one else could be my partner in shouldering the responsibilities the way he does.

You are treasured by the Father

God designed Ralph to have a love of science. Before we met, I didn't know that I could like it just as much. I began to fall in love with Ralph when, for a high school assignment in public speaking class, he gave a presentation about the orbital rendezvous of spacecraft. "Boring," I thought at first. "But he's cute, so I'll try to listen."

Something about his enthusiasm for science attracted me. I admired the way he drew pictures on the chalkboard to illustrate his words. I admired him for making something very complicated very easy for a non-scientist like me to grasp. After we started dating, he showed me that astronomy is fascinating, and when I went off to college, my new interest led me to a very fun job in the campus planetarium.

The Father admires you for what you do as the person he gifted you to be. And he appreciates you for blessing others and for how this, in turn, blesses still more people. One thing leads to another. Only he knows how far-reaching the ripple-effect of your giftedness is. Someday, when you leave this world and join him in eternity, he will tell you. For now, know that he is smiling at you with the most delightful, full-blown, twinkling-eye smile that you can imagine. Well, not quite. It's even better than that!

I think that one of the reasons why Ralph fell in love with me was because I readily received from him the gift of his fascination with science. It had not been that way with his parents.

Ralph built a model of the lunar landing module when men landed on the moon for the first time. Inspired by this monumental accomplishment, he used creativity and his knack for design and engineering to construct it. He had no instructions, no diagram to guide him. He constructed it with materials that he found in the house: tin foil, cardboard, paper towel tubes, etc. When finished, it stood four feet tall.

Then his dad came home from work and grumbled at it. "This is taking up too much space," he said. "Tear it apart and throw this junk away."

His father inadvertently formed in Ralph an image of God as a Father who doesn't admire his children for the good that they do. Ralph thought, far into his adulthood: "I'm basically good, but God's not particularly interested in me, and he is not particularly against me. He ignores me as long as I don't create problems. He's indifferent toward me." This, to him, was fatherly benevolence.

And when Ralph does create problems? "When I screw up, I'm a liability to God, but he picks me up and dusts me off and sends me on my way."

This is not how Abba-Father thinks about us. We are all a gift—a beautiful, irreplaceable gift. Perhaps there's a tear in the old wrapping paper, and maybe the ribbon is askew. If the gift has been dropped by someone, it's broken. But the Father treasures the gift as if it were in perfect condition. He smiles as he holds the gift. His eyes twinkle with joy as he shares the gift with Jesus, who shares the gift with the world.

This is the Father we instinctively long for. Until we discover that Abba is always admiring us, beholding us as a treasure, we're unsatisfied and edgy, easily resentful. We seek reassurance but it's never enough until we hear the Father beam his reassurance.

Ralph says that the most important benefit he gets from the Sacrament of Confession is this reassurance. But all too often, the priest simply says the words of absolution without adding words of reassurance. To Ralph this indicates that he's not truly listening. In contrast, when he apologizes to the people he's hurt and they forgive him, they reassure him that everything's going to be okay. Is it any wonder that this sacrament isn't as appealing to him as God designed it to be?

God has gifted you for ministry

How generous are you with the gift of yourself? At your funeral, will people honor you because of what you did? Will they talk about how God gifted the world through you? Will they discuss with each other the differences you made?

When you come face to face with Jesus at the time you enter eternal life, will you judge yourself unworthy of the fullness of his love because you were stingy with the gift of yourself?

Because you are unique, your ministry is unique. No one besides you can perform this service quite like you. God has matched the perfect ministry to your abilities and the level you've reached in your spiritual growth. He created you for this.

Whatever we have received from him is meant to be shared with others. Years ago I wrote down a note to myself, quoting Catholic lay evangelist David Thorpe: "God wants to fill you to spill you." That is, God wants to fill your life with gifts in order to spill you onto others.

Realize that God sees you as very gifted. Then whenever people ask you to share yourself with them, you can say what Peter said when he healed the crippled man: "What I have I give to you" (see Acts 3:1-10).

As Christians of the 21st century, we are members of a Church that is not just concerned about the souls of others but the well-being of the whole person—spiritually, physically, socially, and psychologically. We are not just concerned about humanity but the well-being of the planet. Ministry is more than trying to get everyone to Heaven; it is working hard to bring all human life to its God-given potential, from the unborn to the elderly, from strangers in the poverty-stricken Third World to the handicapped children in our local schools.

To serve all these needs, the Church is putting out the call for more people, for the use of more gifts, and for the strength of more commitments. As Pope John Paul II said to a group of U.S. bishops in 1993, "the vitality of a parish depends on merging the diverse vocations and gifts of its members into a unity." We are all needed.

Saint Paul wrote: *"Think of us in these terms: as servants of Christ and stewards of God's mysteries"* (1 Corinthians 4:1). We need to periodically examine our lives and ask, "How good of a steward am I with the gifts that God has given me?"

Don't underestimate your value

Too often, instead of listening to God tell us who we are, we believe what our parents, our teachers, and other significant people have said about us. "You'll never amount to anything!" may have been meant as a challenge to encourage us to strive for our full potential, but the child in us absorbed it literally. The words destroyed our self-image. Intellectually, we may have disagreed with the assessments of others, but deep inside, where the child blindly trusts those in authority, the child's interpretation of the words has taken root.

These falsehoods need to be erased by the power of God and replaced with his words. If you were to make two lists, one naming your faults and the other naming your good points, the fault category would be longer, wouldn't it? This is the way most people view themselves after a lifetime of being defined by others. However, this is not the way God sees you; if it were, he would never call you to ministry. Ministries are not built on faults.

Yes, God uses our weaknesses, but not as the foundation of the mission to which he calls us. If he did, our ministries would collapse when times get shaky, like a house on a fault-line during an Earthquake. Rather, God bases our ministries on all that is good in us. How much time have you spent examining what is good in you—and believing it? Let the Holy Spirit teach you about how much the Father values you. He esteems you highly!

God knows us exactly and intimately. We don't. Rather than assume we are so bad, so ugly, or so unlikely to be gifts for the world from the Father, we need to take time to listen to him describe who we really are. We need to ask him to remove the blinders of low self-esteem. Low self-esteem is not humility. It's based on a lie, which says that we are far from being who we're supposed to be. It also says that we will never get there. God, though, esteems us highly, as it is written in Romans 5:8.

> *But God demonstrates His own love toward us, in that while we were yet sinners, Christ died for us. (NASB)*

Yes, we have sinned. Yes, we are far from perfect. But the moment we chose to believe in the redeeming sacrifice of Jesus, the Father esteemed us so highly that he called us saints!

Do you think of yourself as a saint? Saint Paul said that all who are loved by God are saints (see Romans 1:7). Both the Old and New Testaments refer to the people of God as saints. Accept the fact that this is how God sees you. Begin to see yourself that way! To continue to live with low self-esteem is saying to God, "You're wrong about me." How dare we contradict God!

> *As for the saints in the land, they are the excellent ones, in whom is all my delight. (Psalm 16:3 ESV).*

Today's Exercise, Part 2: See your giftedness the way the Father sees it

To better understand how Abba-Father can look at us and see a wonderful gift despite all of our sins and imperfections, it helps to learn how to see others this way. First, we need to realize that, unlike

God, we can only see others skin-deep. We see their faults, not the wounded heart underneath that impels them to behave in faulty ways. With the help of the Holy Spirit, we can see past their faults.

I learned how to do this in the early days of Good News Ministries, back in the late 1990s when we had problems with our first chaplain, Father Ed (the same one who had introduced me to the Eucharist). For twenty years he had been a good friend. However, both of his parents had been alcoholics. The insufficient love he had received from them and the faulty understanding of relationships that he learned from his troubled childhood, compounded by becoming an alcoholic himself and never facing his problems, increasingly interfered with our friendship and with his ministry as a parish priest and as the chaplain of Good News Ministries.

Jesus said we must forgive again and again, "seventy times seven times" (see Matthew 18:22). When I got tired of this and the need to repeatedly forgive him became overwhelming, I begged God to remove him from my life. Instead of cooperating with my wishes, which were based on my own weaknesses, he answered this prayer by giving me supernatural love for Father Ed.

To open my heart to receive this love, my Divine Daddy showed me a vision using the gift of my imagination. I saw a giant, multifaceted gem. The Holy Spirit spoke to my heart: "This is the treasure that Ed truly is, deep inside."

The gem was many-faceted, just like our personalities. Each facet had its own beautiful color. As the light (the Light of Christ) danced on any one of the gem's facets, a color glowed brightly and beamed off into the world. This is how the Father designed us. We make the world a better place when the Light of Christ interacts with any of the facets of our personality.

However, Father Ed's gem was covered with the muck and mud that had been slung onto it whenever someone sinned against him since his earliest childhood. When his parents and others taught him wrong ideas, they slapped more muck onto him. And when he himself chose to sin, he added more mud. He was now so covered with muck and mud that I couldn't see the gift that God had created him to be.

God could see it, though. And from that moment on, so could I.

The Sacrament of Confession wipes the muck off of our inner gem. Healing through counseling and reading books like this one further cleans up our gem. Unlearning the wrong ideas that the world teaches, replacing them with the truth that comes from the Holy Spirit, is also necessary to let our gem shine in all its splendor.

Until others do the same with their gems, if we remember what exists under the muck, it becomes supernaturally easy to see past their faults. And now we understand how Abba-Father can look at us and all of our faults and see a wonderful gift.

Scripture tells us what this gem looks like. The famous love chapter, 1 Corinthians 13, gives us a good description. Here's what verses four through seven tell us about our giftedness:

- Love is patient
- Love is kind
- Love does not envy
- Love does not boast
- Love is not proud
- Love does not dishonor others
- Love is not self-seeking
- Love is not easily angered
- Love keeps no record of wrong-doings
- Love does not delight in evil
- Love rejoices with the truth
- Love protects
- Love trusts
- Love hopes
- Love perseveres

Rewrite this list, substituting the word "Abba" (or "God" or "the Father" or "Papa," whatever your favorite name for him is) in place of "love." For example:

- Abba is patient
- Abba is kind

* * *

Next, rewrite it again, this time adding yourself to the end of each description. For example:

- Abba is patient with me.
- Abba is kind towards me.

* * *

Finally, rewrite it one more time, now replacing the word "love" with yourself:

- I am patient.
- I am kind.

* * *

This list describes your gem! This is how Abba-Father sees you. Now, with the help of the Holy Spirit, continue what you've already begun: Get rid of the muck that interferes with the glow of your gem so that you can become the gift to others that the Father created you to be.

And meanwhile, remember that what others cannot yet see, Abba-Father sees. And he is very delighted!

DAY 15

The Father Delights in You

ABBA-FATHER DELIGHTS in you because he knows your heart. He knows the good that is in your heart. He knows you better than you know yourself. He knows his own presence within you.

Let them praise his name with dancing and make music to him with timbrel and harp. For the LORD takes delight in his people; he crowns the humble with victory. (Psalm 149:3-4 NIV)

We understand way too little of how very much God delights in us.

Even when he is displeased with our behaviors, he knows that we are more than that. He is abundantly pleased with the redeemed saint who is temporarily hidden beneath our sin. Understanding this frees us to delight in his goodness. It frees us from the limitations we've projected onto our Father. It frees us to accept his abundant generosity toward us.

It's good that we are aware of our shortcomings and faults because it leads to repentance. But if we focus on how displeasing we are to God, we get stuck there. Our progress is thwarted in becoming who the Father created us to be. And the times when we *are* aware that he's delighted with us are too brief, too few, and quickly forgotten.

We need to remember that the Father's all-knowing awareness

of us sees not only what is faulty and sinful in us but also what is good and delightful in us. Even while we are in the midst of a rebellious disregard of his Divine Will—if we have accepted Jesus as our Lord and Savior, and if underneath the surface of our human frailty we desire to follow him and become like him—God knows. God sees. God celebrates all that is good in us.

Think about where the goodness in you came from. Everything that is good comes from God himself. This is why, when he looks at you—if you've received the Sacrament of Baptism and you've freely chosen to accept and embrace what Jesus did for you on the Cross—the Father sees his own divine grace in you. He sees his own presence within you. Therefore, how can he not delight in you?

Saint Rose of Lima (1586-1617) said, "If only mortals would learn how great it is to possess divine grace, how beautiful, how noble, how precious. How many riches it hides within itself, how many joys and delights!"

Many people find it hard to believe that the Father is delighted with them. This is usually rooted in the discipline they received as children. Those who were hugged after punishments and were reassured of the parent's love find it easier to know the Father's delight. It's more difficult for those who felt condemned more often than they were affirmed. Meanwhile, our Divine Daddy affirms us more than he condemns us. If there is anything that *can* be affirmed, he affirms it. He doesn't fail to praise anything worth affirming. We just need to learn how to notice it and accept it.

How to notice God's affirmations

1. We need to first be able to dial into his goodness: his true nature. We can only do this after we've accepted how different he is from the imperfections of the humans we've known, *and* we've delineated those differences (like you did earlier in this 30-day journey to the Father's heart).
2. We need to forgive ourselves for our own imperfections. If you find this too difficult, seek the help of a therapist or a mature Christian friend who understands what you're experiencing. And start by forgiving yourself for not forgiving yourself!
3. We need to forgive those who gave us wrong ideas about God's true nature. Your forgiveness is a decision, not a feeling. Nor is it

based on the remorse of those who have hurt you. Do you want to see them reach Heaven some day? Then pray for that as you forgive them and let go of your right to expect remorse.

4. We need to have a good and consistent prayer life. Not memorized, rote prayers (these have their value, but we must not limit ourselves to a formulaic relationship with God). A good prayer life includes conversational prayer. For example, start your day by chatting with the Father: "Good morning, Abba-Father!" Thank him for what he's going to do with this day. Ask him to bless the day, and repeat this throughout the day as situations come up that need his divine touch. When you become aware that you're constantly connected to God, and you find yourself talking to him throughout the day, even in the midst of busy activities, it becomes natural to notice the Father's affirmation.

   Saint Anthony of the Desert (251-356) said, "The vision of the holy ones is not fraught with distraction: 'For they will not strive, nor cry, nor shall anyone hear their voice' (Matthew 12:19, Isaiah 42:2). But it comes quietly and gently that an immediate joy, gladness, and courage arise in the soul. For the Lord who is our joy is with them, and the power of God the Father."

5. We need to accept the Father's affirmation. It might feel like we're not being humble, but the truth is that it is very humble to hear and know God's affirmations. Remember this: True humility means acknowledging what God is doing in your life while seeing what is good in you because of his grace. It is not holy to condemn ourselves after we've been forgiven. If we've repented and we've received his grace through the Sacrament of Confession, and especially if we have followed this up with some form of penance (reparation), then there is no condemnation from God; therefore, neither should we condemn ourselves.

In Christ there is no condemnation

For God did not send his Son into the world to condemn the world, but to save the world through him. Whoever believes in him is not condemned, but whoever does not believe stands condemned already because they have not believed in the name of God's one and only Son. (John 3:17-18 NIV)

The Father did not send his Son Jesus to Earth to condemn anyone. Sacrificing one's life in order to condemn the person you died for does not make sense. Ask any soldier or police officer why they risk their lives. Only psychotic persons would endanger their own lives in order to kill someone they've condemned. Our protective forces risk their lives to *protect.* That's their top priority. And where did this character trait come from? Their Divine Father, of course.

Yet we feel condemned whenever we feel guilty about a sin. Why is that?

Most of us are harder on ourselves than we are on others. We expect more from ourselves. We demand more and feel horrible when we let ourselves down. At first, this seems right. Being scrupulous is holy. And we've learned that being easy on ourselves is unholy (it's self-indulgent, rooted in the sin of pride).

We also know that it's unholy to usurp God's role and decide for ourselves what is sinful and what is not. ("I'm okay, I'm not really sinning."). Well, good! God is delighted that you know this.

Usually, the reason why people rationalize that their sins are really not sinful is because they're afraid of feeling condemned, which translates to feeling unloved, which translates as proof that they are unlovable. But this is the voice of the Accuser, the Devil. Jesus taught very clearly that sin is sin, evil is evil, and holiness cannot be negotiated. He also set us free from condemnation by suffering and dying on the Cross.

If we fail to grasp what it means to be saved by Christ, it's easy to believe that we're never good enough no matter what we do. For some, this makes it impossible to forgive themselves. When we don't feel happy about ourselves, we try to find happiness in how others treat us. Then of course we never get enough affirmation, and when we do get it, we feel embarrassed and unworthy.

When we sin, guilt confirms that we deserve to be condemned. When we innocently make a mistake, this, too, seems to confirm that we deserve to be condemned. So, we condemn ourselves for making the mistake when, instead, we should realize that our mistake is really just another learning tool. And when we suffer unjust, unfair, or unkind situations, if an inner voice tells us that we're being punished, again we feel condemned.

The truth is: You were freed from condemnation when you accepted the idea that Christ sacrificed his life on the Cross for *you.*

When we sin, we are guilty of doing something evil, and when we repent, we return to the freedom gained by Christ. But too often guilt becomes shame. Shame is the feeling that we are evil, which is not to be confused with "regret" that motivates us to avoid committing the same evil again.

Guilt informs us that we have done evil, regret motivates us to avoid evil, and shame tells us that *we* are evil. Shame continues to condemn us long after we've been forgiven. Guilt tells us the truth about ourselves, regret invites us to grow from it, and shame lies to us and paralyzes our growth.

The truth is: There is no shame in realizing that we've sinned, because facing it frees us to become who we really are. Who are *you* really? Thanks to your baptism and the presence of the Holy Spirit within you, you are holy! Your inner gem is holy (as you discovered on Day 14), and thanks to the Sacrament of Confession, the muck has been cleaned off. So, of course, the Father is delighted with you—even though you haven't yet polished your gem to perfection. Only when we reach Heaven are our gems shining brightly—totally clean and perfectly polished.

We learn from life how to know God's delight

Family vacations during my childhood involved four weeks of traveling across the U.S. by car. We saw wonderful sites: the Grand Canyon, Yosemite Park, the giant redwoods of California, glaciers and mountains and lakes and oceans. We had fun times on a dude ranch one year and on a houseboat another year.

This family history nurtured in me a fascination for God's many and varied creations. I felt close to God the Awesome Creator when I stood at the base of a waterfall cascading from a high mountaintop. I felt close to God the fun-loving Daddy when I marveled at stalagmites and stalactites in caves.

What have you admired in nature and how has this aided your relationship to the Father?

My family's vacations also instilled in me the value of expanding my awareness to the cultures and sites outside of my small, local world. My little world was little indeed. I didn't even see people of other ethnicities. The three channels on my home's black-and-white television didn't help much to improve that limitation during the late 1950s and early 1960s. Then we went on a trip that took us through a city where I saw African-Americans for the first time.

"Look!" I exclaimed. "Chocolate people!" After chuckling at my naiveté, my parents explained that these were people who happened to have darker skin. From that starting point, I grew up without racism. I learned that everyone from every culture is a precious child of God with great dignity.

What funny experiences in your life taught you something about God?

When we traveled to the Grand Canyon and hiked along some of its trails, my dad's love for adventure coupled with the parental fear of disaster ("Don't stand any closer to the ledge than that!") gave me an image of Daddy-God as fun-loving and adventurous but also protective.

In what ways were you protected during childhood? Can you see God in those experiences?

These family vacations required many hours on the road. To afford them, we ate donuts and pastries for breakfast in the motel room. Then we drove until lunchtime, finding a rest stop with picnic tables and a playground so that I and my younger brother and sister could run and burn off our restlessness. Mom served us sandwiches and cookies. An hour later we were back on the road until around four o'clock when we'd find the next motel. We ate dinner in a restaurant and Mom shopped for the next day's breakfast and lunch.

Many problems can happen on a long trip like that. At one of the rest stops, my brother Kurt took off his wristwatch, laid it down somewhere, and then ran off to play. He didn't remember it again until we were back in the car several miles down the road. So, we returned to look for it. We wondered: "What if someone else found it and took it?"

Dad, anxious about losing valuable time, was upset about Kurt's carelessness. I silently prayed that my brother would find the watch to redeem himself.

I'm the one who found it. I said to the Lord, "But I asked for Kurt to be the one who finds it." In my heart, I heard his response loud and clear: "You, my beloved child, were the only one who prayed for help."

Did anything like that ever happen to you? Stop reading this and recall a time when you tried to help someone by praying for them—or, if you didn't have faith during childhood, you were *hoping* for them—

and you were the one who ended up knowing the solution to the problem. Because you cared, God gave you the wisdom that was needed. This is evidence that the Father was very delighted with you. He celebrated your gift of caring. He enjoys partnering with you. Rejoice with him!

Of course, my family's vacation trips weren't perfect. They didn't always teach me good things about Father God. I learned a few things that I later had to unlearn. For example, one day, heavy rains flooded the streets that we needed to drive through. My dad said he was afraid the brakes would get wet and fail. His white-knuckled hands on the steering wheel showed how worried he really was.

In the back seat, I silently prayed for protection. I didn't pray out loud in case I'd be shushed. The rain soon stopped, the roads drained, and the brakes stayed clear of the wetness. Finally relaxing, my dad said, "Well, I guess Terry was praying." I did not feel complimented. There was no thank-you attached to his words. Perhaps he truly was appreciative, but my perceptions were skewed by my frustration that I was the only one with the reputation of praying for divine help.

This frustration increased back home. My dad lost his temper often, and I wondered why he didn't turn to the Lord for help when he felt so stressed out. He was a man of God, a minister. Why didn't he show "the peace that passes understanding" that I'd heard so much about in Sunday school? I wanted a daddy who would be a good guide for my spiritual growth but, by the grace of God, I sometimes understood spiritual matters before my dad did (such as the importance of praying for help during a rainstorm).

The problem is, he didn't want to learn from a little kid. And when I became a teenager, my frustrations turned into rebellion, which turned into arguments, which turned into losing the arguments and getting punished for sassing back.

This pattern caused me to feel repeatedly misunderstood. The father I longed for was often not what I needed him to be. So, I doubted that Father God was someone I could turn to for understanding. And I became hyper-sensitive toward anyone who misunderstood me, or disbelieved me, or accused me of being or thinking differently than the way I saw myself. It sent me into an emotional tailspin until I met the real Abba-Father and learned how to listen for his voice telling me what he really thinks of me.

At first, this might seem dangerous. God sees our faults more clearly than everyone else. We know he can condemn us for a long list of what's wrong about us. But that's never the first thing he tells us—not if we have allowed him to adopt us.

He says, "You are my beloved child, with whom I am very pleased."

He is also pleading, "Go and sin no more," because he knows how much we are hurting ourselves by choosing to sin. He knows how much we're damaging his other beloved children. He suffers the yearning heart of a father whose son or daughter has been separated from him. He is angry at what our sins are doing to us and through us to others.

But as I've said in previous chapters, he sees beyond the bad to embrace and encourage what is good in us. When Abba-Father looks at what is wrong in us, he also sees our potential. He looks at us through the lens of Christ's sacrifice on the Cross, which we have embraced. He sees what we've been doing to improve. He is happy about every step we take in the right direction, following Christ and learning from him. He's looking at who we really are, deep in our hearts, in our souls, where he dwells. He's looking at our gem—the beloved child he created.

Sometimes people accuse us of a sin that we did not commit. Or of doing something worse than we really did. Or they condemn us for making an innocent mistake. In each situation, Abba-Father comforts us. He says, "I feel your pain. Come let me hold you on my lap, little one. Cry on my shoulder until your tears are done."

If we try to comfort ourselves, we never feel comforted. Often self-comfort is attempted through self-justification. We tell ourselves, "What I did was understandable. I'm not to blame. I tried my best. It seemed right when I did it, and I still think it's right, even though deep down I know it's not." We torture ourselves with self-doubt and self-recrimination at the same time that we're telling ourselves that we did no wrong.

"I'm good!" we cry and never quite believe it.

Instead, if we let Abba-Father comfort us, healing begins. When we have such a good prayer life that we can hear him telling us why he is delighted with us, even when we feel bad about ourselves (***especially*** when we feel bad about ourselves), we can focus our energies on handling the situation the way God wants us to.

We know we are good because the Father made us good. We know that Jesus took our sins upon himself on Good Friday. And the Holy Spirit strengthens what is good in us. With this threefold dependence on God, we no longer need to prove our goodness to our accusers. We can be satisfied that God is satisfied with us.

Dancing with the Father

Ralph and our daughter, Tammy, used to go to father-daughter dances, a yearly parish event. Even when she was the oldest girl there, she was not too embarrassed to enjoy these "dates" with her dad. And Ralph was delighted that she wanted to go dancing with him.

I believe that our Divine Daddy wants to go dancing with us every day. Any sort of adventure that puts a smile on our face is a vacation with him. He knows that we need a break from routines and, when the difficulties of life are draining us, he wants to restore us by giving us a good time that leaves us with good memories.

We miss a lot of opportunities to go dancing with the Father simply because we don't go looking for them. Maybe we think we must press on through the troubled waters until we reach the other side where we will flop onto the beach exhausted. Or perhaps we look at the to-do list and jump into the next thing that needs our attention without slowing down enough to pray for a play break.

When we were young, school days included recess because teachers understood that the interruption of serious study with some laughter-producing fun could improve students' attention in class. Don't you think God understands this even better? We all need recess! We all need time to play—and our Divine Daddy wants to play with us.

Did Jesus have playtime with the Father? As an adult? In the midst of his seriously important ministry? Surely he did! What do you think Jesus was doing as he walked on water during the storm? I imagine that he had quite a lot of fun with that. As far as we know, it was the first time he had done it. And since he was continually talking with the Father, I wouldn't be surprised if their conversation went something like this:

Jesus: "Hmmmm, my disciples are halfway across the Sea of Galilee and a storm is brewing. They're going to get scared real soon. Abba, I'd better catch up with them."

Abba: "I'd give you a speedboat, but that won't be invented for a couple of thousand years yet. It would freak them out if they heard you come roaring toward them with a powered engine at the back of your boat. Just start walking toward them."

Jesus: "On the water? How awesome! Will my sandals get wet, or will I be hovering slightly above the surface of the water? But hey, this is just as freaky. My disciples will think I'm a ghost."

Abba: "Sure, that's okay. We'll use it to teach them something about faith. Let's get going."

Jesus puts one foot and then another onto the water and laughs: "Hahahaha! Those fish never saw anything like this before."

Abba: "Look over there! I'm making a really big fish jump out of the water to entertain you. This is fun!"

Jesus: "Yeah, I saw that! It was a very colorful fish. You make very beautiful creations."

Abba: "Thanks. Remember when the leviathan was formed? I had Jonah in mind when I designed that one."

Jesus: "Hahahaha, a big wave just splashed me. The storm is getting worse. The disciples won't see the humor in this—yet. There they are. They're going to notice me soon."

Can you imagine Abba treating you the same way the next time a storm brews in your life? It's good to take time to have fun with your Father. Make a concerted effort to develop this kind of relationship with him. A good way to start is by thinking of his playfulness whenever you're doing something that's fun.

Blessed Karl Leisner (1915-1945) said, "Without the love of God and joy in my soul, I will accomplish nothing. With God, I will have everything in me! Give me the strength, Lord!"

Today's Exercise, Part 1: Play a game with Abba-Father

One of my favorite activities is to take a walk through the woods. Along the way, I look for interesting shapes in the tree branches. ("Oh, look at that, Abba! It's wonderful that You made it grow that way. If I were young again, I'd climb up there and sit on that branch and get really quiet and wait for a bird to perch near me.") I smile at the wildflowers. ("Thank you, Abba! You grew those flowers there for me to enjoy.") I notice that the clouds are tinged with gold. ("Hahahaha, that cloud is shaped like a fish! And so shiny!")

Playtime with God is an important kind of prayer. Yet it's so neglected. When we take time to pray this way, we get in touch with how much he delights in us. And in this, we receive healing. We get re-energized. We grow holier because, while we're dancing with the

Father, we can't hear the Devil's temptations.

Blessed Giuseppina Nicoli (1863-1924) expressed it this way: "Joy is a great remedy. I recommend it to you, and I do so very enthusiastically . . . ! Be joyful! I say it again: be joyful! When we are joyful, we are less aware of evil and are cured more quickly. Cast all your cares on God, He is the best of fathers and will look after you as well as possible."

Observe the beauty in nature that God has placed around you. He loves you so much that he gives you beautiful things to look at. They are signs that God is with you. Abba-Father gives you special treats every day to prove that he is attentive to your every desire, your every thought, your every worry, and all of your prayer requests. For example, imagine that you're walking down a lane and you see a ray of sunlight shining through the dense trees. This is God giving you something enjoyable to look at, to bless your day, and to remind you that you are connected to him, because he cares about you so much.

Yes, my friend, God delights in *you*. Look for the many ways that he's revealing this to you.

The Father's hand is in every little thing that goes right and every big thing. Coincidental timing that benefits you shows that he's involved.

Ask the Holy Spirit to reveal to you how much the Father cares about you. The more your personal relationship with the Holy Spirit grows, the more easily you will become aware that the Father delights in you. This is one of the many reasons why the "baptism of the Holy Spirit" (the fully enlivened personal relationship with the Holy Spirit) is an important part of a well-rounded Christian life. The Holy Spirit will increase your awareness of how much the Father is revealing himself to you through the things around you and in the circumstances of your life every day.

For the first part of today's spiritual exercise, you'll need to go outside. If it's a sunny day with clouds in the sky, follow the instructions given in the next paragraph. If you cannot do this now, do it at your earliest opportunity.

When you go outside, sit down. Better yet, let your inner child control this exercise: *lie down* on the grass if you can. Look up at the clouds and study them. Imagine that Abba-Father is sitting (or reclining on the grass) near you. Play the cloud-image game with him. He designed these clouds. What shapes do you see in them? What do they morph into when the shape slowly changes? Make a fairy tale story with him from what you see.

If possible, stop reading now and go outside or look through a window to do this exercise.

* * *

The Father appreciates your goodness

Remember the gem that he sees in you. The next time someone gets mad at you—justifiably or wrongly—take time out to meditate on your Divine Daddy's opinion of you. He approves of everything that is good in you. He appreciates the good that you're doing. Even when you mess up, if you're willing to admit it and rectify it, he wants to lighten the mood. He is eager to resume the dance.

When others get upset with you, what prevents you from being aware of how delighted Abba-Father is with you? Is it a long-ago parental voice scolding you, telling you that you're not good enough to make God happy? Or maybe you were taught that God is always scowling at us, disapproving of us because we are sinners. It's very powerful—and freeing—to identify the messages that we're believing when we don't realize that God delights in us.

There's an important balance between facing our sins so we become holier and appreciating (without the sin of arrogance) how holy we have become.

> *Be perfect, therefore, as your heavenly Father is perfect. (Matthew 5:48 NIV)*

We are all called and anointed to reveal the Father to others by imitating Christ. The fact that we fail at this repeatedly is far less important to the Father than the effort we put into succeeding. If today you are a little holier than yesterday, you are fulfilling the call to holiness. This is the perfection of Christian living. It's progress, and that matters a lot to our Father. He cherishes every little footstep forward on the path of holiness. He is delighted with every little bit of effort, and he dances over every big and difficult effort.

In the Bible, the word "perfect" is used to mean fullness. God's perfect love is the fullness of love. God's perfect timing is the fullness of eternity interacting with the clocks that we have on Earth. By the same standards, the fullness of your Christian life on Earth is a journey to the destination of Heaven's perfection. Step by step. One day at a time.

There are a million reasons why we deserve to be condemned rather than applauded. However, when we think God is condemning us, if we've accepted what Jesus did for us on the Cross, and if our desire is to grow in holiness, then the voice of condemnation is not his. It's the Devil who's the Accuser (re-read Day 11). And Jesus has given us the power to silence the Accuser. In Revelation 12:10-11 (NIV), we learn that if we have placed ourselves at the foot of the Cross to receive deliverance from our sins by the blood of Christ, we successfully triumph over the Accuser's attack of condemnation:

Now have come the salvation and the power
and the kingdom of our God,
and the authority of his Messiah.
For the accuser of our brothers and sisters,
who accuses them before our God day and night,
has been hurled down.
They triumphed over him
by the blood of the Lamb
and by the word of their testimony.

The Devil wants to distract us from the good that we do. Abba-Father wants to increase our holiness by affirming the good that we do. Even when he tells us what's wrong about us, he tells us what's right about us. He encourages us to be who we really are, the beloved child he created and adopted. He's not pointing at the sins we've committed. He's pointing the *way out* of it. He's taking us by the hand to guide us to the path of repentance that leads to great rejoicing.

And the moment we step foot on that path, headed in the right direction (the heavenly direction), the Father dances. The angels dance with him. And the saints in Heaven join the party.

Suppose one of you has a hundred sheep and loses one of them. Doesn't he leave the ninety-nine in the open country and go after the lost sheep until he finds it? And when he finds it, he joyfully puts it on his shoulders and goes home. Then he calls his friends and neighbors together and says, 'Rejoice with me; I have found my lost sheep.' I tell you that in the same way there will be more rejoicing in heaven over one sinner who repents than over ninety-nine righteous persons who do not need to repent. (Luke 15:4-7 NIV)

Today's Exercise, Part 2: God's affirmation

Think of a recent incident when someone got upset with you. What do you imagine Abba-Father would like to say to you that will affirm your goodness and renew your joy? Write it down in the format of a letter that he is writing to you. Start with, "Dear [insert your name] My beloved child . . . "

He's not going to justify your sins. He's not going to agree that you're blameless. He's not going to condemn the people whom you blame for the problems you're dealing with. But he does want to build you up so that you can feel good about moving forward in holiness. Put his affirmation into writing. Feel free to imagine him saying what you long to hear him say but you're not yet sure he is saying. If what you write does not contradict scripture and the teachings of the Church, it's safe to assume that the Father himself is behind the words that come to you.

* * *

And now, here's a bonus gift that your Divine Daddy wants to give you so that you can hear his affirmation whenever you need it. Download "**Love Notes from God**." This document contains 16 healing and inspiring scriptures adapted into "love notes." To use it:

1. Print out all eight pages on colored paper.
2. Slice each page in half to separate each love note.
3. Fold each love note in half to hide its contents.
4. Place them in a basket or decorative box and mix them up.
5. Once a day or whenever you need to hear the Father's affirmation, ask him to choose one of the love notes for you. Then pull one out and make it part of your prayer conversation.

To download it, go to **30DaysToTheFathersHeart.com/lovenotes**.

DAY 16

The Father's Compassion

THE FATHER IS FULL of compassion for you. Compassion is not something that we have to wait for. Compassion is not something we need to be good enough for. Jesus gave us a parable that describes what the Father's compassion looks like. The story of the Prodigal Son (Luke 15:11-32) illustrates that compassion fills the Father's heart even while we are still far off-track in the Christian life.

> *But while he was still a long way off, his father saw him and was filled with compassion for him; he ran to his son, threw his arms around him and kissed him. (Luke 15:20 NIV).*

What don't you like about yourself? Do you still feel ashamed of your sins, and is this making you wonder if Father God is keeping you in misery because you don't deserve better treatment?

The parable of the Prodigal Son assures us that the Father cherishes us no matter what we've done. He waits, full of fatherly yearning, for us to turn away from our sins and turn toward him. That's all we need to do; just turn around. And the moment we do that, he *runs* to us! He wastes no time but immediately embraces us, welcomes us, and kisses us with his super-abundant love.

The prodigal son had not yet asked his dad for forgiveness when he felt forgiveness wrap around him like a warm blanket. His confession came afterward. This is how the Father treats us. When we sin, he waits for our repentance with eager anticipation. He feels the pain of our absence. His fatherly heart yearns for the moment when we'll realize that we're better off with him than in the pigsty of our sins.

Why does he treat us this way when he knows we will so easily fall back into sin? He sees our future. And yet he does not hold our future sins against us. He embraces us in the here and now. That's compassion!

This is what it means to be an adopted child of God. When the Father looks at us who are his adopted sons and daughters, he doesn't focus on what we've done wrong. While we are still in the state of sin, his focus is on the horizon line while he awaits our turn-around. He focuses on the steps we make in the right direction. And he is driven by compassion to run and meet us, wherever we are, and to embrace us in a divine welcome-back hug, *and* to brace us up in our weaknesses.

Because of this, we can stop feeling ashamed of ourselves. We can give God's compassion to ourselves. At the same time that we're feeling convicted to repent, rather than beat ourselves up over what we did wrong (which is the Accuser attacking us again), the Father wants us to be compassionate to ourselves just like he's being compassionate. This does not mean that we make excuses for our sins. No, it means that just like Father God is focused on our turn-around and celebrates our repentance, so should we. Instead of unceasingly wallowing in regret, we can learn from our mistakes, and we can grow stronger in our commitment to live as the saints that God gifted us to be when we were baptized.

When my imagination illustrates the story of the Prodigal Son, I see the son limping toward home. He's walked a long distance on an empty stomach. He's weak and barely able to trudge through the last few miles of the journey home. His father runs to him and cries tears of joy and relief while hugging his son. Then he provides his own strength to support his son for the rest of the journey home.

Abba-Father is bracing you up, too, in your weaknesses—even before you conquer that persistent sin that makes you feel so unworthy. In his tremendous compassion he is giving you powerful support.

Such compassion is unimaginable for those of us who were abused or neglected or rejected by parents. And even in homes where the parents were full of compassion, to the child, discipline feels more like animosity than compassion. A good parent gives children a welcome-back hug after they've learned their lesson or showed a desire to improve. But if we grew up in a home where we did not feel our parents' compassion during punishments, we're probably projecting their character flaw onto God's Fatherhood.

When our prayers go unanswered or we suffer a problem that makes life unceasingly difficult, we automatically assume that God is lacking compassion. We think we're being punished.

It's true that God disciplines us, but this always comes from a heart that yearns for us to become our best selves, which is also our happiest selves. The Father's heart weeps when we sin. He knows that sin is destroying us in ways we cannot yet see. And he longs for us to spend eternity at Home with him. He is all-goodness, and so he has to chastise us.

He does *not* chastise us by refusing to answer our prayers. That would require him to stop being good, which is quite impossible. We block or delay the answers to prayers by the choices we make and by rejecting God's ways of dealing with whatever we're praying for.

The word "chastise" comes from the Latin word *castigare*, which means "to set or keep right" or "to make pure." Punishments that Father God initiates are chastisements that are designed to get our attention and make us turn to the Son who took our sins and nailed them to his Cross. By the blood he shed for us on Good Friday, we are purified from every sin that we genuinely want to overcome.

The word "compassion" means "to suffer with." The Latin word *com* means "with, together." The Latin root of "passion" is *pati*, which means "to suffer." Therefore, we need to realize that in every chastisement, the Father suffers with us.

He is not the parent who sends an erring child to the corner; he takes us to the corner and sits with us there. He is not the parent who teaches a lesson by making the child suffer; he is the Father who takes us to the Son who chose to suffer for us.

When we accept this tremendous act of love, Jesus and the Father give us the Holy Spirit who teaches us lessons in a most victorious way. Thus, all things—including our sins—are made to work together for our good because our Father delights in turning something evil into something holy (see Romans 8:28).

Fearing God as the Ultimate Punisher makes us vulnerable to the false promises that are offered by the world. The Devil plots to take advantage of our weaknesses, and those who believe that God does not have a compassionate heart toward them get tricked into putting more trust in themselves than in God. They embrace the world's moral relativism. Their reasoning (unconsciously perhaps) is: "I'll decide what's right and wrong because my way is more compassionate and tolerant than the God of the Christians."

Sadly, we Christians often contribute to this by conveying God as uncompassionate. We do this when, in our holy desire to help others turn away from sin, we scold them or preach at them. We have the right intentions but the wrong delivery, usually because we're not reaching out to them from a place of humility. We feel superior to them. But if we convey that we're sharing the truth from our experiences of learning how to overcome our own sins, we become the Father's voice inviting them to change. This is why Jesus said:

> *Why do you look at the speck of sawdust in your brother's eye and pay no attention to the plank in your own eye? How can you say to your brother, "Let me take the speck out of your eye," when all the time there is a plank in your own eye? You hypocrite, first take the plank out of your own eye, and then you will see clearly to remove the speck from your brother's eye. (Matthew 7:3-5 NIV)*

We also contribute to a false image of the Father when we get judgmental and legalistic. Jesus said, "Woe to you, teachers of the law! . . . You have neglected the more important matters of the law: justice, mercy and faithfulness." (See Matthew 23:23.) We need to become better at conveying *love, mercy, and compassion* with the truths that others are rejecting or neglecting.

This is what chased Betty, a young woman in my parish many years ago, away from the Catholic Church. She had begun attending RCIA classes to become Catholic. When she learned that the Eucharist is Jesus himself, she began attending Mass daily. And she was so hungry for Jesus that she got into the communion line and received the Eucharist like everybody else. Her sponsors saw this and told her that she was not allowed to do it yet. Betty never returned.

Her sponsors were correct to stop her, but was there a way they could have done it and made Betty feel welcome and connected to Jesus in the Eucharist? They wanted to do what was right, but is it always right to enforce the rules exactly the way they're stated?

Because the Eucharist is Jesus, it's blasphemous to receive him in Holy Communion when we are not in full communion with the Church. This means that if we are in unrepentant sin when we consume the Eucharist, we are making a mockery of this Sacrament. If we receive Jesus in the Eucharist but don't believe that it is Jesus, we're rejecting him and the teachings of the Church. If we want to go to Mass because Jesus is in the Eucharist while refusing to accept the Pope's authority, we're denying the validity of communion as the Body and Blood of Christ in the Eucharist *and* in the Church.

How should Betty's sponsors have handled her desire to receive Jesus in the Eucharist? From my own experience of becoming Catholic, I can tell you that once someone has discovered the truth about the true presence of Jesus in the Eucharist, the burning desire is very strong. "Give me Jesus! Why do you want to keep me away from Jesus?" is a common cry among new believers.

What might God the Father say to them? Do we picture him as a stern Father legalistically insisting on perfect compliance with the rules of the Church? That looks more like a disciplinarian than a compassionate Daddy. It is true that God is both. However, if our first impulse is to view him as disciplinarian, we will continue to have difficulty connecting with him. His heart will seem all too closed to us.

What's the solution to Betty's dilemma? Saint Paul wrote:

> *"We who are strong ought to bear with the failings of the weak" (Romans 15:1 NIV).*

And then he spoke the truth with compassion:

> *"I myself am convinced, my brothers and sisters, that you yourselves are full of goodness, filled with knowledge and competent to instruct one another. Yet I have written you quite boldly on some points to remind you of them again . . . " (verses 14 and 15).*

Paul affirmed what was good in the people of the Roman church, and at the same time he gently but firmly challenged them to change their ways. This is how to teach the truth with compassion. Betty needed to feel compassionate understanding from her sponsors. She needed to be affirmed in her eagerness to receive the Eucharist. And she needed a good explanation of why it's better to wait until she finished RCIA.

What a challenge it is to speak truth with compassion! If you're like me, the hardest time to feel compassionate is in the moment of dealing with someone's difficult behaviors. Our failure to be compassionate indicates that we've been relying on our own limited abilities. We need to open ourselves to let the Holy Spirit fill us and empower us with the Father's compassion. Then we can give *God's* compassion to others.

This becomes easier when we first understand God's compassion for us personally.

The Father's compassion is visible every day

Shout for joy, you heavens;
rejoice, you Earth;
burst into song, you mountains!
For the Lord comforts his people
and will have compassion on his afflicted ones.

But Zion said, "The Lord has forsaken me,
the Lord has forgotten me."

Can a mother forget the baby at her breast
and have no compassion on the child she has borne?
Though she may forget,
I will not forget you!
See, I have engraved you on the palms of my hands;
your walls are ever before me.

(Isaiah 49:13-16 NIV)

Think of someone who has been very compassionate toward you. The Father gave you his own compassion through that person. Who has shown you compassion today? That's the Father reaching out to you. Who was compassionate yesterday? That, too, was Abba-Father's compassion.

Because I didn't get enough compassion from my human father during childhood, I found what I needed in Nana and Pop-pop (my maternal grandparents). God in his great compassion gave me grandparents who doted on me and favored me and listened to all of my complaints with sympathy and compassion.

During visits to their home, Nana and Pop-pop always took their grandchildren to church. On one of those Sundays, I heard the song

"How Great Thou Art" for the first time. I loved it! It's an inspiring song that stirred up within me a strong connection to God. My soul was pulled into it, and I felt the Father's love embrace me. I felt his power, made available through his compassion, in the words of the song, enhanced by the melody.

> *O Lord, my God, when I in awesome wonder,*
> *Consider all the worlds Thy Hands have made,*
> *I see the stars, I hear the rolling thunder,*
> *Thy power throughout the universe displayed.*

Because I enjoyed lying on the grass at night to look at the stars, the song said to me that God loves me so much he gave me the night sky. Because I wasn't afraid of thunder ("That's God having fun bowling" was the fable that my parents told me to explain the booms), the song said to me that God puts drama into rainstorms to entertain me. And because I had learned that God is bigger than the universe, the song said to me that his power was awesome. I felt that power in this song.

After church, I asked my grandparents if there was any way I could have that song. This occurred in the 1960s. Today you can find it online and buy it on CD in music stores and Christian bookstores. Back then, it was not readily available. Nana and Pop-pop took me to music stores, but it was not there. It became Nana's mission to find a vinyl record of it for me. Although she never found a recording of it, her persistence and determination made a huge impression on me.

Who has worked hard to make a wish or dream of yours come true? This is an example of the Father's compassionate love.

"How Great Thou Art" is still one of my most favorite songs. Whenever I sing it in church or hear it on my phone's music app and join in, I feel instantly more connected to the Father. I also feel connected to Nana. She passed away in 1977, and I can almost hear her singing it along with me. I feel her closeness and her joy and her worship in this song. I also feel her compassion *and* God's compassion.

The Father's compassion is with us every second of every day. To become more aware of it we only need to think of the people who have shown us compassion. He gave you his compassion through them. But their examples are only a tiny portion of what the Father is actually pouring out to you.

Learning to love with the compassion of Christ

Another example of the Father's compassion comes from within ourselves.

One of the advantages of being adopted by God the Father is that we have the opportunity to learn from our Big Brother, Jesus. He teaches us how to be a true child of God. During the 1980s, I continually asked Jesus to enable me to love others the way he loves them—no matter what they've done. For several months, I continued to pray and wait for his help.

At that time, I did not know God the Father very well. I had met the Holy Spirit, and it was my trust in the Holy Spirit that gave me confidence to believe that Jesus would answer this prayer. I knew it was important. Without this gift, this ability, this connection to God, I would not be of much use to the Kingdom of God. Without divine help I could not activate this gift. I just could not muster up, by my own efforts, unconditional love for everyone I encountered.

Going to the Sacrament of Confession for this didn't change me. Although this sacrament does give us supernatural graces to overcome the sins that we cannot conquer on our own, more was needed from me. Compassion for others, especially for those who cause troubles, requires that we first truly desire to be like Christ in regard to love.

Abba-Father needed to discipline me, which is to say that he was *discipling* (teaching) me. I learned what it means to be disciplined by God compassionately. The Father's discipline is firm but kind, compassionate, and educational. Unlike the punishing disciplines of our human parents, God's discipline doesn't hurt; it only helps. He doesn't scold us; he empowers us to change. And so, the Father trained me.

In the first phase of my lesson, I faced the question: Did I really, truly want to receive this gift—enough to persistently pray for it?

I said yes and kept praying.

Several months later, while attending a Catholic Charismatic conference, I went to the Sacrament of Reconciliation again to confess not loving everyone like Christ loves everyone. The priest gave me an easy penance: "Say one Our Father prayer and three Hail Marys." Dutifully, I went to the makeshift chapel where Jesus in the Eucharist was present for adoration, and I knelt to fulfill my obligation.

Due to the faith-building environment of the conference, I felt especially close to God. This made it easy for my heart to hear the Lord speak to me. And it seemed that he wanted more from me than the penance assigned by the priest. He was about to give me a test. Would I be willing to do whatever he asked of me?

One of the people attending the conference was a woman from my parish. She served as a leader of the prayer group, but she belonged to a local Wiccan coven. I did not like her. I certainly did not *love* her. Or rather, I did not know how to love her the way Jesus loves her. I felt angry at her for mixing the Christian faith with witchcraft. I thought, "How dare she call herself a leader of the prayer group! She's a demonically influenced fraud!"

Abba-Father asked me, "Will you love her?"

Gulp! How? I wanted to obey God. I wanted to be able to love her. This was a good example of what I had been praying to be able to do. So, I replied, "If You help me do it, I will."

What he said next startled me. "When you see her, give her a hug and tell her that you love her." I knew it was the Lord speaking. It's definitely not what I would have said to myself. And the voice was full of compassion for me as well as for the woman I disliked.

"Nooooo! Not that!" The idea repulsed me. At first, I ran from the idea, but I allowed Jesus to wrestle with me. After struggling for a while, I feebly gave the Lord my yes and braced myself for the encounter.

Strangely, I never saw that woman again at the conference. Afterward, I asked the Lord if I should look for her at church to give her the hug. With a smile, which I could feel as clearly as any of my own emotions, Abba-Father told me that I had passed the test. It wasn't about the hug; it was about my willingness. That made me very happy!

The Father had asked me to give compassionate love to someone I greatly disliked, while at the same time he protected me. The Father showed me through the test that my prayer had been answered. He also taught me that loving someone unconditionally does not mean we have to start liking them. Nor does it mean that we have to spend time with them or submit to their abuses.

This became a turning point in my life. I no longer felt the need to continue asking for the gift. God had delivered it and I had received it, and, thanks to the test, I knew without any doubt that I had received it.

Since that day, compassion towards others has come more easily, even naturally. Not by my own effort but by the grace of God. He had given me his own compassion toward others. And because it is a grace, it has been a permanent gift. I've been repeatedly tested throughout the years that followed.

Tests from God are not like tests in school. They are not given to us to find out if we will succeed or how terribly we will fail. Each test is meant to teach us something important. My willingness to love others unconditionally has been repeatedly tested, and each time it has deepened my relationship with God while it increased my ability (by depending on God's grace) to love all others unconditionally.

These tests always come from the compassionate heart of the Father. They reveal his compassion for me as I share his compassion with others. God's help for passing the tests has remained steadily available.

Every time we reach our limit in loving someone, we can turn to the Lord and ask for supernatural help to love the way he loves. And he supplies this help every time. Of course! It is who he is. He is compassion itself. He is the source of our compassion for others. He wants us to be like him, and he wants us to deliver his tender compassion to others.

Listen to Dawn explain how well this works for her: "I have been able to catch myself thinking more about why the other person might do something that I am not liking. It is hard to take the plank out of your own eye, but praying to be more compassionate and thinking about God loving that person, asking me to love him/her helps. I then have my feelings soften and then I'm able to be more compassionate."

The tender mercy of the Father's compassion

Saint Michel Garicoits (1797-1863) said,

> What does Our Lord preach to us? Tenderness everywhere—in the Incarnation, His holy Childhood, the Passion, in the Sacred Heart, in every inch of His person, both internally and externally, in His words, in His looks . . . What must be the foremost characteristic of our spiritual life? Christian tenderness. Without this tenderness, we will never possess this spirit of generosity with which we must serve God.

The Father's discipline is always compassionate. You know it's our Divine Daddy when a challenging message is delivered with his patience, kindness, and support. It only feels unpleasant when we resist it. The more we want to fight him on it, and the more we want to do the opposite of what he is trying to teach us, the more painful the discipline feels. But it is not the Father who inflicts this pain. It is our own struggle against him. We inflict the pain upon ourselves.

Case in point: the prodigal son of Jesus' famous parable. Why do you think he felt afraid to go home when his life-choices turned out so miserably? What we know about his father—the joyful and tender mercy that overflowed enthusiastically to his lost son upon his return—was not new. Surely both of his sons had witnessed it for many years. Like Abba-Father, whom the father in the story represents, compassion was already part of his nature.

The prodigal son's fears were based on shame, self-centeredness, and self-justification.

Shame blinds us to the truth. Shame—the fear that we are too sinful for the Father to bless us—prevents us from remembering that the Father's nature is to wait for us with a yearning heart and open arms.

Wanting to do things our own way and only for our own sake—self-centeredness—keeps us turned away from God's compassion. The prodigal son was rebellious, wanting to run his own life (look where *that* got him). Perhaps he feared that returning to the family home meant letting his dad have control.

To justify his loose living, he would've had to find ways to blame his father. He would've come up with stories about how his father had driven him away from home. This is what self-justification does to a person: It exaggerates the truth and reinvents memories; it manipulates the facts to the sinner's own advantage.

None of this is a fun way to live. It seems to work for a while, and then the reality of life in a pigsty makes us miserable. It was not the father who inflicted this pain on the prodigal son. The son inflicted it upon himself. It was the consequence of his decisions.

He inflicted pain upon his father, too, but the father handled his suffering with undying compassion. The son, lacking compassion for his father (and was there a mother, too?) could not imagine that his father waited with forgiveness and compassion. He could not understand such compassion nor believe in it because he did not have it within himself. And so, he shut himself off from the family, inflicting upon himself yet another pain, although he would deny this; he would have blamed his father for this, too.

There are many sons and daughters like this in today's world.

I've heard the stories and read the prayer requests of countless Christian parents whose grown children have behaved like the son in the parable. Some still live at home or in visiting distance, but they are emotionally and spiritually far away. They have closed themselves off from the love that waits for their return, because their self-justifications have been lying to them, telling them that condemnation or control or mistreatment is what awaits them, not compassionate love.

When they finally get desperate enough to stop this vicious cycle of feeling hurt and justifying themselves, they discover the compassion that has been there all along—the tender, merciful compassion of God the Father expressed through the family. In the parable, the father (and unseen mother) never stopped loving the son, even while they suffered from their son's divisiveness. And even while they felt hurt by the son's lack of concern for their feelings.

The father's unconditional, faithful love was his gift to the son even while the son was rejecting it. The gift that the son gave to his dad upon his return home was an open heart that was ready and willing to receive the love that had always been available.

The overflow of compassion

The Greek word for "compassion" that was used in the parable implies that the father's heart, at the deepest level, was moved by the problems of his son. The father could not help but wait with great yearning for his son's return. He wanted to reach his son with the love that could make a difference. He wanted to improve his son's life. He wanted to restore joy to him. Though his son rejected him, he was really his best ally.

This is God's compassion. Abba-Father is deeply motivated to be our best ally.

When we experience that depth of compassion, we become motivated to give others the same compassion (not condemnation, not retaliation) when they choose sinful lifestyles and justify it while rejecting us.

With the Father's compassion overflowing from us, we compassionately love those who lash out at us, push us away, or abandon us. We become like our Divine Daddy when we yearn for reconciliation and a safe, peaceful, active relationship. We need to remember that they are caught in the terrible cycle of making wrong decisions and feeling the need to justify them. While they are in that cycle, there is little we can do to convince them that we can be their ally.

There will be moments now and then, opportunities that are all too brief, when we can reach across the divide and give the gift of compassion. But until they are ready to break out of the cycle, we will soon be rejected again. We need to wait like the father in the parable, offering to God our yearnings that go so deep they become tears. This is a very powerful prayer.

Tears that are cried during prayer are very valuable, like droplets of diamonds. There's nothing wrong with getting emotional and pouring our sorrows upon God. When your heart is heavy with grief, Abba expects you to share the burden with him. Give yourself permission to really let it all out, from deep within. The Father cherishes your prayer diamonds. And he cries with you. He waits with you for your prayers to finally be answered.

This is compassion.

The day will come when the waiting finally ends. The prodigal will be spotted while he is still far off and God the Father will go running toward him, taking you along. The Father will dance and rejoice because, at last, he is able to give his love to the one who needed it but feared opening himself up to it.

Take to heart these words by the father of John the Baptist (see Luke 1:78-79):

> *In the tender compassion of our God*
> *the dawn from on high shall break upon us,*
> *to shine on those who dwell in darkness and the shadow of death,*
> *and to guide our feet into the way of peace.*
> *(From the Canticle of Zechariah in the Benedictus)*

The depth of compassion that we feel for those who are hurting themselves is a sharing in the compassion of Father God. Let's thank him for the experiences that help us to understand the depth of his compassion for us. For when we have suffered like the prodigal son's dad did, we will feel a tiny, itty bitty portion of what Abba feels—for each of us.

Today's Exercise: Identify the Father's daily compassion

List the times when people showed you compassion. Start with childhood memories but include recent occasions.

Then read through your list and say, "When ___ showed me compassion, it was the Father's compassion for me."

Don't rush through this. Meditate on it. Reflect on how you felt each time. The Father's compassion is all over it, through it, and underscoring it.

DAY 17

Abba-Father Wants to Hug You

ARE YOU AWARE OF God's touch? The tender, caring touch of the Father reaching out to you. The hug you need when you feel discouraged or lonely. Or the hug of his compassion. Father God touches us every day in big and small ways. He gives us congratulatory pats on the back. He comforts us when we feel depressed. He lifts us up when we stumble. He holds our hands when we stroll down the street admiring the clouds, the trees, and the flowers. And when we get hurt, he wipes our tears, and he kisses our aches.

> *Praise be to the God and Father of our Lord Jesus Christ, the Father of compassion and the God of all comfort, who comforts us in all our troubles, so that we can comfort those in any trouble with the comfort we ourselves receive from God (2 Corinthians 1:3-4 NIV).*

How important his touch is! God designed us to be hugged. We *need* hugs—even for our very survival. Abandoned babies in institutions die from lack of touch. Marriages wither from lack of hugging. Children grow up with poor self-esteem from lack of physical nurturing.

Jesus knew how important touch is. Look at how often he healed people through his physical touch. When he healed lepers, he touched them. Their disease was so contagious that it was illegal for lepers to mingle where people could touch them. But Jesus not only healed their skin, he also healed them emotionally and psychologically by giving him what they needed most—human touch.

Do you know how to identify the Father's hug? Do you know how to feel the hug of an invisible Daddy? Usually, it happens in unexpected ways, at unexpected times. We miss it, however, if we're distracted by our own ideas of how he should answer our prayers. If we have tunnel vision, seeking only what we think should happen, he reaches out to hug us, but we think he slapped us.

How would you recognize a hug from God?

For me, his hug is sort of like an emotional awareness of God's presence encasing me in silent affirmation. It's contemplative prayer without necessarily going into a contemplative state of mind. It's as if the air around me, which is pregnant with God's activity (as described on Day 8), has become as thick as ocean water without being oppressive, and God's activity within it is named "comfort."

It's not something we can become aware of unless we pause what we're doing and seek it. "Daddy, I need a hug!" Whether in a peaceful moment or in the midst of turmoil, it's a prayer that is always answered immediately. God is the inventor of hugs. He wants to hug us a lot more than we know.

Even right now he is hugging you!

Immersing ourselves in the hug of the Father comes easier for those who were raised in huggy families. However, some of us have been hugged inappropriately. Others, like myself, were not hugged warmly. This can make it difficult to feel and enjoy God's hugs.

I come from a non-huggy family. Sure, I was held as a baby and, as a child, I sat on my mom's lap. I felt loved and nurtured by both of my parents. But I have no memories of sitting on my father's lap. I have no memories of running to him when I felt hurt or anguished, no recollection of his arms protectively pulling me in to comfort me.

The only memory association I have with my dad's lap is a game he played with my little brother. He liked to sit Kurt on his lap and invite me or my sister to sit next to them. Then my dad took Kurt's little hand and "punched" us with it. It was a very light and playful tap, but my sister and I did not enjoy it. My dad enjoyed it a lot.

Imagine the misconceptions that this taught me about God the Father:

1. He is more fond of other children than he is of me.

2. His idea of playfulness is at my expense.
3. He doesn't care if something he does makes me unhappy.

While I was growing up, my relationship with my dad was impaired by his coldness. His hugs were formal and stiff. It seemed to me that he really didn't want to hug me. I knew that he loved me, but I also knew, instinctively, that something important was missing. I interpreted it as Dad withholding love from me.

My mom's touch felt comforting, especially when I was ill. But too often when I needed a hug to calm me from crying after I had been scolded for misbehaving, my dad sent me to my room to deal with it alone. More than anything else at that moment, I longed for a parent to come and check on me and give me a reassuring hug. Not getting it, I turned to my Best Friend Jesus. I felt his closeness in that room. This deepened my relationship with him.

How does one heal from the absence of hugs? In sharing my personal story, I'll demonstrate a very effective way to heal.

It happened several years after I became an adult and sought the help of a spiritual director. Irene Huber taught me how to receive inner healing from Jesus.

In prayer, I imagined that I was back in my childhood bedroom. I remembered being a teenager, alone and crying. This time, I invited Jesus into my room, and I imagined what he looked like. Visualizations like this, done in the context of Christ-centered prayer after asking for the anointing of the Holy Spirit, are very real encounters with Jesus. I envisioned him opening up the bedroom door the way I had wished my parents would have done. He came in, sat next to me, and listened to me complain about my troubles. Then he asked (through the Holy Spirit's anointing on my imagination) if I were willing to forgive my parents.

Knowing that this is the door to healing, I said yes. Next, I envisioned Mom entering the room.

"What would you like to say to her?" Jesus asked me. So, I proceeded to tell Mom, in my imagination, how I felt and why. Then she asked me to forgive her. I did and we hugged with tears from both of us.

A word about how this works: In real life, I have not had this conversation with Mom. Before my healing, I didn't know how to approach her. After my healing, it felt unnecessary to bring up.

Anyway, forgiveness is never about the other person; it's about us letting go of our hurts. It's about letting go of the other person's emotional hold on us that exists in our hearts. Until we forgive, we are chained to the damage that was done to us. The other person today might be completely different, remorseful, or long gone, but they are still inside our heads continuing to do damage. This is not their fault anymore; it's ours.

Through the visualizations of the inner healing process, we forgive and let go of their emotional hold on us. When we're finished, we're ready to move forward renewed, restored, and free.

When I felt Mom's hug in my visualization, it was Abba-Father who was hugging me for real.

Next, my dad entered the reimagined room of my childhood. I went through the same process of forgiving him: I told him why I was angry at him, what I had needed from him, and why it was so important to me.

Imagining him asking for my forgiveness was harder to do than it had been with my mother, so I envisioned Jesus coaxing it out of him. At last, I heard the words, "Please forgive me," and I said, "I do forgive you." Then we hugged like I had never felt hugged in real life. My Divine Daddy was giving me the best embrace that I'd ever had from a father.

By the time I was ready to open my eyes and end the visualization, I had changed. I no longer felt any pain or sorrow about being sent to my room to cry alone. And I had moved a lot closer to knowing Father God as a wonderful hugger who embraced me with deep, compassionate love.

Today's Exercise, Part 1: Experience God's hug

My dad was not a hugger because his dad had not been a hugger. It's no wonder that my brother and sister and I never felt close to our paternal grandparents.

My maternal grandparents, on the other hand, were very embracive with their love. Visiting them was an emotional heaven for me. I learned a lot from them about what it's like to be hugged by God (although I didn't know it at the time).

Write a list naming those who have hugged you best. Then describe what you liked about them. This is a description of what God is like!

* * *

The psychology of hugs

In the early 1980s, a popular author/speaker known as "Doctor Hug" got my avid attention because his mission was to spread awareness about the importance of hugs. Due to my family background, I thought that Dr. Leo Buscaglia was providing our world with a breakthrough in modern psychology. He said, "Hugs make you feel psychologically more secure and together." He added, "Hugs are the key to happiness." And he said, "Everybody needs a hug. It changes your metabolism." (Source: **facultyweb.ivcc.edu/rrambo/eng1001/quotes.htm**)

To me, this was Big News. Life-changing. For many of Dr. Buscaglia's readers and listeners, he provided some much-needed "permission" to get the hugs that God designed us to need.

Parents who hug their children warmly, securely, and appropriately convey what God the Father's hug is like. When a hug says, "I care about you," it fosters trust. In the home, good hugs open the door for good communication. The children feel safe talking to their parents about life's difficult times or the mistakes they've made. The same is true in our relationship with Abba-Father: Good hugs in the home reflect God's compassion. Good hugs in the home foster trust in God.

For those of us who grew up without good hugs, the good news is: It's still very possible to feel the hugs of our Divine Daddy. It just takes learning how to recognize them.

In some cultures, nobody hugs. Maybe this is why there is so much war in the world and fighting in homes.

Jeanie says, "It wasn't until after I moved to the South [in the U.S.] that I saw people hug upon greeting one another and leaving one another's company. As I saw others hug, I liked the acceptance and the love it showed. It took me a while to feel comfortable receiving and giving a hug to someone other than a boyfriend, but I got with the program!"

Gift Nyirenda says, "In my childhood days, hugging was not a common phenomenon in Malawi due to strong African cultural values. A normal way of affirming how someone feels here is a handshake, usually a heavy, long one. Recently with televisions we see the meaning of a hug. I have learned to accept it as part of normal social life, and I now do it more often."

For my husband Ralph, Dr. Buscaglia's message was nothing new.

Ralph comes from a large, huggy family. When we began dating, I drank up his hugs like a thirsty camel. After we founded Good News

Ministries in 1995, people who attended our events nicknamed him "The Power Hugger." I smiled at that, because I felt pleased that I could benefit from his hugs every day. But then I began hearing that my hugs were weak. The people I hugged felt like I didn't really care about them. Whoa, this was my complaint about my dad's hugs!

Those who cared enough to speak this out loud to me were right. They blessed me with the truth. Until that moment, I hadn't realized that my hugs were different from Ralph's. So, I began to pay attention to how Ralph hugged. His embrace revealed that he genuinely cared. I cared, too, but I didn't communicate it well in my hugs. Ralph's hugs were physically generated by strong arms. My arms only lightly wrapped themselves around others—my hugs were wimpy and thereby communicated a wimpy concern for others.

Ralph's energy surrounded those he hugged; I withheld my energy. Ralph's hugs lingered; he instinctively knew how long to give a hug—long enough to provide warmth and healing without overdoing it beyond the recipient's comfort level. I behaved like I couldn't wait to break free of the hugs that I gave.

So, I asked Ralph to teach me how to become a good hugger. And he did.

Do you know a good hugger? Go get a hug! It will be the Divine Father hugging you. Do you give good hugs? Realize that you have a ministry of hugging, a very special calling. You give the Father's hug to everyone you reach out to.

Dawn says, "My best hugger is a friend that I would only meet at conferences maybe once or twice a year. We nicknamed her the 'Hug Lady.' She hugged everyone, and you could see the hesitation in some. But after her hug, you could see the difference it made. Her personality is steeped in genuineness. You leave feeling better every time you receive her hug."

That's the Father! His hugs leave you feeling better every time you experience them.

Ralph's hugs are an excellent example of what our Divine Daddy's hugs are like. God's fatherly embrace holds us and surrounds us with the strong arms of his compassion. God is not wimpy. His concern for each of us is energetic and full of life. His hugs are protective, warm, and safe—always.

Physical hugging is necessary for a healthy life. It helps the body's immune system. It relieves depression. It reduces stress. It helps us sleep better at night and invigorates us during the day. It rejuvenates us when we're weary. God designed our bodies to benefit from hugs. Our minds and our moods, too, are improved by hugs. All of these benefits are God's deliberate design.

Spiritual hugging is likewise necessary for a healthy *faith* life. When a parent, spouse, or friend gives us a really great hug, this is Abba hugging us through them.

Gift Nyirenda says, "Hugging here [in Africa] entails a sense of closeness and relationship that people have (you cannot hug a stranger). Spiritual hugging gives more freedom and peace of mind because you learn the essence and value of the other person through forgiveness and reunion. Jesus Christ is an all-time brother who is always ready to mediate in such a reunion. And when you hug that other person again, there is so much joy in your heart, in Heaven, and in your life too. We were not born to be enemies, but to live love and share it as often as possible."

Spiritual hugging helps our soul's immune system, strengthening us against temptations. It relieves depression even more effectively than physical hugs. It reduces stress because it reinforces our trust in God's helpfulness.

Spiritual hugging also helps us sleep better. Sometimes when I've had an especially difficult day, I ask Ralph for a super hug before going to bed, and then I imagine that my pillow is the lap of Jesus.

Spiritual hugging invigorates us to bear the crosses we carry. On good days it energizes our joy. On bad days it comforts us.

The science of hugs

In 2015, researchers from Carnegie Mellon University in Pennsylvania examined the effects of hugs on 404 healthy adults. Participants were exposed to the virus of the common cold. The researchers found that those who had social support (the concern of family and friends) stayed healthy. Furthermore, the study revealed that when social support is expressed through *hugs*, people's resistance to sickness increases by 32%. And of the participants who caught the cold, the ones who were hugged more than the rest suffered less severe symptoms.

"Hugging protects people who are under stress from the increased risk for colds [that's] usually associated with stress," stated Sheldon Cohen, professor of psychology and the lead author of the Carnegie Mellon research. Hugging "is a marker of intimacy and helps generate the feeling that others are there to help in the face of adversity."

Taken to the spiritual level, hugging is a marker of intimacy with God and generates an awareness that God (Father, Son, and Holy Spirit) is our ally in the face of adversity.

Hugs release the hormone oxytocin from the hypothalamus in the brain, which influences our moods, behavior, and physiology. Oxytocin is often called "the bonding hormone" because it promotes attachment in relationships. When Ralph or I have a bad day, we like to turn to one another and say, "You (or I) need some oxytocin." Then we join in a strong, friendly, lingering hug. Abba is in that hug. We always feel better.

Oxytocin improves our mood by increasing the levels of the feel-good hormones serotonin and dopamine. This produces a calming effect and reduces depression and anxiety. The benefits extend throughout the body. It decreases the heart rate and lowers the stress hormones cortisol and norepinephrine. A 2015 study from King's College in London also found that oxytocin acts like an analgesic. Researchers subjected participants to brief radiant heat pulses that were generated by an infrared laser. They learned that oxytocin reduces pain intensity.

God created oxytocin. I believe that this is part of the reason why prayer reduces pain and promotes healing. Prayer is how we hug God and how we open ourselves to receive a hug from God. It gives us a good dose of supernatural oxytocin.

Pray with a friend for supernatural oxytocin and add a hug for a good dose of natural oxytocin.

Today's Exercise Part 2: Feel hugged by Abba-Father

God designed our bodies to benefit from hugs. Therefore, it's very healing to learn how to feel the hug of our Divine Daddy. It begins by meditating on his loving presence. While you've been reading this book, how often did you experience an "Aha!" moment of feeling closer to Abba-Father? *That was a hug!*

When you go to church and feel peaceful there, that's a hug.

When you go to Confession and come out feeling forgiven, that's a hug.

When you talk with a friend about a problem and feel better afterward, that's a hug.

When you feel comforted by an assurance that he is with you to help you face adversities, that's a hug.

When you've been falsely accused and you sense God affirming your goodness, that's a hug.

When you get frustrated and stop to pray, and a feeling of peace comes over you, that's a hug.

Spend time now recalling the various ways that God has helped you, especially within the past day. Which of the above has happened to you? And what else? Write about them, keeping in mind that your Divine Daddy was hugging you each time.

* * *

Make a habit of looking for Abba-Father's hug every day. Your intimacy with Abba will increase. And you might even become physically healthier!

DAY 18

Prayer Requests as an Exchange of Love

DO YOU THINK THAT your prayer requests are not answered fast enough? Or that God ignores your prayer requests? Do you suppose that God is withholding any good from you because you're not perfect? By now (if you haven't skipped any chapters of this book) you know that this isn't true. However, worry is easily triggered when our prayers are not answered. They are triggered by old messages from which we have not yet been completely healed.

For the Lord God is a sun and shield;
the Lord bestows favor and honor;
no good thing does he withhold
from those whose walk is blameless.
(Psalm 84:11 NIV)

Father God is your Doting Daddy. You are favored. There is nothing he wouldn't do for you; this includes sending his Son Jesus to Earth to suffer and die for your sins so that you won't have to. If he did that for you, of course he'll do anything else that will help you spend eternity with him in Heaven. Whatever you ask, if it's within his Kingdom, he will do it for you. It's never a matter of, "Will You, Father?" It's always a matter of trusting him for the "when" and "how."

In Psalm 84, do you get stuck at the word "blameless"? Okay. Who among us is totally blameless when we pray? Not me. Not you. Not anyone on Earth. To get unstuck so that we are free to enjoy fruitful prayer lives, let's look at what "blameless" means in scripture. It's *not* synonymous with the word "perfect." So, keep reading Psalm 84. The next verse gives us a clue about what it means to be blameless before the Lord:

Lord Almighty, blessed is the one who trusts in you.

To be blameless before the Lord means that we are trusting him. It does *not* mean that we never sin. What it *does* mean is that we *prefer* not to sin. We *prefer* to be holy. We *prefer* to be like our Abba-Father. And we *repent* every time we realize we have sinned.

For example, in the story of Job we read that he was "blameless and upright; he feared God and shunned evil" (Job 1:1 NIV). Only Jesus totally avoided sinning (because he was God) and Mary his Blessed Mother (because she was conceived without the effects of Original Sin). Job is like the rest of us. He was considered blameless because he preferred the ways of God even when he was grievously tested.

Do the following words of Psalm 101 sound like you?

I will not look with approval
on anything that is vile.

I hate what faithless people do;
I will have no part in it.
The perverse of heart shall be far from me;
I will have nothing to do with what is evil.

Whoever slanders their neighbor in secret,
I will put to silence;
whoever has haughty eyes and a proud heart,
I will not tolerate.

My eyes will be on the faithful in the land,
that they may dwell with me;
the one whose walk is blameless
will minister to me.

No one who practices deceit
will dwell in my house;
no one who speaks falsely
will stand in my presence.

Every morning I will put to silence
all the wicked in the land;
I will cut off every evildoer
from the city of the Lord.

Those were verses 3-8 (NIV). Now let's look at the preface to it, verses 1 and 2 (NIV):

I will sing of your love and justice;
to you, Lord, I will sing praise.
I will be careful to lead a blameless life -
when will you come to me?
I will conduct the affairs of my house
with a blameless heart.

King David wrote this song and sang it heartily to the Lord. He meant every word. But don't think he was perfect. He was blameless but he was definitely not guiltless. We too are blameless if we love the Lord more than we love the ways of sin and we work at growing in holiness daily.

As you look at Psalm 101, rejoice in the descriptions that portray you. The Father is patting you on the back for getting this far on your spiritual journey. Take everything else to the Sacrament of Confession. Make the commitment to work on these areas until you can check them off the list too. The Father will be very, very pleased with your commitment. He has given the Holy Spirit to you so you can make great progress in holiness. This is what it means to be blameless.

Prayer is like a love letter

When you ask for something in prayer, does it feel like you have to make God change his mind about something? "Please, God, heal my friend who has cancer." As if he didn't want to do it, but maybe since you asked, he'll do it anyway.

Let's dig a little deeper. What I'm really asking you, my friend, is: How strong is your trust? How much do you trust in the Father's goodness—his goodness toward *you*? After you say "amen," do you get up from your prayer chair feeling lighter, happier, and joyful because you've put the whole matter into the Father's hands?

I hope that by the end of this chapter, your prayer times will feel like—more than ever before—an exchange of love between you and the Father. What matters most is the time spent in prayer, not what you prayed for. Is it quality time? Like you're sitting on your Divine Daddy's lap, and you really don't want this time to end.

One of my very special times with Abba-Father is first thing in the morning when I'm out in the yard with my dog. The day is fresh. It's a new beginning, and since I love new things, I delight in the newness of the day with all of its potential still ahead of me. So, I start my prayers by admiring the colors of the sunrise or the dew on the grass (my slippers are getting wet, but that's okay) or the fresh scent of rain that's lingering on the leaves of the trees (I'm glad it stopped raining before the dog needed to go out). This is a wordless prayer. This is my morning dose of giving love and receiving love with the Father.

Then I say out loud, "Thank you, Lord, for the gift of this day. Bless this day and help me to return it to You as a gift that You will enjoy."

At this point, I start slipping off of Daddy's lap. My mind wanders as I watch the dog. Oops! Okay, refocus.

Back securely in his arms, I go through a series of other morning prayers, which I continue while I'm on my porch sipping hot tea. It's a personal liturgy that I call "Teatime with the Lord."

My other most favorite special time with Abba-Father is what I shared with you on Day 12, the Golden Moment of Holy Mass.

These and other prayer times are very comfortable. Very intimate. Very relaxed. But don't think it's always like this for me. I still have prayers of angst—the type of prayers that are based on worry or fear or trials. I'm still working toward the goal of making all of my prayer times to be love exchanges that include prayer requests instead of prayer requests that include an exchange of love.

When I was a teenager, I sometimes wrote notes to my parents and left them on their bed pillows. I did this after an argument had left me feeling unheard or misunderstood. When I failed to get my point across with spoken words, I put them into writing. This sometimes had good results. My parents read these notes after the heat of the moment had passed; they sought me out to discuss it further and calmly.

This was like a prayer request that included an exchange of love. In contrast, my love letters to Ralph were like love exchanges that sometimes included requests.

Have you ever written a love letter to Father God? This will be the spiritual exercise for today. But first we need to get rid of some misconceptions and reinforce your trust in God. By living consciously—paying attention to the misconceptions we need to replace with God's truth—we grow in faith, joy, and trust in the Father's love.

Prayer is not so much a conversation with God as it is an exchange of love. Much can happen in our prayer requests that have no words. It's the language of the heart. In his tremendous love for us, Abba-Father's heart mingles with our hearts, placing within us his desires, which we in turn offer to him as prayer requests—often without realizing that he placed the desire within us in the first place.

When a bad situation is worrying you, how do you pray about it? Worry is a red flag warning us that there are triggers that we still need to dismantle. Are you worried that the situation might never end or that it will end badly? This happens when we do not fully trust God. Are you worried that God doesn't care, doesn't listen to you, or is waiting for you to reach sainthood? This, too, happens because we don't fully trust God.

"Can you add a single hour to your life by worrying?" Jesus asks, rhetorically. "Since you cannot do this very little thing, why worry about anything else? Look at the birds. Your heavenly Father feeds them. Are you not much more valuable than they?" He sighs. "Of course you are! So, seek first the Kingdom of God and his righteousness, and then you'll receive everything you need. Don't worry about tomorrow. Just focus on today. Each day has its own troubles." (See Matthew 6:26-27, Luke 12:26, and Matthew 6:33-34.)

Saint Marie V. Therese Couderc (1805-1885) put it this way: "God always gives more than we ask."

Do you suppose that God is withholding anything good from you? Why would he do that? Is it because you're not doing everything the way he says you should? That would be like saying he refuses to be good to you until you're good. Do you see how silly that is? You'll never be good enough, but so what! It's quite impossible for God to be "not good." Ever. Not for any reason.

None of us can walk without blame every day of our lives and every moment of our days. This is why Christ has given us the gift of the Sacrament of Confession, which is also appropriately called Reconciliation. And this is why the Catholic Mass includes a Penitential Rite. The Penitential Rite fully absolves us of sins unless we are not willing to change. (Grave sins, which have pulled us so far from grace that we've endangered our eternal souls, need more than a public rite. They need the full Sacrament of Reconciliation, one-on-one with God through a priest.)

Of course, the Penitential Rite is a meaningless ritual if we don't consciously bring to mind our sins and desire God's forgiveness. And since the Penitential Rite is short, zipping by too fast for a good examination of conscience, we should arrive at Mass prepared for it. For example, when I realize I've sinned again, I send a quick, quiet prayer to the Father: "Hey, at the Penitential Rite tomorrow, this is what I need you to forgive. Thanks, Abba!"

All of the various life-changing elements of the Holy Liturgy of the Eucharist give us the opportunity to walk without blame. Continually participating in Mass can produce an ever-increasing holiness. Daily Mass speeds up the process. If it's available where you live but your schedule interferes with getting to daily Mass, ask God to make it possible. If your circumstances suddenly change, don't complain but realize that God is working another miracle in your life.

God does not withhold good from you just because you're imperfect. That is more of a human trait than a divine trait. He even answers the prayers of sinners! Jesus often healed a person first and *then* told him or her to "go and sin no more." He didn't wait for people to prove their holiness before giving them a miracle. He didn't back then, and he still doesn't; he hasn't changed.

What matters to God is that we put real effort into growing in holiness, one day at a time, one small step forward at a time.

Praying in the name of Jesus

Jesus said, "Which of you parents, if your son asks for bread, would give him a stone? Or if he asks for a fish, would you give him a snake? If you give good gifts to your children, imagine how much more your heavenly Father wants to give good gifts to those who ask him!" (See Matthew 7:9-11.)

When you were a child, who did you go to first when you wanted your parents to buy something for you? My kids went to their dad first. Ralph would complain to me that the kids treated him like a "walking wallet," but he enjoyed doting on them. He liked being generous with them. (He still does.) I, on the other hand, tended to be more practical. I needed to be convinced that it was a good decision.

Abba-Father does not need to be convinced. If it's good for us (or for whomever we're praying), the answer to our prayer requests is on its way, already planned out. Although it might take some time to implement, God's creative power went into action the first moment we began to turn our thoughts to asking him for help. And if what we desire in prayer was placed in our hearts by the Father's heart, you can believe with all confidence that he's already doing something about it.

But do we always see him this way? Any time we cajole him or try to make a deal with him, we're acting on the misconception that his mind needs to be changed. For example, if we promise, "I'll start going to daily Mass if You give me that financial help I've been waiting for," we're assuming that he needs to be bribed. We might not realize we're doing it, but a prayer that contains no bribe would go like this: "I'll start going to daily Mass because I want to grow in holiness, and I want to feel closer to You. Thank You for the financial help You will provide at the right moment from the right source."

God wants to answer your prayers because you are you. He cherishes you even with all your faults. Every prayer request would literally start with a "thank you" if we understood this.

Prayer is an exchange of love with the Father.

Another misconception we sometimes have is that God sorts through our prayer requests like he's stingy. Any time we list all the reasons why a prayer request is important, we are treating God as a father who is not eager to generously dote on us.

Jesus urges us to expect the Father to answer our prayers out of his great love for us.

> *In that day you will ask in my name. I am not saying that I will ask the Father on your behalf. No, the Father himself loves you because you have loved me and have believed that I came from God. (John 16:27-28 NIV)*

Notice that Jesus said we are to take our prayer requests *directly to the Father*—in his name.

Why his name? What does it mean to ask "in the name of Jesus"? Why not all three Persons of the Trinity? Remember that Jesus is our Mediator. Therefore, we go through Jesus to reach the Father. As we pass through Jesus, we are cleansed by the blood of his sacrifice. When the Father looks at us and our prayer requests, he sees us as the beautiful gem that he created.

And the Holy Spirit is our Advocate. When we don't know what to pray because of the intensity of the problem or because we don't have enough information upon which to base our prayers, the Holy Spirit delivers to the Father the wordless yearnings that dwell deep in our hearts.

To pray *in the name of* Jesus means to pray in the personality of Jesus, and in the love of Jesus, and in the sacrifices of Jesus, and in the Sonship of Jesus—and in everything else that is Jesus. During the time when the scriptures were written, doing anything *in the name of* someone was to do it on his behalf.

Too often, we tack the name "Jesus" at the end of our prayers like it's an exclamation point or like we're stamping our request with a seal that makes it officially Christian. We treat it like a magic word even though we know that prayer has nothing to do with magic.

The name of Jesus does have power. But the power is in his authority over evil, his authority to implement the Father's will, and his authority over our lives. And praying "in the name of Jesus" is powerful only when we say it in the context of an exchange of love. There are many men in this world who are named Jesus, especially in Latin America. The name itself has no power.

Many years ago, I learned from an ex-Satanist that Devil worshippers infiltrate Christian churches quite often, but only where the people lack personal relationships with the Holy Spirit and are therefore not active in the gifts of the Spirit. Without the Spirit's charism of the discernment of spirits, they don't recognize the evil that's in their midst. Satanists blend in, pretending to be Christians. They even baptize their children.

"How does this not save them from Satan?" I asked my friend.

"Easy," he said. "When they say the name 'Jesus,' they think of some guy in South America."

Praying in the name of Jesus means that we are to pray like Jesus prayed. We communicate with Abba-Father, like Jesus did, in a father and son (or daughter) exchange of love. Our asking for his divine help is then an expression of our love for the Father as well as for whomever it is that we're praying. Our requests are communicated with an awareness that the Father is loving us more deeply, more actively, and more adoringly than any human ever could.

We don't ask in order to change God's mind, for he already wants what we want if it's good and if it will bring his Kingdom to Earth more fully. Memorize this! *He already wants what we want!* Imagine that. Petitioning God is only a matter of communicating—in a mutual exchange of love—what we already both want!

The problem is that most of us need help arriving at this truth.

We have been tricked into disbelieving it by the examples that gave us wrong information about God. Once again, we need to differentiate between God the Father and human fathers. Our human parents and other people have not always given us what we requested, even when it was God's will that they should. We've learned since early childhood that we can increase the likelihood of getting what we ask for by throwing temper tantrums, promising better grades, or making a convincing argument. Manipulation works—but not with God. And then we wonder why God is letting us down.

Manipulation is not love. God never manipulates us. Sure, he manipulates circumstances, but he lavishes upon us such freedom of will that it's impossible for him to even consider manipulating us into doing his will. His love is completely unconditional.

On the other hand, conditional love is built into our experiences so deeply (often called *codependency*) that it seems perfectly natural to expect it from God and to apply it to how we treat God. Watch out for manipulation sneaking into your prayers! For example, praying a novena (a set of prayers for nine days) can be either a sacrifice of time motivated by love or an attempt to bribe God ("If I do this prayer dutifully for nine days, You will give me what I want.")

The first time I prayed a novena as a new Catholic was in the late 1970s. I offered it for a loved one who had signed a contract to buy a condo in a nudist community. For all kinds of reasons, I worried about this. The urgency of the matter motivated me to try a novena of the Rosary. Amazingly, after only three days, the deal collapsed, and she changed her mind.

I wondered, "Am I required to finish all nine days of this novena?" Of course not. Sometimes we do need to fulfill our commitment by completing the novena, but God is not a legalist. The novena is not a contract, nor is it a bribe. My willingness to make a sacrifice of time because of love for my friend was all that the Father had wanted from me.

God gives us the desires of our hearts

Abba-Father's greatest desire for us is to live by faith, hope, and love: the faith to trust him, the confident hope of spending eternity with him, and the love that we receive from him here and now, which we share with others. Anything you desire that aids these three essentials of faith is a desire that God has planted in your heart.

A popular type of manipulation today is to bury a statue of St.

Joseph upside down when selling a house. In 1994, Ralph and I put our New Jersey house on the market so we could move to Florida. When too many months passed and the situation was getting dire, friends advised us to bury a St. Joseph statue. "Surely that gives him a headache!" I joked. "Why would he want to be buried in the yard and upside down?"

Ralph and I considered the truth behind the superstition: St. Joseph is the Patron Saint of the home. So, we sat down together, held hands in prayer, and asked the Father, in the name of Jesus, to sell our house quickly. We asked St. Joseph to pray for this, too. Thirty seconds after we said "amen," the phone rang. It was a real estate agent. She had a client who wanted to see our house. A half hour later, they arrived. By the end of the day, they gave us a contract to buy the house.

As much as St. Joseph is patron of the home, Abba-Father is infinitely more so. God already wanted our house to sell. Remember, he already wants what we want if it's good and if it will bring his Kingdom more fully to Earth. By moving to Florida, although we didn't know it yet, we would build Good News Ministries of Tampa Bay, which has gone global and is still very active.

Take delight in the LORD, and he will give you the desires of your heart. (Psalm 37:4 NIV)

Put the emphasis on "give." When we are in a good Father-child relationship with Abba, he puts his own desires into our hearts. We do not need to convince him with temper tantrums or promises to become better Christians or any convincing argument. *He* had the idea first and then *he* convinced us!

Every prayer (including petitions) should be an intimate dialog with the Father. For example:

Human: "Good morning, Abba! Thank You for the gift of this day. Please help me get that job I applied for, or else my family is going to suffer financial disaster."

Abba: "Trust me, my beloved child. That company will make you miserable. But I did place in you the desire to find work. Look elsewhere."

Well, usually God does not give us a forewarning so clearly. However, we do understand that the words "trust me" come with a darn good reason. The thing is, are we going to trust him so much that we relax? I don't mean we fall asleep waiting. We have to keep our eyes open and our prayer-ears listening for God to say, "Now! Go there. Do that. Knock on that door and it will be opened for you." Meanwhile, we're relaxing in his superior plan, his wisdom, and his genuinely deep concern for each of us.

While waiting for the results of our prayers, it's easy to wonder: What if I miss opportunities when I relax? What if by relaxing I become lazy? What if by relaxing I don't try hard enough? What if by relaxing the problems get worse because I'm trusting too much in God? These questions especially come to mind when we've tried our best and nothing happens, or it gets worse.

In reality, "nothing" never happens. In other words, something always happens whenever we entrust our prayer requests to our Father. It only feels like nothing happens because it's too soon for the fantastic plan that God is implementing.

Trusting God so much that we actually relax is not the same as doing nothing. We must try our best to be part of the solution to the problems we pray about. God wants a partnership with us. If we have a personal relationship with the Holy Spirit and we have the charisms that come with it, we can rely on the Holy Spirit to guide us on what to do, when to do it, and what to say. But remember that he gives this kind of help exactly when we need it, not sooner (see Matthew 10:19).

A popular saying is, "God helps those who help themselves." This can be misleading. Many people assume that they must first do everything possible and then leave the rest to God. The danger with this is that we too easily put ourselves in charge. We plan and plot and try to make a difference, and then when we fail, we finally turn to God for help. God wants a partnership with us that gives him the lead.

To entrust our prayer requests to Abba-Father is to relax in his love. It's an active (not passive) relaxation. It's a peace we feel while praying in joyful hope as our guardian angels tell us, "God's got this." It's a quiet readiness to spring into action when the Holy Spirit says, "Now! Go and do . . . "

When you pray in the name of Jesus, think of: "in the *love* of Jesus—my love for him and his love for us and Jesus' love for the Father and the Father's love for the Son." Praying in the *love* of Jesus is powerful because of the concern he has for us and the authority he has over evil. This authority came from the Father's love and is empowered by the Holy Spirit in an outward activity of love.

Praying in the love of Jesus also means "I want what Jesus wants," knowing that Jesus sees a much bigger picture than we do regarding the circumstances of our prayer request. Jesus wants what the Father wants, and the Father wants what Jesus wants. Praying to the Father in the name of Jesus is a loving union of divine desire.

Such prayer is effective because God is already speaking the answer of the prayer into reality. He desired it before we did, and he planted this desire in our hearts. We have but to participate in the loving union of divine desire by asking, thanking, and trusting. We entrust the timing and the ways and means to God (all three Persons of the Trinity).

The breaking of this union of love is what blocks the process of answered prayer. It happens often and all too easily. Any time we insist on doing things our own way, we are interfering with the holy union of divine desire. Likewise, praying for others is probably the most difficult challenge because their free will blocks God's plans. It's much easier to pray for the rain to stop!

Summer in Florida where I live has thunderstorms nearly every day. When it's raining, I usually ask God to stop the rain at my destination by the time I reach it, and sure enough, I receive what I asked for. Jeanie has a similar relationship with the Father. She experiences miracles nearly every day. She says, "I ask our Lord to free up a parking spot for me as I enter a super full parking area. Since God is a God of details, I even ask him for the small, incidental stuff, and often get it!"

Perhaps you, too, have discovered how easy it is to receive a miracle in matters that don't involve interference from the free will of others. Do you have people in your life for whom you've been praying a marathon of pleas for many years? And you're still waiting? God is waiting, too—but not passively.

I had been praying for 20 years for a loved one to return to the faith and to his family. During that time, Abba-Father has continually ministered to me. When I cried, I climbed into his lap and he comforted me, and I felt his tears.

This, by the way, is how to wait with faith, hope, and love instead of doubt, anxiety and fear. We climb into the embrace of our Divine Daddy. We continue praying with determination and sometimes with tears. We give our tears to the Father. We meditate on his compassion, his power, or whatever aspect of his goodness that we need from him at that moment.

Saint Nilus of Sinai (d. 430) advised: "Do not grieve if you do not at once receive from God that which you ask. He wishes to benefit you still more by making you persist longer in your patient prayer before Him. For what can be higher than to address one's converse to God and be in communion with Him?"

And Bishop Robert Barron has said:

> One reason that we don't receive what we want through prayer is that we give up too easily. What could be behind this rule of prayer? Augustine said that God sometimes delays in giving us what we want because he wants our hearts to expand. The more ardently we desire something, the more ready we are when it comes, the more we treasure it. The very act of asking persistently is accomplishing something spiritually important. So, when the Lord seems slow to answer your prayer, never give up.

Several times I've asked God, "What's the point of praying for this same person again today? You've got it. I've turned him over to you. Is it right to do this every day or does it mean that I haven't truly entrusted him to you and let go?"

His reply: "You have been experiencing a small portion of what I feel about the countless people around the world who are choosing a life of sin instead of turning to Me. This is union with Me. Thank you."

On other occasions he's replied with: "Every prayer you offer to Me for this person is like a gold coin being dropped into a piggy bank. The size of this bank keeps expanding as you keep praying. Someday, when this person turns back to Me and your prayers for him finally reach fruition, this bank will break open and the contents will pour over him, showering him with My Grace. The more you pray, the more glorious will be the graces he receives."

He has also told me: "This man will do great things for My kingdom." I heard that one almost audibly. So instead of waiting with grief or anxiety, I wait with hope and peace. I trust in the future reality that Abba-Father has revealed to me. God, who lives in eternity where there are no calendars and no clocks, has already answered my prayers. Time just needs to catch up with reality.

One day, about 15 years after this man chose to follow the voices of demons, I heard in my heart, very distinctly: "It is good." In that very instant I received more than those three words. God wasn't telling me that this man's choices were good. He was telling me that it's good for the family that he was not actively in our lives. And that was just the first of many benefits.

Simultaneously, in that moment of hearing "it is good," the Father filled me with so much peace that it completely and permanently replaced all of the anguish I had been suffering for so long. I never asked him to relieve my suffering in this way. He gave it to me because he cares.

No prayer is unproductive when it's an exchange of love with Abba-Father. In all of my unanswered prayers and in everything that I've waited for, God has worked miracles. And I've learned important lessons, many of which I've been sharing with you in this book.

Jeanie's story explains what happens when we pray persistently:

> For many years one of my brothers was an active alcoholic. After losing several jobs and returning to drinking after a court-ordered rehab program, he finally lost his driver's license permanently due to repeatedly driving intoxicated and having a car accident. I thanked God that he didn't injure or kill anyone. About 35 years of prayer passed before he stopped drinking! When I asked him why and how he did it, he said he just decided to stop and then did it. As sorry as I was to see how he had ruined a period of his life, I'm thinking that God wanted *my brother to desire* to give up drinking.

Today's Exercise: Write a love letter to Father God

Immerse yourself in the love exchange that exists between you and your Divine Daddy. Start by thinking only about his goodness. He has so much goodness to share with you! Begin your love letter with thankful appreciation for the ways he has been good to you. Tell him what that feels like. (Of course, he knows it already, but this writing exercise will help *you* know it more surely.)

Feel free to tell him everything and anything you want him to hear. However, when describing problems, instead of being a faithless complainer, thank him for already implementing a plan—even though you cannot see it yet.

Do you know what he is telling you in reply? Remember, prayer is an exchange of love. It's not one-sided.

Father God is saying to you, "I've got this. Thank you for joining me in waiting for time to catch up to reality. And all those beautiful words you wrote about my goodness? I feel the same way about you. I see that same goodness in you, even when it's buried beneath sin. I know your heart and it is joined to My heart. Come and sit with Me awhile, My precious child. Let's bask in the love that we have for each other."

DAY 19

Abba Is on Your Team

WHO FIGHTS FOR YOU? Defends you? Protects you? No one on Earth as much as your Divine Daddy does. Who wants to enter into your heart, your story, your journey through the everyday trials of life? No one on Earth as much as your Divine Daddy does. He is on your team, and there is no better teammate than God.

By now on your 30-day journey into the Father's heart, I hope you can picture God as a Good Father who is at your side assisting you in every difficulty. However, this is still a very limited view of him. Not only is he at your side; he is actively pouring his grace into your life and into the troublesome situations that you've been praying about.

> *If God is for us, who can be against us? He who did not spare his own Son but gave him up for us all, how will he not also with him graciously give us all things? (Romans 8:31-32 ESV)*

"If God is for us, who can be against us?" When you read this, which word stands out strongest to you: "if" or "for"? Many of us look at the word "if" and mentally translate it to, "I *hope* God is for me. I hope he *is* on my side."

The truth is this: He is always for us. In our trials and challenges, he is always rooting for us, cheering us on, and applauding us enthusiastically because he wants to give us the confidence we need to keep pushing forward to victory. He always wants what is best for us. He always does everything that we allow him to do in making our lives better *and* in preparing us to spend eternity with him in the most glorious way.

I call on you, my God, for you will answer me;
turn your ear to me and hear my prayer.
Show me the wonders of your great love,
you who save by your right hand
those who take refuge in you from their foes.
Keep me as the apple of your eye;
hide me in the shadow of your wings.
(Psalm 17:6-8 NIV)

By his grace—not by our merits—we are favored by our Divine Daddy. He is like any good father who graces his beloved child's life with goodness, but more so. Much more so than any human you and I have ever witnessed. Would you give your son a stone when he asks for bread? Would you give your daughter a snake if she asks for a fish? Jesus said, "If you, then, though you are far from perfect, know how to give good gifts to your children, how much more will your Father in Heaven give good gifts to those who ask him!" (See Matthew 7:9-11.)

Who else is on your team? Who is advocating for you? Who is giving you good counsel? Consider the most annoying problem that you've been working through. Who is supporting you in prayer? Who has given you ideas for possible solutions? Who has confirmed that you're on the right track or, if need be, that you're on the wrong track?

Each person in your life who has been helpful to you in any way is the activity of the Father sharing his gifts with you. Among the gifts that he brings to your team are full knowledge and perfect wisdom. He's keeping an eye on the bigger picture that you cannot see. He's causing circumstances to fall into place to make difficult situations easier (unless the harder way will produce better results).

In 2012, Ralph and I brought my parents into our home so that we could help them deal with the challenges of aging. However, before the necessity of doing this came to our attention, we had begun to build a new house. One of the obstacles that nearly blocked the project caused a design change that, at first, was very disappointing.

Our team included the builder (who prayed for us nearly as earnestly as we did), contractors (some of whom did shoddy work), the mortgage broker (who helped us get financing after other banks turned us down), and our future neighbors. God was the first member of the team. Ralph and I had invited him into the project the moment we began to consider finding land to build on.

Unbeknownst to us, God foresaw the needs of my parents—as well as my needs and Ralph's needs—and made good use of the so-called "obstacle" that ruined the design we had planned. The change enabled my parents to have their own home within our home, with separate porches, separate living rooms, and other features that gave us privacy.

God treats everyone with dignity, and the new design gave everyone a dignified way to live together without always being together. We've all been very grateful for this!

Abba-Father collaborates with us

Four years after we moved into our new home, my dad's strength was almost gone. Despite this, he decided that it would be nice to take a walk down our long driveway. His mind was set, so off he went without telling us.

Abba-Father knew what would happen next. As a good teammate, he had impressed upon me (during the intimacy of my morning prayer time) that I should work from home that day instead of driving to the office. I thought it was just laziness that kept me home. I didn't "feel like" driving that day.

Well, my dad fell before he reached the end of the driveway, and thanks be to God I was there to take him to the hospital. X-rays showed that he had broken his neck, but (thanks be to God again) not so severely as to paralyze him.

From the hospital, he went to a rehab center. Several months later, he had to be moved to an assisted living facility. As always, God—our #1 teammate—was working on our behalf to prepare a place that was right for my dad and for the rest of us. (Note: God rarely sends a text message revealing his plans. We had to do legwork that took us to his solution for our problems.) Mom and I checked out a couple of large facilities, but just two miles from our home was a 6-resident assisted living house. If he could live there, he'd receive more individualized attention and at a more affordable price. Plus, taking Mom there for frequent visits would be easy on Ralph and me.

Thanks be to God, a bed in that house opened up just as my dad's time at the rehab center expired.

You can be sure that your Divine Daddy has been actively working as your Best Teammate whenever your plans get altered for the better and you did nothing to make the change happen. In fact, you actively worked to keep and fix the original plan. The good news is: With Abba on your team, what goes wrong goes right. With Abba on your team, there's always a better plan in the works.

Judy experienced Abba's collaborative spirit in her marriage. During her childhood, she continually heard her parents argue and threaten each other. Whenever her dad returned home from work, her stomach cramped because she feared another fight between her parents. Although there was no physical abuse, there was plenty of emotional cruelty.

She says, "For as long as I can remember, I prayed to God during their arguments and afterward. He was my refuge, along with Mother Mary. I trusted him and hoped he would change things for the better."

However, God did not change her parents. He could not, since they did not submit themselves to his help. But Abba-Father did not ignore her prayers. As the best teammate she could ever have, he changed *her*.

Psychologists tell us that we tend to repeat the behaviors of our parents, even when those behaviors are unhealthy. Judy wanted to escape the pattern set by her parents. She chose to get a college degree so that she would not have to be dependent on a man and get stuck, like her mother, in a situation that she could not walk away from.

Judy was not interested in getting married, but Abba-Father wanted to make her life even better. "He gifted me with my husband," she says. "Today, I see how the grace of God affected my life. God protected me from falling into the unhealthy patterns that I experienced when young—and I had a good partner in marriage to help. I believe this only occurred by the grace of God."

To realize what we can rightly expect from Abba-Father, let's ask: What does a good collaborator look like? To answer this, let's look at what God as a collaborator is not. How are we inadvertently blocking his teamwork? What misconceptions need to be replaced by the truth?

Sometimes we treat God more like he's a dictator than a collaborator. In our desire to do what's right and receive what's best, we might pray, "What is Your will, Lord?" This is *not* a good way to pray—*if* we become paralyzed waiting for God to point the way.

He might be saying, "Go for it! What do *you* want to do? There are other options, but what you're thinking of doing is good. I approve. Count Me in." We don't hear that if we want certainty and prefer to abdicate our responsibility on the team.

A better way to pray is: "Here's what I'm thinking is best, Lord. Guide me. Fill me with Your Holy Spirit as I figure this out. You have my permission to change my ideas about it."

If, in his wisdom, he knows that we're making a bad decision, he warns us: "No, not that; let Me point you in a different direction." If we don't hear it and therefore make a bad decision, he says, "Don't worry! You've asked for My help. I'll put a stumbling block in your way. You won't get very far in the wrong direction."

With Abba on your side, it's safe to proceed in striving for a goal. It's safe to follow a dream. It's safe to work on a project that appeals to you. The reason it appeals to you is because (if it's not a temptation toward sin) Abba is the one who planted in you the desire for it. He gave you the idea. He gave you the talents that are needed for it. He gave you a passion for it. This is how his spirit of collaboration works.

My daughter, Tammy, created a theater production company, and Ralph sometimes got involved. He spent many hours at her side sawing and hammering to build sets and to co-engineer mechanical props. Tammy is good at it, but he has many more years of experience and know-how. Regardless, because it was Tammy's production, he didn't try to take over.

This is a good picture of Abba-Father's relationship with us. He's a collaborator, not a dictator. He's a team member, not a tyrant. He's much better at being the head of the committee than we are, but he doesn't push his authority on us nor "lord it" over us, although he certainly has a right to.

If a project, a ministry, or a goal of ours does not work against the mission of Christ, if it does not lead to sin, and if it pleases him, he will always join us in the effort. He joins us! He does not micromanage us.

Abba's team spirit

Collaboration is very important to God. He is first and foremost a collaborative team of Father, Son, and Holy Spirit.

Then he extended this teamship to include humans:

> *So God created man in his own image, in the image of God he created him; male and female he created them. And God blessed them. And God said to them, "Be fruitful and multiply and fill the Earth and subdue it, and have dominion over the fish of the sea and over the birds of the heavens and over every living thing that moves on the Earth. (Genesis 1:27-28 ESV)*

When Jesus came to Earth, he recruited a team, developed them into a community, and trained them to extend his mission. He told his disciples to pair up (the spirit of collaboration between humans) and go ahead of him into the villages, preaching, healing, and casting out demons (see Luke 10). He collaborated with their ministries by giving them his authority to succeed. He instructed them to take nothing along except a walking staff—not even money or extra clothes—making it necessary to rely on the collaborative spirit of the townsfolk.

Why do you think Christians have not been changing the world nearly as much as evil forces have been changing the world? It's because we have not been very collaborative. We have not imitated God's team spirit. The Church, which is the Body of Christ on Earth, has spent the last 500 years splintering into increasingly more and more denominations and non-denominations. Parishes have been divided into "my ministry" and "your ministry."

The truth is: We can still work together as collaborators. Our diversity does not mean we have to be unproductive. We're supposed to behave like we're on the same team.

> *For through Him we both have access to the Father by one Spirit. Therefore, you are no longer strangers and foreigners, but fellow citizens with the saints and members of God's household, built on the foundation of the apostles and prophets, with Christ Jesus Himself as the cornerstone. (Ephesians 2:18-20 NIV)*

It's very important that, when we serve in ministries, we behave like we are all part of the same Body of Christ. When we work together, we accomplish more than we ever could separately.

> *For just as each of us has one body with many members, and*

> *these members do not all have the same function, so in Christ we, though many, form one body, and each member belongs to all the others. We have different gifts, according to the grace given to each of us. (Romans 12:4-6a NIV)*

This is why I love to connect with leaders of other ministries. Sadly, my efforts to invite collaboration are often met with silence—not even an email saying, "Thanks but no thanks. We'll pray for you. Please pray for us."

While writing this book, I visited the leader of a prayer team of a neighboring parish and handed him a brochure about Good News Ministries. I hoped to explore what God might want to do if we collaborated. If nothing else, we could pray for one another. But the man refused to accept my brochure. He wouldn't even look at it. I mean, the polite thing would have been to smile, take the brochure, put it aside, and throw it away after I left.

Surprised by his reaction, I tried to explain my motives, fumbling with my words. But he cut me short. The rest of the meeting was awkward and fruitless. Analyzing it afterwards, I realized that the Holy Spirit had not given me words to speak. It would have been pointless.

How do you think our Divine Daddy felt about this?

Jesus told us what to do about uncollaborative, uncooperative people: *"If any place will not welcome you or listen to you, leave that place and shake the dust off your feet as a testimony against them"* (Mark 6:11 NIV).

Sweet Abba made good come from the rejection I suffered that day. He used it to reveal to me how deeply it grieves him and even *angers* him when opportunities for collaboration are ignored, neglected, or rejected.

Everyone who's a leader in ministry is very busy. I'm one of them. I know "busy"! But that's not a good excuse for ignoring the call to be collaborative with others. The lack of teamwork on individual committees and within ministries handicaps their mission. The lack of teaming up with other committees and other ministries handicaps the Church and the overarching mission of Christ.

The most common reasons for this lack of collaboration are (1) "I'm too busy; there's too much to do just keeping up with my own responsibilities," (2) "Teaming up with someone outside of my jurisdiction just doesn't fit into the plan," and (3) "I feel threatened by the prospect of someone coming in from outside; they might try to take over and change things."

The answer to the first and second reasons is: We're not adding more work. We're simply networking and discovering how we can help each other by sharing the wisdom, expertise, and connections we've gained. Doing this might actually save time and reduce workloads.

The answer to the third reason is: Collaborating does *not* mean merging ministries. It *does* mean joining as a support network where we can at least talk things over, share expertise, and pray for one another.

This is God's nature. Abba is on your team, ready and eager to share his wisdom, open doors of opportunity, and enable you to accomplish far more than you could ever do without him.

Abba-Father sides with you when others hurt you

God sides with us every time others reject us, misjudge us, or wound us in any other way. Listen to Roseann share her story:

> I have a vivid memory of when I was in third grade and I was wrongly accused of stealing from the milk money collected that I helped collect. A fourth grader had the duty of collecting milk money from the combined class of third and fourth graders. He collected from three and a half rows of students then told me to finish collecting from the remaining students. All of sudden, the teacher, a Religious Sister, stood by my desk and told me to leave the room.
>
> As soon as we both were outside the classroom door, she grabbed me by the collar of my uniform blouse and yelled at me. At first, I really did not know what this was about. Then she called me a thief. As she continued to yell, a classmate came out of the lavatory and must have heard what was being yelled.
>
> When it came to be lunch time, this girl went home for lunch, and I too went home for lunch. While at home, this girl reported the incident to her mother who, in turn, drove her daughter back to the recess yard where a majority of girl classmates were playing. The mother informed the students that I was a thief and warned them not to play with me.
>
> As I entered the schoolyard, the group turned and looked at me. In a few minutes, the bell rang to end recess. As I got into line with these fellow students, one of them told what this mother had said.

I felt so alone. Even before this incident, I had only a few playmates. Now it seemed like everyone stayed away from me.

I just wanted the school day to be over. I wanted to go home. When the school day ended, I ran home to tell my mother. My mother reported the incident to the parish priest that night. No recompense was made. The only result was that that Religious Sister did not return the following school year.

Roseann experienced through her mother what God the Father's support for us is like. It's a shame that the parish priest did not, and he will be held accountable for that when he meets Jesus face to face and Jesus says, "What you didn't do for the least of mine, you failed to do for Me" (see Matthew 25). His guilt is worse than the Sister who unfairly accused, judged, and condemned Roseann. And it's far worse than how her immature classmates responded to the misinformation.

Why? Because God cares about us so much that he gets angry at those who hurt us. He has placed people into positions where they can help, and he wants to serve us through them. So, when they shirk their responsibilities, he is blocked, we remain hurt, and their sin spreads. God sees their inner gem, which was made in his image, but he is greatly disturbed by the muck that's on their gem—muck that they are now throwing at us—and he stands by us, defending us. He holds them accountable for the damage.

He said, "If someone will not listen to the words that my prophet speaks, I will hold him accountable" (see Deuteronomy 18:19). Roseann's mother was the Lord's prophet when she sought justice from the parish priest.

Jesus warned his apostles-in-training about how a priest should handle those who are in his care.

> *Jesus said to them, "The kings of the Gentiles lord it over them; and those who exercise authority over them call themselves Benefactors. But you are not to be like that. Instead, the greatest among you should be like the youngest, and the one who rules like the one who serves. For who is greater, the one who is at the table or the one who serves? Is it not the one who is at the table? But I am among you as one who serves. (Luke 22:25-27 NIV)*

Let's unpack that.

- "The greatest should be like the youngest" is a common theme of Jesus. For example: "The first shall be last" and "The greatest should serve the least" and "Whatever you do to the least of My sheep, you do unto Me." Clearly, God is on the side of Roseann and her mother, and when the priest did not side with them, he failed to be a good representative of God the Father.
- "The one who is at table" foreshadows the table of the Eucharist, i.e., the altar at Mass. Roseann and her mother were parishioners "at the table." The "one who serves" is the priest, just like Jesus who taught very clearly, by word and example, that the priest is a servant.

So how does the Father feel about the failures and sins of clergy and others who are in Church leadership positions? It's bad enough when a non-Christian mistreats us. It's far worse when the mistreatment comes from someone who claims to be Christian but is controlled by evil passions and influences. And it's far more terribly worse when it comes from someone who stands up before the world in a position of "I represent Jesus in what I do."

Our Father said in Ezekiel 34:2 (NIV), *"Woe to you shepherds of Israel who only take care of yourselves! Should not shepherds take care of the flock?"* In verse 4, he said, *"You have not strengthened the weak or healed the sick or bound up the injured."* And then in verses 8 through 10:

> *As surely as I live, declares the Sovereign Lord, because my flock lacks a shepherd and so has been plundered and has become food for all the wild animals, and because my shepherds did not search for my flock but cared for themselves rather than for my flock, therefore, you shepherds, hear the word of the Lord: This is what the Sovereign Lord says: I am against the shepherds and will hold them accountable for my flock.*

And notice what he said in verse 16:

> *I will bind up the injured and strengthen the weak, but the sleek and the strong I will destroy. I will shepherd the flock with justice.*

This is what it means to have God on our team! The Father is quite stern with those who are in positions of helping—especially in leadership positions—yet choose not to strengthen the weak or bind the wounds of the injured, which includes those who have been emotionally injured or those whose reputations have been injured.

He is speaking about you, his beloved child, in Psalm 91:14 where he says, "Because he loves me, I will rescue him; I will protect him."

To those who have hurt you, he says, "I have tried to rescue you, too, but you rejected Me when you rejected My beloved child. Because of your stubbornness and your unrepentant heart, you are storing up wrath against yourself. The day of My Divine wrath is coming to you! My righteous judgment will be revealed. I will repay each person according to what they have done. You will receive My wrath and anger because, instead of seeking Me wholeheartedly, you are self-seeking, and you reject the truth and follow evil!" (See Romans 2:5, 6, and 8.)

To you, he says, "Because of your persistent desire to do good, and because you seek My glory and you honor Me and you want the immortality that comes from My Son Jesus Christ, I will give you eternal life." (See Romans 2:7.)

When we seek help from our Divine Daddy, he is already at our side, delighted that we're depending on him. He comes to us even before we realize we need him. He sent his own Son to us to serve as the Good Shepherd who goes after the lost to rescue them. He is swifter than we are at recognizing our needs, and he springs into action to do something about it.

If you think you have earned the Father's wrath and don't deserve his collaborative help, take this to heart:

The Father tells you, "This is what you are saying: 'My offenses and sins weigh me down, and I am wasting away because of them.' But as surely as I live, I take no pleasure in the death of the wicked. I prefer that they turn from their ways and live. Turn! Turn from your evil ways!" (See Ezekiel 33:10-11.)

And he continues: *"If someone who is wicked repents, that person's former wickedness will not bring condemnation"* (Ezekiel 33:12 NIV).

So, you see, there's a dividing line between the one who makes God angry by hurting one of his beloved children and the wounded child whom God defends. If we truly want to be holy, yet we sin, Abba knows our hearts and cherishes our good intentions. But the one who thinks more of himself than he does of the wounded one and has no desire to repent, that evildoer earns God's anger.

We've all been wounded by unrepentant friends, family, co-workers, priests, teachers, and classmates. In most cases, we don't witness God's wrath against them. But don't let your limited vision trick you into assuming that Abba-Father doesn't care about your sufferings. The story isn't over yet. The Father cares about his lost children as much as he does his hurt children. "Love is patient," as 1st Corinthians 13:4 reminds us. It might take some people a lifetime to repent, and the Good Father waits for them.

Meanwhile, Abba is giving you a way to be healed from your sufferings. It begins with forgiveness. He taught us through Jesus that we don't withhold our forgiveness while we wait for and hope for their repentance. We forgive in order to be healed. We forgive in order to be set free from the chains of their evildoings. Forgiving others works miracles for us.

Some of those who've hurt us might reject God's love even after death and end up in Hell. If you could see the Hell they are headed for now, you'd devote the rest of your life to praying for their salvation.

Abba optimizes your opportunities for success

Abba-Father sees problems and opportunities coming before you do, so he has been preparing you to handle them. It's happened to me many times. Think about how it's happened to you.

In 2006, I served my parish as Evangelization Coordinator. The RCIA Director resigned (due to work conflicts) from the wonderful work of bringing new Catholics into the Church. Abba-Father told me that the pastor was going to ask me to add this work to my responsibilities. This advance notice gave me time to ask the Holy Spirit what my answer should be. I preferred keeping my parish duties limited to part-time hours because I also had responsibilities in Good News Ministries.

When the pastor called me into his office, I knew what he was going to ask me, and I was ready with the answer. Serving as RCIA Director turned out to be one of my most-favorite-ever parish ministries.

I had sought God's wisdom and direction. But I was not a puppet pulled by strings in the Father's hand. Rather, we were a team. Here's how we worked together on this:

When the RCIA position opened, I had three options, all of which God presented to me as good choices. How did I know this? I recognized God's voice by the stirring up of divine energy within me. When a thought or idea originates from God, it comes with a passion to do it. When it's demonic, if we are followers of Christ and are filled with the Holy Spirit, the idea is unsettling and makes us feel uneasy. When it's simply our own thought process, any initial excitement about it fades as we pray while we give God time to make his Divine Will known.

My three options were: One, continue serving part-time as Evangelization Coordinator; two, quit and focus full-time on Good News Ministries, or three, take on full-time parish work.

The Father nudged me to "say yes" to the third option, but it was not a command. It was a clear but soft yes. If I had chosen to answer the pastor's call with "no," it would not have been a sin. But God's "say yes" did come with a caveat: The full-time work would be temporary. The Father knew that the day was coming when he would ask me to focus entirely on Good News Ministries.

When it was time to leave parish work one year later, I initially resisted. I loved what I did; I didn't want to give it up. But by God's grace I became more and more uncomfortable with staying there. And when I finally did quit, the timing was perfect for the woman who replaced me.

Throughout it all, God had my back. I wanted a clear "yes" or "no" from him about quitting, but he wanted me to make the decision. When the lack of a clear answer caused me to procrastinate, Abba-Father nudged me. Meanwhile, he continued working through me to powerfully evangelize the RCIA candidates and catechumens.

If I hadn't quit, Good News Ministries would not have grown into what it is today. This was Abba-Father's first choice for me, but he didn't command me to quit. If I had stayed in parish work, he probably would have blessed that too—for a while. What mattered most is that I wanted to do the Father's will. Because he knows what's best, he has my permission to guide my decisions. And he gives me freedom to participate in how his Divine Will manifests in my life.

That's teamwork. That's the spirit of collaboration.

Today's Exercise:
Discern God's guidance

Think about the last time you were indecisive after seeking God's guidance. Could it be that your indecisiveness came from Abba approving of multiple options? How did his collaborative spirit reveal itself?

DAY 20

The Father Reveals His Love Through Signs and Wonders

HOW OFTEN DO YOU see God's hand intervening in your day? The Father reveals his love through signs and wonders. We see it in the uncanny coincidences that make a difficult situation easier. He reveals his love in the perfect timing of an unexpected phone call from just the right person while we're wondering how to accomplish a goal. He sings to us through the songs playing on the radio that minister to us.

> *We must pay the most careful attention, therefore, to what we have heard, so that we do not drift away. . . . This salvation, which was first announced by the Lord, was confirmed to us by those who heard him. God also testified to it by signs, wonders and various miracles, and by gifts of the Holy Spirit distributed according to his will. (Hebrews 2:1-4 NIV)*

God the Father reassures us through many signs. He wants us to know that he is actively involved in our lives. He does this to build our faith and help us keep our salvation. He wants us to know that he really does care about us and about each situation that is troubling us, because signs are testimonies worth celebrating to build the faith of others.

The Father's concern for us is not supposed to be a mystery. It's not supposed to remain hidden. Our faith is made stronger when we realize that Abba-Father is with us.

On Day 8 of this journey into the Father's heart, I shared the story of how Abba gave us a sign that he approved of our purchase of land to build our house. I mentioned the sign of the unusual timing of the scientist from the Environmental Protection Agency showing up while the land surveyor was there, which made his job easier.

If Ralph and I had not been asking the Father for knowledge of his Divine Will, we would not have been looking for signs. It's important that this is the motivation for our sign-seeking. Signs can be too easily misinterpreted. We can make wrong assumptions about circumstances and coincidences. Demons can give us false signs. And we too easily overlook God's signs.

To detect genuine signs, we start with the humility of realizing that we can misread signs. We ask the Father to correct our thinking if we misinterpret a sign. And always (except in cases of emergencies) we wait for Abba to give us multiple signs: one sign confirms another.

For example, while we were still searching for land to buy, we jotted down the phone number of a builder whose signs we saw next to new construction projects. Mind you, there were other builders who had signs too. We "just happened" to take note of one particular builder. And it turned out that he was Catholic, like us, and he believed in prayer to help get projects done, like we did.

By itself, this was just a nice happenstance. Combined with the timing of the scientist and the surveyor and other signs (such as the hawk feather that I'll tell you about shortly), it was an important message from the Father.

Merry, the Indonesian woman who shared on Day 9 her discovery of Abba's blessings in the struggles she dealt with, received a sign from God in the color teal. She writes:

> I suddenly developed such fondness for the colour teal. Every time I saw any objects in teal colour, my mood just lit up. One day, I woke up with this strong desire to go to the chapel in my area, just to sit in front of the tabernacle and spend time with God. I went to the chapel in the morning. After praying for a while, I walked closer to the tabernacle and kneeled, then bowed my head to the floor to worship

> Jesus hidden in the Consecrated Hosts [that were behind the closed door of the tabernacle].
>
> As I bowed my head to the floor, I saw a small object in teal colour. (I assume it was the tip of a mechanical pencil.) I had no idea how that could be on the floor. The floor was always clean. I was so surprised. I was stunned. At the same time, I felt very special. God had given me a present, just for me, to remind me always of him. During my hard times or when I am in doubt, I always come back to that small object and remind myself that God cares for me.

Many people have experienced God's signs reassuring them. We especially need this after the death of a loved one. Here's the story of what happened to Dawn and her family after her brother passed away. She says:

> Our family's grief has been naturally overwhelming at times. During a celebration of our father's 80th birthday, most of the family (about 28 of us) gathered for a weekend at a camp on a lake. Each morning we were greeted by a beautiful red cardinal that perched on a narrow metal frame. It seemed impossible for a bird to land there. It would knock on the window, seemingly at us. We waited each day to see this curious action of the cardinal. That was 4½ years ago. To this day, when we go to this camp we are greeted by a cardinal. We have decided it is God's way of sending us a beautiful memory of our brother.

Abba's wonderful purposes

A sign is a means of communicating instructions or a direction to follow—like a stop sign or a highway marker pointing to the next exit. Our days are full of signs of God's presence; we just need to pay attention and learn how to interpret happenstances. But Abba-Father gets even more dramatic than that. He enjoys working wonders in our lives—miracles.

Gift Nyirenda from Malawi says:

> If we walk with God on our side, signs and wonders are a testimony that will always accompany us. I was desperate to find a job after getting married, just to support

> my family. I applied for different jobs related to my studies, but nothing seemed to work. I gave up and wrote no more applications. All of a sudden (without expectation) I got a phone call from someone I did not know inviting me to go and start teaching at a certain institution immediately. I could not believe how that worked, but there I was, teaching. I rose to be the Principal (Head Teacher governing all operations of the institution).
>
> To this day, I keep the faith that God does watch over us. Despite our little efforts, he will see us through the challenges we face. I know God is always watching over me and my family.

What do you suppose was the Divine Purpose behind the miracle that Gift received? Did God intervene just so Gift could support his family? No, there's more. There's always more. With God, there are always multiple benefits. Multiple purposes. Think about the testimony Gift's story became. It became an opportunity to evangelize everyone who heard it. Abba-Father wants all of his children to learn how he takes care of those who develop a close relationship with him.

As you read this chapter, the stories of others will trigger memories of your own experiences of God filling your life with his presence. When you remember something, pause to think about how your story can reveal the Father to those around you.

Revealing the Father is why Jesus worked many signs and wonders. The miracles proved the divinity and authority of Jesus—and all the Jews knew that divine authority comes from the Father. When we accept the divinity and authority of Jesus, we embrace the Father.

The miracles of Jesus helped people get to know Abba as he truly is: Yahweh, the God who is full of compassion, love, and helpfulness. Simultaneously, the Father's ultimate purpose for miracles was to reveal who Jesus is. Every miracle was (and still is) an invitation to understand that (1) Jesus and the Father are one, and (2) Jesus is the way for us to reach the Father and spend eternity in Heaven.

Most of the miracles that Jesus performed very purposefully addressed human needs: healing diseases, healing grief by raising loved ones from the dead, feeding empty stomachs, and setting free the victims of demonic control. His purpose was to show the Father's compassion for us in our human condition. It's God's love meeting us in our human suffering.

In the miracles of Jesus, we see a Father who is deeply affected by our pain.

> *When he went ashore he saw a great crowd, and he had compassion on them and healed their sick. (Matthew 14:14 ESV)*

In the miracles of Jesus, we see a Father who is moved to compassion because his children are suffering. He does not sit idly by, telling us to "just deal with it and offer it up." He is much more involved than that. He's a Daddy who kisses away our "ouchies."

> *On another Sabbath he went into the synagogue and was teaching, and a man was there whose right hand was shriveled. The Pharisees and the teachers of the law were looking for a reason to accuse Jesus, so they watched him closely to see if he would heal on the Sabbath. But Jesus knew what they were thinking and said to the man with the shriveled hand, "Get up and stand in front of everyone." So he got up and stood there. Then Jesus said to them, "I ask you, which is lawful on the Sabbath: to do good or to do evil, to save life or to destroy it?" (Luke 6:6-9 NIV)*

This scripture is packed full of signs and wonders:

1. The man with the withered hand did not ask Jesus for a healing. God's desire to reveal himself through signs and wonders does not depend on how we ask for it or whether we even try.
2. Jesus reacted to the misconceptions of the Pharisees and teachers. He felt compassion for the injured man while also feeling upset about the uncaring attitudes of the leaders of the synagogue.
3. Jesus demonstrated the Father's compassion by showing and then stating that the needs of people are more important than overly strict interpretations of the Sabbath law.
4. Jesus gave a name to their overly strict interpretation. He called it evil.
5. Everyone who heard what he said and saw the miracle he performed had the opportunity to be changed by it.

Imagine what the man with the healed hand did next. It's very possible that he began to follow Jesus everywhere. He was hungry to learn more about this miracle worker who cared about him so deeply—just like you might be if someone came along, singled you out, and showed you tremendous concern by miraculously healing you. Perhaps he was there when Jesus said, *"Anyone who has seen Me has seen the Father. The words I speak are not from My own authority. Rather, it is the Father, living in Me, who is doing his works through Me."* (See John 14:9-10.)

In the miracles of Jesus, we see a Father who cherishes his children who have such a close relationship with him that they are always listening to him.

> *For there is nothing hidden that will not be disclosed, and nothing concealed that will not be known or brought out into the open. Therefore, consider carefully how you listen. Whoever has will be given more . . . (Luke 8:17-19 NIV)*

May's story is an example of this. She loved taking care of her three grandchildren while their parents worked. One morning, her daughter-in-law called very early to ask her to take three-year-old Thomas to the doctor. Of course May said yes. But when her son (the child's dad) dropped the children off later than normal, he explained that Thomas had thrown up before leaving home and had to be cleaned up.

"Now," he said before hurrying back to his car, "there is no need to take him to the doctor because, after he threw up, his fever broke and he's feeling better."

May sent the two older grandkids off to school and then looked at Thomas sleeping peacefully on the couch. She reasoned that he was tired because he'd had a rough night.

What happened next can only be explained by a good connection between Abba and his daughter, May. She describes it this way: "Now you will all agree that any of us mortals would have to be insane to pick up a sleeping child and for no visible reason take him to the doctor. *Much less the emergency department.* However, I did just that."

She prayed the *Memorare* (a prayer that reminds us that the Blessed Mother of Jesus is ready to help us) on the way to the hospital. She says, "I truly felt like turning around, as I did not know what reason to give them for bringing him in. But something kept me going."

After they arrived, "Thomas walked with me from the parking lot to the emergency room. I felt stupid about my reason for bringing him. But in the short time while we waited for triage, he went into septic shock. The nurse took him from me and ran inside with him. His bowels and kidneys had shut down. His skin stopped getting oxygen. They worked on him for hours."

The staff congratulated May for saving her grandson's life. She told them who it was that actually saved his life: "Our God whose mercy is boundless."

Then one nurse said, "Yes it was God, but you were open to his instructions."

If May had not followed through on the urging that she had felt in her spirit—an urging that seemed illogical and unlikely—she would have soon found him dead on the couch. His window of recovery was only twenty minutes, and May had taken him to the hospital before that window had started its countdown.

One minute he had been walking through the parking lot like a normal kid. The next minute his fever went through the roof along with his heart rate. The room was full of nurses, each finding a vein, because time was crucial. His nails turned blue, his skin marble. Antibiotics were pushed directly from a syringe into his vein. One nurse was unwrapping the sterile syringes—countless syringes—while another nurse pushed them into the vein.

May held the oxygen mask to his face as her grandbaby lay weak on the bed. An x-ray machine was rolled in. His left lung was full of pneumonia. Heart medication was given to him and they called for a helicopter to be ready so that, once his heart stabilized, they would transfer him to a world renowned children's hospital.

When his heart finally stabilized, he started improving faster than any of the doctors and nurses thought possible. There was no longer a need to transfer him. He stayed in this hospital only four days.

Faith is a gift

"What do you want me to do for you?" Jesus asked the blind man.
"I want to see."
"Go," said Jesus. "Your faith has healed you."
Immediately the man received his sight. Then he followed Jesus.
(See Mark 10:51-52.)

Wait a minute! Did you notice what Jesus said just now? "Your *faith* has healed you." So does that mean that if we don't experience miracles it's because we don't have enough faith? It would seem so. Jesus often said, "You of little faith! Why are you afraid?" (Matthew 6:30) and, "You of little faith! Why did you doubt?" (Matthew 14:31) and, "If only you had faith the size of a mustard seed . . . " (Matthew 17:20).

Because of this, we assume that we must be diligent about increasing our faith. We turn faith into a project—a spiritual exercise. We work at it and work at it and yet make little progress.

The good news is: Faith is not a project. It's a gift. It's not something we do. It's something that Abba did for us when he created us in his image and then adopted us because we turned our lives over to him. He gave us what he has. Faith is our inheritance as long as we accept what Jesus did for us on the Cross.

Jesus destroyed the barriers between Heaven and Earth. He brought Heaven to Earth when he walked the Earth. *("The kingdom of God is at hand,"* he said in Mark 1:15, *"so repent and believe the good news!")* He showed us the door to Heaven when he died on the Cross, and when the Father resurrected him he opened that door. And then, after Jesus ascended to Heaven, he sent to Earth the Holy Spirit so that we could receive and enjoy our Heavenly inheritance while we're still on Earth. Faith is a gift of the Holy Spirit (see 1 Corinthians 12:9).

God gives faith to everyone who has the humility to follow Jesus. Remember the rich young man in Matthew 19:16-22? He turned away from Jesus, downcast because Jesus had asked him to give away his Earthly possessions in exchange for the treasures of Heaven. The young man did not have the humility to listen to what Jesus was trying to teach him. He was not interested in learning that love is the greatest wealth of all and that God's love is so extravagant it far surpasses every Earthly thing.

Lacking the humility to learn, the young man did not receive the gift of faith. God wanted to give it to him, but the man stubbornly trusted in his possessions and in his own efforts instead of the faith that Jesus revealed.

The gift of faith comes from the Father through the Holy Spirit thanks to what Jesus did for us. *"Anyone who believes in Me, as promised in scripture,"* Jesus said, *"will have the Holy Spirit flowing from within them like rivers of living water"* (see John 7:38-39).

After his resurrection, Jesus blew his life-giving breath onto his disciples and said, *"Receive the Holy Spirit"* (see John 20:22). On the Feast of Pentecost, after Jesus ascended to the Father, this breath of Jesus blew through the locked-up room where the disciples waited and prayed, and the Holy Spirit arrived like fire.

The Holy Spirit is still setting the followers of Christ on fire. We are still in the era of the Holy Spirit. And so, to be a Christian means that we receive—*and use*—the gift of faith as well as other gifts that come from God's Spirit. Why? Simply because the Father loves us so much that he'll do anything we let him do if it draws us closer to him.

"If you have faith the size of a mustard seed," Jesus said, *"you could command a mountain to move and it would be moved. Nothing would be impossible for you."* (See Matthew 17:20.) Why? Because our Good Father wants to help his children have strong faith. Life-changing faith. World-changing faith!

Jesus also said, *"It is the Father dwelling in Me who performs the works you've seen Me do. Believe that I am in the Father and the Father is in Me. Truly, truly, I tell you (this is important, listen up), everyone who believes in Me will be able to do the same works that I've been doing. In fact,* **you will be able to do even greater things**, *because I am going to the Father."* (See John 14:10-12.)

Why did he make this astounding promise? Because a good relationship with Father God through the help of the Holy Spirit is astounding! This scripture should deeply convict our hearts. Are we taking Jesus seriously? Or are we perhaps saying, "Who, me???" while looking around us to see if Jesus meant it for someone else.

Read the Book of Acts to see what Christian faith is supposed to look like. We should go running to the Sacrament of Confession for being mediocre compared to those people. We need to repent of ignoring and disbelieving what Jesus said in John 14:12 because the world very much needs Christians who reveal the Father through signs and wonders, like Jesus did. The people in our homes and parishes and workplaces need to learn what God the Father is really like.

Tragically, we have been influenced by the world around us. We've been living in the so-called age of science and reason, which has become—regarding matters of faith—the age of extreme skepticism. And yet, if we look for it, and if members of the Body of Christ communicate and collaborate in the sharing of testimonies, we find plenty of evidence that Abba is still sharing his love through signs and wonders.

Every day, ask the Holy Spirit to increase in you the gift of faith for miracles.

One Sunday evening, Ralph and I spoke to a youth group in a parish of our diocese. Afterward, a girl came up to us wanting to be prayed over for a healing. A year prior to this, she had been in a car accident that damaged her left shoulder. Even after physical therapy, she still could not raise her arm much.

"Will you ask Jesus to heal me?" she said.

Ralph and I both thought, "Oh no! She's expecting a miracle. Who am I to try it?" And then we looked at each other with resignation. We couldn't shoo her away. So, we began to pray for her. After a few minutes of pouring God's Fatherly love over her and commanding her arm to be healed in the name of Jesus, the Holy Spirit inspired Ralph to say, "Raise your arm. How high can you lift it now?"

She raised her hand—it went all the way up!

Ralph and I were as astounded and as overjoyed as she was.

Just before Jesus ascended into Heaven, he gave these final words as an exclamation point at the end of a very important chapter of salvation history: *"Go out into all the world and preach the gospel. Signs will accompany those who believe: In My Name they will drive out demons, speak in new tongues, pick up snakes without harm, and drink deadly poison without getting hurt. They will lay their hands on the sick, who will then be healed."* (See Mark 16:15-18.)

Evangelization is the mission of Christ. Signs and wonders are part of this mission because they prove that God is real and that he truly cares about us. Saint Paul tells us in 1st Corinthians 12:7, "To each of us the manifestation of the Spirit is given for the common good."

In verse 9, Paul specifically names faith as one of the gifts of the Spirit. He names other gifts, too, all of which empower us to be effective partners with Christ in his ongoing mission.

These gifts are supernatural wisdom, words of knowledge that do not come from our own heads, healing the sick, working miracles, prophesying to deliver God's messages, discerning the presence of evil spirits, speaking in a language that is not our own, and interpreting what was spoken in the unknown tongue.

As with all spiritual gifts, the gift of faith named here is given to us for the purpose of edifying others. Those who have the gift of faith are an inspiration to everyone around them—and a challenge to those who do not want to humble themselves and become followers of Christ. We show by our confidence in God that, no matter what happens, God is real, God cares, and God will back up our faith by turning everything, including bad things that happen, into good *("God works in everything for the good of those who love him,"* Saint Paul assures us in Romans 8:28).

The gift of faith for miracles is a fearless reliance on God's promises. This fearless reliance is not a self-built courage. We don't have to work and struggle to overcome the fear that God will fail to answer our prayers. We only have to realize that we have been given this gift and we have to make ourselves available as stewards of his gifts. Then we leave the rest up to God.

Abba builds our confidence

Signs and wonders are the Father's blessing on our decisions to faithfully live the gospel in our daily lives and to share it with others. He wants to activate in us the Holy Spirit's gift of miracle-working faith.

We often talk about *increasing our faith*. We might say, "Your testimony about how God answered your prayers has increased my faith." This is wrong language. Faith does not need to be increased! Even a mustard seed-size faith is enough to move mountains. When the Holy Spirit gives a gift, he gives it fully.

What needs to increase is our confidence in God's love, in his caring support, and in the promises he made.

Confidence grows by paying attention to all the *little* ways that Abba intervenes in our lives. We have big prayer requests and huge concerns. We're waiting for God to act in a mighty way. But when we focus on these, the waiting is hard. The waiting seems too long and we lose confidence in God's support.

Instead, look for the little interventions. That's when we discover that Abba's supportive hand is everywhere. Every day. And so our confidence grows.

One of my favorite ways to experience Abba as a Father who dotes on me is my raindrops prayer. As described in Day 18, I often ask Abba to stop the rain at my destination when (or before) I get there. Even if it's pouring when I leave my house, it's almost always a light drizzle or no rain at all when I arrive. And each time, I grin and thank the Father for blessing me once again.

There are countless ways that Abba dotes on us. And because we often fail to notice, he likes to repeat the gesture. Therefore, if something keeps catching your eye, ask the Holy Spirit what Abba is trying to tell you. For example, when Ralph and I began to draw up plans for building our house, I began to notice hawks. We'd be driving to the store, talking about the house, and a hawk would fly across the street in front of us. On another day, we were worried about not finding a bank that would give us a construction loan, and a hawk perched on a tree in the back yard just when I happened to look in that direction.

Hawk sightings became so frequent—at just the right moment—that I wondered if it was all just coincidental or if God was doing it. So, I asked the Holy Spirit. Not long afterward, I told a friend about it, and together we analyzed what a hawk might represent. What are hawks especially good at? They have keen eyesight, so much so that they can see tiny details on the ground from very high places. Like God!

From then on, hawk sightings reminded me that God is watching over every little detail and therefore we have nothing to fear.

This came in very handy one day when it seemed like we would have to cancel our plans to build the house. I was walking my dog and all of a sudden the air above us became filled with a flock of hawks circling and circling. But hawks don't flock! This had only one explanation: Abba was getting my attention again. Big time. He wanted me to feel very reassured that he was still watching over the details and that there was nothing to fear.

I praised him, "Thank you!" And immediately all the hawks disappeared. They flew away, I guess. I didn't see where they went. They were just *gone.* They had delivered God's message and were no longer needed.

Several months later, while the new house was under construction, I stopped by one morning to see the progress. After looking around, when I returned to my car, there was a hawk feather sticking up from the gap where the driver's door meets the frame of the windshield. It was jammed in there in exactly the right way to stand perfectly upright.

Think of how unlikely that is. If not for the hand of God placing it there, the feather would have had to float down exactly right, with the breeze exactly in the right direction and speed, and with the tip of the shaft pointed straight down when it landed on the car exactly in the gap.

I still have that feather. Every time I touch it, my confidence in God's caring support gets reinforced.

Today's Exercise: The signs and wonders in your life

Abba-Father wants his children to know that signs and wonders are a normal expression of his love. He doesn't reserve it only for the holiest among us nor for a select few wonder-workers. It is to be expected of those who live by faith.

I believe that one of the reasons why so many people have left the church of their upbringing and why so many of the unchurched are not even curious about the faith is because most believers are not revealing God's love through signs and wonders. The message we give: Either God doesn't care enough to work miracles or he's not real.

Human fathers (and mothers, clergy, and others in authority) are called to reveal what God the Father is like. This important responsibility requires being active in a life of faith. Jesus said this includes signs and wonders. Why? Because our testimony affects the eternal lives of others.

Jeanie found an opportunity to teach her four-year-old son about God's helpfulness when he accidently dropped his stuffed bunny out of the car window.

"We drove back to that area of the neighborhood and looked all around," Jeanie says, "but the bunny was nowhere in sight." She considered introducing her son to praying to Saint Anthony to ask God for help in reuniting him with his bunny, since he is the patron saint of lost items. But she hesitated. How disappointing it would be if the bunny didn't show up.

Then she decided to use that as a teaching moment and asked God to do with it as he wanted.

"About three weeks passed and our family went to our neighborhood club for dinner one evening. When we walked in the door, off to the side on an entry hall table sat my son's bunny! I just gloated and told the family that God honors our prayers and those of saints."

What are your stories about signs and wonders? Start a notebook of testimonies. How has God revealed his love to you in miraculous ways? Find someone to share a story with today.

DAY 21

Walking Through the Garden of Life with Abba

HAVE YOU NOTICED THAT in a garden it is easier to experience God than nearly anywhere else? Praying while sitting in or working in a garden is a direct connection to our Creator. Why is that? Because it's a return to the Garden of Paradise, the Garden of Eden. The close relationship that God intended to have with all of his human creations was first brought into reality here. He wants to restore for us the closeness that our first parents, Adam and Eve, lost.

> *Then God said, "Let the land produce vegetation: seed-bearing plants and trees on the land that bear fruit with seed in it, according to their various kinds." And it was so. . . . And God saw that it was good. (Genesis 1:11-13 NIV)*

One of my favorite chores is mowing the lawn. It's good therapy. In the summertime, it gives me a weekly opportunity to turn something scraggy and problematic into a smooth expanse of beautiful green. As I'm riding the mower, my inner child remembers playing in the expansive, green yard of my grandfather's childhood home. It's a wonderful memory. It instantly restores the feeling of being accepted and free to be myself.

When my parents came to live with Ralph and me, my dad sometimes commented on how much I enjoyed mowing the lawn. He said that it made him reminisce about how much he used to enjoy mowing. And then he always added: "I liked it so much that I never let anyone else do it."

Why did he like it *that* much?

During my teen years, he grew a vegetable garden in the side yard. It became one of his hobbies. I didn't pay much attention to it and he didn't invite me to. Only after I bought my first house did I discover the joy of planting seeds, impatiently waiting for them to sprout, and finally delighting over them as they turned into something on my dinner plate with a better flavor than anything I bought in a store.

I was participating in God's miracle of creation as well as the generosity of his abundance. My zucchinis grew huge and multiplied so much that I gave them away and still had too many!

> *Then God said, "I give you every seed-bearing plant on the face of the whole earth and every tree that has fruit with seed in it. They will be yours for food." (Genesis 1:29 NIV)*

> *Do not neglect to do good and to share what you have, for such sacrifices are pleasing to God. (Hebrews 13:16 ESV)*

Blaise from Uganda tells the story of how Abba-Father used his garden to help someone realize his great love for her:

> Recently, after planting in one of my gardens of 10 acres, I looked around and saw a lady. I didn't know her history, but I invited her to have the other 10 acres of land for planting beans. I wanted her to plant beans because this would improve the nitrogen in the soil, which would benefit my fruits. It was a 50-50 deal, but to her it meant a lot more. She wondered how a stranger could give her all that land.
>
> Some of the people who found out about it were not happy. I wondered why. Then one day she came to thank me. She said that she never expected anyone on Earth to love her and give her such a generous offer. She explained that she had been rejected by her husband 20 years ago and the whole community turned against her. Now she saw a miracle in her life: God had brought someone to show her his love. She told me that my offer had given her peace and

> joy simply because she felt God's love. She felt that he treated her special, choosing her to have that free land instead of anyone else in her village.
>
> Praise God! You don't know how high you are raising up a soul when you share generously. You don't know how much you will show God's loving closeness to someone.

As we can see from Blaise's story, a garden can produce not just plants but miracles too. The woman he helped received the miracle of hearing God choose her above all others.

God's voice is easier to hear in a garden—or out in any beautiful place in nature—than anywhere else. Perhaps you have other special places where it's easier to hear your Divine Daddy speaking to you, such as going on retreat or talking to a spiritual director. Not everyone can own a garden, but anyone can decorate a room with pictures of flowers and some live potted plants, and use it as a prayer room.

The only place better is where we can adore Jesus in the Blessed Sacrament of the Eucharist, for (as we learned on Day 12) he is the gateway to Heaven. He is our Mediator opening up communication between us and the Father.

It was in a garden that God spoke to a friend of mine to give me a message that I had not heard directly. This occurred in 1978 while I struggled with becoming Catholic. Though I longed to receive Jesus in the Holy Eucharist, I still heard in my heart the old Protestant messages telling me that I should never become a Catholic.

I had met my friend Mary in a Catholic Charismatic prayer group. Although I became very involved in this group, I still could not hear him inviting me to become Catholic. The noise of my Protestant upbringing drowned out his gentle, Fatherly voice.

Mary knew of my struggle. One day while tending to her garden, she heard God say very distinctly, "Tell Terry to plant her roots in My soil." She knew he meant the Catholic Church, and so did I when she gave me the message.

However, at first she resisted telling me. She replied to God, "But she won't like hearing this." And she wondered if it was just her imagination speaking—a voice she could ignore.

"Tell Terry to plant her roots in My soil," the Father's voice boomed more vehemently.

"But what if she won't believe me?" Mary wondered.

"Tell Terry to plant her roots in My soil!"

So she got up from the garden, went inside, picked up the phone, and called me. When I answered, she said, "Terry, I've got something to tell you. I almost didn't call you because I don't think you'll like hearing this. God told me to tell you this while I was gardening. He had to tell it to me three times before I agreed to call you."

"What is it?" I asked. I knew my friend was not the type of person who exaggerates or hears false messages. Normally, when someone says, "God gave me a message to tell you," they're really trying to impose their own will into it. They want to be God's prophet out of egoism, not humility. But Mary was not like that.

As soon as she gave me the message, I knew beyond all doubt that God was speaking through her. I knew it because I recognized the message. Father God had already been whispering into my heart, through the Holy Spirit, the command to stop attending Catholic Mass as a Protestant.

A few days after Mary's phone call, I contacted the priest of the parish that Ralph and I had been attending. He gave me instructions and brought me all the way into the Catholic Faith. And what a joy it's been to enter into the fullness of Christianity with all of its sacraments and other advantages of being Catholic!

Can you guess why Mary heard God's message for me in a garden—and not anywhere else?

One of my childhood's greatest treasures came from my grandmother. Nana gifted me with a small, framed picture of garden flowers. Imprinted on it was a little poem:

The kiss of the sun for pardon,
The song of the birds for mirth,
One is nearer God's heart in a garden
Than anywhere else on earth.

Although I had not yet planted my first garden, these words resonated in my soul throughout my teen years. I didn't know why at the time.

It's part of a longer work by Dorothy Frances Gurney (1858 - 1932), an English poet and hymn writer. Her father was an Anglican priest. Her husband, Gerald, was also an Anglican priest, but the two of them became Catholic in 1919. Perhaps she was my first patron saint!

God's Garden

The Lord God planted a garden
In the first white days of the world,
And He set there an angel warden
In a garment of light enfurled.

So near to the peace of heaven,
That the hawk might nest with the wren,
For there in the cool of the even
God walked with the first of men.

And I dream that these garden-closes
With their shade and their sun-flecked sod
And their lilies and bowers of roses,
Were laid by the hand of God.

The kiss of the sun for pardon,
The song of the birds for mirth,—
One is nearer God's heart in a garden
Than anywhere else on earth.

For He broke it for us in a garden
Under the olive-trees
Where the angel of strength was the warden
And the soul of the world found ease.

"The Lord God planted a garden in the first white days of the world"—the Garden of Paradise in which "God walked with the first of men." God's first desire for his relationship with humans was to be in close communion, walking together and talking as a loving Father with his beloved child. Today when we walk through a garden or any beautiful place that he created, we re-enter Abba's first desire for us. Jesus restored this communion when he broke open the gate to Paradise through his "yes" in offering himself as a sacrifice for our sins in the Garden of Gethsemane "under the olive trees."

God has been walking through gardens with people since he first created humankind. He planted the first garden ("their shade and their sun-flecked sod and their lilies and bowers of roses, were laid by the hand of God") and intended it to be a place of friendship and nourishment, feeding both the soul and the body.

Do you know what the first sin of our first human father was? Disobedience, yes. He ate from the tree that God had forbidden. But it's a much larger problem than that. We know that our first mother succumbed to temptation because she listened to the seductive tricks of the serpent and she allowed herself to be fooled by him. But what was Adam's temptation?

Our first father—like many fathers since—failed to serve his family as their protector against evil. Adam represents the man who has been given the truth but does not protect his soulmate (and by extension, their children) from the lies of the Devil. Where was Adam when Eve saw the serpent? And listened to the serpent? He *was with her* (see Genesis 3:6). Silently watching. Silently cooperating with the lie because he did not speak up. Silently agreeing to the sin when he accepted the evil fruit that Eve gave to him.

What then do you suppose was Adam's image of God? A Father who is silent when temptation strikes? Remember that Adam hid from God after the sin. He thought that he actually could hide! He is the father who teaches by his own behaviors the misconception that we can do whatever we please because the Father doesn't see us; God is not always with us.

What was your human father's prayer life like? His church involvement? His sharing of the faith with the family? How did he handle temptations? What did he teach about holiness and about how to handle temptations? Did he lead the family in fighting against evil? Or did he leave that mostly to the wife while he sat idly nearby, satisfied with his worldly pursuits and personal ideas of what's good and what's bad?

How did your parents show you God's garden?

We've been looking at the human authority figures who have negatively affected our image of God's Fatherhood in order to identify the misconceptions that we hold about Abba and for the purpose of seeing and understanding him more clearly. It's equally important to look for examples of how the humans in our upbringing have given us a good picture of Abba—and thank them if we can.

My parents had introduced me to the beauty of nature as soon as I was old enough to travel with them on vacation. Every summer, they took the family on an adventure that invariably included nature's wonders. We hiked mountain trails and we row-boated across lakes.

One year, my parents gave me a camera for Christmas. This initiated a lifelong fascination with photography, which for me is the art of trying to capture a moment of God's splendorous presence.

I have always felt closest to God when looking at the graceful lines of rolling hills and the jagged intrusion of rocky mountaintops against soft skies. Or the colorful array of flowers carpeting a field. Or the pattern of waves on the beach gently smoothing out stones over the long course of time.

Another treasure from childhood, which still adorns a special place in my house, is one of my first needlepoints. It says, "Seen as God sees them, all things are beautiful."

How did I learn the truth of that? From the perspective I have now, looking back over six decades of my life, I realize that my Divine Daddy had walked with me through all of the beautiful places I visited.

Here in Florida, there's a wildflower called lantana. When we moved into the house we built, lantanas decorated the yard and we cultivated them as bushes. Much of our property is wild, and it's intriguing to walk through it and notice how it changes every month and every year. A group of wild-grown Apostle Irises popped up near our driveway; how appropriate! And our yard, which had been nothing but weeds and dirt patches when we built the house, was sodded by God himself; the grass amazingly spread to full coverage, starting from a few shoots that we didn't plant.

You've felt it, too, right? The gracefulness of a flying bird captures our attention, and deep in our soul we feel the grace of God. The old adage, "stop and smell the roses," is an invitation to slow down from our distractions and busy agendas to connect with God the Creator-Father. He is walking beside us always, but we are not always aware. The beauty of nature was designed by God to make us aware.

The lessons of nature's beauty

Why do we waste so much time in front of the television when we could be delightfully entertained sitting in our back yards watching the shows that God produces? And they're all commercial-free! The dewdrops on the screen that covered the lanai of my previous house were, in my opinion, far more interesting than sitcoms, talk shows, and violent "action" movies. When the sun hits these tiny globes of water, they sparkle like shiny diamonds, and when God touches them with a gentle morning breeze, they twinkle like glittering stars. It's fun to watch!

It was also awe-inspiring. Just think, God placed those dewdrops on my lanai screen for me to enjoy! He created them with me in mind!

It's sad that we miss a lot of the shows he produces. Many are never seen by human eyes. What a waste! So many dewdrops never get appreciated.

Ahhh, but that's not true. God sees every dew drop in the entire world, and he thoroughly enjoys watching them twinkle in the sunlight. He started entertaining himself with dewdrops long before he created people with whom to share the spectacular view. Right now, wherever there are dewdrops, he's grinning from the pleasure they are giving him.

If he gets this delighted over simple dewdrops, imagine how wonderfully happy he feels about *you*. You are far more important to him than mere drops of water. Nothing that's good about you escapes his notice. He smiles over every nice gesture, every kind deed, every helpful outreach, every use of your gifts and talents, every God-designed personality trait, every prayer, every virtuous goal and dream, and everything else that reflects his holy nature. He gets more excited by you than what he sees in nature.

Think of the last time you walked by a stream. God carved the Earth to put that stream right there, knowing that someday you'd be there to see it. What's your favorite place in nature to visit on a day off or on a whole vacation? God created it to give you pleasure, to uplift you, and to give you respite from the stresses you've endured. Which window in your house do you most enjoy looking through? What do you see outside? God knew you'd eventually live in this house when he designed that masterpiece of a view.

Your Divine Daddy did all of this in order to help you sense his nearness. That's how special you are to him!

When tragedy comes like an earthquake and destroys some of the beauty in your life, Abba wants to give you his fatherly comfort to lean into.

When stress becomes overwhelming, Abba is inviting you to walk with him through a quiet garden somewhere far from the deafening noises of the world.

When a loved one breaks your heart, Abba is offering to you his heart—where butterflies gently flit on a soft breeze as a reminder that it's good to curl up in a cocoon while waiting for a new and better life to begin.

When a difficult decision challenges you with uncertainty, Abba is inviting you to find a quiet, beautiful place where you can be alone with him. He will speak to you. Shhh! Too many thoughts? Gaze at a leaf growing on a tree. See how it's attached firmly to the branch by a thin stem. When the branch sways in the wind, the leaf you're watching moves in harmony with the branch and all the other leaves.

Jesus spoke of himself as a vine to which we are attached. (See John 15:1-4.) Since he only said what the Father wanted to convey, we know that Abba is using the tree you now see and the leaf that catches your attention.

"I am the branch," he says. "You are that leaf. Apart from me you can do nothing but fall to the ground and wither. Together, we move in harmony. Relax in this truth and then think about the decision you're facing. Which choice peacefully floats on the breeze with Me? Which option does no harm to the other leaves? I've planted the answer in your heart, like a flower that will soon open and spread the fragrance of My love into the world."

Your spiritual garden

Jesus taught us that the Father is like a farmer sowing seeds:

> *As he was scattering the seed, some fell along the path, and the birds came and ate it up. Some fell on rocky places, where it did not have much soil. It sprang up quickly, because the soil was shallow. But when the sun came up, the plants were scorched, and they withered because they had no root. Other seed fell among thorns, which grew up and choked the plants. Still other seed fell on good soil, where it produced a crop–a hundred, sixty or thirty times what was sown. (Matthew 13:4-8 NIV)*

If we are fertile soil, Abba-Father plants seeds within us, waits patiently for them to sprout, and delights over us when we bear good fruit.

Our reactions to life's happenings reveal what kind of soil we've cultivated for our lives. Our reactions are based on how much we truly believe that God loves us and cares about us in all things and no matter what.

For example, if we are chronic complainers, our soil is shallow. In other words, our relationship with the Father is shallow. When life heats up, our trials burn up any trust in God's Fatherhood that has sprouted. We need to examine why we assume that difficulties are evidence that God does not care about us. This requires digging deeper into the soil and fertilizing it with the truths about God's Fatherhood that you've been learning throughout this 30-day journey into the Father's heart.

Furthermore, if our dirt has been trampled down by people who cruelly walked all over us, making us hard and our hearts cynical, and if we remain unhealed of this degrading treatment, the seeds of love that the Father sows in us are easily stolen away by the Devil who is telling us that we don't deserve better treatment or that we must seek revenge.

If we get angry easily, especially when we are unable to control our circumstances or we're unable to control that other person who has been sinning against us, this means that our lives are thorny. The Father keeps planting seeds of his blessings within us, but our prickly attitudes choke the growth of these blessings. We need to examine why we get so easily upset. We need to consider why controlling our circumstances and controlling other people makes us feel good. The answers, when revealed in the light of truth, become machetes chopping a path through the thorns.

Sometimes we listen to the truth only on the surface of the soil because we've been hardened by falsehoods. We hear the truth, but the winds of distraction, or turmoil, or false impressions blow it away. For example, we hear that God forgives us when we repent, but we have a hard time admitting our sins because when we were children we didn't understand the love behind the punishments that our parents meted out. Thus today we'd rather fool ourselves into thinking that a sin is not a sin in order to avoid what is really a wrong image of God the Father.

If our dirt is rocky—if we're hardheaded and hardhearted, and if we like throwing hard words at others—the seeds of love that God sows in us won't reach the soft soil underneath where the roots can grow. We need to be pulverized by the hardships of life (and you thought your life shouldn't be so dramatic). The setbacks and persecutions that so easily make us falter in our faith will either harden us or teach us compassion—it's our choice.

Sometimes we accept the truth joyfully but it doesn't last. We feel God's love only while life is easy. When the rocks stub our toes, we forget about Abba-Father's love and we try to deal with the problems our own way. We get rid of the person who's hurting us. We jump to solutions without praying for discernment. We get angry with God instead of seeing our sufferings as a connection to Christ on the Cross.

Sometimes we listen only half-heartedly to the truth. We let worldliness, anxieties, or cravings choke it off. We know about God's love, but we neglect to quiet down long enough to bask in it. We get too busy with our own agendas, too busy solving problems, or too busy rushing into decisions and the fulfillment of our desires. We fail to wait on God's perfect timing and wisdom.

To let the truth sink in deeply where it reaches fertile ground, we have to dig out the falsehoods that we believe and we have to learn why they are false. When the truth penetrates into the depths of our hearts, our lives become fertile soil and we bear good fruit—and lots of it! If our dirt is fertile ground for new growth, and if we let Abba-Father nourish us with his Word and refresh us with his healing waters, his love will sprout within us. Our awareness of being loved will grow and grow until it blossoms, and we'll produce a bountiful harvest of great love for others because what we receive is meant to be shared.

Fertilizer for your garden

Rich soil is fertilized soil—and you know what fertilizer is made of, right? Oh, how stinky it smells!

The natural fertilizers that hit the proverbial fans in our everyday lives can enrich our soil. For example, when we're so busy that we don't take enough time to sit quietly with the Lord and pray, life gets harder. Things go wrong. Mishaps bump into us—or rather, I should say, we stumble into mishaps because we're not paying attention to God's directions. How stinky must life get before we slow down and listen to the Lord?

When we don't take time to humbly listen, our hardened hearts are like the path that's been packed down so hard (usually from other people trampling on us) that the seeds lie on the surface as bird food. God's help never has a chance to take root in us.

When we do ask God for help, he doesn't answer our prayers like a magic genie. He waits to see how much we're willing to trust him. Our Divine Daddy wants to increase our trust. The only way for that to happen is for us to discover that trusting him—despite obstacles, fears, and personal wishes—really does produce good results. But if our faith is rocky, we soon begin to tell God how he should solve our problems, as if we know better than he does!

Sometimes we listen to what others are telling us instead of trusting the Father's voice. If what we hear in prayer does not contradict scripture and Church teachings, we should dare to trust it. We all have good-intentioned advisors amongst our friends and family who have not heard what the Lord is telling us; their worldly or misinformed advice is like thorns that choke out the truth. Our soil can be rich and fertile, but if we don't trust what God is telling us, the seeds he gave us will have no chance to do any good.

To succeed as rich soil that produces good results, benefiting from God's abundance, we have to submit to his hoe, letting him turn under everything bad that happens to us so that it rots into fertilizer that nourishes us and strengthens who we become.

The community garden

Nancy experienced a better understanding of how to have a good faith life when Jesus spoke to her in her imagination during dinner one day. She says:

> I was eating coleslaw with my fried shrimp and God said, "Look at the coleslaw. What's the main ingredient? Cabbage! The coleslaw started out as a head of cabbage. Has the cabbage changed in any way because of the other ingredients that it's mixed with? Not at all. It's still cabbage. But you didn't ask the waitress for a head of cabbage; you ordered coleslaw. Why? Because cabbage that's chopped and mixed with mayonnaise, vinegar, salt, sugar, and spices appeals to the taste buds much more than a plain piece of cabbage."
>
> I wondered, "Yeah . . . so what's your point, Jesus?"
>
> "The cabbage in the coleslaw is no less than what it was created to be. But if it had not given up each stage of its existence (the seed dying in fertile soil to become a sprout, the sprout growing into a head, the head chopped into slaw, the slaw mixed with other produce), it would not have become a delightful salad for your nourishment."

Nancy's parable of the coleslaw points out that true Christian faith is more than just sprouting as seedlings from good soil. Faith is bland unless it becomes part of a salad, mixing what's good about us with the good in others for the sake of nourishing those who want Jesus to minister to them. Or to put it another way: Faith is pointless unless we put it to use as part of a parish community and other faith-based groups that have a mission of serving others.

As seeds, we sink into the fertile soil alone, but we don't sprout alone. Growing requires Father God's participation as he waters us and gives us warm sunshine. However, our strongest flavors that help others in the biggest way come from the hardships we've endured. So Jesus comes along and plucks us out of the comfortable ground to do an important work for his Kingdom.

Meanwhile, life on Earth chops us into slaw, ruining our nicely shaped cabbage head. Instinctively, we try to pull ourselves back together. Even if we understand the value of using our troubles for the good of others, we're still shredded and our flavor is still limited. We need to mix it up with others. We need to find people who are like mayonnaise and spices for us. We need to become part of a community of other vegetables and fruits. (Yes, even people who are "fruits" and "nuts" add flavor to the salad!)

Only as a community can we offer the world a taste of what God's kingdom is really like. Only together do we make a good harvest in the Kingdom of God. Christ's love, power, and salvation are revealed through our teamwork and collaboration with one another, not through our isolated individuality.

Today's Exercise:
Identify what the Father has planted in you

Think about the richness of your soil. Notice what's growing in your daily circumstances. What decisions and behaviors are producing God's love and nourishing others? Here is where you truly believe that God loves you.

DAY 22

Satan's Goal: Destroy God's Fatherhood

To ensure the healing of our father-shaped wounds while we purify our image of God's Fatherhood, it helps to realize how the wrong image is continually being inflicted upon us. Major influences in the culture we live in have been severely undermining the image of fatherhood for a long time.

> *Sing to the Lord a new song, / his praise from the ends of the earth, / you who go down to the sea, and all that is in it, / you islands, and all who live in them. / Let the wilderness and its towns raise their voices; / let the settlements where Kedar lives rejoice. / Let the people of Sela sing for joy; / let them shout from the mountaintops. / Let them give glory to the Lord / and proclaim his praise in the islands. / The Lord will march out like a champion, / like a warrior he will stir up his zeal; / with a shout he will raise the battle cry / and will triumph over his enemies. (Isaiah 42:10-13 NIV)*

God designed his own warrior nature into the hearts of men. He calls them to stand up strong in zeal, raise the battle cry, and triumph over the Devil for the sake of their families, for the protection of the Church, and for the conversion of the world. Men are wired to be champions. It's not surprising, then, that the Devil has been redesigning manhood.

For the past several decades in the U.S. where I live—and elsewhere in cultures that have been influenced by the U.S.—there has been a strong and pervasive effort, in the name of "equality," to make men less masculine, more feminine.

Allie Stuckey of Prager University explains this in-depth. She says, "The growing problem in today's society isn't that men are too masculine; it's that they're not masculine enough. When men embrace their masculinity in a way that is healthy and productive, they are leaders, warriors, and heroes. When they deny their masculinity, they run away from responsibilities, leaving destruction and despair in their wake." (see **youtu.be/U-kxdyJs6y8**)

Feminized men are passive men. Passive men don't stand up to evil to stop it. Passive men don't lead their children to Christ. Passive men don't make heroic sacrifices for their family, parish, community, or country.

So, who do you suppose is most delighted by this? Who is the primary influencer behind it? Who gains the most by mocking and destroying traditional fatherhood? The Devil, of course.

If anything can be labeled as the primary strategy of the Enemy, this is it: Destroy human fatherhood to destroy God's Fatherhood. It's a *coup d'état* to take over as the illegitimate father of the human race. As stupid and unrealistic as it is (because God will never be defeated), demons have been waging this war for eons.

The war began when one third of the angels got upset over God's plans for the human race.

> *Then another sign appeared in heaven: an enormous red dragon with seven heads and ten horns and seven crowns on its heads. Its tail swept a third of the stars out of the sky and flung them to the earth. (Revelation 12:3-4 NIV)*

The word "stars" has long been used in Jewish literature to refer to angels; both the stars and the angels are called "the Hosts of Heaven."

> *Then war broke out in heaven. Michael and his angels fought against the dragon, and the dragon and his angels fought back. But he was not strong enough, and they lost their place in heaven. The great dragon was hurled down–that ancient serpent called the devil, or Satan, who leads the whole world astray. He was hurled to the earth, and his angels with him. (Revelation 12:7-9 NIV)*

This battle was fought before the creation of humankind; Satan was already present in his fallen state when he tempted Adam and Eve in the Garden of Eden. Why did angels become demons? Why did they choose to fight God instead of remaining in the splendor of his magnificence?

The full picture of Satan's rebellion is unknown to us, but theologians have given us a lens into why it happened. Saint Thomas Aquinas proposed that Satan sinned by desiring to be "as God." But why was he so interested in usurping God's role as the Father of the human race?

According to the general consensus of theologians and mystics, angels were created with full knowledge. Their awareness of God and his plans was not limited by physical brains like we have.

"The Church teaches that Satan was at first a good angel, made by God" (*Catechism of the Catholic Church,* paragraph #391). He was also called Lucifer, or "light bearer," when he was a good angel (see Isaiah 14:12-15).

In full knowledge of what God planned for the world, all the angels knew that humans would be created with a lower nature. They also knew that the Second Person of the Trinity, Jesus the Son, would unite himself to humans by becoming the Divine Incarnation, God living as a man. And they knew that all the hierarchy of Heaven must bow in adoration to the Incarnate One and be subject to the authority of this God-Man. Furthermore, they knew that they would be given the vocation of serving humankind.

This was too much for Satan and some of the other angels. They committed the life-changing sin of pride and rejected God's wisdom on how good it would be for angels to serve humans. But despite their repulsion of this servitude, the reality remains: They are still subject to humans who unite themselves to the authority of the Divine Incarnation. (Feel free to laugh at the irony of this.)

> *The seventy-two returned with joy and said, "Lord, even the demons submit to us in your name." [Jesus] replied, "I saw Satan fall like lightning from heaven. I have given you authority to trample on snakes and scorpions and to overcome all the power of the enemy; nothing will harm you." (Luke 10:17-19 NIV)*

Because the demons decided to rebel against God's plans with full knowledge of how wrong they were, and they understood with clarity that it would lead to eternal separation from God, their choice was irrevocable. "There is no repentance for the angels after their fall" (*Catechism* paragraph #393).

Their rebellion continues to this day, and in our lifetimes we have witnessed the increased activity of the war they have been furiously waging against God. However, they know they can never defeat God. So, they turn their anger, hatred, and battle strategies toward those who were the reason for their fall: the humans they do not want to serve.

Enemies invade countries that don't belong to them in order to take over and claim the land as their own. It's the same with our supernatural enemy: Demons invade human lives with the goal of taking over, stealing from God, and destroying the Kingdom of God (as ridiculous and impossible as this is) to pervert it into their own kingdom. The Church is both their primary target and their primary demise, since this is where the Kingdom of God reigns strongest. However, all humankind is their target. Demons hate even those who do not unite themselves to the Divine Incarnation. And those who are not united to Christ are the weakest and easiest to conquer and enslave.

Satan's number one priority is to replace God's Fatherhood over humankind with his own evil fatherhood. Therefore, it's no surprise that human fatherhood has been under attack in insidious and obvious ways. Jesus called Satan "the father of lies" (see John 8:44). By invading human fatherhood, demons invade God's Fatherhood and try to make *him* look like the liar.

They take advantage of our limited awareness. They know we like to supplement what we don't know with whatever will fill in the blanks. They know we are prone to getting wrong ideas about Father God based on what human fathers are like. They use our human limitations against us, creating false images of Father God, thus interfering with and even destroying the beautiful Father-child relationship that God wants to have with humans.

This demonic strategy not only weakens families but also prevents many of us from discovering and embracing God as the True Father.

Roseann's story reveals how the Devil undermines God's Fatherhood even in good Christian families:

> My parents were 17 years apart in age. They were very good Catholics but they did not have a devoted love for one

> another. My mother fulfilled both parenting roles because my father worked a lot of hours, including weekends, to provide well for our family.

The father of lies says, "Hey dads, you're not being a good father unless you provide well for your family. Your family needs and deserves a bigger house, a car for every driver in the family, and expensive vacations. To give them what they want, work harder. Work longer."

> I gained my father's attention when I began to play sports. He came to as many games as he could. But my mother never came to my games. She was so busy doing all the chores of the household, even cutting the lawn while omitting the tender, precious moments of bonding with her children.

The father of lies says, "Hey mothers, your children need to learn to be unselfish. They should realize that you don't have all the time in the world to give them. Every chore is important. The house must be kept clean. What will the neighbors think if they come in and see dusty shelves, toys strewn about, and old newspapers piling up on the end table? And by the way, don't ask the children to do your chores. They can't do it as well as you can; you'll only have to re-do it anyway."

> When my father wasn't working, he was doing charitable works for the church. Charitable works had been my father's life when he was single.

The father of lies says, "Church activities and charitable works are highly commendable. You sin if you don't make them a top priority. Therefore, they take precedence over all family activities."

Roseann's parents seem, on the surface, to be good people. And they were, but the Devil hated them for it and took advantage of their vulnerabilities. Like many well-meaning parents, they believed the Devil's sneaky lies that the culture had normalized. Mixing good parenting with worldly ways is like punching a hole in a soccer ball. One good kick and the ball (or the children's image of God's Fatherhood) deflates.

Roseann explains how it happened to her:

> There was a lot of quarreling between my parents. My father did not like my mother telling him what to do or what

> was needed. Quarreling really hurts the love atmosphere needed for a good and enriching family life. The biggest stumbling block in my relationship with Father God is the fear of disagreements.

Regarding how the culture normalizes the Devil's strategies, she says:

> I believe that men no longer know how to be fathers. In today's culture, so many men are missing in their role as fathers. And many mothers desire to be like men: having jobs or careers equal to men, having girls' weekends, drinking alcohol equal to men, not taking the time to raise their children in the formative years of life. And more families are divorced rather than married once and for life.

We can see the effects of damaged fatherhood in the divorce rate. Separated parents often, however inadvertently, diminish the role of fatherhood. When dads are portrayed as the bad guys by hurt and angry moms, children usually develop a wrong idea about fatherhood. When dads spend their weekend custody visits focused only on having fun with the children, the authority and leadership of fatherhood gets lost.

Fatherhood is undermined when the husband does not serve as the head of the family. It happens when his God-given authority is ignored, rejected, abused, or supplanted. God's design for the family is for both mother and father to discuss things openly with each other, seeking God's will together, submitting to one another respectfully, and using fatherly authority as an extension of God's authority to empower what is decided. But in many homes today, the mother is dominant; she takes control by having the last say. The children are directed by the father to "go ask your mother," or the opinion of the father is overruled by the mother-in-law or the wife, who has the louder voice.

Certainly abortions destroy the value and importance of fatherhood, as they destroy the human life of the unborn child, who was created by Father God himself. Abortions rob both parents of the family life that God had wanted to bless them with, which further devalues fatherhood.

There are many insidious ways fatherhood has been undermined, which most of us have blindly succumbed to. We meant well, we thought we were doing what's best, but in fact we inadvertently cooperated with the Devil's strategies. Let's reveal them so that we can draw closer to God *and* so that we can help others meet the real Father God. If you find any of these revelations uncomfortably true for you, remember that Abba-Daddy is holding his arms out to you, wanting to draw you into his love and his way of loving. Don't let the Devil accuse you; let the Holy Spirit convict you. Take steps to break free from what is not like God's Fatherhood, little by little, one day at a time.

Ready? Consider how materialism undermines fatherhood: Careers are often prioritized as more important than parenting. Modern-day lifestyles often create the assumption that luxuries—such as a nicer, bigger house, a TV in every room, and expensive vacations—are good for the children, but let's be honest. It's a treadmill that inadvertently undercuts family life and prevents people from seeing God as a Father who cares more about us than anything else.

And here's another uncomfortable truth: The picture of God as a warm, loving Daddy who holds us close to his heart begins to be blurred at the very beginning of childhood if the baby is not held enough. It happens when babies are toted around in portable car seats more often than they are carried in the arms of their parents. It happens when infants are bottle-fed solely for the convenience of the mom instead of being nursed. It happens when their formative years are spent with babysitters who are not family members, even though both parents are alive. And it happens when family interaction in the home is replaced by TV shows and video games.

There are many more ways that worldly culture has opened the door to the infiltration of Satan's anti-Father strategies. It's not surprising, then, that God Fatherhood is disrespected by many adults today. Our society is full of adults who are still seeking the father they needed during childhood while at the same time ignoring God, the only Perfect Father. They miss out on his love because they think that faith in him is irrelevant. Having accepted the Devil's lies, they decide for themselves what is right and what is wrong, thus usurping God's authority. And thus, the Devil has enlisted them in his fight to destroy God's Fatherhood.

Television's role in the downfall of fatherhood

Consider what the history of television reveals about Satan's strategy. When I was a child, a popular sitcom on television was

"Father Knows Best." In the 1950s and early 60s, the culture was much gentler than today's. The father of lies was in the early stages of corrupting modern culture. His influence was not as widespread as it is today.

TV shows told stories of intact families, and we laughed at the foibles of children who still had a lot to learn. We all knew that the stories did not depict real life, but that's why we enjoyed them. They gave us an escape that reassured us of what the ideal should be. Family entertainment gave us a picture of what families could strive for.

By the time I became a teenager, the culture began to glorify rebellion against parents, Christian morals, and anything else that stood in the way of a self-centered worldview. Divorce was given approval in child-friendly family shows. Women were often depicted as smarter than men.

Some shows dared to tackle important social justice issues, such as racial equality. This was good, but they didn't stop there. Whenever a rebellious mindset is in control, it *invents* injustices—like the fallen angels did when they believed it was unjust of God to ask them to serve humans. A common scene in family shows was (and still is) a battle of wits between parents (usually divorced) insulting each other while the children turn it into an opportunity to get what they want (of course without suffering any emotional wounds). Thus evil is made to seem good and good is made to seem evil.

A prime example of entertainment being used as a battle tactic was the very popular 1970s show "All in the Family." Archie, the father, was a very prejudiced bigot who dominated his wife and needed to be corrected by his smart-mouthed daughter and her out-of-work, somewhat stupid husband. The feminist daughter represented the new world that viewers were being invited to forge, where women are supposedly better than men and women's rights are supposedly more important than everyone else's, including the rights of children. (The legalization of abortion in the U.S. occurred two years after this series began.) Archie Bunker represented everything that viewers didn't like about their own fathers. By laughing at the stupidity of Archie, we could stop crying—however briefly—about the hurts we suffered in our childhoods.

Little by little, fatherhood was increasingly undermined. By the 1980s and 90s, while my children were growing up, TV sitcoms often portrayed dads as buffoons. The kids were smarter and wiser than the parents. TV characters who were divorced became more prevalent. And the trouble-making ex (always the father) was either undeserving of family life or else he was blatantly uncaring. At best, he was absent.

And then came shows in which fathers portrayed the glorification of corrupt moral values as if this were a good thing. They were womanizers or lazy drunks or hustlers or con artists or selfish connivers. Lust replaced love.

And think of the abundance of shows, both comedies and dramas, that featured childless couples. If any did have children, their families were almost always very small. The message: Children are unimportant.

Next on Satan's agenda: TV shows that normalize homosexual love and children being raised by gays and lesbians. At the same time, clergy and other teachers of the Christian Faith have failed to put enough effort into explaining why homosexual love falls far short of the love of God. There hasn't been enough faith formation about the goodness that God intends for the holy bond of marriage between one man and one woman who are committed to each other for life. Although Pope Saint John Paul II emphasized it in his teachings about the theology of the body, they've not been disseminated through good faith formation in every church community. And so, there's plenty of room for Satan's agenda to infiltrate even the Church.

Fatherhood has lost its godliness. However, Father God is not going to let the Enemy keep winning. He is already working a plan to restore holiness to fatherhood and to families. We'll look at this in upcoming chapters.

Of course, television was not the only tool that the Enemy has successfully used. The history of TV merely gives us a clear timeline of the undermining of fatherhood.

The destruction of true fatherhood has even infiltrated the lives of Christians, for two reasons. One, we are taught by the culture in which we live, with its subtle, decades-slow creep of moral relativism invading our thoughts and ideas. Two, the Church has failed to teach and glorify holiness in families as strongly as the Devil has worked against it. This is why so many people today need to read this book and find help from our Divine Father.

Thankfully, there have been signs of a reversal of the fatherhood-destroying trend. One example was the popular series "Last Man

Standing," which first aired in 2011. Despite its mix of Christian morals mingling with worldly ways, and conservative-minded characters with liberal-minded ones, fatherhood was usually handled with respect. After it was cancelled in 2017, so many fans clamored for its return that another network rebooted the series a year later.

Dealing with the Devil

We who love the Lord our God and embrace his Fatherhood want to save unborn children from abortions. We want to promote marriage as the union of one man and one woman. We want to help young adults realize that children are gifts who are more important than self-centered goals.

However, I believe we will not be able to win these battles until we first help others gain respect for fatherhood. Nor will many of our evangelization strategies work without it. We don't like hearing this because it sounds too discouraging. So, let's examine this more closely.

Consider how culturally-influenced people react when countercultural Christians stand up for the truth about abortion, homosexual marriages, and other hot topics of morality. You probably loved ones who fail to understand the truth because they don't understand God's Fatherhood—his loving, protective fatherhood. The truth feels threatening to them. This means God feels threatening to them. They don't know that he has their best interests at heart. They don't know that all of his commandments, as revealed in sacred scripture and the traditional teachings of the Church, are prescriptions for a life that they'd be thrilled to live if only they would trust him.

We could say to them what Jesus said:

> *Why do you not understand what I say? It is because you cannot bear to hear my word. You are of your father the devil, and your will is to do your father's desires. He was a murderer from the beginning, and does not stand in the truth, because there is no truth in him. When he lies, he speaks out of his own character, for he is a liar and the father of lies. (John 8:43-44 ESV)*

Satan knows that with the loss of respect for human fatherhood comes the corollary loss of respect for God's Fatherhood, leading to an increase of sin and estrangement from God.

If we're going to reverse this trend and heal family wounds by uplifting fatherhood, we have to introduce people to Abba-Father—the real Father as he truly is. To turn our world around by evangelizing it, changing hearts for Christ, we have to help people heal from their wrong images of God's Fatherhood. And this begins by purging our own false images of God from our thinking.

After 21 days of working your way deeper and deeper into the Father's heart, shedding the various ways that you've misunderstood God because of misperceptions caused by imperfect parents, how much closer to him do you feel now? Granted, it's a process that needs to continue long after you finish reading this book. When we've thought one way (the misconceptions) all of our lives, the old ideas have formed deep ruts. Your new understanding of God's Fatherhood has given you new wheels for your journey through life, but they will repeatedly slip into the ruts. This is normal. This is not a problem as long as you remember to stop, readjust the track you were thinking, and consciously work at creating new ruts. The longer you use your new insights about who Abba-Father is and how much he cares about you, the deeper the new ruts will become and, therefore, the easier it will become to stay in the new way of thinking.

What if everyone you know overcame their misperceptions, too? How would a better relationship with Abba-Father change their lives? How would it impact *your* life? Multiply this out to everyone they know. Then imagine it rippling out to others and eventually to even more people. How would this change the world?

This is what the Devil wants to make sure will *not* happen. Demons are aggressive about stealing God's children from his Kingdom. They are constantly trying to turn people away from the Divine Father and to keep them away from him. They are thieves who want to kill and destroy any type of fatherhood that reflects God's true nature (see John 10:10).

It's no accident of societal evolution that the image of fatherhood has been undermined more than motherhood or childhood.

God's strategy

God gave protection to his image when he gave the commandment that protects families: *"Honor your father and your mother"* (see Exodus 20:12). Regardless of how imperfect our parents were—how abusive, rejecting, or trouble-making—we defeat Satan and his strategies by honoring them.

What does "honoring" look like? It does not mean overlooking the ungodly ways of our parents. Nor does it mean justifying their sins with remarks like, "Well, he treated me the same way his own parents treated him; it's what he learned." While this is true, it's also true that each person is given the brains and opportunities to choose to break free from the problems of their upbringing. Each person has the freedom to do what is right: to heal from and overcome the bad behaviors they learned. (The exception to this is when demons have taken possession of a person; an exorcism is needed before they can have such freedom.)

Forgiveness is our first step in becoming free of a parent's unholy and unhealthy behavior patterns so that we don't fall into the trap of imitating their patterns. It's a common problem: We can abhor a parent's behavior, declaring that we will never treat our children the same way, but we end up being all too much like that parent. Forgiveness is not enough to break the mold. We have to consciously and deliberately watch for the sins of the parent getting repeated in our behaviors and then go to the Sacrament of Confession to receive God's supernatural grace in overcoming it. With the help of the Holy Spirit, and the Sacraments of Confession and the Eucharist, we can succeed in becoming the wonderfully good person God created us to be.

Honoring our parents does not mean putting them on a pedestal or even praising them publicly. It's doing good to them, whether they deserve it or not, because of their inherent dignity which God gave them.

It's doing acts of love, not just saying that you love. It's being concerned about their needs and doing deeds of caring. Many people today claim to love their parents while actively rejecting them; this indicates that the Devil has gained access to them. They have succumbed to the very prevalent lies of the father of lies and thus became his pawns of division and the destruction of fatherhood.

Even the worst of parents are to be honored as God commands. This does not mean that we respect them. In fact, everyone has to earn respect, even parents. God commands us to honor our parents regardless of whether they have earned our respect.

Nor does "honoring" our parents mean ignoring their sins and unhealthy behaviors. Whatever they're still doing that should get stopped or healed or changed: If we can help them overcome it, great. If we cannot, we need to set boundaries and enforce them. We need to protect ourselves from being manipulated by Satan's strategies. And if we have children in our care, we need to protect them, too.

Jesus commanded us to love our enemies (see Matthew 5:44). Let's face it, he was talking about our parents, too, not just criminals, terrorists or that nasty boss at work. A parent is an enemy whenever he (or she) does anything that opposes God's Fatherhood. And because Abba-Father cherishes what is good in us, parents are enemies when they oppose our God-given dignity.

To love our enemies, we have to first forgive them—even if it's seventy-seven times (see Matthew 18:22) every day. The next step is to do good to them or for them—even if the only good we can do is pray for them. When we do this, we defeat the Devil!

Forgiveness is often difficult, but it becomes easier when we realize that we are not approving of their sins. We don't have to wait for them to become remorseful. Forgiveness is the act of relinquishing to God our desire to retaliate or to see them get punished. It's choosing to let go of the hurts that chain us to what they did wrong, so that God can heal us. Forgiveness sets us free from the hold they have on our emotions.

Once we're free, we can honor them by reaching out to them with unconditional love. We can honor them by connecting to the heart of their soul, which was created in the image and likeness of God. We can focus our relationships on what is good in them. We can give them the love that God has given to us.

In doing this, a miracle happens. We become even more aware of Father God's love for us. We feel closer to Abba than ever before.

> *Then Peter came to Jesus and asked, "Lord, how many times shall I forgive my brother or sister who sins against me? Up to seven times?" Jesus answered, "I tell you, not seven times, but seventy-seven times." (Matthew 18:21-22 NIV)*

The problem is that people don't change as quickly as we want them to, and some people don't change at all—at least not that we can see. To be able to forgive them seventy-seven times, we have to make the conscious decision to respect and love people the way they are right now, even while disapproving of and disliking what they do. If they never improve, can we love them anyway? If their lack of improvement causes us more problems, can we love them then?

Forgiveness is not based on what others do, but on what we need. Forgiveness releases us from the hold that their sins have on us. It's a decision to protect our joy and not allow others to control our feelings. And for this to happen, our forgiveness must be sincere. We can say with our lips that we've forgiven others, but if our happiness depends on others changing, we remain frustrated and angry. Ongoing anger is a sign that our forgiveness is only lip-deep.

Joy through forgiveness is dependent upon God, not on what others do or don't do. We choose to forgive based on the love that God has for sinners, not on whether they deserve it. And then, because we've given them mercy, we receive God's mercy and we're released from the emotional chains that have bound us to the damaging effects of their sins.

This often is enough to heal our pain. When it's not, we might need the help of a therapist. The nature of the pain is frequently multi-layered, especially when dealing with childhood hurts. To be fully healed we need to identify one layer at a time and choose to forgive several times.

To protect ourselves from the return of pain, or when the person we forgive is still actively repeating their offense, it helps to examine why we feel hurt even after we forgive. Ongoing pain comes from unmet needs. As long as we keep wanting others to meet those needs, we feel hurt over and over again. However, *nobody* except God can meet all of our needs. Unless we look to God for all that we need from others, the pain of our wounds is going to control us until the day we die.

To defeat the Devil, we merely have to do the opposite of what he wants us to do. He wants to divide you from God; therefore, love God with all your heart and all your mind and all your soul, passionately, without being lazy about it or half-hearted. And the Devil wants to divide families; therefore, forgive the family members who have sinned against you. (Note: Enforcing safe boundaries is not being divisive. The person you need to protect yourself from is the one who caused the division. You can love them unconditionally and do good for them from afar. This, too, defeats the Devil.)

Today's Exercise: Write a letter of forgiveness

Think of the parent who most damaged your thoughts about God's nature as Father. Write a letter to that parent without ever showing it to him or her. In the letter, explain how the damage was done and why this hurt your relationship with Abba-Father. Then, in writing, give forgiveness to that parent. Include a prayer that asks God to forgive this person as well.

Don't just think about it; write it. This will activate the cortex of your brain, resulting in a quick calming of your emotions.

You can repeat this exercise for the other parent and anyone else who has given you wrong ideas about God's Fatherhood.

If you need to recall what the wrong ideas about God are and what the truth is, review the previous chapters of this book.

DAY 23

The Tears of Abba for Your Healing

Do you know yet how much Abba-Father cares about you? As your Perfect Father, he cries when you cry. He feels the pain that parents feel when their child suffers. He longs to give you healing.

> *Oh, that my head were a spring of water and my eyes a fountain of tears! I would weep day and night for the slain of my people. (Jeremiah 9:1 NIV)*

When my daughter, Tammy, was sixteen, she had to endure major back surgery to straighten her spine. As her parents, Ralph and I endured the waiting room with some difficulty, waiting for assurance that everything had gone well. Sometimes my mind drifted to the operating room and I imagined her lying there with her insides exposed and bleeding. Quickly I diverted my attention—it was too much!

However, this was nothing compared to how I felt during her first few days of recovery. As she suffered in the hospital bed, the morphine drip that relieved her pain was not nearly enough to make her feel good. She hurt so bad that she cried and she was very angry that Ralph and I had put her through this.

I wanted to cry with her. I wanted to hold her in my arms, but I couldn't because the bedrails, the tubes, and monitors blocked me. I wanted to make her pain go away, but I was powerless.

To pull myself together, I took a little respite in the hallway. Still emotionally exhausted, I re-entered her room. When she saw me, she furiously vented her pain at me. I wanted to be strong for her and find a way to comfort her, but I couldn't and I began to cry. So I ran from the room and sought out the hospital chaplain. I cried deeply and uncontrollably in his office. I thought I should be at Tammy's side and felt guilty that I couldn't be there right then.

My tears poured out from the deep well of empathy that I felt for her as her mother, which had been accumulating since the doctor first told us that she needed surgery.

When a parent suffers the pain of watching a child in pain, it's an immersion into the loving heart of the Father. We're experiencing a tiny portion of how our Divine Daddy feels when any of his children suffer.

Does it surprise you to picture Father God crying? All of the emotions we feel—if they are healthy, come from caring, and are rooted in love—come from God. We feel a tiny portion of what he feels. Every time you were hurt by one of your human parents or some other authority figure, or by any other person or situation, Abba-Father cared so much that he cried the tears of a totally empathetic parent—he cried *for you.*

Imagine how he feels watching his children suffer the destruction that comes from their sins. He knows that they are killing their souls and are headed to an eternity without him. The pains of Hell are far worse than any earthly suffering.

Tears are very fatherly. Saint Paul wrote about his tears in his letter to his spiritual children in Corinth:

> *For I wrote you out of great distress and anguish of heart and with many tears, not to grieve you but to let you know the depth of my love for you. (2 Corinthians 2:4 NIV)*

We cry for others because we care. Abba-Father cries for us because he cares—more than we can imagine.

The tears of Abba are why he sent Jesus to us as healer and why he gave him the mission of bringing us to Heaven. To accomplish this, Abba would have to watch his most Beloved Son suffer the torture of a flesh-ripping whip and an excruciatingly painful crucifixion.

When Jesus dined with his disciples at the Last Supper, the Father knew what lay ahead. How do you think he felt about it? When Jesus rose from the table and left the building to go to the place of his betrayal, how did the Father feel then? In the Garden of Gethsemane, Jesus cried out to him, begging to be spared the pain of the scourging and crucifixion but nonetheless willing to do whatever the Father asked of him. Jesus cried so deeply that his sweat was like drops of blood (see Luke 22:44). How did the Father feel about denying his Son the rescue that he had prayed for?

He felt what any parent would feel who has to watch their child suffer, but he felt it more deeply and more keenly than you or I ever could. I believe that Abba-Father cried throughout the ordeal. He did not cry for himself. He did not cry because of any pain that he himself felt. He cried because Jesus was in pain. And he cried because many people were going to live and die rejecting what his Son did for them.

Jesus is still in pain today. He said, "Whatever you do to the least of these, you do to Me" (see Matthew 25:31-46). When others hurt you, they hurt Jesus. When we hurt others, we hurt Jesus. And the Father cries in deep parental love for Jesus as well as for those who have been hurt *and* for those who inflict the pain.

The Father cries whenever we wound Jesus through our flaring tempers, our prejudices, our judgmentalism, our injustices, our selfishness, or anything else that inflicts suffering upon others. When we betray Jesus by hiding our faith in public, the Father cries again. And when we repent of our sins and seek reconciliation with Jesus, we delight the Father. He dances!

God, of course, is multi-dimensional, never feeling just one emotion at a time. While the hammer drove spikes into the hands and feet of Jesus, Abba-Father cried and simultaneously rejoiced that the resurrection was coming. He knew the difference that Jesus' suffering would make in your life and mine. And he knew what it would do for everyone else who accepts this gift.

Abba's tears can heal you

Think about the tears of Abba—especially the tears that poured from deep within his soul for *you*. This can heal you.

He sorrows over the wounds that were inflicted upon you. He cried when you were a child suffering from something that should never have happened. Knowing this can set you free from the misconception that he is a stoic authority figure who is doing nothing except waiting for you to get into a better mood.

For every tear that you've shed because of evils that others have inflicted upon you, Abba-Father has shed many tears. Yes, he knows the future healing you will receive. He knows the good that will come from the bad. He knows that his Son Jesus took your wounds with him to the Cross so that you could be healed. But knowing what's good does not stop him from feeling extremely sad when something bad happens to you.

Abba-Father wants you to pour all of your sadness into his heart. Sorrow expressed in prayer is very valuable. Our tears are like precious diamonds to him; they are not bullets that shoot our frustrations Heavenward to force God to hurry up and make things better. Each tear is itself a prayer.

Since God will not go against anyone's free will, he will not stop every abuser or betrayer. We cry out, "God! You can make this stop. Why are You not stopping this?" And as bad as we feel, he feels it more. He cries for you and he suffers the pain of watching his other child make hurtful decisions. His other child is so far away from him spiritually (at least in regards to how you've been hurt) that he cannot hear the Father's loving voice offer him a better life. Nor can he hear the Father's angry voice command him to stop hurting you. Nor can he hear the Father's invitation to find healing from the wounds that contributed to his hurtful behaviors.

What old wound in you still hurts? What disappointment in childhood did you suffer because your human father was not like God the Father? What damaged your image of God? What makes you angry about how you've been treated? Is there anything that this 30-day journey into the Father's heart has not healed yet? Anything that still brings tears to your eyes when you reflect on it deeply enough?

Climb into Daddy-God's lap and cry about it. Or visit him in any way that suits you, and let yourself cry on his shoulder. This is a prayer!

Sorrow expressed in prayer is very valuable. It's prayer beyond words. When you surrender your anguish into the heart of the Father, your tears are very precious prayer-diamonds that he treasures. He says, "You are precious in my eyes. I honor you. I love you. Do not be afraid, for I am with you" (see Isaiah 43:4-5).

To surrender means you've quit trying to change what you cannot change. You might still wish you could, but you're giving God clearance to move in and comfort you no matter what does or does not happen.

Abba's peace can heal you

Surrendering is usually not easy. But the sooner we realize that we cannot change the person or the situation that's causing us to suffer, the sooner we can let go of it and receive healing. I once had a good friend of many years who suddenly was no longer a friend upon whom I could rely. We used to have wonderful conversations about living the faith. We had shared our spiritual journeys with each other. I had been able to confide in him when I needed help discerning God's will. He had helped me discover what God wanted me to learn from my trials. He was also a good friend to my husband Ralph.

When the reality of the end of this hit me, I turned quickly to my Divine Daddy. I felt his compassion but I cried out, "Why? How did this happen? What can I do to make it better?"

I could not make it better. There was nothing I could do but surrender it to God. And this was a process. Over the course of the next couple of months, I cried several times because of the loss of the friendship. It took me that long to get over the shock of it ending. There was no apparent reason for the change. And talking to him about it only made it worse. Oh, we remained "friends" but only in a cordial way.

We met for lunch one day to catch up on family and work news. By the time we left the restaurant and went our separate ways, I had finished surrendering to God my desire to restore what we used to have. It had become obvious that we were no longer on the same page in discussing matters of the faith. What was important to me was not something that he wanted to think about, let alone talk about.

As I walked to my car, I remembered the scripture about walking away from those who don't listen to us:

> *As you enter the home, give it your greeting. If the home is deserving, let your peace rest on it; if it is not, let your peace return to you. If anyone will not welcome you or listen to your words, leave that home or town and shake the dust off your feet. (Matthew 10:12-14 NIV)*

Let's paraphrase this in the context of losing friendships:

> *As you visit someone, give him your Christ-like greeting. If he is deserving, the peace of Christ will rest on him; if he is not, the peace of Christ will return to you and comfort you. If anyone will not welcome you or listen to your words, leave that person and shake the dust off your feet. Go instead to those who are genuinely good friends–those who listen to you and who care about you.*

The moment I shook off my desire to get back what was lost, I felt peace. And the peace provided healing. Today, if this friend wants to restore our friendship, I'm open to testing it. But he can only pass the test if God has worked in him to make it happen. This is what it means to surrender something to Abba-Father.

Abba's compassion can heal you

Knowing how Abba-Father feels about your tears can give you great comfort. In his omniscience, he sees what lies ahead. He has a plan to turn the evil that has happened to you into a blessing that's far greater than the amount of suffering you've endured. There is much reason to rejoice, and yet he is joining you in your sorrow—he is so full of compassion!

To become more aware of this compassion, we first need to discover what's interfering with our view of it. To do that, we should ask ourselves: "What am I focusing on?" There's a fine line between holy tears and self-pity. If we remain focused on our woes, we become paralyzed in self-centered misery, which never really heals. If we remain focused on the people who have hurt us and what we expect from them, we become blind to the compassion of God and we only get more frustrated. To escape this trap, we need to let go of the other person's hold on us. We need to forgive.

Remember, forgiveness does not mean that what the other person did was okay. Nor does it necessarily mean that we're reconciling with them, because that might be unsafe or impossible.

We forgive others because God has forgiven us. We forgive because we want to be free of the other person's control of our emotions. We forgive because we know that others do bad things because bad has been done to them, and we know that there's a divinely-designed gem under all the muck of their sins. We also know that they are being controlled by the wrong messages that formed their behaviors and the sins that others committed against them. We feel sad that they have not opened themselves yet to the Lord's healing love.

Holy tears come from a heart that's in pain—not only for ourselves but also for those who have hurt us. We realize that the evil they have done to us comes from a deep hole in their hearts caused by not receiving all of the love that they needed. They know less about God than we do, and we feel sorry for them because they have not yet opened themselves to the compassion of Abba.

To whatever extent we feel sorry for them, this is but a tiny bit of how the Father feels for them.

By gaining a better understanding of how Abba feels, we begin to see things as God sees them. This can be helped along by the Holy Spirit.

Abba's vision can heal you

God desires to share with you a view of the bigger picture that he sees. Part of that picture is the good that will come from what has been bad.

Sufferings are devastatingly terrible when they're pointless and unfruitful. Abba-Father always wants to turn grief into joy. Therefore, he only allows us to suffer in ways that have the potential to become beneficial to us *and* to others. He gives meaningful value to our pains by embedding within them a mission—a purpose—that will minister to others and which will also bring the Kingdom of God more fully to Earth.

In the same way that Jesus provides salvation to us through what he suffered, our sufferings can be used to help others. The sacrifices we make, the forgiveness we give, and the healing that we've experienced are united to the mission of Jesus. When we look for ways that our sufferings can benefit others, we discover the ministry that Abba-Father wants us to use as a victory cry.

This is a measuring stick that will show you whether you are doing well or poorly in your spiritual growth. When you learn to appreciate suffering because you know there's a value to it, you are doing well. In fact, when we appreciate suffering, we appreciate God, and by appreciating him, we please him greatly.

Searching for the bigger picture that heals is usually most fruitful when we discern it through the help of a trusted friend or a professional counselor. God speaks to us through them, and when he does, we can more easily recognize that the message was not merely a product of our own wishful thinking.

Joanne is a long-time friend of mine who knows something about my dad, our father-daughter relationship, and the caregiving that Ralph and I gave him during his final years. Her prayer support has meant a lot to us, but in two short sentences she said something to me that made a huge difference. I felt their healing impact in a way that only happens when God is the author of the message.

She said, "You didn't get the father you needed. Your father got the daughter he needed." Suddenly, it no longer mattered that my dad had not fathered me the way I needed. A higher purpose came delightfully into my awareness. God had put me into this family for a mission that no one else could do like I could do. You, too, have a mission that no one else can do like you can do.

To help me fulfill my mission, Abba-Father gifted me with a spiritual director who led me through the inner healing that opened me to the Father's perfect love (as described on Day 2 of this book). He also gave me a difficult friend who—through his alcoholism and codependency—taught me important lessons that helped me become my dad's caregiver. And Abba did many other things that enabled me to respond to my dad in healthy, loving, holy ways. All of which helped me to write this book for *your* benefit.

Today's Exercise, Part 1: The bigger picture

Consider the bigger picture of a situation in which someone in your past caused you to suffer and you still feel the pain of it today. How have your experiences with it benefited someone else? This is far greater than simply finding relief for your own heartbreaks. Armed with this knowledge, you can discover that the past no longer drags you down. The past becomes fuel for a greater purpose. And this purpose becomes fuel for the healing you need—and for the healing that others need!

* * *

Knowing Abba's Divine Will can heal you

One of the stumbling blocks that prevent us from moving forward in healing is the question: "Why me? Why do I have to suffer this?" Jesus answered this in a revelation to the mystic Luisa

Piccarreta. She lived from 1865 to 1947 in Italy and is known as the "Little Daughter of the Divine Will." She is being considered for canonization as a saint and is currently defined as a Servant of God. Confined to her bed since the age of 16, she offered her sufferings to Jesus for the salvation of sinners. Unable to eat, she miraculously survived on nothing more than the Holy Eucharist.

Jesus often visited her, and on January 30, 1909, he said:

> My daughter, in almost all of the events that occur, creatures keep repeating, over and over again: "And why? And why? And why? Why this illness? Why this interior state? Why this scourge?" And many other whys. The explanation of "why" is not written on Earth, but in Heaven, and there everyone will read it.
>
> Do you know what "why" is? It is egoism, which gives continuous food to love of self. Do you know where "why" was created? In Hell. Who was the first one that pronounced it? A demon. The effects produced by the first "why" were the loss of innocence in Eden Itself, the war of untamable passions, the ruin of many souls, the evils of life. The story of "why" is long; it is enough to tell you that there is no evil in the world which does not carry the mark of "why."
>
> "Why" is destruction of divine wisdom in souls. And do you know where "why" will be buried? In Hell, to make them restless for eternity, without ever giving them peace. The art of "why" is to wage war against souls, without ever giving them respite.

Jesus is not forbidding the question but rather the *continuance* of the question. It can be very helpful to investigate why something has happened so that we can learn from it. But when it becomes a lament, a complaint, then we are doubting God. We are assuming that he does not care enough to make things "right" (according to our own idea of what should happen). We are disbelieving that he is involved in what is happening to us.

By grumbling about what has happened, we presume to know a situation better than God does. We behave as if our will is more important than Divine Will.

There's nothing wrong with being unhappy about a situation—especially when it occurs due to someone's rejection of Divine Will. Our sin begins when we dwell on it instead of looking for the good that God can bring from it. We sin by being inconsolable, blocking our Divine Daddy from giving us his love and compassion—blocking him by insisting that we cannot be happy until he does what we want him to do.

It is *not* sinful to be dissatisfied with earthly imperfections, i.e., the trials that occur because we live in a world that is no longer the Garden of Eden. We have a natural longing for Heaven. We were created to live there with God for all eternity. It's our true home, and instinctively we know it. That's why we complain when we experience something unheavenly here on Earth.

Sin sets in when we expect perfection even though perfection is only possible in Heaven. We cry, "God, I'm tired of this trial! When are You going to make it end?" We complain, "God, You obviously don't understand how bad this problem is for me. Can't you see I'm suffering here? Oh God, when are you going to make that person change so that I can enjoy my life better?"

Complaining is an indication that we've let our heavenly expectations push aside our earthly need to trust God.

Worse, when we complain to others, we're spreading our distrust. As soon as we become aware that grumblings are welling up within us, or as soon as we feel dissatisfied with life here on Earth, we need to surrender our complaints to the loving heart of the Father. We must take our complaints directly to God. No one else. (The only exception is a counselor or friend who can help us become more holy and healed.)

When our complaints disappear into God's compassionate heart, our frustration dissipates. It's absolutely amazing! Try it! Pick a complaint and let it melt into God. He's wrapping you in his warm and caring hug. He understands you. He knows what injustices have caused you to suffer. He is receiving your complaint and replacing it with peace or restfulness or joy or hope or ___. What good gift is he giving you in exchange for entrusting your complaint to him?

I cried out to God for help;
I cried out to God to hear me.
When I was in distress, I sought the Lord;
at night I stretched out untiring hands,
and I would not be comforted.

"Will the Lord reject forever?
Will he never show his favor again?

Has his unfailing love vanished forever?
Has his promise failed for all time?
Has God forgotten to be merciful?
Has he in anger withheld his compassion?"

Then I thought, "To this I will appeal:
the years when the Most High stretched out his right hand.
I will remember the deeds of the Lord;
yes, I will remember your miracles of long ago.
I will consider all your works
and meditate on all your mighty deeds."

Your ways, God, are holy.
What god is as great as our God?
You are the God who performs miracles;
you display your power among the peoples.
(Psalm 77:1-2,7-14 NIV)

Complaints mean that we've forgotten how much God is already blessing us.

But to be fully healed, we must go beyond the complaints. We must even go beyond surrendering them to the Lord. Not only should we stop complaining about our crosses, we must love them.

> *And he said, "The Son of Man must suffer many things and be rejected by the elders, the chief priests and the teachers of the law, and he must be killed and on the third day be raised to life." Then he said to them all: "Whoever wants to be my disciple must deny themselves and take up their cross daily and follow me." (Luke 9:22-23 NIV)*

And how can we love our crosses? I passed an important milestone in my spiritual journey when my spiritual director, Father Williams, listened to my complaints and said, "You must embrace your crosses." How? By realizing that they unite us to Christ—to the Passion of the Christ, which he willingly and lovingly suffered for us.

Not every cross that we carry is a cross that God has assigned to us. Probably most or all of the father-wounds that we've dealt with in this book were not what God wanted you to experience. But he did freely choose to permit them so that he can turn them into many blessings for you and for others. He delights greatly in mocking the

Devil who thought he could take advantage of you.

Some crosses are to be dropped quickly. Some are to be endured for a season. Some are a beautiful gift from God to make your holiness shine. Abba-Father will help you figure out which is which in your life, usually through a spiritual director or a Spirit-filled friend who listens to your pain and understands your heart.

Today's Exercise, Part 2: The final steps to healing

Some of us need more ways to progress in healing than what I'm presenting here. If this book is leaving your wounds feeling open, exposed, and raw, please run (don't walk!) to the nearest priest, spiritual director, or therapist. Abba-Father cannot complete his mission of providing you with healing unless you cooperate with the full plan.

Now let's do a spiritual exercise that can help you receive his healing compassion.

Begin with this prayer:

Come Holy Spirit and fill me. Come Holy Spirit and renew me. You have my permission to change me. Jesus said that he would give us the Helper, the Holy Spirit, whom the Father would provide, to teach us all things, as Your Word promises in John 14:26. Come Holy Spirit and open my eyes so I can see more fully what the Father sees. Anoint my imagination so I can envision what the Father wants to show me. Open my ears to hear the Father's voice, and help me to know that the words, which sound like my own, are really his. Open my heart so I can receive the healing that the Father wants to give me.

† In the name of Jesus Christ, amen!

Now the Holy Spirit will anoint your imagination. Trust it. I'm going to lead you through a visual prayer.

Imagine that Jesus is sitting next to you (he really is, of course). In front of you is a red brick pathway leading up to a huge castle door. Can you see the castle? This is the King's palace.

Jesus stands up and invites you to walk with him to the castle door. Imagine that you get up and follow him. When the two of you reach the door, you see how huge it is. It's made of gold. How can anyone open this heavy, giant-sized door? For Jesus, it's easy. He simply touches it and it swings wide open.

Now imagine a red carpet inside the door. It's leading to a throne. The King is seated upon his throne and he is smiling at you. A big "I'm so proud of you, my beloved child" smile. This is your Divine Daddy!

He says, "You are most welcome here, my child, for I have adopted you. You are a prince/princess. You belong here. Come closer. I care so much about you that I want to hear all about what's bothering you."

Walk forward on the red carpet. If you have trouble getting started, let Jesus carry you or hold your hand as he leads the way.

Imagine reaching the base of the huge throne. When you look up at the King, he seems too huge to fully see. But his hand is reaching out to you. A safe, caring, gentle hand.

The moment you accept his helping hand, you find yourself on his lap. Take time to imagine what it looks like and what it feels like.

Then tell him about the pain you feel from the wounds you've been thinking about. Tell him about it from the depths of your heart—the well from which your tears flow.

Notice the tears of Abba.

No one else cares about you to the extent that God does. No one possibly can. His love is more. Always much more. Full and complete. Perfect.

Go back and look at what you've written in the exercises of this book from previous days. Tell Abba about them. Read what you jotted down in the second column of the exercise on Day 2. Thank Abba for being the Perfect Father.

The final step toward healing is to let God fill in the gaps that were left by human imperfections. This is a lifelong journey.

DAY 24

The Tears of Abba for Lost Souls

HAVE YOU EVER WONDERED how God feels about the lost souls in your family? You pray for them because you yearn for their salvation. You even ache for them, knowing that their sinful lifestyles are separating them from the God who loves them and they are endangering their eternal souls.

> *When Israel was a child, I loved him, /and out of Egypt I called my son. / . . . It was I who taught Ephraim to walk, / taking them by the arms; / but they did not realize / it was I who healed them. (Hosea 11:1,3 NIV)*

Saint Padre Pio of Pietrelcina said, "Oh the souls! If you knew how much they cost! . . . God runs after the most stubborn souls. They cost him too much to abandon them."

One of my college professors was an avowed atheist. I became friends with Professor Kirk when I joined the campus planetarium staff. He directed the shows and taught me how to channel my creativity into sharing the science of astronomy. As our friendship grew, I shared with him my belief in Jesus, and he listened because of our friendship. But he would not give faith a try.

Then Ralph and I wedded. Less than two years later, I discovered the miracle of the Eucharist and became Catholic. Shortly after that, we both discovered the anointing of the Holy Spirit, and my faith became more alive than ever. Then, during a visit to my parents' home, which was near the college I had attended, I learned that Professor Kirk was in the hospital dying from cancer. So, I went to visit him.

On my way to the hospital, I prayed for his soul. Unexpectedly, a vision overtook my mind. I saw Jesus leaning over my friend's hospital bed, crying. Tears streamed down his cheeks. He sobbed with an inconsolable yearning because this man was still rejecting him and he would soon face the eternal consequences of his decisions.

The scene shook me to the core. I wanted to comfort Jesus, but there is no comfort I could offer that would replace the pain of the loss of a person's eternal soul.

When I arrived at the hospital, Professor Kirk was delighted to see me. He asked, "Can you heal me?"

"No, I can't," I replied. "Only Jesus can do that."

"Well, forget it then. I don't want anything to do with Jesus."

And I knew that Jesus was still leaning over the hospital bed, crying.

Abba-Father was crying with him. His tears were (and are) united to every parent who understands that something terrible is happening to a beloved child and there is nothing they can do to stop it. The gift of free will includes the option to choose a loveless eternity.

Why would anyone reject the love of such a Father?

Meanwhile, I stood at Professor Kirk's hospital bed and felt entirely inadequate. I searched for words that might make a difference. It was very heartbreaking to see Jesus weep. I wished that I had learned how to engage the faithless in such a way as to open their minds to the truth and open their hearts to God's love.

Wouldn't you like to know how to do this too?

I suspect that my professor and most others who reject the Christian faith have never been properly introduced to the real Jesus. They adopt key misconceptions about him that make belief in him seem disadvantageous. They're basically good people and have very loving hearts. They are more like Christ than they realize.

So, what keeps them away from Jesus?

And then there are those who believe in Christ but they don't go to church or do much else with their faith. I suspect that many of them have never been properly introduced to God the Father. He's not an authority in their lives because they want to be their own authority over right and wrong. They don't realize that he's a Doting Daddy and that his commandments are really blessings.

We who have a good relationship with Jesus are called by the Father to continue the mission of Christ, equipped and empowered by the Holy Spirit. Abba-Father's yearning desire to embrace his lost loved ones is manifested through us. The ache you feel for those who are rejecting a lifestyle of faith is a tiny portion of Abba's ache. When you grieve for them, you are tasting the salt of Abba's tears.

God is counting on you to work with him in bringing lost souls to his outstretched arms. All baptized Christians are called to be apostles. As disciples, we learn the faith. As apostles, we share the faith. During Vatican Council II, 2,500 bishops wrote the *Decree on the Apostolate of Lay People* to help us understand how important the lay faithful are as apostles. The decree starts with a mind-blower:

> *In its desire to intensify the apostolic activity of the people of God the Council now earnestly turns its thoughts to the Christian laity.*

The opening sentence shows how much the bishops cared about the role of lay people in the mission of Christ: *"In [the Council's] desire . . ."* they wanted "*to intensify*"—stir up, make hot, increase—our "*apostolic activity.*" In other words, they reminded us that we're part of an apostolic Church while implying that there's more we should be doing.

As a Protestant girl watching her dad lead congregations, I knew how much time he put into preparing his sermons. I knew that he prepared each service and printed up the bulletins. I often helped fold those bulletins. His ministry was what I admired most about him. And so I often envisioned myself behind the pulpit and thought it would be very fulfilling to follow in Dad's footsteps.

The desire to go to seminary and become a Protestant minister had disappeared by the time I went to college. It was not the path that God wanted me to take, so he suppressed that desire. Then, after I became a Catholic, he let it loose. He uncapped the well. But now the desire took the shape of lay ministry. I jumped through every door that opened to me within the Catholic Church. And there were many such doors over the next 40-plus years.

After the founding of Good News Ministries (this story was shared on Day 9), Ralph and I got a personalized license plate for our car. We still have it. It reads: APOSTLE. It's a great discussion-starter!

Every Christian is an apostle. In the Decree on the Laity, the bishops wrote:

> *From the fact of their union with Christ the head, flows the laymen's right and duty to be apostles (paragraph 3).*

They explained that, as members of the Christian Body and with Christ as our authority and guide, we have been privileged with the right—and commissioned with the duty—of making *"all men partakers in redemption and salvation, and through them to establish the right relationship of the entire world to Christ"* (paragraph 2). And:

> *A member who does not work at the growth of the body to the extent of his possibilities must be considered* **useless** *both to the Church and to himself.*

Wow! Useless! The first time I read that, it convicted me to the core. I became more energized than ever to serve the Father in the mission of Christ. I made a promise to him: "I don't want to waste any time doing something that does not somehow advance Your Kingdom on Earth. I want even my dying to serve You (somehow; I leave that up to You, Father)."

God designed all of us to do important work for the Kingdom of Christ. My energy comes from the Holy Spirit. This is what a normal Christian life is meant to look like. Living this way makes us feel much closer to the Father than everything else we do. We can be handicapped by past traumas that were inflicted on us by father-figures, yet still feel very close and very special to our Divine Daddy. The determination to be *useful* to the Church bypasses every obstacle on the journey into the Father's heart.

Being useful to God means you are collaborating with him. It means watching for the doors that he opens for you—doors of opportunity where you can be who you really are with the gifts and talents he has given you—and saying yes to moving forward. It means discovering how you can put to good use what you have learned in your journey of healing from the past. It means finding ways to glorify God in even the most mundane of daily chores and the most unpleasant of duties.

Love that goes nowhere is not love. Love is an outward-moving gift that yearns to give itself to the beloved. *"The only thing that counts is faith expressing itself through love"* (Galatians 5:6 NIV).

How, really, are you expressing your faith? Are you using every gift, every talent, and every skill to share God's love? Are you using your resources for the growth of the Church?

Think of a time when you were asked to do something and you turned it down because you thought you weren't qualified. Let's imagine that a request went out for someone to organize a Bible study for children. You ignored it because you were afraid that you might get in over your head. Your fears were stronger than your love for the children, and that made you useless.

When we respond in fear, we're useless because we underestimate the God who offered us the opportunity to work for him. We've forgotten that he's powerful enough to help us accomplish the task. If God thinks we can do it, then of course we can do it, as long as we keep in touch with him and allow the Holy Spirit to function through us.

The essence of being an apostle is giving to others what we've received from God. This is why the bishops who wrote the decree on the laity stated that we are to put *"at the service of others the grace received . . . as good stewards of God's varied gifts"* (paragraph 3). They based this on 1 Peter 4:10, which says: *"Each one should use whatever gift he has received to serve others, faithfully administering God's grace in its various forms"* (NIV).

Whatever we've received, it came from God to bless us and so that we could use it to bless others. We are funnels of his blessings. As they pour into us from God, we pour it out to others. And if we do everything he inspires us to do (nothing more, nothing less), he will never deplete our resources. We can't possibly be more generous than God is. Being generous means that we give ourselves the opportunity to experience Abba's generosity to us.

What is apostolic activity?

The Decree on the Laity says:

> *The Church was founded to spread the Kingdom of Christ over all the earth. . . . Every activity of the Mystical Body with this in view goes by the name of 'apostolate' (paragraph 2).*

In other words, everything we do that glorifies God is an apostolic activity. The *Catechism of the Catholic Church* lists many kinds of activities that can be apostolic: our prayers, family and married life, daily work, relaxation of mind and body, and even the hardships of life *"if they are accomplished in the Spirit"* (paragraph 901).

When our daily activities become spiritual sacrifices, they become holy actions, and by this we consecrate the world to God. Do you see how important you are? Your everyday apostolic activities are consecrating the world! And that includes your loved ones who right now are far from God. By offering up your holy actions to Abba-Father on behalf of someone who needs sanctification, your good deeds are prayers themselves. Your good deeds wipe the tears from Abba's cheeks.

Scripture commands us to make sure that everything we do glorifies God. Otherwise it's useless:

> *Whatever you do, whether in word or deed, do it all in the name of the Lord Jesus (Colossians 3:17 NIV).*

Doing it in the name of Jesus means that we are branches of God's love, and we are staying attached to the vine, who is Jesus:

> *I am the true vine. . . . No branch can bear fruit by itself; it must remain in the vine. Neither can you bear fruit unless you remain in me. (John 15:1,4 NIV)*

Therefore, all of our activities or deeds that are not apostolic result in no lasting fruit. They're useless.

The bishops wrote: *"The fruitfulness of the apostolate of lay people depends on their living union with Christ"* (paragraph 4). Jesus said: *"Apart from me you can do nothing"* (see John 15:5).

Does the time you spend watching television glorify God? If not, it's a worthless use of valuable time. Recreational activities can glorify God (for example, if they recharge us so we can be enthusiastic in our servanthood), but if they keep us from our apostolate, they can be useless.

True apostles are identified by the following fruits; these come from paragraph 4 of the decree.

1. We are hidden in God. We do not glorify ourselves. Therefore, the people around us see Jesus, not us, and by seeing Jesus they meet the True Father. If we're in a powerful, public role, such as being the boss at work or the president of the parish council, the

way we lead teaches others what Jesus is really like.

2. We are free from the slavery of possessions and we accumulate riches that last forever. Materialism does not rule us. If we have something that another person needs, we are happy to give it away.
3. We exert all of our energies in extending God's kingdom, and our Christian spirit is an energizing force in the world. Will people remember us as someone who richly affected their lives? Will they recall how we made a difference everywhere we went?
4. In difficult times, we persevere because we *"consider that our present sufferings are not worth comparing with the glory that will be revealed in us"* (Romans 8:18 NIV). When a service we do is attacked by someone's bad opinion or by demonic interference, we take it as a sign that what we're doing is important and so we continue it to completion.
5. With the love that comes from the prompting of God, we do good to everyone (see Galatians 6:10). If our neighbor is a bad-mouthed grouch, we evangelize him by mowing his lawn and finding other ways to serve him.
6. We strive to please God rather than people. Perhaps a friend wants you to join him at a movie that has pornographic elements. When you say no because you don't want to waste your time and money on a movie like that, he mocks you and calls you a religious fanatic. Nevertheless, you stand your ground because you care more about what God wants you to do.
7. We are always ready to follow Christ, even when it means giving up something or getting persecuted. In other words, we're willing to carry the cross with Jesus. It's painful to spend money to fix a neighbor's broken car, especially when we'd rather buy something for ourselves. What's worse is when our relatives get mad at us for not using the money on our own family. But we rejoice because, more than ever, we feel the Father's joy.
8. We nurture Christian friendships in which we mutually support each other in all our needs. The way we care for one another (e.g., "Your need is as important to me as it is to you") shows the world what the Father's love is all about.

These fruits are non-verbal ways of evangelizing. To help others open their hearts to Abba-Father's love and his ways of parenting us, we need to have words that help their minds understand the truth, accompanied by the fruits of our faith that can nourish their souls. Your words and your fruits must come from your own experiences so that you are genuine and they know it. Being genuine is very powerful in getting others to trust you so that they will listen to you.

Did you ever reject Jesus? Did someone help you come back to the Lord by their patient and persistent efforts? Share your story with them!

Are you someone who is patient, kind, compassionate, selfless, and on fire with your faith? To be effective in helping Jesus bring lost souls to the Father, we have to live the faith like we really believe what we profess. We need confidence to speak up about the advantages of being Abba's adopted child.

Jesus told us in Luke 12:11-12 that there is no reason to worry about what to say, for when the opportunity arises, the Holy Spirit will give us the words. Is your relationship with the Holy Spirit active enough yet to rely on his help?

To be effective, we need to care about the souls of others so much that we cry when they reject Jesus.

> *I am speaking the truth in Christ–I am not lying; my conscience bears me witness in the Holy Spirit–that I have great sorrow and unceasing anguish in my heart . . . for the sake of my brothers, my kinsmen according to the flesh (Romans 9:1-3 ESV).*

Who's your Professor Kirk? Which people in your life are making Abba weep? Do you pray for their salvation with the passion of heartfelt anguish? That's the starting point. That's the foundation for all evangelization efforts. Without this, the best words don't make a difference.

Sadly, we can be the best evangelizers and some people will still choose to turn away. Why is that?

Anger at the root of faithlessness

There might be a million reasons that contribute to a person's rejection of Christ, but for the purpose of this book, let's look at the effects of father-wounds.

As you know, we are living in an increasingly angry world. The shootings in schools and malls give evidence of this, as do all the riots, the heated political arguments, the court cases, and anti-Christian persecutions. Underlying this anger are unhealed wounds.

Nearly everyone has some amount of unresolved anger that goes back to the unmet needs of childhood. And it leaks out. It always eventually leaks out. Have you ever lost your temper over some little thing and then wondered why you reacted so strongly?

We might think that we have all of our anger issues under control. We might even have nothing but good memories of childhood and feel no reason for anger. Or perhaps we've accomplished a lot of healing and we truly experience Abba as the Perfect Father who gives us all the love we need. But still lurking in our subconscious psyche are influences from the past that, when awakened, bring out the ugly in us.

The frown of a grocery store clerk might trigger an impulse to become self-defensive and rude. Why? Because unhealed wounds release the infected puss of anger. When a new circumstance reminds us of old traumas, disappointments, or heartbreaks—wham!

We're usually not even aware of the connection.

The clerk's frown might unconsciously remind us of the angry face of a parent who was punishing us, making us feel insecure about ourselves. We want everyone to like us, even strangers, but here's someone whose frown seems to be announcing that we are unlikeable. This is rooted in the misconception that we are bad. Our parents probably communicated that it was our behavior that was bad, not us, but as children (and sometimes even as adults!) we internalized it, took it personally, and concluded that we are bad and therefore unlikeable.

The normal reaction to the reawakening of "I'm bad" is to get self-defensive (which is a plea to be seen as a good person) and rude (which is anger trying to make the other person seem less good than we are).

Similarly, anger is at the root of faithlessness, because there's a father-wound triggering the desire to reject God. The parent's frown becomes God's frown. The unbeliever reacts to an invitation to go to church as if puss were leaking from an old wound: "God knows how bad I am, so why would I put myself into a church where I feel disliked? No, I'm going to protect myself by making up my own mind about what's good and what's bad. I don't want religion to be another parent controlling my life."

Can you hear the anger in that reaction?

Fatherhood's role in finding faith

When we know, really know, that Abba loves us no matter what and that he sees everything that's good in us and delights in it, anger no longer interferes with our faith. By searching for our anger-triggers with the help of the Holy Spirit, we can disable them. By giving Abba-Father time to minister to us, we can be healed. If only everyone knew this!

Well, *you* now know it, and so the Father is asking you to share it with someone who is ready to listen to you. You've shown compassion and you've been laying the groundwork by asking the Holy Spirit to anoint his (or her) heart and you've offered up good deeds as a prayer for his (or her) sanctification. Because of this, "*They will know that I am the Lord, when I break the bars of their yoke and rescue them from the hands of those who enslaved them*" (Ezekiel 34:27 NIV).

> *Then Jesus told them this parable: "Suppose one of you has a hundred sheep and loses one of them. Doesn't he leave the ninety-nine in the open country and go after the lost sheep until he finds it? And when he finds it, he joyfully puts it on his shoulders and goes home. Then he calls his friends and neighbors together and says, 'Rejoice with me; I have found my lost sheep.' I tell you that in the same way there will be more rejoicing in heaven over one sinner who repents than over ninety-nine righteous persons who do not need to repent." (Luke 15:3-7 NIV)*

Do not be discouraged when your efforts to bring lost souls to the Father seem to fail. Jesus described the Father as a shepherd who never stops trying. However, he counts on *us* to persistently join him in going after the lost.

Imagine what happens to those who have had especially traumatic childhoods. Even if their families were churchgoers, they will not know God as he truly is without first receiving a lot of healing through therapy. Spiritual healing usually comes after emotional healing. Abba cannot minister to those who distrust him. He cries for them like any good father who does not have access to their suffering child.

Because fatherhood has been undermined throughout society for multiple generations, trust in God is at its lowest point. Father-wound anger is exploding everywhere: in riots, road rage, and other demonic upheavals. The Divine Daddy who wants to hug their wounds away cannot reach them, though they are most in need of his mercy.

And so the anger escalates. While Abba reaches out to them saying, "I have what you seek," those who need it most don't know that they can look for it, and when they don't seek it, they can't find it.

On April 24, 2008, about a mile from my home, a 16-year-old boy named Kendrick waited for his mom to pick him up from the library. Unfortunately, at that moment she was getting out of jail after being arrested for driving without a license.

Kendrick had grown up without his father. When he was seven, his mother began dating a man who soon moved in with them. The boy suffered abuse from both. Later, an investigator would find more than 40 scars on his body.

One Christmas, this "stepfather" smashed all of Kendrick's Christmas gifts to punish him for doing poorly in school, while his mother did nothing to rescue the holiday.

When he was 13, the boy's unresolved anger exploded in public. He grabbed a tree branch and attacked a beautiful white egret until the bird was limp on the ground. Then he redirected his anger to a duck. When officers arrested him, a witness said, "Even though this act was serious, it's my hope this young man gets some help and isn't lost in the system. He just needs someone there for him after school."

He never got that help. Three years later, Kendrick's anger exploded again while waiting for his mother to pick him up after school. He often waited for her at the public library that was next to his school, while playing the video game *World of Warcraft*. On the day of his mother's jail time, the library closed and the boy continued to wait: alone, hurt, and angry. The evening grew dark. He saw the headlights of a car turn into the library's driveway. At last! But no, this was not his mother. The driver was a teenage girl. She parked near the front of the library, stepped out of the car with a couple of books in her hand, then walked toward the book drop-off box.

Kendrick rose from his bench. The girl slipped the books into the box and turned toward her car, telling her girlfriend on the cellphone that she saw a "weird guy" near the front of the library. Suddenly, he grabbed her and twisted her arm behind her with a tight squeeze. He yanked her away from the car and, as she squirmed and began to scream, he hit her so hard across the face that she felt dizzy. He hit her again and again until she blacked out. Then he dragged her behind the library and raped her.

When the police found her, she was comatose and near death. She survived, but the boy's angry attack had irreversibly damaged her brain. The girl, who was 18 at the time, has regained her mind and her memory, but she is still unable to walk, talk, see, or eat on her own.

Kendrick is now serving a life sentence in prison.

Abba cried for both of them. And for their families. As Saint Pio of Pietrelcina said, God did not abandon them. He ran after them, hoping that they would stop and seek him so that they could find him.

Jesus said, *"Seek and you will find. . . . Which of you, if your son asks for bread, will give him a stone? . . . Your Father in heaven will give good gifts to those who ask him"* (see Matthew 7:7-11).

And the Father said, *"When you search for Me with all your heart, you will find me and I will restore you"* (see Jeremiah 29:13-14).

The girl's mother, Vanna Nguyen, found God during her daughter's rehabilitation. The relationship she'd had with her father made it easy to believe in the goodness of God the Father. Vanna had grown up in Saigon, Vietnam. In 1975, when the Vietnam War ended, her father was captured by South Vietnamese soldiers and imprisoned. Five years later, he returned home.

One night, he pulled Vanna close to him and whispered in her ear, "We can't survive here. You need to leave." He had made a deal with a local fisherman to smuggle his daughter out of the country. She would go to America to live with an aunt.

Vanna became a U.S. citizen, married, and gave birth to two daughters. The second child, Queena, is the one who was brutally attacked.

Although Vanna had lived much of her life without a father, her memory of him was as a loving protector. This was a good start for eventually finding the love of Abba while she cried with aching love for her wounded daughter. Raised a Buddhist, she turned to the Christian faith in her daughter's rehab center. Abba-Father helped her turn bitterness and anger into forgiveness and hope.

"I think if not for God, we may have all fallen apart long ago," Vanna wrote on a website dedicated to raising funds for Queena's huge medical expenses (joinqueena.com). She believes that she and her daughter have been called by Christ to be light for the world (as Matthew 5:14 describes). She says she knows that this is what is most important. It has been difficult, but she has learned to trust Jesus for Queena's future.

Best of all, she has witnessed the healing that God has given to Queena's heart. Despite what happened to her (and remembering it), and despite her handicaps, Queena has a joyful spirit. She has an unshakable determination and a constant smile that has inspired adults and children all around the world.

How did it happen? Are people like Vanna and Queena specially chosen and prepared by Abba-Father for this? Would you or I be able to choose faith in God if something like this happened to us?

All of us are chosen to have this kind of faith, and all of us are prepared by God for whatever we're going to face. Faith is a gift of the Holy Spirit. Trust is a decision we make. The kind of faith that Vanna has comes from her decision to trust God and her desire to lean on him. She is a child who has a healthy relationship with her Divine Daddy.

We, too, can have this kind of faith for every trial we endure. There's a supernatural strength that's given to us by the Father through the Holy Spirit. Having a personal relationship with the Holy Spirit (also known as "baptism in the Spirit") makes a huge difference! So, does turning to faith-filled friends, a spiritual director, and possibly even a good therapist. When any of these are missing from our lives, we suffer more.

The heart of the Father

Vanna nearly lost her child to violence. Abba-Father knows what it is to lose a Son to violence. But not all violence is physical. Spiritual violence—the destruction of a soul—is a terrible, terrible tragedy. Many parents have lost their children to the faithlessness of today's culture. Abba-Father knows what this loss feels like, far more than we do. He is more upset by it than any human parent could ever feel. He longs to spend eternity with every son or daughter he's created, and he knows the mortal danger their souls face if they continue to stay away from him.

We look at a violent abuser like Kendrick or his mother or his stepfather, and we see anger that repulses us. Abba sees a wounded soul in danger of being lost forever.

We look at abortion-rights women screaming against pro-life Christians, and we see their hatred and stubborn refusal to accept the truth about abortion. Abba sees lost children who need healing and deliverance from their fears.

We look at shooters who kill dozens of school children and steal every child's right to feel safe. Abba sees these killers as children who were not safe in their own homes.

He is not justifying the evil they do. He does not excuse their sins nor overlook them. However, if only he could reach them, embrace them, and heal them, then there would be less violence in the world. He cries for them, longing for entry into their hearts.

Like any good parent.

Have you ever loved someone who refused to accept your love? How do you feel about it? You're loving them passionately with a suffering love like Jesus experienced in his Passion. Did you know that if someone has nailed you for embracing Jesus and rejecting their faithless lifestyle, you have invisible stigmata? Think about it: When someone refuses to let you reach out to them with your love and God's, you are nailed with Jesus on his Cross. The pain you suffer is your stigmata.

At first, when someone rejects our love, we feel bad for ourselves. We want to be in a mutually loving relationship. We hate rejection. We mourn what we desire but cannot have. However, Abba's love, which dwells within us, makes us feel bad for those who reject us. We mourn for them because we know that deep down in their hearts they desire to be loved completely and unconditionally, and we know that they have closed themselves off from it through their bad decisions, misconceptions, and anger-fed attitudes.

This is a love that's united to Abba's heart. When we unite ourselves so intimately to his heart that we mourn for lost souls with tears, he smiles. He receives our unity as a hug, which is an echo of the hug that he is giving to us.

Today's Exercise: Pray for lost souls

Write a list of all the lost souls in your life. Then pray for them using the following prayer or your own adaptation of it. I recommend praying it immediately before the Rosary, which is the Blessed Mother's weapon for breaking the strongholds of the demonic forces that have imprisoned your loved ones.

But first recall who you are to the Father:

The Spirit of the Sovereign Lord is on me,

because the Lord has anointed me
to proclaim good news to the poor.
He has sent me to bind up the brokenhearted,
to proclaim freedom for the captives
and release from darkness for the prisoners,
to proclaim the year of the Lord's favor
and the day of vengeance of our God,
to comfort all who mourn,
and provide for those who grieve in Zion–
to bestow on them a crown of beauty
instead of ashes,
the oil of joy
instead of mourning,
and a garment of praise
instead of a spirit of despair.
They will be called oaks of righteousness,
a planting of the Lord
for the display of his splendor.
(Isaiah 61:1-3 NIV)

A Prayer to Free the Captives

Father God, I pray that You would teach me to yield myself to Your Spirit. Holy Spirit, teach me to trust You as a living Person who leads my life and my prayers. Help me to understand Your ministry and power. I long to see a demonstration of Your power in my life just as the Apostle Paul did (1 Corinthians 2:2-5).

I thank you that You indwell, seal, sanctify, and empower me. You guide me, teach me, and pray through me. Help me to partner with You in everything I do. Transform my life completely with Your power. Make me sensitive to Your promptings, and teach me to partner with You in prayer in a deeper way. Bring effectiveness to my prayers for the salvation of ___.

I thank you that through Jesus Christ the darkness vanishes as I pray for lost souls. Thank you, Holy Spirit, for convicting the world of sin and for inspiring righteousness. I pray that You will soften the hearts of ___. Remove the spiritual blindness from their eyes, and help them to understand the truth about You. Bring them to repentance and salvation (Acts 3:19). Help me to be Your light in their lives.

Help me to let my light shine before them, that they may see my good deeds and glorify my Father in Heaven (Mathew 5:16). Show me how to be Your witness and how to show acts of love to them. I believe that You are working in their lives even as I pray. I promise to persevere in prayer until ___ are safely in the Father's arms.

In the holy name of Jesus, amen.

DAY 25

Saints and Mystics Reveal the Father's Heart

THE HEART OF THE Father is breaking. It grieves him to see so many of his precious children fall into Satan's hands. He cherishes even the worst evildoers more than we can imagine. Abba-Father has been reaching out to them in countless ways, including through saints and mystics.

> *God is mighty, but despises no one; / he is mighty, and firm in his purpose. . . . But if people are bound in chains, / held fast by cords of affliction, / he tells them what they have done–/ that they have sinned arrogantly. / He makes them listen to correction and commands them to repent of their evil. / If they obey and serve him, / they will spend the rest of their days in prosperity / and their years in contentment. / But if they do not listen, they will perish by the sword / and die without knowledge. (Job 36:5,8-12 NIV)*

When the Father's love doesn't reach the hearts of his lost children, he extends his mercy. When that doesn't work, he disciplines them. Chastisements are the lion's den that we walk into when we turn away from God. When our lives get torn apart by the lions of sinful decisions, we either turn to God for rescue or we let the lions devour us.

Our sins create our chastisements (the lion's den) but it's our Good Father who chooses how we are disciplined (how we are bitten). He sets us up to succeed, not to fail. He permits the Devil to torture us when we open ourselves to demons—but only in ways that have the potential to sanctify us.

It pains Abba deeply to discipline us, just like any good parent who punishes the child out of heartfelt love and concern. And like every good parent, he reluctantly but firmly expresses his love through anger when nothing else works. It is anger towards the lion and it is anger over the sin that put us into the lion's den. Our Divine Daddy hates all sins because they feed us to lions.

When Jesus said to Peter, "Get behind me, Satan! You're a stumbling block to me; you're not thinking about the concerns of God, but merely human concerns!" he was angry. Was he calling Peter "Satan"? If he was, then his anger was directed to Peter. Or was he calling out Satan who used Peter to try to tempt Jesus to forego his mission? (See Matthew 16:23.)

I imagine that Jesus saw the Devil standing behind Peter. The Devil had used Peter's vulnerabilities to trigger a rebuke against Jesus: "Never, Lord!" Peter had said. "You shall never go to Jerusalem and let them kill you!" (Satan tried to tempt Jesus throughout his ministry, not just at his 40-day fast at the beginning of it.) So, Jesus rescued Peter by getting the Devil off his back. And he reminded the Devil that he, Jesus, will always be out in front winning battles for his followers.

Abba's anger is never vindictive, hateful, or spiteful. It's the wrath of a warrior king who stands up to the enemy and demands the evil to stop. While he does this, if we are in any way on the enemy's side, we too feel his anger.

> *Endure hardship as discipline; God is treating you as his children. For what children are not disciplined by their father? If you are not disciplined–and everyone undergoes discipline–then you are not legitimate, not true sons and daughters at all. Moreover, we have all had human fathers who disciplined us and we respected them for it. How much more should we submit to the Father of spirits and live! They disciplined us for a little while as they thought best; but God disciplines us for our good, in order that we may share in his holiness. No discipline seems pleasant at the time, but painful. Later on, however, it produces a harvest of righteousness and peace for those who have been trained by it. (Hebrews 12:7-11 NIV)*

Let's take a look at how this happens. We all have conversion stories, i.e., turning points in our lives when we repented from something that was sinful and more fully embraced the True God to follow his path of holiness. How did God get our attention? Often it's by "hitting rock bottom," a hardship or trial that, from God's perspective, is a loving chastisement.

They almost always involve a mystical experience. For me, it was the supernatural gift of instantly believing that the Eucharist is truly Jesus Christ in person (which I described on Day 12). For others, it can be much more dramatic.

Alan Ames is a recovered alcoholic who had been raised Catholic but was far from God. Then he had a mystical experience that revealed the love of Abba-Father most clearly. Afterward, he became a supernaturally gifted mystic with a ministry of healing, speaking, and writing. He receives messages from the Holy Trinity and from saints. He has the written support of his archbishop in Perth, Australia: first Archbishop Barry Hickey for 17 years and then Archbishop Costello and Auxiliary Bishop Don Sproxton.

Listen to his story as told to Christine Watkins for her book, *The Warning: Testimonies and Prophecies of the Illumination of Conscience*, published by Queen of Peace Media. As you read it, look for Abba-Father's love in the events that unfolded.

> In 1993, when I was forty, I traveled frequently for my job as a sales manager for a pharmaceutical company in Perth, Australia. On one of my work trips, I flew to a city called Adelaide and went through my monotonous routine of checking into a hotel and sitting on the bed to watch television. Though normally a heavy drinker, I hadn't downed any booze because I didn't generally consume alcohol on a work day.
>
> While I was watching the evening news, all of a sudden, directly in front of me appeared a horrific-looking man who reached his arms forward and began to choke me. He had dark skin and bulging eyes, with lips drawn back in a snarl that exposed his ghastly teeth; but I was less concerned with his appearance than the fact that he was strangling me!
>
> I tried to use my martial arts moves against him, having been captain of the Australian team in the Aikido World Championships, but my hands passed right through his

body. Nothing I could do would stop his stranglehold. After a few minutes of useless fighting, the veins in my neck were about to burst, and I believed I was taking my very last breath.

Then an audible voice in my head said, "Pray the Our Father!"

That was the last idea I would have come up with, but in desperation, I started to pray it, and the strangling stopped. Then I stopped and the strangling resumed. Every time I ceased to pray, the strangling started, and every time I resumed, the strangling stopped. To add to this nightmare, I was trapped and couldn't move. I tried repeatedly to get out of the hotel room, but the terrifying man kept me pinned in a stranglehold—and this went on all night.

The experience was so strange and frightening that I thought I'd gone mad: "That's it. I'm absolutely crazy." I'd heard of people who drank in excess and would see pink elephants traveling up the wall, so I figured I was one of them. Then I saw my neck in the large hotel mirror. To my amazement, it was bruised; therefore, I couldn't deny the attack was real. Yet I couldn't accept it either.

The next day, I heard the same voice in my head that had told me to pray the Our Father. He told me he was an angel whom God had sent to help me. I didn't believe in the existence of angels. To me, they were nothing more than make-believe fairies. He said God had sent him because God loved me and wanted my love.

"If God exists," I answered back to this "fairy" in my head, "surely he wouldn't love someone like me!" I had good reason to think I was a poor candidate for love. God had always been the furthest thought from my mind, and troublemaking the first.

His Catholic mother tried to raise him in the Faith, but he rejected it. He couldn't believe that God was real.

At age twelve, I started drinking alcohol and was brought before a court judge for taking money out of the candle box in St. Edmund's Church in Edmonton, London. At age fourteen, I had the worst record of all the students at

> a Jesuit school in Stamford Hill and was finally expelled for stealing.
>
> I thought the only way I was going to get treated with any dignity was to follow in the footsteps of my father: an aggressive, alcoholic gambler. People were frightened of him and gave him a grudging respect, which he gained through violence. I copied his habits, including his constant drinking, because alcohol gave me good feelings and numbed me to all the bad things in my life. But the next day would always come, when everything felt worse, so I would drink again to drown the consequences.

Alan joined a motorcycle gang and became extremely violent. After marrying, he got a job by lying. He became very successful and earned lots of money.

> I lived for power, money, and a good time at all times. But suffering always dragged down my dreams because my pleasure came from sin and addictions, with their lingering imprint of pain, hurt, loneliness, and emptiness.
>
> My life was a dark one when the angel started to visit me. Even when I heard his voice, I still didn't believe that he existed, so I said to him, "Prove you are real." And he did. He started to tell me of different things that would happen in my life, which I shared with my wife—and to our amazement, they all came true. The angel was gentle, but I didn't listen to him; therefore, in his stead, God sent in the big guns.

One night, St. Teresa of Avila appeared to him.

> She proceeded to give me a kick up the back side, saying I needed to change my life completely to avoid going to Hell, which she then described in frightening detail. That woke me up. Before then, Hell was only a made-up myth to trick people into living better, but now, if that place existed, I certainly didn't want to go there. . . . Then she revealed what could also be mine: she told me all about Heaven. "That is where I want to go!"
>
> "You can reach paradise," she said to me, "anyone can. If you live your Catholic faith, you are guaranteed Heaven." Then she insisted, "Pray, pray the Rosary!" and asked

> me to go get one.
>
> I didn't want to pray. Prayer was boring, so I looked for excuses: "Where can I get rosary beads at this time of night?"
>
> "There is a shop around the corner that is open and sells rosary beads."
>
> "At 9:30 at night? That's impossible!"
>
> "You go there!"
>
> "This is totally nuts," I thought to myself, as I walked outside. Turning the corner, I saw a religious shop. It was open, and they were stocking inventory. St. Teresa directed me downstairs where many rosaries were on display. I couldn't believe it. She showed me a brown rosary, which I later discovered was the color of the Carmelite order to which she belonged. "Get that one!" she urged.

Back in his hotel room, rosary in hand, he continued to argue with St. Teresa.

> "You must pray," she said, "and you must pray the Rosary because you risk losing your soul! You are going to Hell unless you change!" Needless to say, she won the argument.
>
> I didn't really know the Rosary, so she explained to me how to pray it. She said that I should see it as a window into the life of God on Earth, that I should place myself beside Jesus and walk with Him through His life. By doing so, His grace would reach inside of me and touch me in a powerful way.
>
> "Every prayer of the Rosary," she told me, "is a step away from evil and a step toward God. See the Rosary as a chain you are hanging around the neck of Satan, which will weigh him down and break his grasp on you."
>
> From my first Rosary prayer, I felt a peace, a happiness, an excitement within. I couldn't stop laughing, and I couldn't stop crying. No drugs or alcohol could have given me what I was feeling at that moment. The more I prayed, the stronger this feeling became, until suddenly, I had finished fifteen decades.
>
> . . . From the moment I started to pray the Rosary, Satan's grasp on me weakened. My addictions fell away, and

I had many of them—alcohol being the primary one. This is nothing I did, but a grace from God. Anyone who has been addicted to alcohol knows how hard it is to quit, and I stopped immediately. In moments of temptation, when I felt weak and so alone, hurt, rejected, and unloved, I was freed and strengthened by remembering St. Teresa's words to me: "Every time you feel a desire to do wrong, think of Jesus. Just think of His Name, think of Him suffering on the Cross, or see the Host before you. Keep concentrating on that and you will see your desires fall away."

One day in 1994, Jesus came to him in a vision.

Before me was Jesus on the Cross, telling me he loved me and he wanted to forgive me. It was the greatest day in my life, but also the most difficult because I was shown how all my sins, from childhood to the present, had contributed to his suffering and dying. There were so many of them! It seemed as though I was sinning every second of my life.

I saw that every time I had hurt someone, I was hurting Jesus. Any time I told a lie, I was lying about Jesus as he suffered and died. Every time I gossiped about people, I was below the Cross with those gossiping about Jesus as he hung in agony. Any time I made fun of others, I was making fun of Jesus as he died for me. Even the smallest sin, even the thoughts I had toward others—of dislike, anger, hate, or frustration—seemed so big. And to see my grievous sins was absolutely terrible.

Jesus showed me the state of my soul, which was putrid. He revealed how my sins not only hurt other people but often led them into sin, such as when they tried to imitate me or responded with anger or violence. I felt so ashamed, so unworthy and offensive. I wanted to run away but couldn't, and Jesus wouldn't leave me. Worse yet, he kept telling me he loved me and longed to forgive me.

. . . For five hours, I cried and cried, curled up on the floor, sobbing like a baby, begging Jesus, "Let me die, let me die!" To see his Blood running down his face as he called out to me through his suffering, "I love you, and I want to

> forgive you," was the deepest pain I've ever felt in my life.
>
> Eventually with his grace, I built up the courage to ask for his forgiveness. Reaching out across a chasm of shame, I said, "Forgive me, dear Jesus."
>
> "I do forgive you," he answered. At that moment, I felt a tremendous weight of sin being lifted from me. His love touched my soul in such a wonderful way that I never wanted to lose his presence again. Possessing him, I knew, was the most important thing in life. I felt refreshed, renewed—a different person! I couldn't stop telling Jesus that I loved him and wanted to love him forever. I knew I could never hurt him again purposefully, and I never wanted to be away from him. I fell in love with Jesus that day, and I totally committed my life to God.

Then Jesus told him to go to Confession.

> When I came out of the confessional, Jesus said, "Understand that when you don't confess all your sins, you hold onto the pain and hurt and suffering that comes with them. If you do not confess all of your sins, it is easy for Satan to lead you into more sin because you are not only left feeling bad about yourself, but you also have that sin residing on your heart, on your very soul. It remains a weakness there, a doorway where evil can enter and lead you further away from God. It is also important that you continue to recognize your mistakes, and once you do, come to Confession and ask for forgiveness. Do not push them aside and say they are not important. Understand that it is important to get rid of every sin."

Since then, God has sent Alan around the world to lead others to the same repentance and purification. To prove that his story is real, God has revealed himself by healing people in Alan's audiences as he prayed for them. Alan has often wondered, "Why me? There are so many good people who come to church because they love God, so many religious people, yet You are talking to me who has been so bad, who *is* so bad. I just don't understand."

The answer: "It is because God loves you, and he loves you the same as anyone else. The only difference is how much you love God. Also, God appearing to you, someone who was so far away from him, shows that his love is there for everyone, even the worst sinner, not just for a select few."

The Illumination of Conscience

Alan Ames experienced an illumination of conscience when God revealed to him all the ways he had wounded Jesus throughout his life. This is something we'll all experience when we die and, as the saying goes, our entire lives flash before our eyes. However, contrary to popular worldly opinions on this, it's not a movie depicting all the scenes of our lives. It's not a fun, amazing memory-jogger. It's an illumination of conscience.

According to the Bible, when we die, the veil of our understanding is removed. We can see things clearly. We can see things we didn't understand before.

> *See what kind of love the Father has given to us, that we should be called children of God; and so we are. . . . Beloved, we are God's children now, and what we will be has not yet appeared; but we know that when he appears we shall be like him, because we shall see him as he is. And everyone who thus hopes in him purifies himself as he is pure. (1 John 3:1-3 ESV)*

The same thing can happen any time throughout our lives:

> *But whenever anyone turns to the Lord, the veil is taken away. Now the Lord is the Spirit, and where the Spirit of the Lord is, there is freedom. And we all, who with unveiled faces contemplate the Lord's glory, are being transformed into his image with ever-increasing glory, which comes from the Lord, who is the Spirit. (2 Corinthians 3:16-18 NIV)*

The illumination of conscience is the veil being lifted. Look at what Saint Alphonsus de Liguori said about it:

> When the soul enters the kingdom of the blessed, and the barrier which hinders its sight is taken away, it will see openly and without a veil the infinite beauty of God; and this will be the joy of the blessed.
>
> Every object that the soul then will see in God himself will overwhelm it with delight; it will see the rectitude of his judgments, the harmony of his regulations for every soul, all ordained to his divine glory, and its own good.

> The soul will especially perceive, in respect to itself, the boundless love which God has entertained towards it in becoming man, and sacrificing his life upon the cross through love of it. Then will it know what an excess of goodness is comprehended in the mystery of the cross, in the sight of a God become a servant, and dying condemned upon an infamous tree; and in the mystery of the Eucharist, in the sight of a God beneath the species of bread, and made the food of his creatures.
>
> In particular, the soul will perceive all the graces and favors shown to it, which, until then, had been hidden. It will see all the mercies he has bestowed on it, in waiting for it, and pardoning its ingratitude. It will see the many calls, and lights, and aids that have been granted to it in abundance. It will see that these tribulations, these infirmities, these losses of property or of kindred, which it counted punishments, were not really punishments, but loving arrangements of God for drawing it to the perfect love for him.

Saint Alphonsus described what happens when the veil is lifted for a holy person, i.e., all of us who have been following Jesus as our Lord and Savior, all of us who have been repenting from our sins. Alan Ames is an example of what happens to sinners who are willing to repent.

What about those who are not (yet) willing? Many saints and mystics have spoken of a worldwide, sudden illumination of conscience affecting everyone, all at the same time, from every religion and creed, including atheists and the worst of evildoers. Everyone will see their entire lives through the eyes of Abba-Father. They will see, like Alan Ames did, how terribly they wounded Jesus with even the smallest of sins.

This book would be too long if I were to sidetrack onto the stories of these saints and mystics and their messages. I'll cover just a few.

The Prayer of Divine Illumination

You have loved ones who have rejected Jesus. We all do. You know people who have embraced the lies of the Devil without realizing that they have endangered their lives here on Earth as well as their immortal souls. They need divine illumination!

In fact, we all have been tricked into believing, to some extent, the lies of the Devil. We sin because we do not understand that God has a different way, a better way. We, too, need an increase of divine illumination.

According to messages given by our Blessed Mother during her various apparitions over the past century and longer, we can be sure that God has a plan to rescue the world from darkness. Many Spirit-filled priests and others who have the charism of prophecy are echoing what saints and mystics have said: God is planning to provide a supernatural illumination. He is going to purge humankind from its very pervasive evils by sending a flood like in the days of Noah, but this time it will be the flood of the Holy Spirit! God is going to make it known to everyone on the Earth that Jesus is Lord and he is the only way to Heaven, so that everyone can decide with eyes wide open whether to follow him or not.

Several days before the Feast of Pentecost in 2020, during my morning meditations, I felt inspired to write the following Prayer of Divine Illumination. It's provided here to help bring about the Great Illumination in your loved ones and into your own life. It can be an effective weapon against the darkness that has pervaded our world.

It begins with an Act of Contrition. It has three decades of prayers: one to Jesus, one to the Father, and one to the Holy Spirit. The decades are separated by the prayer for mercy that is often used in the Rosary. And it finishes by seeking the help of Holy Mary and Saint Joseph.

The Act of Contrition
O my God, I am heartily sorry for having offended You, and I detest all my sins, because I dread the loss of Heaven and the pains of Hell. But most of all because they offend You, my God, who are all good and deserving of all my love. I firmly resolve, with the help of Your grace, to confess my sins, to do penance, and to amend my life. Amen.

To Jesus (pray this 10 times)
Oh come Lord Jesus with Your Divine Light!
Come shed Your Great Illumination into the darkness of this world.
Come anew with Your Spirit of Truth to save us from the deceits of the evil one.

Once between decades:
Oh my Jesus, forgive us our sins, save us from the fires of Hell; lead all souls to Heaven, especially those most in need of Your Mercy.

To the Father (pray this 10 times)
Father God, enlighten our minds, that we may be set free.
Enlighten our intellects, that we may understand the Truth more fully.
Enlighten our wills, that we may embrace Your Divine Will.

Oh my Jesus, forgive us our sins . . .

To the Holy Spirit (pray this 10 times)
Come Holy Spirit and fill us.
Come Holy Spirit and renew us.
Come Holy Spirit and activate Your Divine Gifts in us, especially the gift of discernment

Oh my Jesus, forgive us our sins . . .

Hail Mary, full of grace, the Lord is with you. Blessed are you among women, and blessed is the fruit of your womb, Jesus. Holy Mary, Mother of God, pray for us sinners now and at the hour of our deaths.

O Glorious Saint Joseph, spouse of the Immaculate Virgin, obtain for us a pure, humble, and charitable mind, and perfect resignation to the Divine Will.

In the name of the Father, and the Son, and the Holy Spirit, amen.

Words from our loving Mother

God has been sending the Blessed Mother to us for a long time, most especially in the past 200 years. A little over 100 years ago, she gave some very powerful messages in Fatima, Portugal, and since then, her sightings or apparitions have increased. Her messages have been filled with pleading, like a mother urgently warning her children of danger as she tries to point them to the safety of Jesus. She's repeatedly said that the world needs to repent, we all need to pray more, and people who are away from Christ need to come back to Christ.

She repeats this message everywhere she appears.

On May 13, 1917, the Blessed Virgin Mary began to appear to

three children in Fatima: Lucia dos Santos, and her cousins Francisco and Jacinta Marto. These appearances are well known for the three secrets, and many books, articles, and websites cover them. In particular, I recommend to you the Vatican document published by the Congregation for the Doctrine of the Faith, entitled *The Message of Fatima*. It was published at the beginning of the third millennium when Pope Saint John Paul II decided to make public the text of the third part of the "secret of Fatima." This document includes wonderful prayers by John Paul II, who consecrated the world to the Blessed Mother.

"*The power of this consecration* lasts for all time and embraces all individuals, peoples and nations. It overcomes every evil that the spirit of darkness is able to awaken, and has in fact awakened in our times, in the heart of man and in his history," wrote Archbishop Tarcisio Bertone, SDB, Secretary of the Congregation for the Doctrine of the Faith.

Our Lady of Fatima gave us three tasks. If enough people were to do these, she promised, they would bring peace to the world:

1. We must be sorry for what we've done wrong; we must put God first in our lives.
2. We must pray the Rosary each day for peace.
3. We must make sacrifices for sinners so they will know and love God.

Father Stefano Gobbi, founder of the Marian Movement of Priests and a mystic, went on pilgrimage to Fatima in 1972. At the shrine, he prayed for certain priests who had renounced their vocations and were attempting to rebel against the Catholic Church. He heard Our Lady's voice urge him to gather other priests who would be willing to consecrate themselves to the Immaculate Heart of Mary and remain strongly united to the holy pope and the Church. This was the first of hundreds of inner locutions that Fr. Gobbi would receive over the course of his life.

From 1988 to 1996, Our Lady gave him five messages concerning the illumination of conscience. The first took place on May 22, 1988, which was the Feast of Pentecost. She spoke of Abba-Father's plan to enlighten even the most rebellious of sinners.

> With his divine love, he will open the doors of hearts and illuminate all consciences. Every person will see himself

> in the burning fire of divine truth. It will be like a judgment in miniature, and then Jesus Christ will bring his glorious reign in the world.

On June 4, 1995, which again was the Feast of Pentecost, she said:

> Tongues of fire will come down upon you all, my poor children, so ensnared and seduced by Satan and by all the evil spirits who, during these years, have attained their greatest triumph. And thus, you will be illuminated by this divine light, and you will see your own selves in the mirror of the truth and the holiness of God. It will be like a judgment in miniature, which will open the door of your heart to receive the great gift of divine mercy.
>
> And then the Holy Spirit will work the new miracle of universal transformation in the heart and the life of all: sinners will be converted; the weak will find support; the sick will receive healing; those far away will return to the house of the Father; those separated and divided will attain full unity. In this way, the miracle of the Second Pentecost will take place. It will come with the triumph of my Immaculate Heart in the world. Only then will you see how the tongues of fire of the Spirit of Love will renew the whole world, which will become completely transformed by the greatest manifestation of divine mercy.

Prior to this, the Blessed Mother began appearing in San Sebastián de Garabandal, Spain, on July 2, 1961. She spoke to four children: Conchita González, Jacinta González, Mari Loli Mazón, and Mari Cruz González. In October, she told the children about a Great Miracle that was coming. Conchita later reported:

> In order to prepare us for the Great Miracle, a supernatural warning, coming directly from God, will occur. The Warning will appear in the sky and will be visible to the whole world. It will be understood by everyone at the same time, regardless of their state of life or knowledge of God.

For those who stay close to Christ, it's an illumination of conscience and it will unveil the glory of God in a fullness we've never seen before. For evildoers, it will be a warning. When they see everything they've done through the eyes of Abba-Father and they realize how much they've wounded Jesus, will they be happy about those wounds? Or will they repent?

Janie Garza is a visionary and locutionist with the visible stigmata (the wounds of Christ) on her body. Born in 1955, she has authored *Heaven's Messages for the Family*. In 2006, her bishop gave his full approval to continue speaking and spreading the messages she's received.

In 1994, Saint Joseph appeared to her and said:

> The Truth is the Eternal Father. You cannot live in sin and say you know the truth, for you cannot have two masters. You must choose to live in darkness or to live in the light. For those who believe that they live in the light but continue to break every Commandment given by God, to these souls, I, Saint Joseph, say that these souls will not be able to see the state of their souls and live.

From all of my studies about the illumination of conscience, it seems to me that if your loved ones who've been rejecting Christ have shown evidence that they do love, they do care, and they do feel bad for the wounded, then the illumination will alarm them the way Alan Ames was alarmed. Seeing what they did to Jesus will horrify them. (This includes seeing what they did to Jesus every time they hurt you!) They will repent. If it happens at the moment of their death, they will gladly enter into the purification of Purgatory. If it happens in a global miracle, they will spend the rest of their lives on fire for the Lord and God will turn their rebellion into ministry.

St. Joseph told Janie:

> Share with them that the Eternal One is calling them to return to him and to accept his love and mercy, to amend their lives and to live the messages of prayer, fasting and conversion. All who repent will receive special graces to enter into the Sacred Heart of Jesus and the Immaculate Heart of Mary. To all who repent, God will shower his mercy on them. No one will be turned away, for God loves all his children.

Today's Exercise: Write your story of conversion

Spend some time recalling the various times you experienced a significant repentance. Ask the Holy Spirit to refresh your memory. Even ask your Guardian Angel to refresh your memory!

Many of us have had a profound turning point. Others reading this have had only gradual spiritual growth from the day they were born. But all of us have sinned. All of us have discovered a need to seek Abba's forgiveness.

Did any of these occasions include a mystical encounter with the Lord? If this has happened to you, share it with someone you know who is struggling in their relationship with God. Remember, everything that Abba-Father gives to us is meant to be shared. He gave you a conversion story. Don't hide it! Glorify God with it.

DAY 26

Saint Joseph as the Image of God's Fatherhood

ONLY ONE SAINT STANDS out as the best human model of God's Fatherhood. Saint Joseph is the best ally for men who want to be good husbands and fathers. And yet we know so little about him from the Bible. Only recently has devotion to Saint Joseph become popular. Why now? It's because of all that Satan has done to destroy the image of fatherhood. Abba-Father is giving Saint Joseph to the world as a remedy for all of the demonic strategies against marriages and families.

> *When Joseph woke up, he did what the angel of the Lord had commanded him and took Mary home as his wife. (Matthew 1:24 NIV)*

Joseph is taking into his "home"—his fatherly care—anyone who asks for it. If Mary is our mother, then Joseph is our father representing God the Father. We who have been adopted through baptism to become children of the Divine Father are also adopted by the only human father who is perfect. How did your dad fail you? What did you seek but not get from the father-figures in your life? Joseph has all of the qualities you've longed for.

His job, however, is not to replace God as the father we need. His mission is to be the human image of Abba-Father, replacing the flawed image we've carried around since childhood. His greatest desire is to replace Satan, the father of lies who has tricked the world into rejecting God's Fatherhood.

Sometimes we mistakenly think that the Devil is the polar opposite of God. We think that Satan is the ultimate nemesis of God, and God is the ultimate nemesis of Satan. This is not true. God already won the battle—long before Jesus defeated Satan on the Cross. The war is being waged between the Devil and the children of God (all humans). Jesus died for *us*, to set us free from the captivity of evil.

The Devil's true nemesis is the one who is nicknamed "Terror of Demons": Saint Joseph.

Men are warriors. God created them to have victory in their blood. Therefore, Joseph is a warrior: the strongest fighter in the army. Jesus is the army's General, the Commander-in-Chief. Joseph is the army's second in command, the Deputy Commander or Executive Officer. He uses the authority of the General to go up against the enemy and win. And since Satan's war is being waged against us humans, Jesus has sent a human to lead us through the battlefield and take back territories that the Devil has stolen.

Jesus referred to this when he said, "The gates of Hell will not prevail against My Church" (see Matthew 16:18). He wasn't talking about the enemy's aggressions against the Church. Gates don't attack. Gates protect. Our mission on the battlefield is to attack the gates and knock them down. Our mission is to make breakthroughs that free Satan's captives. With our Commander-in-Chief, we proclaim as our own mission statement the same scripture he read aloud at the start of his public ministry:

The Spirit of the Sovereign Lord is on me,
because the Lord has anointed me
to proclaim good news to the poor.
He has sent me to bind up the brokenhearted,
to proclaim freedom for the captives
and release from darkness for the prisoners
(Isaiah 61:1 NIV, quoted in the New Testament at Luke 4:18)

Yes, this is your mission statement too! Jesus taught me this many years ago. My book *Overcoming the Power of the Occult* had just been published and I'd been invited to speak to a Catholic youth group about the occult games they liked to play with. When I arrived at the meeting room, the youth minister handed me a bible while opening it to any random page. He asked me to lead the meeting with scripture. Guess what scripture passage his bible fell open to! Yup, the one I just quoted above.

At that moment, Jesus told me (and the Holy Spirit filled me with certainty all the way to my core) that this was my mission statement and the calling of every Christian.

That night, some of those teenagers left for home set free from the lie the Devil had tricked them into believing: that they could safely play with the Ouija board and other games of the occult.

How Saint Joseph wins battles for us

Jesus gave us his mission and he gave us his authority over evil so we can succeed in the mission.

> *For the grace of God has appeared that offers salvation to all people. It teaches us to say "No" to ungodliness and worldly passions, and to live self-controlled, upright and godly lives in this present age, while we wait for the blessed hope–the appearing of the glory of our great God and Savior, Jesus Christ, who gave himself for us to redeem us from all wickedness and to purify for himself a people that are his very own, eager to do what is good.*
>
> *These, then, are the things you should teach. Encourage and rebuke with all authority. (Titus 2:11-15 NIV)*

Saint Joseph was all of those things—self-controlled, upright, and godly—and he is our role model. When we purify our lives from sin, we gain Christ's own authority to stop the tactics of the Devil, first in our personal lives and then in the lives of others according to the mission he gives us. The Devil becomes afraid of us!

Saint Joseph, armed with the authority of Christ, is leading the way to victory. He guides us in knocking down the gates of Hell. He is advancing our invasion into Satan's territory to reach victims of the battle, i.e., those who've been trapped by the Devil's lies.

This does not include rescuing those who are already in Hell. There is no redemption for them. It's too late for them; they have made their choice. The people who are still alive and have been seduced by demons into following them into the earthly territories of

Hell—these are the prisoners we're going after.

The earthly territories of Hell are all of the fortresses of evil from which Satan's minions go out and spread lies, steal God's children away from him, and infect the world with evil. They are the headquarters of Planned Parenthood, Communism, the occult, sexual deviancy, and other portals to Hell.

Saint Joseph does not fight political wars, but he does lead an army against evil agendas in politics. He does not fight in courtrooms, but he does fight against the evils that brought cases to trial. He battles for souls anywhere that the Devil invades. His weapon? The truth! The truth about who God is. The truth about what it means to be a child of God. The truth about Jesus conquering the Devil throughout his earthly ministry and especially on the Cross.

Remember how Jesus defeated the Tempter in the desert (see Luke 4:1-13). He spoke the truth about each scripture that Satan twisted. He countered each lie with the truth. The most effective way to resist the Devil is to crush his lies with the truth and then act on the truth.

Look at how the battle is won in James 4:1-8 (ESV):

> *What causes quarrels and what causes fights among you? Is it not this, that your passions are at war within you? You desire and do not have, so you murder. You covet and cannot obtain, so you fight and quarrel. You do not have, because you do not ask. You ask and do not receive, because you ask wrongly, to spend it on your passions. You adulterous people! Do you not know that friendship with the world is enmity with God? Therefore, whoever wishes to be a friend of the world makes himself an enemy of God. Or do you suppose it is to no purpose that the Scripture says, "He yearns jealously over the spirit that he has made to dwell in us"? But he gives more grace. Therefore it says, "God opposes the proud but gives grace to the humble." Submit yourselves therefore to God. Resist the devil, and he will flee from you. Draw near to God, and he will draw near to you. Cleanse your hands, you sinners, and purify your hearts, you double-minded.*

What are the weapons the Lord gives us as we follow Saint Joseph into battle? This scripture gives us four. (1) Commit firmly to being on God's side: God gives grace to those who are at enmity with the world. (2) Resist the Devil: Never believe his lies but counter them with the truth and act on the truth. (3) Draw near to God: Pray, pray, pray! (4) Repent of your sins: The Sacrament of Confession demolishes the Devil's strategy against you while it strengthens your resolve to remain on God's side of the battle.

With the Blessed Mother, Saint Joseph is asking for prayer, penance, and holiness. In her apparitions, she has been telling a sinful world that we can no longer live in enmity against God. She has been begging people to change their lives. Joseph is totally united to her in this message. Prayer, penance, and holiness is exactly how we successfully spread the Kingdom of Christ in a demonized world.

As Patron Saint of the family, Joseph goes into every home where he's invited and—with the authority of Jesus—he leads us to defeat the Devil. He assists in taking care of the children. He helps strengthen marriages. He teaches men to imitate him. He also joins in with the prayers of parents whose adult children have strayed off into Satan's territories.

Satan fears Saint Joseph because, though a mere human, he is the perfect image of God the Father. After Jesus and Mary, there is no one whom Satan runs away from more speedily than Saint Joseph.

However, to benefit from Saint Joseph's warrior-fatherhood, we need to pull him out from the shadows and give him a place of importance in our homes, in our lives, and in our churches. He humbly accepts that the Blessed Mother has been in the limelight, but when given the opportunity, he gladly steps out in front to protect us from the enemy's attacks and to help Jesus rescue those lost lambs who have wandered away from the safety of the sheepfold.

Meet Saint Joseph

Saint Joseph has always been recognized by Christians as an extraordinary man, although most of what is known about him does not come from scripture. Throughout the history of the Church, saints, mystics, popes, and others have given us a fuller picture of him. Here is a partial list of the fatherly traits they described. As you read through them, take time to connect these traits to Abba-Father. Saint Joseph, in his perfection as a father, reveals to us what our Divine Daddy is like more so than any other father-figure.

1. **Saint Joseph is perfect in love, humility, and dedication** to his mission of caring for Jesus and Mary, according to many

Fathers of the Church including Saint Jerome and Saint Augustine.

2. **Saint Joseph is authoritative, affectionate, and faithful**, as Saint Augustine pointed out while explaining that, although he was not the biological father of Jesus, he was a true father—a holy father.
3. **Saint Joseph is patient**. Saint Joseph Marello said, "He was always imperturbable, even in adversities. Let us model ourselves after this sublime example and let us learn to remain peaceful and tranquil in all of life's circumstances."
4. **Saint Joseph is a protector**, and this is one of the fatherly traits that scripture reveals. He protected Jesus and Mary when King Herod was trying to destroy the newborn king.
5. **Saint Joseph is a provider**, as we know from his trade as a carpenter. We also see his unfailing determination to provide a safe place for Mary to give birth when all the inns were booked up. Saint John Paul II wrote in Redemptoris Custos, "The growth of Jesus 'in wisdom and in stature, and in favor with God and man' (Luke 2:52) took place within the Holy Family under the eyes of Joseph, who had the important task of "raising" Jesus, that is, feeding, clothing, and educating him in the Law and in a trade, in keeping with the duties of a father."
6. **Saint Joseph has a strong sense of responsibility**, as indicated in the scripture about Mary and Joseph losing track of the Child Jesus for three days. They had assumed he was hanging out with others in the caravan who journeyed with them on the way home from their pilgrimage to Jerusalem. When they realized that he had been left behind, they searched "anxiously" (see Luke 2:48). This is not the anxiety of someone who worries without self-control and without trust in God. It's the anxiety that every parent feels when a child is unwittingly endangering himself.
7. **Saint Joseph is a just man**, as shown in how he handled the news that Mary was pregnant. Being "a just man and unwilling to put her to shame," he decided to send her away quietly. (See Matthew 1:18-24.) Even though the situation was shocking and disappointing, he reacted without anger, fear, or judgmentalism. His decision was based on love and compassion for Mary.

8. **Saint Joseph is always submissive to God's will.** Saint Francis de Sales said, "To be just is to be perfectly united to the Divine Will, and to be always conformed to it in all sorts of events, whether prosperous or adverse. That Saint Joseph was this, no one can doubt."
9. **Saint Joseph is a problem solver.** Imagine the difficulties he had to overcome while the Holy Family lived in Egypt. Saint Francis de Sales said, "Saint Joseph was in a land which was not only foreign, but also hostile to Israelites. The Egyptians resented that the Israelites had escaped from their tyranny, and also that they had been the cause of many of their ancestors being drowned in the Red Sea." To bring his family through those challenges, he had to be a good problem solver. According to the mystical revelations of Blessed Anne Catherine Emmerich, Joseph was often unable to find sufficient work and provide the food, clean water, or proper housing that he wished to give his family. His problem-solving skills kept them alive and unharmed.
10. **Saint Joseph comforts us in difficult times.** Saint Joseph Marello said, "Let us commend ourselves to our good father, Saint Joseph, who is the Patriarch of troubled people, since he himself went through so much trouble."
11. **Saint Joseph helps us pray and worship.** Pope Benedict XVI said, "Joseph fulfilled every aspect of his paternal role. He must certainly have taught Jesus to pray, together with Mary. In particular Joseph himself must have taken Jesus to the Synagogue for the rites of the Sabbath, as well as to Jerusalem for the great feasts of the people of Israel. Joseph, in accordance with the Jewish tradition, would have led the prayers at home both every day—in the morning, in the evening, at meals—and on the principal religious feasts. In the rhythm of the days he spent at Nazareth, in the simple home and in Joseph's workshop, Jesus learned to alternate prayer and work, as well as to offer God his labor in earning the bread the family needed."
12. **Saint Joseph wants to be your father.** In a vision, Jesus said to the Servant of God Sr. Marie-Martha Chambon, "You must call Saint Joseph your father, for I have given him the title and the goodness of a father."

13. **Saint Joseph is available**, placing himself at the service of family life and your spiritual growth. Pope Benedict XVI said, "There is but one fatherhood, that of God the Father, the one Creator of the world, of all that is seen and unseen. Yet man, created in the image of God, has been granted a share in this one paternity of God (Ephesians 3:15). Saint Joseph is a striking case of this, since he is a father, without fatherhood according to the flesh. He is not the biological father of Jesus, whose Father is God alone, and yet he lives his fatherhood fully and completely. To be a father means above all to be at the service of life and growth. Saint Joseph, in this sense, gave proof of great devotion."
14. **Saint Joseph is the most luminous of all the saints**, according to Saint Gregory Nazianzen who wrote: "The Almighty has concentrated in Saint Joseph, as in a Sun of unrivalled luster, the combined light and splendor of all the other saints." (Note: Saint Gregory did not imply that Joseph is greater than Mary. Traditionally, she is not given the title "saint" because she is more than that. She is the Mother of God, a super-category of holiness.)
15. **Saint Joseph was Mary's most chaste husband**. From the beginning, saints and mystics have told the same story about his marriage to Mary. Details vary but the essence is the same: Before they knew that they would someday marry, she had taken a vow to be married to God alone. Joseph, too, had taken a vow of celibacy as an act of devotion and complete surrender to God. Mary was one of the temple virgins serving the Lord since early childhood. Normally the temple virgins were sent home to marry and raise children when they reached the age of fourteen, so the temple priests, recognizing how special Mary was, decided to find her a husband. All the unmarried male descendants of David were brought before the altar presenting a staff. The priests believed that God would give a sign through the staff of the man whom God had chosen for Mary. Joseph's staff sprouted lilies, which is why on holy cards he is often depicted with a flowering staff. He was delighted to take as his bride someone who was as devoted to the Lord as he was; they could both keep their vows of celibacy. Saint Lawrence of Brindisi said, "For just as husband and wife are one flesh, so too Joseph and Mary were one heart, one soul, one spirit."

16. **Saint Joseph is the second Adam**, the perfect Adam, the way Adam was supposed to be. Saint Lawrence of Brindisi said, "And as in that first marriage God created Eve to be like Adam, so in this second marriage he made Joseph to be like the Blessed Virgin in holiness and justice."
17. **Saint Joseph is the spiritual father of all humanity**. Pope Pius XI wrote, "The intercession of Saint Joseph is that of the husband, the putative [accepted] father, the head of the family of Nazareth which was composed of himself, Mary, and Jesus. And as Saint Joseph was truly the head or the master of that house, his intercession cannot be but all-powerful. For what could Jesus and Mary refuse to Saint Joseph, he who was entirely consecrated to them all his life, and to whom they truly owed the means of their earthly existence?"
18. **Saint Joseph is a role model of masculinity.** Jesus as a male child learned from Joseph's fatherhood what being a man, a husband, and a father truly looked like. Every manly trait that Jesus exhibited he learned from Joseph. These traits, in turn, reveal to us what God the Father is truly like. Jesus endured much: Picture Joseph enduring much while he dealt with ordinary townspeople who were far less holy than he was. Jesus stood up to bullies, full of self-confidence without demeaning anyone: Picture Joseph stopping fist fights between angry neighbors, intervening without fear, and with great wisdom. Jesus made many sacrifices before his final, huge sacrifice: Picture Joseph sacrificing his time at work to give the Child Jesus his attention and also sacrificing the material pleasures he could have earned if he had spent more time at work.
19. **Saint Joseph obtains great blessings** for those who invite him into their lives with great devotion. Saint Teresa of Avila wrote, "I have great experience of the blessings which he can obtain from God. I do not remember that I have ever asked anything of him which he has failed to grant. I am astonished at the great favors which God has bestowed on me through this blessed saint, and at the perils from which he has delivered me, both in body and in soul. . . . The Lord wishes to teach us that, as he was himself subject on Earth to Saint Joseph, so in Heaven he now does all that Joseph asks."
20. **Saint Joseph has unlimited power to help us**. Saint Thomas

Aquinas wrote, "There are many saints to whom God has given the power to assist us in the necessities of life, but the power given to Saint Joseph is unlimited: It extends to all our needs, and all those who invoke him with confidence are sure to be heard."

The world needs Saint Joseph now more than ever.

Ralph and I enhanced our marriage and our relationships with Father God by consecrating ourselves to Saint Joseph through a 33-day spiritual exercise using Father Donald Calloway's book called *Consecration to Saint Joseph: The Wonders of Our Spiritual Father* (published by Marian Press). I highly recommend this to everyone who wants to stand firmly on God's side of the battle and receive Saint Joseph's protection. Consecration is both a devotion and a commitment. You can consecrate yourself, your marriage, your family, your home, and your work to Saint Joseph. You can place yourself into the hands of the best human father ever.

Father Calloway explains why this is so important:

> In our day, Jesus wants the Church to know, love, honor, and seek refuge in the spiritual fatherhood of Saint Joseph. There has never been a time in history when God's people have needed Saint Joseph more. Why? Simply put, the majority of men no longer know or understand what it means to be a gentleman, let alone what it means to be a good father. Children have grown up with poor examples of fatherhood, if they have grown up with a father at all. Contraception, pornography, abortion, gender confusion, moral depravity, empty churches, morally corrupt clergy, and cultural chaos are only a few of the fruits of a society that lacks real men and fathers. Jesus wants to draw our attention to the spiritual fatherhood of Saint Joseph in order to right these wrongs and bring order back to the Church and the world.

In looking at how much Saint Joseph is needed today, Father Calloway compares him to his biblical namesake, the great patriarch Joseph, the son of Jacob. Saint Lawrence of Brindisi said of this:

> The former Joseph was holy, righteous, pious, chaste; but this Joseph so far surpasses him in holiness and perfection as the sun outshines the moon. "Pharaoh, the mighty

> king of Egypt, exalted Joseph and made him the highest prince in his Kingdom because he stored up the grain and bread and saved the people of his entire kingdom. So, Joseph saved and protected Christ, who is the living bread and gives eternal life to the world."

Father Calloway adds:

> Today, there is a worldwide spiritual and moral famine on the Earth. Souls are dying because of a lack of spiritual nourishment. Hearts are broken; marriages are ruined; lives are destroyed; children are murdered in the womb; and truth and common sense are in short supply. The spiritual and moral famine in the world is devastating every nation, laying waste to humanity. There is not a single country left that has not been affected by it. What are we to do? To whom can we go to find nourishment for our souls?

"Go to Joseph and do whatever he tells you!" (Genesis 41: 55)

The Devil's overwhelmingly successful attack against our families and his massive infiltration of our world are not a surprise to Abba-Father nor to Saint Joseph. Over the past 150 years, Saint Joseph's importance as the perfect model of fatherhood has become increasingly recognized. Notice how it's evolved:

- In 1868, Blessed Jean-Joseph Lataste, OP, asked Blessed Pope Pius IX to declare Saint Joseph the "Patron of the Universal Church."
- In 1870, the pope proclaimed that Saint Joseph is the "Patron of the Universal Church."
- In 1879 at Knock, Ireland, Saint Joseph appeared with the Blessed Virgin Mary, Saint John the Apostle, and Jesus (who appeared as the Lamb of God on an altar).
- In 1889, Pope Leo XIII wrote Quamquam Pluries, an encyclical letter about Saint Joseph.
- In 1909, Saint Pope Pius X officially approved the Litany of Saint Joseph (which is included below for your edification).
- In 1917 in Fatima, Portugal, during the final apparition of Our Lady, Saint Joseph appeared with her. He was holding the Child Jesus and together they were blessing the world.

- In the 1950s, visionary Sr. Mary Ephrem was told by the Blessed Virgin Mary (under the title Our Lady of America) that the Church should emphasize a renewed devotion to Saint Joseph. Saint Joseph himself also spoke to her about this.
- In 1955, Venerable Pope Pius XII established May 1st as the Feast of Saint Joseph the Worker.
- In 1958, Bishop Angelo Roncalli, who had a great devotion to Saint Joseph, was elected to the papacy (as Pope John XXIII).
- In 1962, Pope Saint John XXIII entrusted the Second Vatican Council to Saint Joseph.
- Later that same year, the pope added Saint Joseph's name into Eucharistic Prayer #1 of Holy Mass.
- In 1989, Saint Pope John Paul II wrote Redemptoris Custos, an apostolic exhortation on Saint Joseph.
- In 2013, Pope Francis added Saint Joseph's name into all of the Eucharistic Prayers. He also consecrated the Vatican City State to Saint Joseph.

Where does this put us today? Saint Joseph wants everyone to consecrate our homes to him. Now. Our homes are battlefields. The Devil and his minions have been fighting against domestic peace, fighting against children growing up to become holy priests or religious or fruitful parents, fighting against the holy Sacrament of Marriage. And most of all, fighting against the true image of God as our Father.

To help win the battle in your home, set up an adoration chapel or a shrine. We tend to think that adoration chapels are only for churches and must contain Jesus in the Blessed Sacrament. But consider what Blessed William Joseph Chaminade said about Saint Joseph:

> How many times did he, like the lone sparrow, nestle on the roof of that holy temple of the divinity, contemplating this divine Child sleeping in his arms, and thinking of his eternal repose in the bosom of the heavenly Father?

Your home becomes an adoration chapel every time you contemplate the presence of Jesus and praise him. We don't need to see the Eucharistic Host to adore Jesus. He is with us all of the time.

Joseph adored him as he held him in his arms. He adored him as he taught him, played with him, and worked with him. And he invited others to adore him, too. Picture the scene in Bethlehem when he and Mary welcomed the scraggly, smelly shepherds. Picture how he welcomed the magi, though they were not Jews. Imagine how he felt as he watched them give gifts to the baby. And now he is inviting you, too, to spend time each day adoring your Savior and giving him gifts.

This is what a good father does. He helps his children to know and adore Jesus. He is concerned about their eternal salvation.

The prayers of a father for his children are very powerful—but only when he is firmly and completely on God's side of the battle. Half-heartedness weakens his authority. Wholehearted commitment to his role as God's warrior gives him the authority of Jesus, and with this he leads his family in defeating the Devil.

Today's Exercise: Meditate on the Litany of Saint Joseph

We can get a bigger picture of what Saint Joseph's fatherhood looks like by using the Litany of Saint Joseph. Pause to reflect on each of the fatherly traits that are named here in the titles of Saint Joseph. Stay with each one until you attach them to Abba-Father. For example, how is God the Father "most chaste"? I see this as describing God's purity. So, then I ask: How does Abba's purity affect my life? Why does this make him the most wonderful Daddy ever?

The Litany of Saint Joseph

Lord, have mercy on us.	- *Christ, have mercy on us.*
Lord, have mercy on us. Jesus, hear us.	- *Jesus, graciously hear us.*
God the Father of Heaven,	- *have mercy on us.*
God the Son, Redeemer of the World,	- *have mercy on us.*
God the Holy Spirit,	- *have mercy on us.*
Holy Trinity, one God,	-*have mercy on us.*
Holy Mary,	- *pray for us.*
Saint Joseph,	- *pray for us.*
Renowned offspring of David,	- *pray for us.*
Light of Patriarchs,	- *pray for us.*
Spouse of the Mother of God,	- *pray for us.*
Chaste guardian of the Virgin,	- *pray for us.*

Foster father of the Son of God, - *pray for us.*
Diligent protector of Christ, - *pray for us.*
Head of the Holy Family, - *pray for us.*
Joseph most just, - *pray for us.*
Joseph most chaste, - *pray for us.*
Joseph most prudent, - *pray for us.*
Joseph most strong, - *pray for us.*
Joseph most obedient, - *pray for us.*
Joseph most faithful, - *pray for us.*
Mirror of patience, - *pray for us.*
Lover of poverty, - *pray for us.*
Model of artisans, - *pray for us.*
Glory of home life, - *pray for us.*
Guardian of virgins, - *pray for us.*
Pillar of families, - *pray for us.*
Solace of the wretched, - *pray for us.*
Hope of the sick, - *pray for us.*
Patron of the dying, - *pray for us.*
Terror of demons, - *pray for us.*
Protector of Holy Church, - *pray for us.*

Lamb of God, who takes away the sins of the world,
- *spare us, O Jesus.*
Lamb of God, who takes away the sins of the world,
- *graciously hear us, O Jesus.*
Lamb of God, who takes away the sins of the world,
- *have mercy on us, O Jesus.*
He made him the lord of his household
- *And prince over all his possessions.*

Let us pray:

O God, in your ineffable providence you were pleased to choose Blessed Joseph to be the spouse of your most holy Mother; grant, we beg you, that we may be worthy to have him for our intercessor in Heaven whom on Earth we venerate as our Protector: You who live and reign forever and ever.

Saint Joseph, pray for us.

DAY 27

Reclaiming God's Fatherhood Over the World

HOW'S YOUR JOURNEY INTO the heart of God's Fatherhood? Do you feel differently about him today than when you started? Are you excited about this? Abba-Father is! He's delighted that you've overcome some of the obstacles that have prevented you from knowing him better. He's super happy that you are now embedded more deeply into his heart. And so he says: "Because of what you've discovered, I need you to be My ambassador! There are countless people who are suffering because they don't yet know Me well."

> *And he said to them, "Go into all the world and proclaim the gospel to the whole creation. (Mark 16:15 ESV)*

Have you said yes yet to this calling? Right now, for the purposes of this book, we're zooming in on the mission field of healing people's relationships with Abba-Father by changing their wrong images about him, and by rescuing them from the father of lies. Are you willing to follow Saint Joseph into this battle? We're always eager to say yes when we're thinking about our loved ones who have been captured by the Devil. But are you interested in going farther? Are you willing to fight for the souls of other people's loved ones?

Abba-Father is counting on you! You and I and every follower of Christ are called and commissioned to counter Satan's attacks against fatherhood, marriage, family, and the Church. And here's how to be successful:

1. Purge from your own life the misconceptions you have about God's Fatherhood—*check! Done, although there is more work to do on this.*
2. Consecrate your life to Saint Joseph (and/or Holy Mother Mary)—*covered on Day 26.*
3. Receive the Holy Spirit's anointing.
4. Purify your life, make frequent use of the Sacrament of Confession, and do penances that strengthen your holiness so that your battle armor has no holes through which the enemy can weaken you.
5. Become a clear reflection of God's Fatherhood, examining your conscience about this and asking the Holy Spirit to illuminate your vision about how to do this better.
6. Turn evil into blessings by using the problems and victories you've experienced as energy and motivation for helping others discover and run to the True Father.
7. Identify your gifts and talents, and look for or create opportunities to use them to glorify God.

Receive the Holy Spirit

The Holy Spirit is Christ's Spirit generously given to us so that we can be holy and to continue the ministry that Christ began—especially the mission of revealing God the Father in such a way that others will desire to spend eternity with him. Just like Jesus did. People met the Father through Jesus. People can meet the Father through you now. When Jesus walked the Earth, the Father's true image was revealed by Jesus: how he lived, how he handled conflicts, how he cared, how he forgave, etc. Jesus walks the Earth through you now. Others will discover the Father's true image by how you live, how you handle conflicts, how you care, how you forgive, and so forth.

On our own, we cannot be like our Father enough to convert the hearts of others. We need the Holy Spirit for this. When Christ's

Spirit is alive and active within us, we have Christ's holiness, his faith, his supernatural love and peace, his confidence and endurance, and everything else that we need to become the Father's ambassadors.

> *You will receive power when the Holy Spirit has come upon you; and you shall be My witnesses both in Jerusalem, and in all Judea and Samaria, and even to the remotest part of the earth. (Acts 1:8 NASB)*

Ever since the first outpouring of the Spirit on Pentecost, God has been transforming the world by working through those who serve his Kingdom. When we're willing to be part of this exciting plan, God generously fills us with his Spirit so that we will succeed in everything that he commissions us to do. How well we serve—how much his holiness and power exudes from us—is up to us.

We receive the Holy Spirit during baptism. The reality of this is confirmed and strengthened in the Sacrament of Confirmation. But this is not enough. It's a partnership with God and we have to say yes to it. We have to desire it so much that it directs our thoughts and our actions.

Have you ever been asked, "Are you born again?" Skip that question! Go directly to: "Is the Holy Spirit living within you, activating your faith, inspiring you to holy action?" Having a personal relationship with Jesus Christ is only the first step. A personal relationship with his Holy Spirit is what transitions a sinful person into a holy person.

It was the Holy Spirit who gave the first Apostles unfettered boldness to proclaim God's word. Without this, they were scared and ineffective. Does your faith give you powerful boldness and confidence? Does it motivate you to take action for the sake of those who are suffering from the lack of a close Father-child relationship?

It was the Holy Spirit who filled the first Christians with rejoicing when they faced persecution. Are you able to rejoice in the midst of troubles? If not, ask to be renewed by the Holy Spirit.

It was the Holy Spirit who inspired them to pray and who deepened their prayer life. Is your prayer life in need of help? If it is, then ask the Holy Spirit to fill your prayer time.

It was the Holy Spirit, not a tornado, who blew like a violent wind from Heaven and filled the whole house where the disciples were gathered on Pentecost (read Acts 2:1-4). Do you sense the powerful presence of God when you gather in community? If not, ask for the baptism of the Holy Spirit, and keep asking until the Spirit overwhelms you. (This is best done in community with others praying for the release of the Spirit in you.)

Jesus put the baptism of the Holy Spirit on an equal level with the baptism of water:

> *Very truly I tell you, no one can enter the kingdom of God unless they are born of water and the Spirit. Flesh gives birth to flesh, but the Spirit gives birth to spirit. (John 3:5-6 NIV)*

The two work together: baptism by water cleanses us from sin; the Holy Spirit empowers us to be holy and resist new temptations to sin. Does your faith enable you to overcome repeated tendencies to sin? If not, then let nothing stop you from receiving the baptism of the Holy Spirit. By water, God's holiness has replaced your fallen, sinful nature. By the Holy Spirit, God's holiness has become your true nature.

The Holy Spirit is the key that unlocks our holiness: "No one can enter into God's kingdom without being born of water *and* Spirit. Spirit begets spirit." We can only be Christ-like when his Holy Spirit is alive and active in us. We can only stay on the path to Heaven when the Holy Spirit is our guide. We can only lead the world to God's Fatherhood when the Spirit of Christ reveals him through us.

A common misconception that thwarts our ability to serve as an ambassador of God's Fatherhood is the idea that only some specially chosen people are filled so fully with the Holy Spirit that they live supernatural lives. Do you suppose that the Father has rationed the gift of his Spirit to you? Do you think you have a portion of the Holy Spirit or the fullness of the Spirit?

> *The one who comes from heaven is above all. . . . For the one whom God has sent speaks the words of God, for God gives the Spirit without limit. (John 3:31,34 NIV)*

Jesus said that the Father did not ration ("limit") the Spirit to him. What about us? Peter said that the Holy Spirit has been given to all who obey the Father.

> *Peter and the other apostles replied: "We must obey God rather than human beings! The God of our ancestors raised Jesus from the dead. . . . We are witnesses of these things, and so is the Holy Spirit,*

whom God has given to those who obey him." (Acts 5:29-30,32 NIV)

You and I do not obey God all of the time like Jesus did. Does this mean that the Father gives us less of his Spirit than he gave to Jesus?

Try this question: Is the Father's love ever limited? Can he partially love anyone? Of course not! There is no such thing as "partial love." Love is love! God, who *is* love, fully and completely loves you. So, why does it seem like he gave Jesus the fullness of the Spirit but only a portion to us?

Jesus stayed fully in touch with the Father and was therefore open to receiving everything that the Father wanted to give him. He could hear everything that the Father told him. And he could do everything that the Father wanted to do through him.

When we were baptized into the life of Christ, the Father gave us his Spirit fully. The problem is, we're not fully in touch with the Father. Our worldly attachments and busyness distract us. Our sins build a dam that holds back the waters of the Spirit.

Countless Saints have experienced the power of the Spirit in amazing miracles because they worked hard daily at breaking down the barriers between this world and Heaven. They worked hard at purging out all the sins and distractions that disconnected them from God. "But I'll never be *that* holy," we point out. We give up before we try long enough. We become content with the progress we've made and so we sit down on a cozy wayside bench. We see hard work ahead, and so we turn onto paths that look pleasant and easy.

Thus, we lead mediocre lives instead of miraculous ones. Big dreams about doing amazing ministries become fantasies instead of realities. And instead of achieving great accomplishments that change the world, we severely limit our potential.

The Father is not the one who rations the Holy Spirit to us. We are the ones who put limitations on our service as Abba's ambassadors. Observe the decisions that you make today (and each day) while asking yourself: "Am I choosing the way of holiness? Am I staying centered on God's love for me and my love for him?" Each and every moment!

Making the right decisions—the holy and loving and soul-nurturing decisions—will flood your life with God's Spirit.

A Prayer to the Holy Spirit

Dear Jesus, stir up within me the fullness of Your Holy Spirit. Help me to live in Your holy power. Open my mind to understand Your truths, and open my heart to accept Your truths even before I gain full understanding.

O Holy Spirit, help me to seek, more than anything, the Kingdom of God. Help me to recognize what I am attached to that is not of You, and give me the determination and the strength to let go. I want only You.

O Holy Spirit, help me to face my sinfulness and to feel genuine sorrow for the damage that I have caused. Comfort me as I mourn my need for forgiveness, and give me Your spirit of rejoicing over this new growth. Then, help me to share this healing mercy with all those around me.

Jesus commanded, "Go into all the world and preach the good news." Use my gifts and talents to make a difference. I have my own expectations about what I should and should not do. I now surrender to You my ideas, my limitations, my preferences, and my goals. I want to be useful to You. I want to go where You lead me. Holy Spirit, send me forth gifted and empowered to spread greater awareness of God's Fatherhood.

Come Holy Spirit; renew me. Amen!

Purify your life

Restoring the world to God's Fatherhood happens one soul at a time. Think about the people in your life who are not on the path that leads to Heaven. You feel worried about them because you care. You care because you know what a huge blessing it would be for them if they surrendered their lives to God right now. You wish you could help them experience the compassion, mercy, and helpfulness of Abba-Father. They desperately need it. Perhaps you've even felt the tears of Abba as he longs to pull them into his heart.

We need to repent from being so focused on our own lives that we ignore the tears of Abba. We need to let go of our feelings of inadequacy that make us say, "That's not in my job description as a Christian. That's for someone else to do." We need to awaken the sleeping ambassador within us and ask: "Why am I not doing more to reclaim God's Fatherhood over the world?"

It's a sin to keep the truth bottled up and locked away. The Holy Spirit wants to speak out through us, but we hold back because we don't want to feel embarrassed or criticized. Abba wants to love those who have not been loved enough, but he needs our flesh to do the reaching out and the hugging.

> *You are the light of the world. A town built on a hill cannot be hidden. Neither do people light a lamp and put it under a bowl. Instead they put it on its stand, and it gives light to everyone in the house. In the same way, let your light shine before others, that they may see your good deeds and glorify your Father in heaven. (Matthew 5:14-16 NIV)*

Because we love Jesus and appreciate what he did for us on the Cross, we have the light of Christ within us. But all too often we let the unloving behaviors of others hide this light by darkening our spirits. Do we stay angry when they sin against us—or do we give them the gift of Abba's love? Do we protect ourselves from rejection and persecution by hiding the light—or do we boldly increase the light and take it out into the darkened world?

Abba-Father wants us to work with Jesus to conquer evil by spreading the Light of Truth everywhere, but if we hide our faith under a basket, we imprison the truth about God's Fatherhood.

As much as we have the love of Abba within us, if we're not giving it to others, the lack of its outward movement makes us feel empty. It's like a faucet. Wrap your hand around the kitchen faucet. When the tap is closed, the pipes are full of water, but you can't feel it. Open the tap, let the water flow, and now you feel its power as the water's movement vibrates the pipes. In the same way, we can only feel the fullness of God's love and power within us when we let it flow out to others.

By purifying our own lives and deepening our own relationship with our Divine Daddy, his love pours out from us. Then, everything we do can reveal the Father's true nature to those who are thirsty for spiritual healing. Opportunities occur every day and in ordinary circumstances. Wherever we connect with others—on social media sites, in stores and restaurants, in church, at work—the waters of the Holy Spirit can flow out from us and reveal Abba's true nature.

Become a clear reflection of God's Fatherhood

Many people ask: "If God really exists, why does he let evil happen?" The answer is: because *we* allow evil to happen.

You and I and all Christians are the earthly Body of Christ, and Abba-Father expects us to continue the earthly ministry of his Son. Jesus made this clear when he sent disciples out to surrounding towns and villages during their apostolic training (see Luke 10:1-16) and when he gave his final instructions just before ascending to Heaven (Mark 16:15).

Jesus is still saying to his followers today:

> *You are the light of the world, because I am in you, you are in Me, and I am in the Father. I am the light of the world. Whoever follows Me will never walk in darkness, but will have the light of life. Let your light shine before others, that they may see your good deeds and glorify your Father in heaven (see Matthew 5:14 and 16, John 14:20, and John 8:12).*

If our lives are immersed in Jesus Christ, and if our decisions depend on what he has taught, then we're living in the Divine Light that destroys evil. We have within us that Divine Light. We have within us the ability to conquer the powers of darkness—if only we allow ourselves to become fully brilliant in it, releasing it instead of bottling it up or hiding it under a bushel basket.

You are Abba-Father's ambassador. See how important you are to him!

Christians have been given divine strength—which is the power of the light of Christ to defeat darkness—to open the gates of Hell by dispelling the lies and deceptions that have imprisoned people. We have been given the Holy Spirit (the Spirit of Truth) to defeat the darkness that has been blinding people to the truth. We can and must introduce them to God's Fatherhood (as it truly is), to the salvation he has provided through his Son Jesus, and to his Holy Spirit who changes people's hearts and minds.

"The gates of Hell will not prevail against you" is not a promise. It's a fact. (Remember Matthew 16:18 from Day 26.)

Here's an illustration of just how easily the light of Christ within you can conquer darkness. If you take two boxes, attach them side by side, and then punch a hole between them, what would happen if you put a lamp inside one of them? Would the darkness pass through the hole and diminish the light? Or would the light pass through the hole and enlighten the other box?

See, the power of light is completely stronger than the power of darkness! This is the power of the Light of Truth. This is what we are called to share by the way we live our lives and reveal what God the Father is truly like.

Charmaine saw it happen:

> A friend called to "talk," and at the beginning I was apprehensive. I wanted to protect myself. But as she continued speaking, the Holy Spirit was telling me that this was the reason for my faith experiences. So, I opened up, and the more I shared the lighter she got and the freer I felt. She was actually laughing by the time we were done.

Turn evil into blessings

Who in your life is suffering through a tragedy or difficulty? Realize that they're instinctively seeking a ray of light that will lead them out of their darkness into hope, love, healing, and the restoration of goodness. Saint Teresa of Calcutta said:

> I think everybody . . . knows deep down in their hearts that there is God, and that we have been created to love and to be loved; that we have not been created to be just a number in the world. But we have been created for some purpose, and that purpose is to be love, to be compassion, to be goodness, to be joy, to serve.

You can reveal to them Abba's loving Fatherhood when they're ready to be assured that God cares about them. Ask the Holy Spirit to prepare their minds to receive the truths that will help them find what they seek. And, when Abba shows you that the time is right, ask the Holy Spirit to give you the words to speak.

It's quite normal to feel inadequate when we look at the darkness of lies and misconceptions that are controlling others. This feeling comes from looking at ourselves and being aware of our limitations. Don't do this! Look instead at what you do have: your experiences that have increased your trust in God, *and* your compassion, *and* your opportunities to reach out and speak to those who are hurting, and much more.

If your heart is with God, if your heart loves to serve him, if your heart trusts your Divine Daddy, and if your heart wants to be obedient to his ways, he will raise you up. He is, in fact, already preparing you for something important to do in the battle to restore his Fatherhood to the world.

Be ready! All of your experiences—the good and the bad—can be used as preparation for a special anointing that God wants to give you. How do I know? Because that's the way he works all of the time. He uses everything about today to prepare us for a future mission, even though we're not aware of being prepared, so that we can do greater and greater works for his Kingdom.

Look for the fire that burns because of the hardships you've endured and the healings you've received. This is where God can work most powerfully through you. Don't overlook this fire. Abba-Father put it there for his purposes and plans.

The path he's laid before you might not be clear, but put one foot forward and start moving! God will reveal the next step, and then the next, and then the next.

Consider this: If a hundred years from now you were to be canonized a saint, what "specialty" would be your patronage? Oh, don't balk at this question. Even if you're never officially canonized, you are in fact headed for Heaven because of your love for Christ. What would the people on Earth ask you to pray for when you reach the throne of God?

This "specialty" is what you've been anointed to do now, serving God with your life here on Earth. This is how he will reach some of his children who have turned away from him. This is how he will restore holy fatherhood to families. This is how he will change the world.

Identify your gifts and talents

Jesus revealed to Saint Thérèse of the Child Jesus that the Father is pleased to work with those who become utterly docile to his direction, with total dependence upon him, because in this humble position we are ready to receive his gifts. Anything and everything that benefits the Kingdom of God then becomes possible.

What traits do you have that can be a gift to others? These are traits of your heavenly Father, which he gave to you as part of your inheritance. Do they seem too little and insignificant for the big task of revealing Abba's love to the world? This is not a problem! Abba can and will multiply what you have, like he did when Jesus prayed over the few loaves and fish that fed a huge crowd.

Consider the passion you feel. Have you cried over lost loved ones? Let your concern for them become fuel for your light. Then Jesus, who is your Light, can invade the darkness of lost souls through you. Don't be surprised—or discouraged—if you're not able to make a difference with your own family members (most of us cannot). However, you *will* be able to enlighten the loved ones of other families. So, ask Jesus to send other people to your own loved ones while you become the answer to the prayers of others who grieve *their* lost loved ones.

"Let your lamps be burning ready," Jesus said in Luke 12:35-38. *"Be dressed and ready for service."* Is the light of Christ within you "burning ready"? Not just lit, but ready to join Christ on the adventure of knocking down the gates of Hell and conquering territories of darkness?

What's the fire in you? What do you feel passionate about that's useful to the Lord? Why do you care so much about the souls of others?

The Lord has much need of your gifts and talents, your experiences and skills, and your training and wisdom. He can put it all to very good use. And he wants to! He plans to! But too often we say no because we fail to understand how much he's already prepared us, and so we feel intimidated by the possibilities. We need to trust more in Abba-Father than in our own limited understanding.

There is no one else who can offer to the Kingdom of God exactly what you can offer. You are the answer to the prayers of someone who is lifting up to the Father another lost child. Abba looks at you and knows that you, uniquely, can reach that particular victim of Satan better than anyone else in his or her life. The Holy Spirit will point out to you who that person is—if you ask for eyes to see.

If you feel inadequate and overwhelmed by the task, remember that it's not you who are the source of adequacy. You are not the Savior. You are the vessel of the Divine Love that is more powerful than evil. Where sin abounds, grace abounds the more (see Romans 5:20). God's grace combined with your passion will make a difference despite how small and insignificant your abilities seem to be.

If you've smothered the flame of your lamp with doubts, Abba is offering you a two-step process to reignite your fire.

1. The Sacrament of Reconciliation removes the sin that's been strangling your confidence. It also provides supernatural grace to overcome the natural tendencies of fear, self-doubt, and any lack of concern for the souls of unbelievers.
2. The baptism of the Holy Spirit (or the renewal of it) sets your heart on fire and empowers you to do whatever the Father wants to do through you.

Abba's abundant grace is always readily available to increase your faith, to strengthen your resolve, and to make you successful despite all obstacles. This is what it means to be "burning ready."

It's not we who change the world. It's the divine presence of God within us, burning like a furnace in which no evil can survive.

The love of Abba in you can change the world!

Why does God let evil happen? Because evil has been enfleshed in this world and Abba stops it through the flesh—first through the incarnation of God the Son, Jesus, then through us, his adopted children. But too few of us are actually doing our part.

Abba-Father wants to raise up a vast corps of ambassadors who have the passion to reclaim the world for holy fatherhood. We are needed and called because we now live in a society where Satan's version of fatherhood has made it "okay" to redefine marriage, change gender identity, and seek sexual pleasures outside of marriage. Divorce is considered better than the self-sacrificing hard work of permanent marriages. Personal agendas preclude having children and even murder them in the womb. Marriages fall apart and families with children are raising them without faith. Why? Because we're not doing enough with what we've been given.

Too few have been answering the call to be warriors and ambassadors.

It would be so much easier if Jesus would hurry up and return in his Second Coming to punish all evildoers and whisk us away in a trouble-escaping rapture. However, escapism does not save souls. God has a better plan.

> *Let your light shine before others, that they may see your good deeds and glorify your Father in heaven. (Matthew 5:16 NIV)*

This is how Abba saves souls. This is how he spreads his Fatherhood across the Earth. This is how *we* spread the truth about God's Fatherhood and change the misconceptions that are keeping people away from his love. Abba-Father uses the Light of Christ within us to reveal his love to others in a way that changes their hearts.

When Jesus walked the Earth, he united us to God the Father by revealing the Father's true nature in everything he said and did. This is what we are now supposed to do. As you discover more and more about what your Divine Daddy is really like, through this book and in all the circumstances of your life, you are called and commissioned to share what you've learned so that others may discover it, too. (One easy way to do this is to give them a copy of this book.)

It's more than a calling! It's love. It's the love of Abba made real in you. It's your love for Abba coming to fruition as you give witness to how wonderful God is.

One Sunday morning during Mass, an unkempt woman wandered down the center aisle of church all the way to the front pew. She clutched a paper shopping bag stuffed with what was probably her only possessions. After sitting down, she fell asleep.

After Mass, Ralph and I said hello to her. Our young children, David and Tammy, came with us and observed how we handled the situation. Ralph and I guessed that she had not eaten for a long time, so we invited her to come home with us for brunch.

A conglomeration of thoughts whizzed through my mind: "Was she dangerous? Would she show up at our door again and again begging for more food? Was she on drugs? What does God want us to do? What kind of example do we want to set for our children?"

She gratefully accepted our offer and climbed into the back seat of our car, sitting between our two children. Very politely, David and Tammy made no comment about her smell. Obviously it had been a long time since she had bathed.

In our home, we fed her two breakfasts. When she had finally eaten enough, she asked if she could use our phone to call her husband and children to let them know she was okay. They had not heard from her in many weeks. (This happened before cell phones, when we had to pay for long distance calls.) More thoughts buzzed through my head: "Was the call long distance? What would it cost us? Why am I even wondering about that?"

Through our kindness, we gave the Father's love to this stranger. The Holy Spirit had inspired us to invite her into our hospitality, which was a gift that God had given to us for her benefit at that moment. In the inevitable ripple effect of love, the Father reawakened love in her heart, motivating her to reach out to her family.

We don't know what happened to her after we took her to a homeless shelter. Most of the time, we don't see the results of sharing the Father's love with strangers. But it feels great to be part of God's plan for them. That feeling is a gift from God to us. It's his smile as he dances for joy with us.

Cardinal Emmanuel Célestin Suhard, archbishop of Paris during World War II, wrote in his book *Priests Among Men*: "To be a witness does not consist in engaging in propaganda, nor even in stirring people up, but in being a living mystery. It means to live in such a way that one's life would not make sense if God did not exist."

You are the Father's gift to the world—most specifically to the people he has put in your path. This includes your parents, your children, your coworkers, the stranger who sits next to you in church next Sunday, the clerk in the grocery store, and so forth.

To everyone you meet, Abba is handing them a gift—and that gift is you. Your faith. Your healthy relationship with him. Not everyone will accept the Father's gifts when he offers it to them. Not everyone will accept you as a gift from the Father. But you *are* a gift nonetheless.

> *Each of you should use whatever gift you have received from God to help others. Be faithful stewards of God's grace. When you speak, do so as one who speaks the very words of God the Father, who is revealing himself to others through you like he did through Jesus. Serve with the strength God provides, so that in all things the Father may be glorified. (Paraphrased from 1 Peter 4:10-11)*

Jesus did not stay at home in Nazareth after he began his public ministry, talking about the Father to just a few people. Capernaum became more or less his hometown, but he traveled often so that more people could meet the Father through his actions, his teachings, and his parables. Jesus knew that everyone longed for the Father's love but many had been waylaid by sin and misconceptions.

> *Jesus went through all the towns and villages . . . proclaiming the good news of the kingdom and healing every disease and sickness. When he saw the crowds, he had compassion on them, because they were harassed and helpless, like sheep without a shepherd. Then he*

> *said to his disciples, "The harvest is plentiful but the workers are few. Ask the Lord of the harvest, therefore, to send out workers into his harvest field." (Matthew 9:35-38 NIV)*

You and I are today's answer to that prayer!

Abba's plan

Jesus took his disciples with him on his mission trips. He gave them on-the-job training. He used these experiences to build their faith, unveil the truth, and teach them how to live as children of the Father. He's been doing that with you, too. And everywhere he went, he reached out to others, revealing the Father by being the compassion of the Father, the forgiveness and mercy of the Father, the caring helpfulness of the Father, and the Father's authority over evil.

His plan today is to do that again—through you.

God's love created us. God's love for others is the reason why he gifted us with talents, wisdom, and altruism. In our concern for others, he can reach them through us. You and I have been designed with abilities, passions, and desires that can make a difference in the hearts of those who need help in seeking and finding God.

The best moments in life are when we lose ourselves in the gifts that Abba has given to us. This means using our talents in alignment with his desires, being—just being—what God wants us to be. Who are you when you are "just being" yourself? You are a beloved child of Abba. Having inherited his "genes," the DNA of his divine nature, you have within you the compassion of the Father, the forgiveness and mercy of the Father, the caring helpfulness of the Father, and the Father's authority over evil.

And the world desperately needs this! There are people around you who desperately need it *from you.*

Although Jesus was the humblest person who ever lived, he never hid himself. Yet we think that being humble means hiding ourselves so that we don't draw attention to ourselves. And thus we miss opportunities to evangelize.

When Jesus cursed the fig tree, why did that story make it into scripture? (See Mark 11:12-14 and 20.) Was it to show that he had a temper? Was he demonstrating that when nature does not keep up with the desires of God, it gets punished? The answer is neither. It's in the Bible to teach us that, if we are unproductive and unfruitful when

God wants to benefit from us, *we* are cursed. We are the fig tree that's been cursed with uselessness. What a horrible feeling!

Blessed are we when we work with God to clear up the misconceptions that have been keeping people away from his love. Cursed are we if we are useless to God; our souls wither and die like the fig tree did.

Today's Exercise: Acknowledge your giftedness

Write a list of your traits that could be (and have been) useful to God as a gift to others. It might be as small (seemingly) as a phone call or text message asking someone how they're doing today. And it might be as big as generating ideas for starting or improving a public ministry. Either way, when you offer them to the Father, he greatly appreciates you. Write down everything you can think of, and tomorrow or next week when another one occurs to you, return to your list and add it.

DAY 28

The Father Gifted You to Make a Difference

THE PATH TO THE deepest place in Abba-Father's heart is the road of ministry—in other words, collaborating with him in his works. At the very moment when he conceived you in your mother's womb, from the depths of his Divine Heart your Divine Daddy pulled out a piece of his fatherly love for humankind and handed it to you. And he gifted you with a very special purpose, which he planned long before your life began. A Father-child alliance.

> *Before I formed you in the womb I knew you, and before you were born I consecrated you. (Jeremiah 1:5 ESV)*

The Father is calling out to you, inviting you to take his fatherly love into the world in a way that only you can do. Nobody else can do it like you. This is designed into your DNA. It's why he gave you the parents you have. It's why he gave you life at this particular time in history. He set you apart from others while you were in your mother's womb and called you by his grace. (See Galatians 1:15.)

No matter how young or old you are, Abba wants his fatherly love to reach others *through you.* Throughout our missionary lives, the look and feel of the collaboration with Abba evolves but the purpose is always the same: "Reveal My fatherly love to others."

When we figure out how our alliance with Abba works—what he created us to do—we gladly give up everything else that we thought we wanted to do because nothing is more satisfying than fulfilling this purpose.

You are gifted because the Father created you to be a gift. You are a gift that's growing more valuable every day because you desire to use your giftedness in your special alliance with him. This collaboration is your ministry.

You are unique; therefore, your ministry is unique. No one besides you can perform this service quite like you. You are gifted in a way that no one else can match. Abba has linked your abilities and spiritual growth to the perfect ministry for you.

The question of our calling is not: "What should I do to take God to others?" Rather, the question is: "What should I take *of God* to others? What has he given me to share with them, which will help them know him better?"

When God does something for us, we should not be satisfied with just a "Thank You, Lord"—because he wants more from us. The world needs more. It's important to add, "Lord, what do You want me to do with this gift?"

Whatever we have received from him is to be given to others. As Catholic lay evangelist David Thorpe used to say, "God wants to fill you to spill you." That is, God wants to fill your life with gifts in order to share those gifts with others through you.

Abba wants us to make ourselves available so we can say what Peter said when he healed the crippled man at the temple gate: "What I have I give to you" (see Acts 3:1-10).

As Christians of the 21st century, we are members of a Church that is not just concerned about the souls of others, but the well-being of the whole person: spiritually, physically, socially, and psychologically. We are not just concerned about humanity, but the well-being of the planet. Ministry is more than trying to get everyone to Heaven; it is working diligently to bring all human life to its God-given potential, from the unborn to the elderly, from strangers in the poverty-stricken Third World to the handicapped children in our local schools.

To serve all these needs, the Church needs more people who recognize that the Father has gifted them. As Pope Saint John Paul II said to a group of U.S. bishops in 1993, in today's world, "the vitality of a parish depends on merging the diverse vocations and gifts of its members into a unity." We are all needed. Not all priests realize this, unfortunately, but our local parish should be our starting point for seeking an outlet for the purpose we were born to fulfill.

And if no door of opportunity opens there, then Abba-Father will give you a different door to use. It might be in an existing nonprofit ministry or it might be to simply make your faith available to coworkers at your job. Or the Father might start a new ministry with you.

St. Paul summed up the mission of servanthood with these words: "Think of us in these terms: as servants of Christ and stewards of God's mysteries" (see 1 Corinthians 4:1). We should periodically examine our lives and ask, "God has gifted me. How good of a steward am I with the alliance we share? Am I doing my part?"

Don't underestimate your value

Too often, instead of listening to our Divine Daddy tell us who we are, we believe what our parents, our teachers, and other significant people have said about us. A parent who says, "You'll never amount to anything!" may have meant this as a challenge to encourage us to strive for our full potential, but the child in us absorbed it literally. The words destroyed our self-image, our personal value. Intellectually, we may have disagreed with the assessments of others, but deep inside, where the child blindly trusts those in authority, the child's interpretation of the words has taken root.

We have many false notions about who we are and how important we are to the Father. Joy comes from being set free from lies and embracing the truth. The lies need to be erased by the power of God and replaced with his words. How much time have you spent examining what is good in you—and believing it? Let your Divine Daddy teach you about how much he values you!

God knows us exactly and intimately. We don't. Rather than assume we are so bad, so ugly, or so unlikely to be extraordinary servants of God, we need to take time to listen to him describe who we really are. We need to ask him to remove the blinders of low self-esteem.

Low self-esteem says that we are far from being who we're supposed to be. It also says that we will never get there. Abba, though, esteems us highly: "God demonstrates his love for us this way: While we were still sinners, Christ died for us." (See Romans 5:8.)

Yes, we have sinned. Yes, we are far from perfect. But the moment that we chose to believe in the redeeming sacrifice of Jesus, the Father esteemed us so highly that he called us saints!

Do you think of yourself as a saint? Saint Paul said that all who are loved by God are saints (Romans 1:7). Both the Old and New Testaments refer to the people of God as saints. Accept the fact that this is how God sees you. Begin to see yourself that way! You're a saint who's still being perfected by the pilgrimage to Heaven.

To continue to live with low self-esteem is like telling God, "You're wrong about me." How dare we contradict God! He says, "As for the saints on Earth, they are the glorious ones in whom is all my delight." (See Psalm 16:3.)

Abba has created you for a definite service

Saint John Henry Newman (1801-1890) wrote:

> God has created me
> to do him some definite service.
> He has committed some work to me
> which he has not committed to another.
> I have my mission.
> I may not know what it is in this life.
> But I shall be told in the next.
> I am a link in a chain,
> a bond of connection between persons.
> He has not created me for nothing.
> I shall do good. I shall do his work.
> Therefore, I will trust him.
> Whatever I do, wherever I am, I cannot be thrown away.
> If I am in sickness, my sickness may serve him.
> If I am in sorrow, my sorrow may serve him.
> He does nothing in vain. He knows what he is about.

God does the extraordinary with ordinary people

Abba-Father is more displeased with the condition of the world than you and I are—infinitely more. He is more grief-stricken than we are over the loss of so many souls who have been tricked by the father of lies. You can be sure that he is working a divine plan to rescue the lost in a very fatherly way. And he has gifted you to be part of it!

But while he was still a long way off, his father saw him and was filled with compassion for him; he ran to his son, threw his arms around him and kissed him. The son said to him, "Father, I have sinned against heaven and against you. I am no longer worthy to be called your son."

But the father said to his servants, "Quick! Bring the best robe and put it on him. Put a ring on his finger and sandals on his feet. Bring the fattened calf and kill it. Let's have a feast and celebrate. For this son of mine was dead and is alive again; he was lost and is found." So they began to celebrate. (Luke 15:20-24 NIV)

Place yourself inside the parable of the Prodigal Son. Not as the returning son. You are one of the servants. The Father is saying to you: "Quick! One of my lost children is ready to return to Me. Bring the best robe—the best of what I am offering thanks to you, a gifted partner in My love. Give him what you have that will help him see how much I love him and cherish him. Give him the wisdom, the knowledge, and the benefits of your experiences, shared through your unique set of talents and skills. Help him to see My great joy as I embrace him."

Stop underestimating how important you are to the Father's plan for restoring the world to his fatherly love. God enjoys doing the extraordinary with ordinary people. Do you remember Judas and Ananias from Acts 9:10-19? Many people don't remember them, although they played a very important role in the earliest days of the Church. These were the two who ministered to a most undeserving, mean, and nasty bully whom they should have feared because he was the biggest persecutor of Christians.

Here's their story: One day, Ananias was having a nice, ordinary prayer time, deepening his relationship with the Risen Christ, when Jesus appeared to him in a vision and said:

"I want you to go to Straight Street on the other side of town, to the house of Judas. He's got a visitor there that I want you to minister to."

"Sure. How do you want me to help him?" Ananias may have asked.

"His eyes have been blinded, and I want you to lay hands on him to restore his sight."

"No problem. You've used me to heal people before. I know what to do."

"Yes, but the man I want you to heal is Saul of Tarsus." (We know him as Saint Paul.)

"What? You can't mean that! This man has attacked our brother Christians in Jerusalem! And now he's here in Damascus to arrest all of us! You can't be serious."

Jesus must have sighed, as he surely does whenever we think we understand situations better than he does.

"Go!" Jesus commanded. And so Ananias went.

He and Judas were the first Christians to forgive Paul for his persecutions and to trust him. God had given Judas the mundane ministry of taking Paul into his home. And he called Ananias to heal him and to empower him with the Holy Spirit.

These were two ordinary people, and after we meet them in Acts 9:10-19, we never hear of them again. And yet, what they did had a major impact on the whole world, even to this day. They gave Paul his initial push into one of the most powerful ministries of evangelization for all time.

What kind of an impact can you have on the world as an ordinary person in your alliance with Abba-Father?

I'm convinced that the reason why so few Christians serve God with all their hearts, minds, souls, and energy is because we have an enemy that doesn't want us to do it. He uses the wounds of our past and our misconceptions about God's Fatherhood against us. He uses our sins against us, even after we've received forgiveness in the Sacrament of Confession. And he uses the sins we're still committing when we're only partially dedicated to our sanctification.

The Devil's message: "You're not good enough. You're inadequate. God isn't really asking of you what you think he's asking. It would be better if someone else did it."

Abba-Father's message: "Way to go, Girl! Way to go, Guy! You're simply amazing! That's how I created you to be. Rely on Me and join Me in the great adventure that lies ahead. Together we will do something brilliant!"

When you were a child and your teacher assigned a difficult school project to you, was it easier to do it if your mom or dad cheered you on? Or when you cleaned your messy room and your mother applauded you with a huge smile, didn't it make you want to do more because you delighted in pleasing her? This is how it is with Abba-Father. We have a messy world. God needs hard-working, all-in partners.

Several years ago after Mass one morning, a friend and I chatted in the shade of a tree. During our conversation, she told me that she was getting a vision. This was not unusual for her, and I valued the revelations that came from her visions. This time, she said that she saw me digging in the dirt, sowing seeds and tilling the soil. Jesus, according to her vision, was standing near me, watching me.

As she described it, I could see it, too, in my imagination. However, my interpretation of it was very different from hers. I saw Jesus smiling at me. He approved of me. He was delighted with how hard I was working for his mission.

But my friend said that Jesus was displeased with me. I was working too hard, she said.

Whose interpretation was correct? How could she see Jesus frowning while I saw him smiling?

I took it to prayer over the next few days and felt confirmed in what I had seen. Today, I still see Jesus standing with me in the garden that he gave me to tend. Smiling.

My friend's interpretation was probably tainted by jealousy. I didn't know it then, but she was pushing me away. Afterward, we drifted apart as she repeatedly saw my ministry in a negative way.

Meanwhile, I've continued to sow the seeds that Abba gives me to plant. My energy comes from knowing that I am Abba's gifted daughter and together we have a special alliance that no one else can replicate.

Every day in my morning prayers, I ask the Holy Spirit to renew me and re-energize me. I also go to daily Mass to be renewed, inspired, and reenergized. One day, as I headed to the chapel doors, it occurred to me that I was about to enter a portal into another dimension. The altar and the tabernacle containing Jesus are at the center of this alternate universe. It's the ideal place to spend time with my Divine Daddy while getting renewed and energized.

Sometimes during meditations immediately after receiving Jesus in the Holy Eucharist, my mind travels to the sunny field of colorful flowers where Abba-Father and I often meet up. He is seated on the blanket, smiling at me, arms open, inviting me to come and sit with him. I snuggle up to him and nestle in his white, flowing robes. We talk. He encourages me. His concern for me fills me with joy and new freedom to go back into the world to serve him with all my heart and all my mind and all my soul.

On this particular day he told me, "I'm glad you're here. I have a beautiful day planned for you." Seeing his smile, my energy grew. I happily looked forward to getting back to my office and digging into the work that he wanted me to accomplish. And by the way, whenever I plan to do something that is not in his plans for the day, something happens that interferes with it. More often than not, my schedule gets rearranged, and that's okay. This is my Divine Daddy working with me. He also withdraws from me his Divine Energy when I try to persist in doing what is not on his to-do list.

God needs hard-working Christians who tend to their gardens with all due diligence. With too few of us around, the Devil has been gaining more and more territory as a fake father destroying more and more souls. We all need to say yes to the alliance that Father God wants to build with us for restoring his Fatherhood to marriages, family life, and the Church.

Today's Exercise: Self-assessment tests for discerning your special calling

To help you figure out what you have been gifted by God to do, use this questionnaire. You can download a printer-ready PDF copy of it, which includes space for your answers, from **30DaysToTheFathersHeart.com/tests**.

Test #1: Getting to know your giftedness

Answer the following five questions:

1. Think of any ministry you are currently involved in, no matter how small or insignificant it seems to be. How does this ministry advance the Kingdom of God?
2. Why did God call you (instead of your neighbor, another family member, or another parishioner) to the particular ministries in which you're already involved?
3. What makes you special in the eyes of God?
4. What makes you special to the people around you?
5. What is it about your personality that contributes to this?

Test #2: What paralyzes me from saying yes to the right calling?

The two biggest obstacles are pride and fear. Use the following to determine how much these obstacles interfere in your life. Be honest. If your answer is somewhere between Yes and No, choose the one that is more so.

PRIDE

- Do I think I'm so good at hearing God that I'm always right?
- Am I looking for his answers only in super-spiritual ways and not everyday events or people?
- Do I go overboard in responding to God? Are you doing more than what common sense directs?
- Are my priorities out of order, e.g., thinking material gain and other self-serving goals are more important than service to community?
- Am I waiting for God to reveal the whole picture first?
- Am I waiting to become perfect at hearing all of God's directions?
- Are my motives for ministering wrong? Do I want to glorify myself? Do I count on good deeds for getting me into Heaven? Am I motivated out of guilt?
- Am I waiting for God to tell me what I want to hear?
- Am I waiting for a bigger, more glamorous career?

FEAR

- Am I afraid of what others will think of me if I get involved in a Church vocation?
- Am I afraid God will get mad at me if I respond to his call and then mess it up?
- Am I afraid of misinterpreting God, as if he won't straighten me out?
- Do I believe God has only one "perfect" will for my life and ministry, and if I'm not absolutely sure what it is, it's wrong to try anything?
- Do I think God is hiding his call from me?

- Am I so sure I know what God's will is for my life that I get confused by obstacles in my path and the lack of opportunities to further my career goals?
- Am I afraid of the cost of service? Of not liking his choice for me or being given more than I can handle?
- Am I worried that God isn't concerned about my needs and feelings?
- Am I saying "Yes but—" like Moses?
- Am I afraid that my ministry will be too big or too public or uncomfortable or distasteful?

Test #3: Testing your talents

The following is a survey of your gifts, talents, and personal experiences. It can help point you to what your calling in ministry might be. It's not all-inclusive, nor will it provide the final word for making any decisions. It's to be used only as a guide to help you discern what the Holy Spirit has been preparing you to do, in combination with prayer and other forms of guidance.

Write down the first answer that comes to you; this will be the truest response, hopefully bypassing your intellectual or emotional prejudices. Be assured that God is speaking to you as you come up with your answers.

Questions 1 through 4 focus on where your desires for ministry really exist. Take these desires seriously. God created you to do a unique work that no one else can do the same way. And you are not really satisfied until you are doing what God created you to do.

1. List the ministries you have been involved in. Then, put a star next to the ones you feel most passionate about (the ones that excite you the most).
2. List the ministries you have ever considered doing, even if only for a brief time. Include those you dismissed as impractical or unrealistic. Then, put a star next to the ones you feel most passionate about.
3. What ministries do you see others perform that gives you one or more of these feelings: "I wish I could do that." "I feel there's something wrong with me that keeps me from doing that." "I

envy the person who can do that."

4. What ministries have ever caused you to think: "I would do that, or I could do that, if only . . . "

Questions 5 through 7 reveal areas that have caused you the most growth, the deepest insights, and the greatest ability to help others. In what ministry can you best utilize these?

5. Name the worst experiences you have had in your life: the hardest or longest trials you have had to live through.
6. What experiences or activities in your past led you away from God or caused you to lose faith?
7. What do you regret doing that happened when you didn't know God or when you were away from the Church?

Questions 8 through 10 indicate the know-how, skills, and aptitudes you have acquired. Nothing is ever wasted, because sooner or later, sometimes in unexpected ways, God gives us opportunities to use these for his glory. Could these strengths of yours be used in a Church vocation?

8. What do you enjoy most about yourself? (What gifts do you believe God has given you? E.g., your faith, ability to have good relationships, organizational skills, love for serving, etc.)
9. List the skills you've been educated in through formal schooling, self-education, seminars, etc.
10. List the types of jobs you have held. Put a star next to the ones you enjoyed most.

Question 11 deals with your passions. Whatever you feel passionate about is where you could serve in ministry with zeal. People often burn out in ministry work because they don't have a strong love for it. Follow your heart to the type of service where you really care to make a difference.

11. What bothers you most about this world? (E.g., abortion, euthanasia, poverty, pornography, immoral television shows, lonely people, aging parents, hospitalized children, the popularity of the occult or New Age movement or Satanism, the crime rate, violence in the home, substance abuse, sexual abuse,

the divorce rate, inactive church members, non-Christian cults, adoption issues, bad government, cancer or other traumatic diseases, children who lack faith in God, damage to the Earth's environment, etc.)

Questions 12 and 13 give you a glimpse of how others see you and your calling. Listen to their feedback. They can recognize your areas of giftedness more objectively than you can.

12. Do people admire something about you? What is it?
13. Do people tend to come to you with their problems? Is this because they believe you are a good listener, you care, or you give good advice? What kinds of problems do they come to you with? What is the pattern here?

Question 14 takes a look at your dreams. Where do you think the inspiration for your dreams comes from? God, of course! Dare to put no limits on your discernment process. God will help you refine your dreams and guide you in reaching the right goals once you dare to believe in yourself and in your lofty goals.

14. If money, time, and space were not obstacles, what would you most like to educate yourself to learn? Or what kind of work would you most like to do?

* * *

A Prayer to Become God's Instrument

O, my heavenly Father, I give all of my life to You
in the name of Your Son, my Lord Jesus Christ,
and through the power of Your Holy Spirit.
I have heard You calling me,
and I choose to follow where Your Son leads me.
I want to help others find their way into Your kingdom.
I want to serve others so that they can experience Your love.
Use me.
Use the hurts and sufferings I've endured.
Use the talents, the resources, the time, the experiences, the spiritual growth, and everything else You have given me.
Use me.

Help me to love all people unconditionally so that they experience Jesus through me.
Help me to grow in my desire to love all people.
Today, and every day, help me to decrease so that You may increase in me.
Help me to love purely, humbly, and generously.
Show me how to receive more of Your love so that I have more love to give.
Heal me of every obstacle that holds me back from serving You.
I give You permission to change me.
Here I am, Lord, I want to do Your will.
Amen.

DAY 29

The Majesty of the Father's Love for You

When my mom was four years old, she was taken from her family and placed into the home of foster parents. Ten years later, the couple finally adopted her. In between, she didn't know to which family she truly belonged. This made a lifelong impact on her. Do you feel this way about God's Fatherhood? Are you aware of the benefits of having been fully adopted by the Father in all of his royal majesty? Or are you just in foster care?

> *But when the set time had fully come, God sent his Son, born of a woman, born under the law, to redeem those under the law, that we might receive adoption to sonship. Because you are his sons, God sent the Spirit of his Son into our hearts, the Spirit who calls out, "Abba, Father." So you are no longer a slave, but God's child; and since you are his child, God has made you also an heir. (Galatians 4:4- NIV)*

God the Father is the King of All Creation. He is the King of the Universe. He is robed in splendor and majesty (see Psalm 104:1). Therefore, life with him is filled with his splendor and majesty, his strength and joy (see 1 Chronicles 16:27).

In the many ways in which he differs from your human father

and the other human models of fatherhood, his kingship completes the picture. We benefit greatly from taking time to contemplate his majesty. This is where he most easily (in our thoughts) rises far above everything we've experienced from human interactions. As king, he is like no other; he is far more wonderful than even the best of earthly kings.

When the ancient nation of Israel began to build their kingdom, God was their king. As long as they remained subservient to his kingship and obeyed his instructions as revealed through prophets, they won every battle. They thrived. They grew larger. And then came the fateful day when they looked at other nations and began to covet the leadership of human kings. God warned them repeatedly that human kings would disappoint them and even endanger them. But they insisted, and God gave them what they asked for so that they could learn from their mistakes.

Their first human king, Saul, rebelled against God and caused all sorts of problems. So, God replaced him with King David, a good model (most of the time) of what God's kingship was like. From David's line would eventually come the perfect model: Jesus the Son of God. (Note: Jesus is also called a king—the messianic king—because Jesus and the Father are one.)

Let's consider the traits of a good king and how Abba-Father is the perfection of kingship:

1. **He is the center of the universe.** Ancient civilizations usually laid out their cities and kingdoms around a central dwelling place for the king. When we keep God in the center of our lives, we benefit from his kingship and all that this offers.

   Yours, O LORD, is the greatness and the power and the glory and the victory and the majesty, for all that is in the heavens and in the earth is yours. Yours is the kingdom, O LORD, and you are exalted as head above all. (1 Chronicles 29:11 ESV)

2. **He is never voted into power.** Human kings inherit their positions of leadership from their bloodlines. God the Father voted for us to become citizens of his Kingdom. And he gave us the Blood of Jesus to open the gates of his Kingdom so we can enter. By the Blood of Jesus, we are brought into the bloodline of the king of the universe.

But God shows his love for us in that while we were still sinners, Christ died for us. Since, therefore, we have now been justified by his blood, much more shall we be saved by him from the wrath of God. (Romans 5:8-9 ESV)

3. **A king cannot be voted out of power.** A king is the king for the rest of his life. God is eternal, and no matter what happens, no matter who fights against his kingship, no matter who tries to take the throne for himself, God remains king. We can find great comfort in this when evil seems to be taking over.

   Praise the Lord! / I will give thanks to the Lord with my whole heart, / in the company of the upright, in the congregation. / Great are the works of the Lord, / studied by all who delight in them. / Full of splendor and majesty is his work, / and his righteousness endures forever. (Psalm 111:1-3 ESV)

4. **A king's authority is absolute.** He is the top administrator in charge of making decisions. A good king makes decisions based on what is best for his people. During crises his decisions stand firm, giving stability; he has already determined the outcome and the course to reach it. Likewise, God makes decisions that are based on firm and unchanging principles—and on deep, deep love. We can trust his plan. We can rest assured that all good prayer requests, as they meet with his approval, will be successful.

   My word that goes out from my mouth will accomplish what I desire and achieve the purpose for which I sent it. (See Isaiah 55:10-11.)

5. **His word is law.** A good king doesn't create rules in order to control his people. Nor does he make laws for the sake of enjoying his authority. Rather, he enacts laws that help his Kingdom to prosper and his people to flourish. The Kingdom of God is ruled by the Father of love. Obedience is required for living in his wonderful and holy Kingdom. And we gladly obey because the purpose behind every rule is love. Even the Church's rules that we might disagree with (such as those pertaining to fertility and contraception) are for the purpose of love—a higher love. If this is not obvious, then we need to dig deeper, reading the Church's documents in a search for the love that at first was hidden.

   Keep listening to the thunder of his voice / and the rumbling that

> *comes from his mouth. / Under the whole heaven he lets it go, / and his lightning to the corners of the earth. / After it his voice roars; / he thunders with his majestic voice, / and he does not restrain the lightnings when his voice is heard. / God thunders wondrously with his voice; / he does great things that we cannot comprehend. (Job 37:2-5 ESV)*

6. **His presence is the manifestation of his authority.** When a king attends a meeting or shows up on the battlefield, or when a citizen gets an audience with him, his full authority is present. When we pray to God Our King, his Divine Will is with us. If our prayer requests don't contradict his Divine Will, the full measure of his authority responds. And as citizens of his Kingdom, when we pray for others, we have the right to exercise his kingly authority because the king is always with us. This is especially important to remember when we are battling forces of evil and when we are praying for healing.

   > *Now to him who is able to keep you from stumbling and to present you blameless before the presence of his glory with great joy, to the only God, our Savior, through Jesus Christ our Lord, be glory, majesty, dominion, and authority, before all time and now and forever. Amen. (Jude 1:24-25 ESV)*

7. **He protects his realm.** Since ancient times, when an enemy invaded, kings would act with wrathful aggressiveness. God is protective too. Though he is slow to anger, he is great in power and will not leave the guilty unpunished (see Nahum 1:3). The Lord is gracious and compassionate, slow to anger and rich in love (see Psalm 145:8), setting prisoners free from the Devil's strongholds when they turn to him for help. He is all-powerful and therefore cannot be defeated.

   > *He stores up sound wisdom for the upright / and is a shield to those who walk in integrity– / guarding the paths of the just / and protecting the way of his faithful ones. (Proverbs 2:7-8 ISV)*

What does it mean to be adopted into the King's family?

Saint Paul tells us that through Christ Jesus we are Father God's adopted children. This is his will and pleasure! He gets excited about it. His heart swells with joy thinking about *you* as one of his adopted kids. In fact, he wanted to father you since before he created the Earth!

> *Praise be to the God and Father of our Lord Jesus Christ, who has blessed us in the heavenly realms with every spiritual blessing in Christ. For he chose us in him before the creation of the world to be holy and blameless in his sight. In love he predestined us for adoption to sonship through Jesus Christ, in accordance with his pleasure and will. (Ephesians 1:3-5 NIV)*

Abba-Father gave life to each of us, but our tendency to sin keeps us from fully living as royal children of the King of the Universe. Jesus came to Earth to teach us how to be true children, first by his words and his example, and then he took our sins upon himself and died with them on the Cross. This cleared the way for us to become children who are adopted into the great majesty of God.

> *The Son is the radiance of God's glory and the exact representation of his being, sustaining all things by his powerful word. After he had provided purification for sins, he sat down at the right hand of the Majesty in heaven. (Hebrews 1:3 NIV)*

Jesus shares with us his Holy Spirit, who empowers us to be holy, and the majesty of the Father, by which we are victorious over sin. We have the power of the King's authority to drive away our tempters. This is why Saint Paul could state that Christians are saints, no longer sinners. In Romans 6:3-14 (NIV) he tells us:

> *Or don't you know that all of us who were baptized into Christ Jesus were baptized into his death? We were therefore buried with him through baptism into death in order that, just as Christ was raised from the dead through the glory of the Father, we too may live a new life.*
>
> *For if we have been united with him in a death like his, we will certainly also be united with him in a resurrection like his. For we know that our old self was crucified with him so that the body ruled by sin might be done away with, that we should no longer be slaves to sin– because anyone who has died has been set free from sin. . . . Count yourselves dead to sin but alive to God in Christ Jesus. . . . For sin shall no longer be your master, because you are not under the law, but under grace.*

And look at how he addressed the people in church communities:

> *To the saints and faithful brothers in Christ at Colossae (see Colossians 1:2).*
>
> *To the saints who are in Ephesus (see Ephesians 1:1).*

And:

> *I felt compelled to write and urge you to contend for the faith that was once for all delivered to the saints (see Jude 1:3).*
>
> *Now about the service to the saints, it is superfluous for me to write to you (see 2 Corinthians 9:1).*

The point is: In our natural births, we came into the world as sinners. In the supernatural rebirths of our baptisms, we came into the Kingdom of God—as *saints.* We spend the rest of our earthly lives improving how well we live out our true identity. (Well anyway, that's the King's plan.) Through the Sacraments of Baptism, Confession, the Anointing of the Sick, and the Holy Eucharist, we die to our old sinful ways and grow in sainthood by the grace of God. Only saints can live in the Kingdom of God.

The King has decreed that we are his holy people. He adopted us and now we are royal children. We are princes and princesses of his Divine Kingdom.

> *But you are a chosen race, a royal priesthood, a holy nation, a people for his own possession, that you may proclaim the excellencies of him who called you out of darkness into his marvelous light. (1 Peter 2:9 ESV)*

You are a CHOSEN one: The Creator of the universe has chosen you and given you life. You are a masterpiece of creation!

You are ROYAL: Your Father is King of the Universe; you are his prince or princess!

You are a PRIEST: Whether a ministerial priest or a member of the "common priesthood" of all baptized Christians, you offer spiritual sacrifices acceptable to God. How? Every sacrifice of love, every sacrifice of money or time, every giving of your talents, every offering up of your sufferings, every prayer that you lift up to Heaven: These are your gifts to God, offered for the sake of others.

You are CONSECRATED: Yes, you are holy! Jesus has consecrated you to the heart of his Father's love and to his Holy Spirit's holiness. The word "consecrated" means that you have been "dedicated to a sacred purpose." Wow! Have you discovered your sacred purpose? It's the holy reason why you are still here on Earth.

What it means to be an heir of God's majesty

They speak of the glorious splendor of your majesty– / and I will meditate on your wonderful works. / They tell of the power of your awesome works– / and I will proclaim your great deeds. They celebrate your abundant goodness / and joyfully sing of your righteousness. (Psalm 145:5-7 NIV)

Sinning is a sign that we don't really know who we are. We don't truly know (at the moment of temptation) that we have inherited from our Father the King everything we need, including a holy alternative to what the Tempter is pushing us into. We don't stop to think about what it means to be a beloved prince or princess. In other words, we underestimate the advantages of being a child of the King. We undervalue what it means to be an heir of his authority. We don't realize how much God loves us and how much goodness he is longing to shower upon us.

Consider what often happens to children who are rescued from abusive homes and are then adopted by loving parents. Because these children did not experience unconditional, safe love during their formative years, they have a hard time believing that they are truly loved by the adoptive family. They instinctively long to go back to the family of origin. They sometimes even sabotage their new family relationships.

It's basic human nature. We prefer the familiar over the unknown even when it's harmful. Are you still longing to go back to old, familiar, sinful patterns? Are you still rationalizing that they are not really sins? The goal is to fully embrace your new life in the family of God. Your Almighty King will help you do it. (He brought you to this book, right?)

When do you doubt God's love for you? Our Father is inviting you to discover that he has set no conditions on loving you—he has only UNconditional love for you. You can trust him completely. You can believe that, as your Good King, he will always take good care of you, even while life's circumstances seem to indicate otherwise. This is life as an adopted child. This is life in the majesty of Abba-Father's love. He is always working in the circumstances to eventually produce many blessings for you.

> *For all who are led by the Spirit of God are sons of God. For you did not receive the spirit of slavery [to sin] to fall back into fear, but you have received the Spirit of adoption as sons, by whom we cry, "Abba! Father!" The Spirit himself bears witness with our spirit that we are children of God, and if children, then heirs–heirs of God and fellow heirs with Christ, provided we suffer with him in order that we may also be glorified with him. (Romans 8:14-17 ESV)*

What does it mean that we received a "Spirit of adoption"? This scripture explains that the Holy Spirit of God bears witness (testifies) that we are God's children. We are his heirs, a favored position that comes with a wonderful inheritance. We were born as mere humans, totally lacking God's supernatural nature, but we have been adopted into his royal family with all the riches of our Father's Kingdom—the gifts and talents, wealth of love, abundance of goodness, and everything else that belongs to our Father.

In the Creed, we say that we believe in one God and that he is the Father of all. He was our Father since the moment he created us in our human mother's womb. We were made in his image. He's the only true (i.e., perfectly loving) Father that we've ever had. So—why do we need a Spirit of adoption? It's because we inherited the original sin of our first parents, Adam and Eve. When we were born, we became heirs of their fallen kingdom.

Our baptismal certificate is our adoption paper. The legal validity of it is endorsed by the Holy Spirit and signed with the Blood of Christ.

Every sin breaks the spiritual connection between us and our Divine Creator. It's like the rebellious son who rejects the teachings of his parents and adopts a contrary lifestyle. He cannot break the birth bond. He cannot put an end to his blood connection with his parents, not even if he changes his name. However, the family's spiritual connection has been broken. When the son finally reconciles with his parents, the spiritual bond must be restored: Trust has to be rebuilt and hearts need to be healed.

When we reconcile with God, how can we rebuild trust? He knows that we'll sin again. Although we sincerely want to be good children, he knows he cannot trust us to remain sinless. So, he gave us the Spirit of adoption: The Holy Spirit we received from Jesus brings about our adoption into the royal family. By the Holy Spirit we are empowered to become holy, making us princes and princesses.

This is a gift from the Father's majesty—his tremendous, unconditional love for us. Because of his Spirit of adoption, it doesn't matter that we cannot be trusted. The Father trusts his own Holy Spirit, and "the Spirit bears witness that we are God's children" (see Romans 8:16).

Our Father does not hold our past sins against us. He does not base our future on how we treated him in the past nor on what we're capable of doing again. The past has nothing to do with his acceptance of us. Rather, our Father bases everything on the Spirit of adoption.

Are we sincere in wanting to become holier? That's all that matters.

If we stay connected to him through the Spirit of adoption, as true children of our Daddy-God, we treat others with the same mercy. Have you suffered in a relationship where the bond has been broken and trust has not been rebuilt yet? If that person wants to reconcile with you, choose to show mercy. You can place your trust in the Spirit of adoption—not on human flesh, but on God's own Spirit. It's the only way we can be healthy and holy in our dealings with those who say they want to reconcile with us after they've hurt us.

What it means to be a citizen of Heaven

You know you're going to Heaven, right? It's guaranteed as long as you continue to desire to be a saint, a royal member of God's family, accepting the great sacrifice that Jesus made for you.

> *Everyone born of God overcomes the world. This is the victory that has overcome the world, even our faith. Who is it that overcomes the world? Only the one who believes that Jesus is the Son of God.... And it is the Spirit who testifies, because the Spirit is the truth.... Whoever believes in the Son of God accepts this testimony. Whoever does not believe God has made him out to be a liar, because they have not believed the testimony God has given about his Son. And this is the testimony: God has given us eternal life, and this life is in his Son. Whoever has the Son has life; whoever does not have the Son of God does not have life. (1 John 5:4-13 NIV)*

There are three ways in which the Holy Spirit testifies that Jesus is giving Heaven to us: First, the Spirit overshadowed the Virgin Mary to conceive Jesus miraculously. Second, when Jesus arose from the waters of his own baptism (the "initiation rite" of his public ministry), the Spirit descended upon him. Third, when Jesus shed his blood for us, he commended his Spirit to the Father. When the Father raised Jesus from death, he gave his Spirit to everyone who follows Jesus, and thus the Spirit carries you and me into eternal life.

These three proofs are of one accord. They work together to speak the same message. And now that we've been given the Holy Spirit of Jesus himself, we are the proof that Heaven is real.

> *Remember that at that time you were separate from Christ, excluded from citizenship in Israel and foreigners to the covenants of the promise, without hope and without God in the world. But now in Christ Jesus you who once were far away have been brought near by the blood of Christ. . . .*
>
> *Consequently, you are no longer foreigners and strangers, but fellow citizens with God's people and also members of his household, built on the foundation of the apostles and prophets, with Christ Jesus himself as the chief cornerstone. In him the whole building is joined together and rises to become a holy temple in the Lord. And in him you too are being built together to become a dwelling in which God lives by his Spirit. (Ephesians 2:12-13,19-22 NIV)*

With citizenship comes responsibilities. Do you ever feel like you don't have much value? God's Spirit in you gives testimony that you have tremendous value! Extremely important value! First, when you were conceived in your mother's womb, you were made in the image and likeness of God. By being who God created you to be, you, whom others can see, reveal to the world what God, whom they cannot see, is like.

Second, in the Sacrament of your Baptism, the Spirit descended upon you and the Father said of you, "This is my beloved child, in whom I am very pleased!" Thus you were initiated into the ministry of Christ and you have been sent forth to give his love, healing, and salvation to the world in which you live, work, and serve.

Third, when you allow your sufferings to be an offering of love for others, your sacrifice is visible evidence of Christ's sacrifice. This sacrifice will not destroy your spirit but will purify it and strengthen it. Your continued life in the Holy Spirit will help carry others into eternal life, because your faith will strengthen their faith.

Your testimony of suffering and endurance is evidence that God can resurrect goodness from every bad situation.

How well are you translating this testimony into a language that others can understand? More specifically, in what ways are you giving yourself to others, allowing them to experience what is valuable in you? For example, if you're in a ministry that, in some way, changes the world because you're sharing with others the gifts that God has given to you, then you are the true presence of Christ. And this is how you can be assured that you're going to Heaven. And this is how you take others with you into eternal life.

You know the old saying, "When in Rome, do as the Romans do." We could extend that to: "While living in the world, do as the worldly people do." But God says, "You're a citizen of MY Kingdom now, so do as the saints do. Be a saint in every worldly place that you visit."

Think of what happens when you visit old friends or family who live in sinful or unhealthy lifestyles, or when you spend hours each day working side by side with worldly people. Maybe you were just like them before deciding to become more like Christ.

Now that you've journeyed through spiritual conversion and emotional healing, how easy is it to revert back to worldly and unhealthy ways when you're around them? Do you allow yourself to be infected by their attitudes and bad habits (foul language, for example, or gossiping and bad-mouthing others)? Or do you, instead, behave like the saint that God in his kingly majesty ordained you to be?

Sometimes we think we have to blend in so that we'll be accepted or to make the visit peaceful or to avoid trouble in the workplace. But Jesus the Prince of Peace is the only true source of peace. And it is his desire to make the Kingdom of God known to the people around you.

However, there's a wall of enmity that divides us from those who don't know Jesus (or don't know him well enough to behave like him). Jesus wants to tear down that wall.

> *For he himself is our peace, who has made the two groups one and has destroyed the barrier, the dividing wall of hostility. . . . His purpose was to create in himself one new humanity out of the two, thus making peace, and in one body to reconcile both of them to God through the cross, by which he put to death their hostility. He came and preached peace to you who were far away and peace to those who were near. For through him we both have access to the Father by one Spirit. (Ephesians 2:14-18 NIV)*

Tearing down the wall can be a long process when those on the other side of it enjoy being their own kings. But never give up. Jesus won't! Not until the last breath is gone.

My dad and I were often on opposite sides of that wall. He didn't understand why I became Catholic, nor did he try to understand. He had spent seventy years rebelling against Catholicism and some of the moral values it represents, and he was proud of his rebellion. We disagreed on many things, but I had learned early on that there was no point in trying to open up a dialogue about any of it. When Ralph and I brought my parents into our home to care for them, we sadly discovered that my dad was still unwilling to consider our point of view.

Such closed-mindedness carried over into refusing our advice (and that of his doctors) about how to safely navigate his declining health. This is why he disregarded our warnings and decided to take a walk down our long driveway on that fateful day when he broke his neck.

My dad treasured being in control. *"For where your treasure is, there your heart will be also" (Matthew 6:21 NIV).* He also hoarded vast collections of books, vinyl records, and other possessions. One day he showed me row after row of bookshelves (all of them very full) stored in his brother's basement. He invited me to choose books that my daughter Tammy might enjoy. But he wanted them all back. He had no use for them anymore, but he did not want to let go of them. I silently said to Jesus, "I guess he's going to have a very long Purgatory learning to let go of everything that he can't take with him to Heaven, huh?"

After he broke his neck, we watched how God prepared him for Heaven. Because of his rapidly weakening condition due to the accident, my dad lost more and more control his life. He needed round-the-clock nursing care and facilities that we could not provide in our home, so he also lost the ability to live with his beloved wife. He repeatedly tried to bargain his way to her: "Come live with me and I'll take care of you."

And then, in March 2020, Covid-19 locked him into his small half of the room that he shared with a roommate whom he hated. That's when I saw the first miracle: He peacefully let go of control. He willingly accepted that talking to my mom on the phone every day, instead of seeing her in person, would have to be good enough. To my astonishment, this previously rebellious man was at peace with the lockdown. (More at peace than I was!)

In November the bones of his fingers became infected. He lost the ability to do his only activity: type on his computer. Then he lost a part of his body because one of those fingers had to be amputated. While still recovering from surgery, he had congestive heart failure. His heart could no longer pump enough to give him the energy to sit up. He stopped eating. He lay in bed, curling up into the smallest version of my dad that I had ever seen.

The nursing home allowed Mom and I to visit him because he was nearing the end. He was letting go. Unlike his behavior during pre-Covid visits, he was happy to see his wife but not unhappy when she left.

The most beautiful moment of watching my dad journey towards death was when Mom and I got him to sing with us. His favorite song for all of his life had been the funny 1943 jingle: "Oh, mairzy doats and dozy doats and little lambsy divey. A kiddle divey, too. Wouldn't you?" (It means: "Mares eat oats and does eat oats and little lambs eat ivy. A kid will eat ivy too. Wouldn't you?") So, Mom and I started singing this and he perked up enough to join in. But (and here's the beautiful part) as soon as the song ended, he said, "Let's sing the Lord's Prayer." And so we did.

A few days later, this was the closing hymn of his memorial service.

But I've jumped ahead in the story. My dad continued to linger in his state of letting go. The day he finally passed away was December 8th, the Solemnity of the Immaculate Conception of Mary. That was also the day that Pope Francis announced the start of the Year of Saint Joseph. My dad had never been open to learning why or how Ralph and I could have a real relationship with Mary and Joseph, but now the Good King, Abba-Father, whose timing is always perfect and powerful, was showing me that our prayers for my dad had been answered.

I believe, without any doubt, that Mary and Joseph introduced themselves to my dad and they escorted him to Jesus in the hour of his death.

There's one more miracle to tell you. I chose for the opening song of my dad's memorial service my favorite hymn, "How Great Thou Art." My uncle, who lives where my dad grew up, held a second memorial service, and a friend videoed it. Uncle Merlin also chose "How

Great Thou Art" for the opening song. When Mom and I watched the video afterward, we both heard my dad's voice, loud and clear, singing with great enthusiasm and joyful reverence to the great majesty of God:

> O Lord my God, When I in awesome wonder
> Consider all the works Thy hand hath made;
> I see the stars, I hear the mighty thunder,
> Thy pow'r throughout the universe displayed:
>
> Then sings my soul, my Saviour God, to Thee,
> How great Thou art! How great Thou art!
> Then sings my soul, My Saviour God, to Thee,
> How great Thou art! How great Thou art!
>
> (© 1948 by The Stuart K. Hine Trust CIO)

Every time I replay that video, I hear my dad's voice again. Jesus had thoroughly broken down the wall of enmity.

> *For he himself is our peace, who has made the two groups one and has destroyed the barrier, the dividing wall of hostility by setting aside in his flesh the law with its commands and regulations. His purpose was to create in himself one new humanity out of the two, thus making peace, and in one body to reconcile both of them to God through the cross, by which he put to death their hostility. He came and preached peace to you who were far away and peace to those who were near. For through him we both have access to the Father by one Spirit. (Ephesians 2:14-18 NIV)*

Today's Exercise: Enjoy your royalty

God says, "You're a citizen of MY Kingdom now!" Imagine Abba-Father sitting on a throne. (Ask the Holy Spirit to anoint your imagination.)

1. How big is the throne?
2. What color is it?
3. What color is the kingly robe that he's wearing?
4. Is he wearing a crown? What does it look like?
5. He is smiling at you. What is he telling you about adopting you

and giving you a royal inheritance?

6. Look back at the seven traits of a good king and recall how each of them has been revealed in your life.

DAY 30

Receive the Father's Blessing

On this final day of your journey into the Father's heart, your Very Dear Divine Daddy wants to give you his blessing. A blessing that will stay with you for the rest of your life. A blessing that will carry you into the bliss of Heaven. A blessing that will make a difference today and every time you return to Abba-Father during prayer.

> *But his bow remained steady, / his strong arms stayed limber, / because of the hand of the Mighty One of Jacob, / because of the Shepherd, the Rock of Israel, / because of your father's God, who helps you, / because of the Almighty, who blesses you / with blessings of the skies above, / blessings of the deep springs below. . . . / Your father's blessings are greater than the blessings of the ancient mountains, / than the bounty of the age-old hills. (Genesis 49:24-26 NIV)*

This is his promise. You are a much-loved adopted child of God. With your adoption, you have inherited all that belongs to him. Generously! Abundantly! But what does this mean? In our human experiences, someone has to die before we receive our inheritance. Since Abba-Father is eternal, how does our divine inheritance come to us? Do *we* have to die? Do we have to wait until we reach Heaven before we can receive it?

Our inheritance looks like this: God has made available to us eternal life and every blessing under the heavens and in Heaven. (See Genesis 49:25, Ephesians 1:3, and Malachi 3:10.)

Jesus often said, "The Kingdom of God is at hand." We can correctly interpret that to include: "The full inheritance of God is at hand." Note that Jesus did *not* say: "When you die, if you believe in Me you will enter the Kingdom of God and *then* you will receive your inheritance."

He *did* say, *"I am the resurrection and the life. The one who believes in me will live forever"* (see John 11:25-26). This is the greatest blessing of all. But we need every blessing under the heavens now. Today. Right? Don't you wish you could have Heaven on Earth this day and every day? Isn't that what you're asking for when you ask for God's intervention in the problems of this world?

The good news is: Your inheritance *is* available to you *right now.* Abba-Father desires to give it to you today and every day of your earthly life—as long as you are still following Jesus and doing your best to be the saint that your baptism re-created you to be.

In human inheritances, very often the writers of wills base their decisions on how worthy the inheritors have been. In divine inheritances, Father God bases his decision on our acceptance of Jesus as our Lord and Savior, for it is Jesus who is worthy, not us.

Jesus also said, *"Whoever believes in me, as the Scripture has said, 'Out of his heart will flow rivers of living water.'" Now this he said about the Spirit, whom those who believed in him were to receive (John 7:38-39 ESV).* This is the blessing from Abba-Father that empowers us to be saints. The Holy Spirit helps us to become more and more saintly each day (if we ask him to).

In another scripture, Jesus put this blessing into the context of using our inheritance now, in daily life:

> *Very truly I tell you, whoever believes in me will do the works I have been doing, and they will do even greater things than these, because I am going to the Father. And I will do whatever you ask in my name, so that the Father may be glorified in the Son. You may ask me for anything in my name, and I will do it. (John 14:12-14 NIV)*

We have inherited the right to ask!

The reason why we don't see this blessing fulfilled—the reason why we don't always get what we ask for—is because we have not fully grasped (and believed) that we *are* God's adopted children and that we have an inheritance that's available to us right now. Jesus knew we'd struggle with this, so immediately after telling us we have a right to ask, he explained:

> *If you love me, keep my commands. And I will ask the Father, and he will give you another advocate to help you and be with you forever–the Spirit of truth. (John 14:15-17 NIV)*

A personal relationship with the Holy Spirit is necessary to receive and utilize our divine inheritance. We are impotent Christians if we love Jesus but ignore the Holy Spirit. We live as foster children instead of adopted children of the Father if we neglect learning how to be in a loving relationship with the Holy Spirit.

Another condition for receiving our divine inheritance here on Earth is what we plan to do with what we receive. Every blessing is meant to be shared.

> *Remember this: Whoever sows sparingly will also reap sparingly, and whoever sows generously will also reap generously. Each of you should give what you have decided in your heart to give, not reluctantly or under compulsion, for God loves a cheerful giver. And God is able to bless you abundantly, so that in all things at all times, having all that you need, you will abound in every good work. You will be enriched in every way so that you can be generous on every occasion, and through us your generosity will result in thanksgiving to God. (2 Corinthians 9:6-8, 11 NIV)*

Jesus explains this clearly in the parable about separating the sheep from the goats:

> *Then the King [the Son of Man when he comes in glory] will say to those on his right, "Come, you who are blessed by my Father; take your inheritance, the kingdom prepared for you since the creation of the world. For I was hungry and you gave me something to eat, I was thirsty and you gave me something to drink, I was a stranger and you invited me in, I needed clothes and you clothed me, I was sick and you looked after me, I was in prison and you came to visit me." (Matthew 25:34-36 NIV)*

Eight special blessings

In Matthew 5:1-12, Jesus teaches the Beatitudes. The word "beatitude" means supreme blessedness or happiness, a state of utmost bliss. This is what Jesus desired for us when he preached the Sermon on the Mount. This is what the Father wants to give us as our inheritance—right now. Today.

The first set of Beatitudes (verses 3-6) focuses on our relationship with Father God. They tell us that God is the source of our happiness. The rest of them deal with our relationships with each other. This pattern reflects Jesus' core message: First love God with all your heart and soul and mind, and the second commandment is to love your neighbor as yourself (see Matthew 22:37).

(Note: The Bible version quoted here in bold font is the English Standard Version, ESV.)

1. **Blessed are the poor in spirit, for theirs is the Kingdom of Heaven** (verse 3).

   We are "poor in spirit" when we stop placing our confidence in material security or other false gods (the kingdom of the world). By depending instead on our Daddy-God (the Kingdom of Heaven), we experience his power, his love, and his faithfulness. Think of a time when you died to yourself by choosing to be poor in spirit, trusting in the Father when it seemed easier or more sensible to trust in the things of this world. Remember how much closer to God you felt!

2. **Blessed are those who mourn, for they shall be comforted** (verse 4).

   We "mourn" or "sorrow" when our flesh-nature wants to take the easy path that leads to sin but our spirit chooses to resist and to take the holy path. Our Daddy-God comforts us while we struggle and suffer. His ability to comfort us is limitless. Recall an experience you had fighting against yourself because you didn't want to do something God's way. Did you feel like crying in frustration? Did your flesh-nature mourn when you refused to give in to it? How did God comfort you?

3. **Blessed are the meek, for they shall inherit the Earth** (verse 5).

   We are "meek" or "lowly" when we are submissive to our Father's Divine Will, obedient to his commands. Inheriting the "land" means becoming one of Abba's royal children in the Kingdom of Heaven. What are some rules of the Church that people don't like to obey? Is there a rule that you first disobeyed then obeyed? Why did you change? What effect did it have on you?

4. **Blessed are those who hunger and thirst for righteousness, for they shall be satisfied** (verse 6).

   We "hunger and thirst for righteousness" when we choose to live morally, i.e., when we conform our will to the Father's will. This hunger will be satisfied because the Father gave us Jesus, and Jesus gave us the Holy Spirit who helps us achieve righteousness. Reflect on how you have grown in righteousness. What activities have purified you? Have you ever experienced growth in your ability to love? Did you become stronger morally because you overcame temptations?

The second half of the Beatitudes reflects the spiritual growth that is produced by the first half.

5. **Blessed are the merciful, for they shall receive mercy** (verse 7).

   When we are poor in spirit and place our trust in God's mercy (verse 3), the next step is to give his mercy to others, and this results in the blessing of receiving even more of God's mercy (verse 7). Call to mind some of the contrasts between the world and Christianity; for example, lying versus honesty. When you have chosen the Christian way, see how this shows the purity of your heart!

6. **Blessed are the pure in heart, for they shall see God** (verse 8).

   When we've wanted to sin but we've chosen instead to do what is holy even though it makes our flesh-nature mourn (verse 4), we become pure in our hearts and we can see Abba-Father more fully, i.e., we dwell in the presence of God (verse 8). This purity allows the light of Christ in us to shine more brightly onto others, and they are brought closer to God through the witness of our lives.

7. **Blessed are the peacemakers, for they shall be called sons of God** (verse 9).

   When we are meek (verse 5), we become peacemakers (verse 9), because we no longer fight and argue with others. Consider how God deals with us when we choose the path of sin. Does he fight against us? Sometimes it seems like we're wrestling with him, but it's not God who is arguing: We're the ones who do all the complaining and yelling and struggling. Being peacemakers means we live as his adopted children by handling conflicts the same way our Father does, the same way that Jesus showed us. We love our enemies unconditionally. We turn the other cheek. Reflect on a time when you served as a peacemaker. How did it reveal the Father to the people with whom you dealt? Did you have the opportunity to see the difference it made in their spiritual lives?

8. **Blessed are those who are persecuted for righteousness' sake, for theirs is the Kingdom of Heaven. Blessed are you when others revile you and persecute you and utter all kinds of evil against you falsely on my account. Rejoice and be glad, for your reward is great in Heaven, for so they persecuted the prophets who were before you** (verses 10-12).

   When we strive to live out our true identity as saints—the adopted children of the Loving Father—we become more like Christ. This is a clear contrast to those who don't, and for this reason they persecute us. They convince themselves that they are better than we are in order to avoid realizing that they should give up their old ways and be converted. When was the last time you were persecuted because of your relationship with God? Perhaps someone misunderstood your faith or rejected you or deliberately caused problems for you. Did you feel blessed by it? Did you feel closer or farther from Jesus when it happened? Did you grow spiritually?

It's not easy to live in such a way that we can receive the blessings described in the Beatitudes. It takes great effort, but the Holy Spirit is here to help us, to comfort us, to guide us, and to reward us.

Abundant blessings

One of the functions of ancient kings was to bless the citizens of their kingdoms. Most cultures believed that their kings served as intermediaries between the gods and the people. And so they expected their kings to have the power to bless the people with good weather, abundant crops, healthy children, and prosperity in business dealings.

We, however, have the One True God as our king, and we have direct access to him.

In the Old Testament, we read about the great patriarchs of the faith giving a father's blessing to the eldest son before dying. This was a reflection of God the Father. They believed that the father of the home was directly connected to God the Father. Therefore, whatever blessing the father chose to give to his offspring (usually the first-born son) came with the authority of God. This is why Jacob stole the blessing from his twin, Esau, and why Esau was so upset by the trickery (read that story in Genesis 27). They knew that the blessing was not a wish; it was a guaranteed plan for the future, an inheritance received from the hand of God.

"May God give you heaven's dew
and earth's richness–
an abundance of grain and new wine.
May nations serve you
and peoples bow down to you.
Be lord over your brothers,
and may the sons of your mother bow down to you.
May those who curse you be cursed
and those who bless you be blessed."
(Isaac's blessing to Jacob, Genesis 27:28-29 NIV)

Moses relayed the guaranteed blessings of God to the people of Israel. He proclaimed the inheritance given to those who enter into the covenant with God. In Deuteronomy 28:1-13 (NIV), we find fifteen blessings. As you read them, remember that God has never changed. The needs change, but not God and his blessing. Let this truth sink in: God wants to bless you in the same way, though adapted for your circumstances today.

If you fully obey the Lord your God and carefully follow all his commands I give you today, the Lord your God will set you high above all the nations on earth. All these blessings will come on you and accompany you if you obey the Lord your God:

1. *You will be blessed in the city and blessed in the country.*
2. *The fruit of your womb will be blessed,*
3. *and the crops of your land*

4. *and the young of your livestock–the calves of your herds and the lambs of your flocks.*
5. *Your basket and your kneading trough will be blessed.*
6. *You will be blessed when you come in and blessed when you go out.*
7. *The Lord will grant that the enemies who rise up against you will be defeated before you. They will come at you from one direction but flee from you in seven.*
8. *The Lord will send a blessing on your barns and on everything you put your hand to.*
9. *The Lord your God will bless you in the land he is giving you.*
10. *The Lord will establish you as his holy people, as he promised you on oath, if you keep the commands of the Lord your God and walk in obedience to him.*
11. *Then all the peoples on Earth will see that you are called by the name of the Lord, and they will fear you.*
12. *The Lord will grant you abundant prosperity–in the fruit of your womb, the young of your livestock and the crops of your ground–in the land he swore to your ancestors to give you.*
13. *The Lord will open the heavens, the storehouse of his bounty, to send rain on your land in season and to bless all the work of your hands.*
14. *You will lend to many nations but will borrow from none.*
15. *The Lord will make you the head, not the tail, meaning that, if you pay attention to the commands of the Lord your God and carefully follow them, you will always be at the top, never at the bottom.*

Blessings come to us all the time. Every breath and each heartbeat is a blessing of life. We are blessed whenever we see, do, hear, or feel something that comes from the heart of our Divine Daddy. Thus, we're even blessed in situations that feel like curses, because he is with us, guiding us through it!

To grow stronger in our relationship with the Father, we need to become more aware of our inheritance. We need to look for the blessings he wants to give us. Admittedly, this can be especially difficult to do during hardships. But we succeed when we give it conscious effort and ask for the help of the Holy Spirit.

During troubled times, we must overcome our desire for humans to make things better. We must, instead, look for Abba-Father pointing out the part of our inheritance that we can pick up and use while waiting for him to work *inside* the troubles. Ask the Holy Spirit to help you do this.

The blessings inside the Lord's Prayer

Jesus gave us the "Lord's Prayer" so that we can have a wonderful relationship with our Divine Daddy. The problem is, if we run through it quickly and mindlessly, we miss the blessings that Jesus intended for us to receive.

> *This, then, is how you should pray: "Our Father in heaven, hallowed be your name, your kingdom come, your will be done, on earth as it is in heaven. Give us today our daily bread. And forgive us our debts, as we also have forgiven our debtors. And lead us not into temptation, but deliver us from the evil one." (Matthew 6:9-13 NIV)*

When we pray the "Our Father" prayer meaningfully and mindfully, we submit ourselves into a relationship of complete love with and trust in the Father. The Catechism tells us that having a loving relationship with the Father "has enormous consequences for our whole life" (para. 222-227):

1. **"It means coming to know God's greatness and majesty."**
   No matter how loving, powerful, caring, helpful, and wise we think God is, he is *infinitely* more so. But we box him up in our minds, believing that he is limited because the examples of humans and our understandings of what the Father is like have been limited. When our problems become overwhelming and it seems that God's help is very limited, it's because we imagine him to be who he is not. This is when it's time to pray, "Our Father, give me this day my daily bread, and help me get in touch with how You are loving me right here and now."
2. **"It means living in thanksgiving . . . everything we are and have comes from him."**
   How much credit do we give to ourselves and the hard work we put into getting the good things in life? How much credit do we give to luck or happenstance? The truth is: Good exists because it comes from God. When you pray "Hallowed be Thy name," right after calling God "our Father," pause to reflect on the total

goodness of God's Fatherhood. Then pray it again with the awe of immense thankfulness.

3. **"It means knowing the unity and true dignity of all men."**

   When we really believe that God is the Father of all, we have no prejudices, no feelings of being superior to certain people, no fears of being inferior to others, and no difficulty loving even the most unlikable folks. Since God's love for all people is unlimited and unconditional, being in a close relationship with the Father stirs up within us the same love for everyone. But if we can name someone whom God supposedly does not totally love because he or she is undeserving, we will have a hard time believing that the Father totally loves us, because we, too, are unworthy.

4. **"It means making good use of created things . . . to use everything that is not God only insofar as it brings us closer to him, and to detach ourselves from it insofar as it turns us away from him."**

   Which possessions, which people, which habits, which ideas, and which dreams are hard to let go of? When we truly believe that the Father loves us completely, everything else loses their importance. We eagerly take time to sit in his love, share our hearts with him, and do favors for him. If a neighbor's house burns down, we don't mind giving them some of our own furniture while they rebuild. If our local church asks for more money, we don't mind increasing our donations because we know that the Father is generous with us. What do we love more than God?

5. **"It means trusting God in every circumstance, even in adversity."**

   Do we see blessings in the troubles we experience? We do if we know that God is taking care of us as a Good Father and that he's working a plan to bring good from the bad. What comes to mind when he doesn't answer our prayers the way we want him to and in the timing we desire? Do we say, "Abba-Father, You have a better idea than I do of how to answer this prayer!" Or do we take matters into our own hands first? When we rush ahead of God, we're not taking time to consider all of the resources that we've inherited from our Father. He gives us a better understanding of the situation, patience, sacrificial love, wisdom, the involvement of the right people, the right circumstances falling into place, etc.

The Lord's Prayer as a dialogue

The "Our Father" prayer is most helpful when we slow it down enough to allow it to become a dialogue. For example:

Our Father –

"Yes, My wonderful child? What do you want to ask of Me? I'm delighted that you have come out of your busy day to spend time with Me."

Who art in Heaven –

"I long to spend eternity with you here in Heaven, My blessed child. I'm delighted that you accepted the tremendous gift of My Son's sacrifice. Please don't be lazy about your journey towards Heaven. I will provide you with a period of purification in Purgatory if necessary, through My Great Mercy, but I'd much rather wrap My Loving Arms around you the very moment that you leave Earth. My greatest desire is for you and I to have complete union. Waste no time in reaching My Love!"

Hallowed be Thy name –

"Thank you for acknowledging My Perfect Holiness. When you call on Me and depend on My holiness, My purity, My total and complete love for you, and My inability to ever sin against you, we are dancing together in the joy of our Father-child relationship. Depend on My holiness; it is the source of your confidence. My holiness means that your prayers are being answered in the best way and at the best time."

Thy Kingdom come –

"Everything in My Kingdom is your inheritance, My beloved child. My grace is yours. My generosity is yours. My confidence is yours. My power over evil is yours. What else do you need? If it's something that belongs to My Kingdom, it's yours for the asking."

Thy will be done –

"Trust My perfect timing in everything you ask for. Let go of your ideas of how and when your prayers should be answered. Unite your will to My Divine Will. Repeat this part of the prayer whenever you feel disappointed, or confused about My will for you, or overwhelmed by the invasion of evil in the world. Pray out loud, 'Our Father … Thy will be done. Thank You. I trust in You. Take care of everything.'"

On Earth as it is in Heaven –

"Heaven and Earth unite when you and I unite, My dear one. Your desire to submit everything to My Divine Will brings Heaven into your earthly life. And in that union, you have the fullness of the inheritance that I have given you. Count on it. Watch My Will unfold in unexpected ways and in the wisdom of My perfect timing."

Give us this day our daily bread –

"Tell Me, My precious one, what you need from Me today. Start every day this way. Which of the blessings of Heaven do you seek today? What kind of help do you need? Remember: The measure in which you give to others is the measure you have chosen for yourself. To receive more of My blessings, become more generous in giving."

Forgive us our sins as we forgive those who sin against us –

"What sins do you want Me to forgive today? The measure in which you forgive others is the measure you have chosen for receiving My forgiveness. Do you think I will not fully forgive every sin you confess in the Sacrament of Reconciliation? And in the Penitential Rite of the Holy Liturgy? And in your repentance at any time or any place? I am not a liar. If you still feel unforgiven or unforgiveable, who is it that you have not forgiven? Choose to forgive—even if the one you have withheld forgiveness from is yourself. If you don't forgive yourself, return to My Divine Will which has fully forgiven you."

Lead us not into temptation but deliver us from evil –

"Those who do not ask for My help are seduced by temptations. I have not taken you out of this world yet, and so you face many temptations every day. I am selective about which ones come into your life, because I want to strengthen your fidelity, increase your virtue, and augment your merits. I have given you everything you need for overcoming the lies and seductions of the Evil One. My blessed child, rely on the inheritance I have given you. Each temptation is a test you can ace. Learn from them."

Amen!

"Amen! It is so! I have spoken, with full authority, in total agreement with your prayer."

The Litany of the Father's Heart

Now I would like to share with you a prayer that can help you complete your journey into the Father's heart. You would do well to make it part of your daily prayers. (All the prayers in this chapter are available for download at **30DaysToTheFathersHeart.com/prayers**.) This is a prayer to your Doting Daddy, the loving God who cares for you far more than you can imagine. Afterward, we will end this book with his blessing to you—his response to your prayer.

Father, First Person of the Most Holy Trinity,
Thank You for creating me to be Your beloved child.
Father of the only-begotten Son,
Thank You for loving me so much that You sent Your Son to die for me.
Father who, with the Son, sends me love in the Person of the Holy Spirit,
Thank You for sending me an Advocate who comes to my defense.
Our Father in Heaven,
Be my eternal Father.
Father, infinite majesty,
Thank You for caring about me with all Your might.
Father, infinite holiness,
Thank You for being my Perfect Father.
Father, infinite goodness,
Thank You for not abandoning me when I am struck by evil.
Father, infinite happiness,
Thank You for sharing Your joy with me.
Father, all-powerful,
Thank You for wanting to take good care of me.
Father, all-knowing,
Thank You for doing what's best for me.
Father, present everywhere,
Thank You for being with me in all my trials and all my victories.
Father, all-just,
Thank You for appreciating me for who I truly am when others misjudge me.
Father, all-merciful,
Thank You for forgiving me when I repent of my sins.
Father of love,

Thank You for cherishing me.
Father of beauty,
Thank You for making me in Your image.
Father of wisdom,
Thank You for directing me through Your Holy Spirit.
Father, Divine Providence,
Thank You for watching over me.
You are my Good Father in joy and in sorrow.
You are my Good Father in sickness and in health.
You are my Good Father in prosperity and in adversity.
You are my Good Father in life and in death.
You are my Good Father for all of eternity.
Thank You! Amen.

To go into this more deeply, listen to my podcast about the Litany of the Father's Heart, where I unpack its wealth line by line. Go to 30DaysToTheFathersHeart.com/litany.

The Litany Inside the Father's Heart for You

And now the Father gives you his blessing:

My child,
Thank you for being My beloved child.
My child who follows My only-begotten Son,
Thank you for loving Me so much that you want to spend eternity with Me.
I am your Father who, with the Son, gives you My love in the Person of the Holy Spirit;
Thank you for receiving the Advocate whom I give you for your defense.
I am your Father in Heaven;
I bless you with the full inheritance of being My beloved child.
I am infinite majesty;
I bless you with the fullness of My caring compassion.
I am infinite holiness;
I bless you with all of My being, all of My righteousness, all of My perfection.
I am infinite goodness;
I bless you with the promise that I will never abandon you when

you are struck by evil.
I am infinite happiness;
I bless you with My joy.
I am all-powerful;
I bless you with My divine power to defeat evil and to do all that I call you to do.
I am all-knowing;
I bless you with whatever I know is best for you.
I am present everywhere;
I bless you with My hug in all your trials. I bless you with My dance in all our victories.
I am all-just;
I bless you with My appreciation of your goodness whenever others treat you unjustly.
I am all-merciful;
I bless you with forgiveness in the very moment you repent of your sins.
I am the Father of love;
I cherish you.
I am the Father of beauty;
I have made you in My image, and so you are very beautiful!
I am the Father of wisdom;
I am directing you through My Holy Spirit.
I am Divine Providence;
I am watching over you.
I am your Good Father in joy and in sorrow.
I am your Good Father in sickness and in health.
I am your Good Father in prosperity and in adversity.
I am your Good Father in life and in death.
I am your Good Father for all of eternity.
I bless you! Amen.

About the Author

Although Terry Modica knew Jesus Christ as a close friend since early childhood, she didn't meet God the Father in a personal way until her early adult years. Then it struck her how little she trusted God because she had been projecting onto him the imperfections and limitations of her human father and other authority figures. Getting to know the Divine Father, as he really is, proved to be a challenge. In this book, she shares the wisdom and healing she gained over the next forty years. Mrs. Modica has made it her goal to help people experience the wonderfulness of the True Father.

She is co-founder and Executive Director of Good News Ministries (gnm.org), podcast host, international speaker, retreat director, and author of the popular Good News Reflections on the readings from daily Mass. She has a theology degree and certifications in two Lay Pastoral Ministry institutes.

Other Books by Terry Modica

9-Day Consecration to St. Joseph

FORGIVEN: A Meditation on the Passion of Christ

RADICAL LOVE: Reflections for Couples

Victor: The Novel

Overcoming the Power of the Occult

Daily Prayers with the Saints

The Trail of Roses: A Lenten Journey

Daily Prayers with the Saints

Visit gnm.org/books-by-terry-modica

My Soul Shall Be Healed